THE RESCUE OF THE INNOCENTS

Endangered Children in Medieval Miracles

THE RESCUE OF THE INNOCENTS

Endangered Children in Medieval Miracles

R. C. FINUCANE

ST. MARTIN'S PRESS
NEW YORK

RESCUE OF THE INNOCENTS
Copyright © R. C. Finucane, 1997
All rights reserved. Printed in the United States of America.
No part of this book may be used or reproduced in any manner
whatsoever without written permission except in the case of brief
quotations embodied in critical articles or reviews. For information,
address St. Martin's Press, Scholarly and Reference Division,
175 Fifth Avenue, New York, N.Y. 10010

ISBN 0–312–16213–8

Library of Congress Cataloging-in-Publication Data

Finucane, Ronald C.
    The rescue of the innocents : endangered children in medieval
miracles / by Ronald C. Finucane.
        p.   cm.
    Includes bibliographical references and index.
    ISBN 0–312–16213–8
    1. Children — Diseases — Europe — History.   2. Social history-
-Medieval, 500-1500.   3. Spiritual healing — Europe.   4.Miracles-
-Europe.   5. Children's accidents — Europe.   6. Pediatric
epidemiology — Europe.   7. Medicine, Medieval.   I. Title.
RJ39.F55   1997
618.92'00094'0902 — dc21   96-52278
                                                                CIP

Interior design by Harry Katz

First published: September 1997
10   9   8   7   6   5   4   3   2   1

In Memory of George F. Finucane

CONTENTS

LIST OF FIGURES

PREFACE

As he stood in the coolness of the Augustinian chapter house, a refuge in the midst of Tolentino's noisy streets, once again Berard had to admit to the inquisitors that he could not recall the date of a particular event. While he hesitated, searching his memory for things that happened so long ago, he noticed that the notaries sitting near the three papal commissioners had paused too, their pens poised, waiting. When his testimony ended, they would compare their cursive notes and draw up a carefully written report to be forwarded to the curia in Avignon. Berard knew how this worked, since he himself was a notary.

The pope's men passed to yet another question on their long list of interrogatories, probing his mind in their search for *puram veritatem,* the plain truth. Berard was over fifty, and some of the events had taken place more than thirty years earlier. All that he could remember now, in July of 1325, was that years ago his son Nicholas had been cured of a hernia he had suffered for more than six months; that his daughter Ceccha's throat, so swollen that surgery was considered, had been cured without the knife; that another son, whose whole body used to tremble as his pupils turned upward and spittle collected on his lips, was finally released from an ailment called the falling sickness; and that all these things happened because of Nicholas of Tolentino, the holy man who was buried in the very church in which Berard was giving evidence. Berard also recalled seeing, some twelve years earlier, a noble lady bring her twelve-year-old daughter into the church where, *coram omnibus* —in front of everyone—she cut the girl's tresses and placed the hair at Nicholas's tomb, because he had recalled her daughter "from the dead." The hair, along with some of the girl's clothing, was the grateful mother's offering. Berard went on to describe how over the years he had seen crowds of people, from a great variety of places, come to Nicholas's tomb and publicly swear that they had been blind, or crippled, or possessed by demons, or captured by enemies, or deaf or mute, or afflicted by "many, many" (*multi et multi*) diverse illnesses; they had all been freed of their afflictions because of blessed Nicholas. Some brought one kind of offering, others another kind, according to what they had vowed while praying to the dead "saint."[1]

Berard was testifying before a canonization commission set up by Pope John XXII to inquire into the life and miracles of Nicholas of Tolentino, an Augustinian friar who died in 1305. The records of such canonization proceedings contain an abundance of precise details concerning the daily lives of those who sought help from their saints. The following pages explore reports of "miraculous" benefits bestowed upon one particular group of recipients, medieval children: the healing of an ill child, or the resuscitation of a drowned toddler, or the recovery of an infant whose mother had crushed it while they slept in the same bed. The records tell of family and village reactions, of parents crippled in their grief when sickness attacked their children, of neighbors running to a riverbank to pray next to the "dead" body of a child. We analyze the experiences of 600 children who were rescued, cured, or resuscitated—as it was thought—by the holy dead, and also examine the impact of these wonders upon the children's families. Although there is a great deal of information on medieval childhood dispersed throughout contemporary medical and theological treatises, in medieval prose, poetry, and art, in the biographies of saints as well as of lay personages, and in legal and administrative documents such as coroners' records, wills, and secular as well as canon law, we concentrate in this book on one type of source only, hagiographical records. The sources have been chosen in such a way that comparisons can be made between northern and southern Europe: overall, were the illnesses suffered, or the accidents or injuries sustained, by northern children different from those of southern children? Within families in the different regions, reactions of mothers will be compared with those of fathers, other kin, and neighbors. Did families from the two European regions become involved in children's calamities in different ways? Parental grief, and the forms it took, will be considered as well. Another focus of the inquiry compares medieval children's accidents and illnesses with those of modern children; I believe that this is worth attempting despite the methodological risks involved. The number of questions raised will no doubt exceed the answers provided. Nevertheless, even the questions may be helpful to those who wish to explore this facet of children's history.

Any mention of the history of childhood evokes the memory of a certain French civil servant turned historian, but the shade of Philippe Ariès has been laid to rest for some time now. There is no longer any need to go on proving that childhood was "discovered" centuries earlier than Ariès postulated, or that many medieval parents loved their children—some to distraction—while others were barbarously cruel; we now recognize that there is a distinction between medieval parents' indifference to a child's fate and resignation to that fate.[2] Interest in the history of childhood began to grow especially after the appearance of Ariès's work, published in France in 1960 and translated in 1962 as *Centuries of Childhood: A Social History of Family Life*. Ariès's claims about childhood have been examined critically and, in large part, superseded thanks to the continued work of those who have followed paths opened up by Ariès himself. An excellent example is the classic essay of the 1970s by Mary Martin McLaughlin, "Survivors and Surrogates," in *The History of Childhood*.[3] Further books and journal articles, international colloquia, and collections of essays have followed. The 1980s opened with a publication that provides both a collection of primary sources and a reasoned overview of the topic, Klaus Arnold's *Kind und Gesellschaft in Mittelalter und Renaissance* (Paderborn, 1980); Barbara Hanawalt's book, *The Ties That Bound: Peasant Families in Medieval England* (Oxford University Press, 1986), analyzes thousands of cases presented in medieval English coroners' records, re-creating the ambience of English family life, including the lives of children.[4]

In 1990, Shulamith Shahar published a wide-ranging synthesis that explores a variety of sources.[5] Indeed, considering the nature of the subject, the topic can be approached by various avenues; where Hanawalt used administrative-legal documents, James A. Schultz, for instance, examined more than 200 Middle High German literary texts as the basis for his study of German childhood.[6] Given the genre with which he chose to deal, it is not surprising that Schultz's picture emphasizes not peasant children but the sons and daughters of the German nobility. Work continues: to take but one example, toward the end of the 1990s, the research of Didier Lett, carried out in collaboration with Danièle Alexandre-Bidon, will appear under the title *Histoire de l'enfant au Moyen Âge*.[7] Lett's synthesis will draw upon a variety of medieval sources.

Some of the material in the following pages was presented at Mid-America Medieval Association conferences, at Western Michigan University, and at a seminar sponsored by the Department of Child Studies of the University of Linköping in Sweden. On this last occasion, I had the pleasure of meeting and learning from Klaus Arnold, Barbara Hanawalt, Shulamith Shahar, Christian Krötzl and others. I am grateful to the organizers of those conferences and events and to other scholars who have been extremely generous with their time, comments, offprints, and criticisms. This group includes, but is not limited to, Professors Monica Green, Didier Lett, and Susan Ridyard as well as Drs. Eleanora C. Gordon and Jerome Kroll, whose medical analyses have been very helpful. I must also thank

Ms. Jan Bulman, who, in the midst of her own work as a graduate student of medieval history, took the time to read and critique the form — and very often the substance — of the book, as well as prepare the index. In spite of assistance from so many people, however, I accept responsibility for the errors that no doubt remain. It is hoped that these pages will throw further light on childhood in the Middle Ages, illuminating what David Herlihy called the "corners of the medieval household that historians have found most difficult to penetrate, its cultural and emotional life."[8]

1

INTRODUCTION
··················

The canonization of saints, a process whose oversight was claimed by the papacy in the late twelfth century, was increasingly centralized as more efficient inquisitorial procedures were developed during the thirteenth century. By the fourteenth and fifteenth centuries the procedures, personnel, and goals of such inquests were well organized, in many cases operating alongside unofficial efforts to promote canonizations that the ecclesiastical establishment sometimes repudiated.[1] Ironically, these processes could be used for quite different purposes: in the very year the inquest into the sanctity of Nicholas of Tolentino was initiated in central Italy, 1325, another set of hearings had finally concluded, in the southern French diocese of Pamiers. Bishop Jacques Fournier had used inquisitorial procedures to track down the "Good Men" and their followers in the Pyrenean foothills, where the cancer of heresy was dispersed among little nodes of Cathar heretics at villages such as Montaillou.[2] On the one hand, an inquisition could confirm eternal damnation; on the other, it could verify everlasting sanctity. At Pamiers, inquisitors cleansed souls or sent them to hell; at Tolentino, they could turn a corpse into a saintly relic.

Official mechanisms for establishing sainthood, then, were widely recognized and well implemented by the end of the Middle Ages, generating records that included the sworn statements of thousands of witnesses to the holy lives and posthumous wonders of would-be saints. But saints were "made" in other ways too. Popular admiration of an individual who had lived a holy life, then worked "miracles" after death, could result in visits by pilgrims who left offerings at the grave. Most of these tombs were located in churches, monasteries, and cathedrals, and often the friars, monks, or canons of such places made written summaries of the wonders attributed to "their" holy dead. Their informal records of tales told by pilgrims sometimes included the names of neighbors brought along as witnesses to a miraculous cure or resuscitation from "death." In addition, letters about wondrous events sent to pilgrimage centers were copied into the miracle registers. From time to time a "cure" occurred at the shrine or tomb itself, before the very eyes of the guardian cleric who recorded it. These books or registers of miracles constitute the second main source of data for the present study, along with official canonization records. The informal collections seem, on the surface, less impressive than the records produced by papal inquisitions, where witnesses were sworn on the Bible; where scars and other marks of healing were carefully examined; where conflicting testimony was thrown back at witnesses; where, sometimes, witnesses were dismissed because clearly they were simpletons, apt to say anything. However, even the biased keepers of shrines could be skeptics: in response to a mother's claim that her son had been drowned and then resuscitated thanks to a miracle of Thomas Becket, some of the Canterbury monks shouted *"est, est"* while other monks, less convinced of Becket's wondrous powers in this case, responded *"non, non!"*[3]

Whether recorded at canonization hearings or at saints' shrines, "miracles" are attractive in the richness of their intimate details. There are weaknesses in these records, it is perhaps superfluous to note, as there are in all historical sources. Clearly medieval people's understanding of illness and death is not our own. We might be puzzled by an apparent inability of the villagers and townsfolk of the Middle Ages to decide (to take the extreme example) whether someone was, or was not, dead. On the other hand, because these records are statements of what contemporaries believed, they are valuable reflections of at least segments of a medieval worldview. In addition, when these tragedies happened, undoubtedly—and expectedly—anxious parents tended to exaggerate the seriousness of their child's illness or accident and, at the time of the event, to draw bystanders into their own emotional turmoil. It is futile to expect medieval (or modern) parents or neighbors to describe children's accidental injuries or purported deaths dispassionately. This fact in itself illustrates the strength of the emotional bonds linking children and adults. Many of the cases were reported five, ten, or more years after they had happened. No doubt witnesses distorted the details, unconsciously or not, when trying to recall memories that were both painful and, because of "miraculous" intervention, wonderful. The apparent precision and thoroughness of the formal canonization hearings, often including a physical examination of children—all of this preserved in a neat notarial script—present us with a beguiling veneer of "objectivity." Yet the process, very often tainted by partisanship at many levels, was far from faultless. Finally, many witnesses at papal inquiries and informal witnesses at the shrines described "miracles" in the vernacular, which was then forced into the relatively blunt Latin of the church, a further source of distortion.

Even with their exaggerations and inaccuracies, however, these records — canonization depositions as well as shrine-side claims — are a framework for investigating the involvement of parents and kin, neighbors and strangers, whenever a child was ill, or injured, or thought to be dead. Although what was claimed about "actual" illness and "real" death is problematical, the claims are of historical value. While the "miraculous" core may be unbelievable, the incidental or circumstantial details — the *nonessentials*, as far as most witnesses and shrine-keepers and parents were concerned when reporting these cases — are of primary importance for our purposes.[4] These hagiographical sources are useful supplements to the imaginative literature that usually concerned only the upper crust of medieval society, and to scientific and medical texts that combined traditional lore, going back to Aristotle and the Hippocratic corpus, with scholastic theorizing divorced from practicalities — although there are exceptions. They complement ecclesiastical documents such as canons, penitentials, and sermons that contained generalities about child care and the responsibilities of parents, as well as comments about children and childhood scattered throughout the sprawling corpus of canon law. They even can supplement legal records, such as judicial eyres and coroners' reports. Although the latter usually did not include extensive circumstantial minutiae about children's deaths, they abound, as Barbara Hanawalt has shown, in useful data concerning childhood.[5] Augmenting the wealth of all these records, as Renate Blumenfeld-Kosinski put it, are the miracle collections, "a promising and as yet virtually untapped source of information on family relationships and attitudes toward children."[6]

THE SOURCES

Eight major miracle collections were chosen with the following criteria in mind: the collections should be extensive, which means, ordinarily, that they include at least 100 miracle reports, some of which involve children; they should represent cults of both northern and southern Europe; and they should include both "official" inquisitions (transcripts of the sworn testimony of witnesses who appeared before papal commissioners) and "unofficial" collections put together by those who had charge of a shrine or had some special interest in saint making. Another selection criterion was the contemporaneity of the sources: these were "real" individuals whose deaths and cults were recorded by contemporaries in the central and later Middle Ages. Therefore, there will be no references to St. George, St. Christopher,

St. Uncumber, or any other "saints" whose existence on this earth was more mythical than biological. In addition to the eight extensive collections, several other shorter contemporaneous lists will be referred to, particularly when these include striking or informative examples involving children.

Among the selected major collections of northern European cults is the miracle dossier of Thomas Cantilupe, who died as bishop of Hereford in 1282. His posthumous wonders were investigated by a papal commission in 1307, and he was canonized in 1320. Some of the testimony about his purported miracles was published in the monumental *Acta Sanctorum*.[7] Because that version is marred by many errors and much editorially inspired confusion, however, in the present study reference is made in almost every case to the manuscript that the inquisitors forwarded to the papal curia for further deliberations, MS *Vatican Latin 4015*; in addition, MS *Exeter College 158* was consulted.[8] Another northerner whose official records proved very useful was the mystic Dorothy (Dorotheas) von Montau, who took up the religious life after being widowed in 1390. She died in 1394 and was buried at Marienwerder, some forty-five miles south of Danzig in modern Poland. (The villagers involved in her cult will be referred to as Pomeranians.) A papal commission set up in 1404 heard testimony concerning, among other things, events postdating her death. Although repeated attempts were made to raise her to official sainthood, she was never canonized. Two other major northern European cults were used, but these, unlike the official inquiries into Cantilupe's and Dorotheas's miracles, attracted only unofficial compilers of posthumous thaumaturgy. One is Thomas Becket, England's premier saint, whose death in 1170 was followed by miracles at his tomb. In a speedy process, the dead archbishop was canonized in 1173. Meanwhile hundreds of miracles were said to have occurred at his tomb and in the homes of the English and European faithful. These were recorded by two Canterbury monks, Benedict (later abbot of Peterborough) and William.[9] Between them, they accounted for just over 700 cases of what was thought to be God's divine intervention mediated by Becket. The last of the major northern European cults centered on another important figure of English history, King Henry VI, killed in 1471. His body was buried at Chertsey, but when pilgrims began visiting his tomb, an embarrassment to the government, the corpse was transferred to Windsor. The miracles, recorded over the last two decades of the fifteenth century, contain abundant information on the illnesses and mishaps of late-medieval English children. Henry VI seems to have been as unlucky after death as he had been in life, since attempts to canonize him were shelved after Henry VIII's break with Rome. These four sources, combined with a few lesser collections, provide a total of 311 reports from northern Europe involving the accidents and illnesses of children and problems arising at birth and in earliest infancy.

The southern European cults include that of Louis, a prince of the house of Anjou who became a Franciscan, then (reluctantly) bishop of Toulouse, dying in 1297; his tomb at Marseilles became a pilgrimage center. An official inquisition gathered testimony about his life and posthumous cult in 1307 and 1308, a process that resulted in his canonization in 1317. A second source is the cult of Clare (Chiara) of Montefalco in central Italy (Umbria). An ascetic even as a child, she continued her austerities up to the end of her life in 1308. In a grisly operation carried out just after she died, her heart was removed and cut open to reveal what the amazed women of her convent claimed to be depictions of the instruments of the crucifixion. Testimony about her life and miracles was gathered in 1318-19 by a panel appointed by the pope, but her canonization did not take place until 1881.[10] Another papal commission at work in Italy gathered data on the life and miracles of Nicholas of Tolentino (d. 1305). This Augustinian friar, a master of preaching and healing (even in his lifetime), was buried in Tolentino, some forty or fifty miles from Chiara's Montefalco. In the wake of pilgrimages, posthumous miracles, and requests to the curia, the principal inquisitorial process took place in the summer of 1325 (when Berard, the notary mentioned in the preface, testified). Nicholas was canonized in 1446. The last of the selected major southern European cults was that of Pope Urban V, who was buried in Avignon in December of 1370 but whose bones were translated (moved) to Marseilles in 1371, where miracles were reported. Although many witnesses provided testimony, recorded by notaries in the late 1370s, and additional wonders were noted in 1390, it does not appear that any formal board of inquiry was established by any pope, nor was Urban ever canonized. Nevertheless, the reputed miracles were numerous and, in many instances, very detailed. As a counterweight to the four northern European cults, then, we have identified four major sources of data from southern Europe, which will be augmented by a few additional cults from the South. These southern collections contain 289 reports involving children.

A total, therefore, of 600 cases involving childbirth, accidents, illnesses, and purported deaths of children has been identified in the selected European miracle collections. These 600 constitute the "core" data, the foundation for comments and conclusions reached in the following pages. Although some particularly interesting descriptions have been taken from sources extraneous to the 600-case core, only these 600 were considered in constructing the graphs and formulating statements concerning percentages, or comparative analyses, that appear in this book. In chapter 2, of the 110 core cases, 59 were reported from northern Europe, while the South accounted for 51. Instances of illness were reported for 124 northern children, but 210 cured children were described in the southern cults. The greatest difference, however, is seen in the core cases relating to accidents: the selected northern European collections provided 128 instances, whereas a mere 28 were reported in our sources from the South. Reasons for these differences will be considered in due course. None of the 600 instances came to be written up at a shrine or discussed before a papal commission earlier than the twelfth, or later than the fifteenth, century; a quarter of them were recorded during the thirteenth century, nearly half (45 percent) in the fourteenth century; the twelfth and the fifteenth centuries each accounted for the remainder in roughly equal proportions (about 15 percent). This is a small number of cases, spanning a long period, upon which to predicate firm conclusions. Although the material provides an abundance of anecdotal data, generalizations based on 600 examples must be highly speculative. For these reasons, this work should be seen as an exploratory study, whose tentative findings can be verified, corrected, or negated only through the analysis of many more examples of illness, accident, and "death" involving medieval children.

FAITH HEALING

No matter what criteria are used in selecting these materials, it could be objected that, since these are records of "miracles," and miracles do not happen, the reports are useless as historical sources. For reasons already indicated, however, this is not the case: this study focuses on the ambience of the events rather than the "miracles" per se. In any event, even the most dedicated skeptic must acknowledge, as doctors, psychologists, and anthropologists have recognized for a very long time, that "cures" can result from innumerable agencies. A patient's strong belief in any given therapy, whether administered in modern American or European clinics, in the villages of Nigeria, or in medieval Europe, can result in the alleviation of suffering. When this coincides with natural remission, the termination of self-limiting ailments, or the relief of psychogenic aches and pains, so much the better; the therapy "works." In addition, the power of expectant faith, built up during the course of a journey to a sacred place, could make pilgrimage itself a therapeutic agent. Medieval sufferers who experienced any alleviation of distress, for whatever reasons, attributed this to the saint whose enshrined bones they visited or merely vowed to visit. In addition, as I have shown elsewhere, medieval people's recognition of types and of degrees of illness was usually as imprecise as their definitions of a "cure."[11] Not only that, but this imprecision extended to death itself, which for many medieval Europeans was subject to varying definitions.[12]

The broad envelope of subjectivity surrounding illness and even death extended to the assumption that timing, in such miraculous matters, was not significant. "Cures" that did not manifest themselves for days, weeks, or even months after going on pilgrimage or vowing to a saint could be credited, nevertheless, to the saint in question. A casual attitude toward dates and durations also appears with irritating regularity in other ways, as any medievalist will know: undated charters, or chroniclers' references to events occurring merely *eo tempore* — in, or at, that time. This temporal nonchalance is critical when dealing with the subjects of this book, as seen, for instance, in claims about children lying under the water "all afternoon." The country people of medieval Europe measured relatively short durations in ways that seem to us, in our love of exactitude, to be further evidence of the disconcertingly permeable "boundaries" of their worlds, mundane as well as miraculous. They measured hours and minutes by the length of time it took to walk or to ride a given distance, or to say specific prayers (usually the *Ave* and *Pater Noster*) a given number of times, or to hear a Mass or eat a meal. Those within earshot of a church bell also might be able to identify such canonical hours as the monks or village priest chose to mark, but peasants' references to vespers or matins usually do not help to pinpoint specific times.[13] It also was not uncommon for witnesses to note something happening at "the third hour" or "toward sunset." When the season or month is known, such hints allow us to place events within a general chronological framework only. In short, there is very little chance of determining the precise chronology of children's illnesses or the exact times when they fell into wells or began bleeding as a result of an accident.

"CHILDREN" AND THEIR FAMILIES

Since this study concerns children, definitions of "child" must be established at the outset. This apparently straightforward task is not so simple. For instance, in medieval Germany it would appear that the concept of the "teenager" did not exist as we understand it: "the 'nature of childhood,' whatever it is felt to be, is 'particular' not only to childhood but also to each age and culture. . . ."[14] In our own societies, the point at which a person ceases to be a "child" is not always clearly recognized. Differing definitions are evident in contemporary America and England, for example; childhood tends to last longer in the former country than it does in the latter. As in modern times, the medieval range of terms for children was broad, and usage varied widely.[15] In this book, however, "children" are taken to be individuals age fourteen or younger.[16] Whenever the very common words *puer* (boy) and *puella* (girl) were encountered in the miracles, they were *not* assumed to refer to children unless specific ages were also given or the details made it clear that they were younger than fourteen. In addition, because the word *puer* could be used for newborn girls as well as boys, other details in the miracle narratives, or grammatical indicators, are relied on to establish gender.

Among the 600 examples, cases concerning childbirth and early infancy (110) involved, self-evidently, neonates and infants; of the remaining 490 examples, 155 of the subjects can be defined as "children" from context. The ages of the remaining 335 individuals are specified in the records. As shown in figure 1.1, well over half had not yet reached their sixth birthday. In a few instances, archaeological finds can be set alongside the data arising from our examination of the miracle records, with suggestive (although not conclusive) results. It would appear, for instance, that most of the children exhumed in a Thuringian dig (with burials dating from the tenth to mid-twelfth centuries), and most children who were reported in our sources to have experienced near death and miraculous recovery in northern and southern Europe, fell into the same broad chronological categories: the majority were under five years of age.[17]

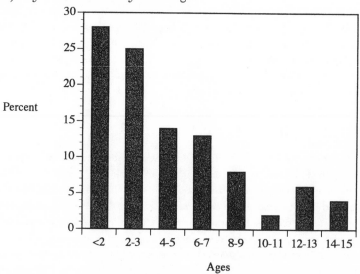

Figure 1.1 Ages specified for 335 children

In this study, then, we are dealing mainly with infants and younger children. Although it is accepted that many medieval parents loved their children and were deeply concerned about their welfare, it is worth exploring an observation by Philippe Ariès that love does not necessarily mean understanding. Does anything in these records suggest that medieval adults recognized a special status for childhood? Was it acknowledged that children possessed unique characteristics? We know that in the seventh and eighth centuries Columban and Bede and, centuries later, Anselm and others recognized the special qualities of children; and we know that the monastic environment was especially conducive to what Henri Platelle called a *"tonalité affective"* regarding children.[18] We know, too, that many child-raising manuals (written by men), such as those by Giles of Rome or Arnold of Villanova, acknowledged the special needs of children. But what of the laity whose lives were spent outside these monastic or literate environments?

The miracles illustrate some common expectations about children. In addition to what they reveal about parental involvement in certain aspects of their children's lives, the narrations and depositions indicate what many ordinary adults assumed about children's physical state or habits, especially those that predisposed them to danger. Adults knew, for instance, that children tended to misinterpret reality or to overreact in unfamiliar situations. Therefore, grown-ups sometimes ignored children's alarmed shouts or tears, which probably led to the children's frustration. Apart from that, this was sometimes an unwise response, as illustrated in a French case. One spring or early summer day two boys were "childishly playing" on the banks of a pond outside their village a few miles from Pontigny.[19] One of them, nine-year-old Humbald, slipped and fell into the water, which was about twelve feet deep. The other, younger boy—not yet at the age of discretion, the narrator explains—seeing that he could do nothing, began crying in his helplessness, "as a child does."[20] Two women in a nearby field ignored him, thinking that he was only childishly pretending to cry.[21] When he did not stop, one of the women ran up and asked what was wrong; upon being told that his playmate (*cognatus,* perhaps kin) had drowned, the woman screamed and the other came over. Eventually, with the help of the village men, Humbald was recovered from the water. When he began moving and "returned to life," the bells rang and the people danced, as the rescued boy was carried into the church; their noisy jubilation could be heard in three surrounding villages. In a similar way, when a little English boy ran into a country pub to tell his mother that a girl had fallen into a fishpond, she disregarded him, ignoring his "childish words"; in a report from Pomerania, Elisabeth took no notice of her little daughter who ran into the house claiming that a child had fallen into a well. When her husband came in with the same news, Elisabeth immediately rushed out to help.[22]

Grown-ups recognized that children were playful and active but without much discretion or judgment. This was particularly true of those younger than seven, which medieval writers generally accepted as the age by which judgment began to be exercised and reason employed. When describing potentially dangerous activities, commentators and witnesses often used such expressions as "thoughtlessly and childishly" and "lacking discretion"; in one case a girl fell into a well, "being of an age when the danger was not understood."[23] In another case Alice of Lonsdale, age nineteen, remembered tripping in a hole in the road when not paying attention to where she was going because, as she said, she was only five years old.[24] Adults realized that certain types of behavior were normal aspects of childhood. This awareness was acknowledged time after time in the miracle reports: children exhibited "childish zeal," "youthful excess," "childish playfulness"; their accidents followed behavior "typical of children" or infants. Eighteen-month-old Thomas fell and punctured his palate while wandering around the house with a sharp stick in his mouth, "the way that playing children do."[25]

CURATIVE TECHNIQUES

Given the purposes of the miracle collections, only a few of the surgeons or physicians who appeared in them were portrayed sympathetically. According to most miracle reports, doctors usually gave up after examining children or, if they attempted any remedies (expensive remedies, as many records are careful to note), their patients were left in the same or even worse condition. Quite apart from the records' biases, such an outcome is hardly surprising, given the state of contemporary medicine. Parents often ministered to their sick or injured children, preparing potions or applying poultices, for instance, even giving "a woman's milk" to a feverish fourteen-year-old boy.[26] While the "official" church ignored most home remedies, it disapproved of some folk cures—the magic, evil incantations, and sortilege about which papal commissioners, examining witnesses to miraculous cures, always asked. Some incantations, of course, were perfectly acceptable: after an eight-year-old boy was run over by a cart, the carters, on their knees with arms stretched heavenward, sent a doggerel-prayer-incantation to Henry VI, "holy and best of kings," to bring them aid and relief.[27] Although "superstitious" adjuncts to healing were mentioned in the miracle reports even less frequently than physicians and surgeons, they must have played an important role in contemporary life. An English couple, for instance, tried to cure their son of fever by placing rings and written charms around his neck.[28] Such charms were usually combinations of geometrical figures and Latin, Greek, and Hebrew words or letters that were strung out in lines of gibberish; for the literate, their incomprehensibility made them seem even more powerful.

While the hierarchy condemned outright "superstitious" cures, the church recognized, although sometimes grudgingly, a whole range of quasi-religious remedies that seemed to arise from magical as well as religious impulses. When describing how a mother "measured" her child, the compiler of Henry VI's miracles remarked that she was going along with a commonplace belief of the laity.[29] The ritual of measuring—a technique used throughout England and in Europe—usually involved taking a piece of thread or string and stretching it out over the afflicted child, from head to foot and sometimes between outstretched hands, while praying for spiritual assistance.[30] In this way the child was thus "measured to" a particular saint. The thread was then incorporated into wax (perhaps after being twisted or coiled), forming a candle to be offered at the designated saint's tomb. In many instances, the very act of measuring was credited with immediate curative or recuperative results. Another rite, widespread in England, was to bend a coin held over a child while vowing to offer that particular coin at a saint's tomb. In one case, a flustered father was so anxious to attain the saint's bounty that he bent a silver coin by pressing it forcefully against his daughter's forehead.[31] A very common means of curing, usually encouraged by the church, was the application of water (dispensed by churchmen) that had come into contact with relics. Water that had washed a saint's corpse or was thought to contain dissolved particles of a saint's body was considered the most potent. Shortly after Becket's murder on December 29, 1170, Canterbury monks began selling water that, they claimed, contained some of the martyr's blood. This water, sold in small lead vials or ampoules worn around the neck or kept in churches or in the home, was used in a great variety of ways, particularly during illnesses. Becket came to be known as "the best physician," an epithet that was stamped on some of the vials. In various ways, accommodating and enterprising Canterbury monks averted any danger that pilgrims' demands for Becket water might eventually deplete the original stock.

These curative rites could be performed at a distance from the holy relics, but many sick, injured, or "dead" children and adults were taken to the shrines where they waited for deliverance. Quite often children were placed on saints' shrines.[32] This was especially true of aborted, stillborn, or suddenly "dead" infants, who were rushed to church and set down on or

near the altar or a holy tomb. Older children taken to shrines for a cure
might stay there until miraculously blessed, or until their parents' patience
was exhausted and they all went home disappointed. Sleeping at curative
shrines, or incubation, was well known in antiquity; forms of this behavior
seem to have been practiced in the Middle Ages as well. It sometimes happened that cripples, the blind, the mute, and the mentally disturbed fell
asleep afflicted and awoke cured, perhaps after a dream or vision of the
entombed holy person.

No matter what particular curative techniques were applied to children—depositing them on tombs, bending coins over them, measuring
them, bathing them with relic water or pouring some into their mouths—all
such endeavors were accompanied by vows. Vows were so essential to the
curative process that very often papal boards of inquiry wanted to know the
precise words used, by whom pronounced, when, where, and in whose
presence. Canonization commissions thus seem to have endorsed the crude
do ut des principle, according to which a pact or "deal" is made with an
invisible power: if you cure my child, I will go on pilgrimage to your
shrine/will offer ten shillings at your tomb/will fast and drink no wine for
three months, and so on. In fact, regardless of what the witness being examined might have been thinking, the pope's representatives were attempting
to establish as clearly as possible that a cure or resuscitation had occurred
because of the invocation of the *particular* dead person whose life and wonders they were currently examining; the making of a vow to that person was
the commissioners' assurance that this had been the case. Sometimes
promises to the uncanonized dead were combined with vows to established
saints as well as to God the Father, Christ, and the Virgin. Vows made over
a child's body were usually pronounced aloud; occasionally a witness
explained that no one had heard her or his vow since these had been "made
in my heart." The records also suggest that it was believed that the words
would be heard more readily in heaven if the vowers were in direct contact
with the earth. In England, for example, after a child fell into a brook,
everyone knelt with bare knees on the earth to pray as best they could. The
procedure is described even more explicitly in the near drowning of a little
girl near Hereford. According to her father, the men removed their stockings
so that they, like the women, could pray with their bare knees upon the
earth. Another witness claimed that everyone removed their shoes, and yet
another stated that some bystanders (both men and women) rolled their
stockings down toward their feet, while others took off both shoes and
stockings before kneeling on the ground.[33] Presumably this added potency
to their prayers: perhaps some deep-seated impulse prompts physical con-

tact with the earth when mere humans address the invisible world—God did, after all, command Moses to remove his sandals.[34]

In most cases the child's parents made the vows. Occasionally, the spiritual condition of the vower was mentioned, as in southern France, where a woman's five-year-old son, seeing her distressed because of an eye ailment, suggested that she kneel and make a vow to Louis of Toulouse in exchange for a cure. This "wise child" topos concluded with the mother responding "Son, I am not worthy for him to hear me, since I am a sinner; but *you* vow."[35] Apart from specific individuals, the vows and prayers of whole classes of people were believed to be especially effective. In one instance these were enumerated: someone sent for the vicar, the aged clerics, and the widows and little children *(parvuli)* of the village to come and pray at the side of a drowned child.[36] In another case one of the women kneeling by an infant's corpse addressed her neighbors as follows: "Are we not five widows here? Let us bend our knees nine times invoking the blessed Thomas [Becket], and repeat the Lord's Prayer nine times in his name."[37] Whether vowing or praying, it was customary to raise the arms and eyes heavenward, a form of Christian prayer more primitive than the folded hands of feudal supplication; occasionally it was stated that the upraised hands were joined.[38] Sometimes suppliants reminded saints of earlier appeals that had been made on behalf of a child or of favors already granted by a saint to a suppliant. Naturally, weeping often accompanied the vows and prayers of parents and others kneeling by an afflicted child.[39]

What objects or activities did people promise their saints? These took a variety of forms, some specific to northern Europe, others to the south. Before examining these differences, we begin with the universal vow of pilgrimage to a saint's tomb, sometimes barefoot. People vowed to go on pilgrimage once, annually for a specific period of years, or even for the rest of their lives. Some achieved a form of temporary asceticism while on pilgrimage by leaving their "inner" garments at home; the barefoot pilgrim, skin chafed by rough wool, thus made him- or herself into a kind of public penitent.[40] Some suppliants vowed to feed paupers or to offer candles at shrines. Images or quantities of wax were promised, but sometimes, too, there were lengths of cloth (perhaps fringed with gold), rings and jewels, even livestock. In addition, in both northern and southern Europe sometimes children themselves were commended, or offered, to saints.[41] After a girl had been pulled from a well, the lady *(domina)* of a village near Pontigny went into the church where villagers had taken her body. The *domina* promised the saint "if you save this girl I shall give her to you, and will concede whatever authority I have over her, and won't for any reason try to sell

her or her heirs' homage to anyone else."[42] Dedications like these are remi-
niscent of the earlier practice of oblation, when a child actually was given to
a monastic order by being taken to the altar and placed in contact with it, to
the accompaniment of a formal statement or document from a parent or
guardian.[43] In Lanfranc's *Monastic Constitutions*, for instance, the child's parents were to wrap his hands in the altar cloth and offer him to the abbot.
Until about the time of Gratian in the twelfth century, these vicarious vows
were binding, regardless of what the child wished when he or she was
older. Such customs were changing during the thirteenth century, and
monastic child oblation, as such, was all but extinct by the fourteenth and fifteenth centuries, although John Boswell suggested that it continued in
other forms.[44] That the custom of oblation was not entirely outmoded in the
later Middle Ages is suggested by two examples from the cures attributed
to Nicholas of Tolentino. In one instance in 1323, a mother vowed a very ill
child to the dead holy man and promised that, if the saint cured him, she
would enter her son in the Augustinian order as soon as he could survive
without her nurturing care. However, he died eight months later.[45] In
another example from the same collection, a father whose infants had died,
one after the other, vowed to name his next son Nicholas, offer him to the
saint on his tomb, take him back in exchange for the boy's weight in wax,
and when he grew up enter him in the Augustinian order, "if the boy wished
it."[46] When the father testified in 1325, his son Nicholas was six months old.

Most children who were brought to tombs and physically deposited on
them seem to have represented surrogate oblations in which the child,
instead of remaining in the service of the saint or the church, returned
home with the parents. On the other hand, children could be left at tombs
symbolically, in what has been called a "rite of substitution."[47] There was the
candle that "contained" the child's measurements; or the weight of the child
victim offered in grain or in wax, as in the case just cited in which a father
substituted wax for his son, whom he "took back" from the saint.[48] Although
such offerings were made for adults too, the various collections suggest that
they were associated more commonly with children. Southern European
cases furnish interesting variations on this theme of pseudo-oblation. Some
parents, seeing their offspring revive after a vow, left the child's hair at the
tomb, as Berard the notary witnessed at Tolentino. This offering becomes
even more significant in view of what the Italian Dominican Giovanni
Dominici (ca. 1356-ca. 1420) wrote in his handbook on child raising, condemning parental pride: "How much time is wasted in the frequent comb-
ing of children's hair; in keeping the hair blond if they are girls or perhaps
having it curled!"[49] Other parents took their children to shrines, stripped

them, and left their clothing on or near the tombs.[50] In an Italian case, a grandfather vowed to take his grandson to a tomb, undress him, leave all his clothing behind, and never take it back.[51] This example suggests that the undressing occurred at the shrine itself, and it raises the possibility that the donors sometimes recovered such gifts of clothing. Children's clothing also was offered in northern Europe, but the ritual of stripping a child at the tomb does not seem to have been observed. In any event, the underlying assumption seems to have been that a vow dedicating a child to a saint could be discharged by leaving a substitute for the child, whether in wax or some other form. As for other differences between the regions, it seems to have been a southern custom for a parent to vow to go to a saint's shrine with her or his—or the child's—hands tied up, symbolizing, presumably, a suppliant's total submission to a saint's power.[52]

Apart from pilgrimages and offerings of hair, candles, grain, or clothing, perhaps the most common gifts to the holy dead were votives, sometimes of silver or gold, but more often of inexpensive wax, made to resemble the part healed or, if the beneficiary was a child or infant, the whole body. The variety among votives was limited only by the imaginations of the donors; one report reveals that a little wax cradle complete with tiny infant was left at a shrine.[53] Usually the gifts were wax eyes, teeth, hands, arms, legs, feet, heads, and the like, often purchased from vendors strategically stationed near pilgrimage centers. In one case a boy ran to buy some teeth from "the one who makes wax images" near the Marseilles shrine of Louis of Toulouse.[54] Such objects, which also might include bits and pieces of humanity (sloughed-off skin from burns, small bones, teeth, vomited-up "worms," cherry pits or bladder stones, even a bit of tissue from a woman's genitals) often were suspended or otherwise displayed around or near the tombs of the holy dead, like trophies.[55] These objects helped to publicize the wonders of the dead and to encourage pilgrims (with their offerings) to visit parish churches and monastic and cathedral naves, transepts, crypts, and choirs. Often, when the monks or canons of such establishments accepted a miraculous report, an extempore sermon was preached, the hymn *Te Deum* resounded, a procession circled the shrine, and the bells rang out. Church bells were especially effective publicizers of miraculous wonders. Testifying in 1325, our notary Berard claimed that only a few months earlier, while in Florence, he was drawn to the Augustinians' church of the Holy Spirit after hearing the brethren ringing their bells to announce a miracle attributed to Nicholas.[56]

2

THE DANGERS OF BIRTH AND EARLY INFANCY

....

Our study begins with the perils of pregnancy and childbirth in the later Middle Ages. In examining pregnancy and neonatal existence, this chapter serves as an extended preface to the analysis of children's accidents and illnesses, since familial interactions that came into play when children were endangered were evident even before birth: premonitions of danger haunted expectant parents, who were well aware that parturition could mean death rather than life.[1] Parents had every reason to be afraid. Although "statistical" data are, of course, unavailable, one can assume that the death rate for medieval mothers and infants was high, reflecting contemporary nutritional and general living conditions, certain assumptions about female physiology and anatomy, the application of relatively rudimentary medical techniques for dealing with emergencies during delivery, and the tending of neonates and mothers in sometimes grossly insanitary conditions. With the additional element of excruciating pain and its anticipation, it is probably safe to assume that a woman's attitude toward her unborn or recently born child was a confused jumble of anxiety, love, fear, regret, hope, and despair—for herself and her infant. As soon as she became pregnant she would be well advised, then, to ward off possible evils through her faith in God and the saints. She might go on pilgrimage to various shrines, hang relics or religious images around her neck, and engage in prayer from morning to night.

STERILITY AND CONCEPTION

Paradoxically, however, a childless woman would have been equally persistent in her prayers to become pregnant. Even if the planets and the waxing moon were just right, even if vows had been made to all the patron saints of childbirth, even if dolls were propped up near the marriage bed to encourage fertility, and even if the couple used four egg yolks, powdered cloves, saffron, and hot oil of roses (as recommended in a late-medieval English medical text), the womb still might remain barren.[2] And if this were so, the couple well knew what to expect from kin and neighbors: sterility brought shame and disappointment. It is likely that church teachings about sexuality, inculcated from the earliest Christian centuries, had by the central Middle Ages instilled in ordinary parishioners the dictum that sex was to be tolerated in marriage for the procreation of children (although virginity was best). Ambivalent about the pleasures of sex, the church preferred that children be brought forth, in James Brundage's words, after "grimly joyless and respon-sible copulation."[3] As the Dominican Nicholas of Gorran (d. 1295) wrote, a woman's only alternative to virginity, should she desire salvation, was to "generate children continually until her death."[4] In such a context, a childless marriage left the couple open to suspicion: perhaps they used contraception, or practiced infanticide, or wantonly indulged themselves in sexual pleasures, possibly enjoying "unnatural" sex (e.g., sexual positions graphically described, and then condemned, in moralists' writings and in the peniten-tials), or had intercourse during proscribed times without regard for the "proper" goal of sexual activities.[5] For many reasons, in medieval Europe the risks of pregnancy and childbirth seem to have been overshadowed by a greater fear of disgrace in marrying and producing no children at all. This universal concern took on added urgency when linked with descent of titles or properties. William, a Lincolnshire knight, brought his wife before the keepers of Becket's shrine.[6] "The Lord," William explained, "closed up her vulva, and removed from me all hope of begetting children." They had been childless for fifteen years, while her youth "flowed away in anxiety." After Becket's death, the two decided to ask help of the martyr. En route to Canterbury, at their very first stop she began to regain the vigor and color of earlier years. As they approached the city the woman (whom her husband never named) had an encouraging dream about Becket; later that year they had a son whom they named Thomas, in honor of their benefactor.

Sterility, impotence, or frigidity—whether affecting knights or peas-ants—could be viewed as a God-sent punishment for some unconfessed sin or as the result of an enemy's curse, or even due to some biological anomaly in one or both partners. A well-known test to determine which partner was responsible for failure of progeny involved placing urine from husband and wife in containers of bran and examining the mess nine days later, to ascertain "whether there is any fault in either one of them or both."[7] Although the existence of such experiments suggests that there was perhaps room for doubt, normally it was assumed that the wife was "at fault." As an English woman expressed it around A.D. 1300, for a long time people thought she was sterile, which made her feel disgraced.[8] After prayers and a visit to Cantilupe's tomb, however, she gave birth within a year — to twins. In this English case a saint did his work quickly, as he did in a southern French example, when conception occurred the same night a vow was made to the dead Pope Urban V.[9] In Italy Riccucia testified before papal commissioners in 1325 that, not having conceived any children, she promised God and St. Nicholas that if she gave birth, she would name the child Nicholas and offer the child's weight in wax at the tomb.[10] That very night *(dicta nocte)*, she continued, immediately after making the vow while in bed with her husband, she conceived a son, duly named Nicholas. The papal commissioners, punctilious as always, asked who was present when her vow was made — they normally asked for names of witnesses to vows or any purportedly miraculous events: Riccucia responded (possibly with a hint of exasperation, given the circumstances) that her husband, who had since died, was there. The papal functionaries continued down the list of questions, or interrogatories, that they had established beforehand. When they asked whether her son still lived, she showed him to the pope's men. He was about eight years old.

Riccucia did not indicate how long she had been married before she conceived, but such information was sometimes provided. Guido, who stated that he was about thirty, and Marguarita had been married for twelve years but could have no children. They made a vow to take a wax image, the weight and length of any child they might have, to the Marseilles tomb of Louis of Toulouse.[11] Marguarita conceived within the year and produced a son who was still living seven years later. Although Guido gives us his age, he also gives us a mathematical-biological conundrum. Guido said that he was *about* thirty years old; he then said that he had been married twelve years without children, until his son was born, at present age seven. This would suggest either that Guido had been married at age eleven (which was possible), or that when he says "about," that is what he means; adding five years to his age creates a more reasonable chronology. However, even while acknowledging the caveat that most medieval people did not know their own ages (including, as J. R. Hale pointed out, late medieval and renaissance kings[12]), occasionally one can hazard a guess at reasons for infertility if the ages, as given, are approximately correct. After being sworn to provide true testimony on September 9, 1325, Pina told papal examiners that she was thirty years old, not adding "about." She went on to tell them that after some four years of childlessness, sixteen years earlier she made a vow in her husband's house, in her mother's presence, that if St. Nicholas would hear her prayer, she would name the child Nicholas and strip it at the saint's tomb, leaving its clothing as an offering.[13] Within a month she began a pregnancy that ended with a daughter, named Nicolucia. If Pina has her dates right, she was married at age ten, well before menarche; therefore, try as she and her husband might, a pregnancy was unlikely.[14] By age fourteen, however, when she happened to make her vow, biological changes (and spousal attentions) wrought the desired result.

Although Pina may have expected too much of her prepubescent body, in general contemporaries were aware of the exigencies of biological development. As expressed by Soranus, an early second-century writer, "One must judge the majority [of women] from the ages of fifteen to forty to be fit for conception, if they are not mannish, compact, and oversturdy, or too flabby and very moist. . . . [Other women less suitable for childbearing included] those who quickly change color, especially if the color deepens."[15] One medieval witness claimed that he had nearly given up after years without children, believing that his wife was sterile although, as he put it, she was still young enough to conceive. Pontius, another southern French witness, swore that he had no offspring after eight years of marriage even though his wife "was old enough for pregnancy." She conceived two months after his vow to Urban V and was still pregnant when he went to the tomb to tell his story.[16] In another case, the female's youth created a problem during delivery, rather than at conception. After suffering labor pains for three days Alienor, a knight's wife, seemed near death, "for she was not yet of the age at which she should have become a mother."[17] Her husband, William of Oxford, especially compassionate "because of the unseasonable conception," tied some Becket relics around her neck, upon which she immediately gave birth to a son. In the early fourteenth century a Montpellier doctor, Bernard de Gordon, noted that birth was difficult for certain women, particularly girls who conceived before they were thirteen.[18]

The ages at which medieval couples married tended to vary with their social level and region, as well as with the epoch in which they lived. The slight evidence provided by the miracles does not allow fine distinctions to be made between early versus late medieval marriages, or between northern and southern European marriage patterns. All that can be offered is a handful of cases which are suggestive rather than conclusive. As for the relative ages of spouses, in twenty accident and illness reports the ages of both parents of an affected child were recorded: in fifteen of these twenty couples, the husband was older than his wife, in five cases by (reportedly) just ten years; but in four marriages, the wife was said to have been older than her husband, in one instance by twenty years. In only one couple were the ages the same (thirty-eight). Such rough statistics are weakened by the tendency of contemporaries to state their ages in round numbers or multiples of five.[19] Altogether, the ages of 128 mothers and fathers were recorded, as shown in figure 2.1.

The figure includes the fathers' ages as recorded in the illness and accident accounts but not in birth and infancy miracles, since very few fathers' ages were provided in those records; it is based, however, on the mothers whose ages were listed in all three categories. The pattern reflects the ages of parents at the time of their child's miracle. Most of the women were just about evenly divided within the childbearing decades of the twenties and thirties. Over half of the fathers, however, were in their thirties; the rest were roughly equally divided among those who were in their twenties, forties, and fifties. It has been observed that, in fifteenth-century Florence, the highest child producing age for women was twenty to thirty-four; for the men, from thirty to fifty.[20] Very few women in their fifties had children younger than fourteen; they were outnumbered, proportionally, by teenage mothers. In sum, if this sample is at all representative, most of the parents involved in these children's miracles were in their twenties and thirties, with most of the fathers in their thirties.

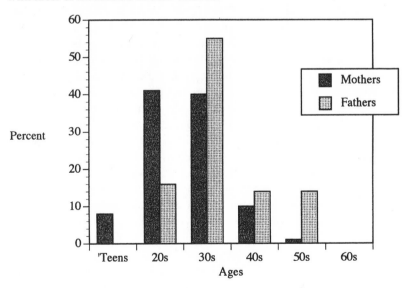

Figure 2.1 Ages of parents, based on 85 reported ages for mothers, 43 for fathers (total 128 specified ages)

Whatever age they happened to be, both sexes seem to have accepted the assumption that women were at fault for not producing children.[21] Presumably this taint also applied to women whose infants, year after year, were stillborn or died soon after birth, as in Barlessa's case. She had had four babies who died immediately after being baptized. Again pregnant and afraid to lose yet another child, Barlessa vowed to present the infant's weight in wax at Urban V's tomb if her newborn lived. Three years after her son was born (he was still alive), she brought eleven pounds of wax to the tomb. Another happy parent offered twenty pounds of wax for the successful birth and continued life of his son, named Urban after the spiritual benefactor; he and his wife had produced several children, but all had been "unable to live."[22] The records are replete with examples of stillbirths and of women who repeatedly went through the long, dangerous process of pregnancy only to see their children born and immediately buried. In the late 1280s Golluthith from Herefordshire claimed that she had given birth seven times, but each time the infant was stillborn. On the eighth occasion, the child was born dead but revived after bystanders measured it to Cantilupe.[23] However, such positive results might not break the unlucky pattern: in 1392 Katherina, then in her late twenties or early thirties, gave birth to a dead son; next year the same thing happened. By 1394, about to give birth again and apprehensive of the same results, she was assisted by seven trustworthy neighbor women. They found that this infant too was dead, lying motionless for an hour. On their knees, all of the women begged for help from Dorothy of Montau. Their vows and prayers completed, the infant started to move and come to life, even as they watched. About eleven years later, when Katherina told the commissioners about this, naming some of the women involved, she added that after giving birth to this child, in the next two years she had two more children, both dead.[24] Sometimes women offered reasons for their "defects": during 1404 Gertrude, a widow of thirty-four, explained that although she had once given birth, she was so impaired from her birth trauma that for five years she remained sterile and, although diligently trying, she was unable to conceive again. In addition to this, her kin abused her for providing no children for their consolation. Finally one of them (or perhaps her husband) vowed to take some wax to Dorothy's tomb. Nine months ten days later she gave birth to a baby girl, named Dorothy out of reverence for the saint.[25] Children mattered to a whole kinship network, and pressures to produce must have been a source of great anxiety within marriage—as in the case of the couple who, after several years of childlessness, were quarreling every day. The wife was so depressed that she "didn't know what to do."[26] When such problems arose among the

rich and powerful, ways could be found to end the marriage. It was probably not so easy for most.

PREGNANCY AND PRENATAL COMPLICATIONS

Let us assume that the desired conception was attained, whether easily and
naturally or only after recourse to saintly or spiritual help, doctors, or medical recipes—of which there were many. It was already ancient lore that special care should be shown to pregnant women, as illustrated in the writings
of Soranus. In his opinion, for example, "the cold bath ought to be used in
moderation . . . , so that no shivering sensation may arise."[27] In some late-
medieval German cities pregnant and lying-in women were given special
legal protection and support.[28] The miracle records also indicate an awareness of this need to treat pregnant women gently, or at least differently. In
England, for instance, when a near-term mother insisted on clutching her
drowned daughter to her, the husband and neighbors were concerned that
the mother's grief, and the coldness of the child's body, might cause a mis-
carriage; and when a French woman asked permission of a male kinsman to
go on pilgrimage, he denied her request since—as he said—she was heavy
with pregnancy.[29] In spite of such solicitude, of course women fell ill or suffered accidents or other traumatic experiences that resulted in miscarriages.
And some experienced even more mysterious postconception developments,
such as the English woman Agnes. The usual nine months came and went,
and then another nine months, during which she could feel no growth.[30] At
last "a certain woman" told the unfortunate Agnes "you have already gone far
beyond the set bounds of pregnancy. The fetus you conceived has not
increased, for it follows the course of the moon . . ." Obviously, something
peculiar had happened: the fetus grew while the moon increased in size but,
as the woman explained, the moon's rays continued to affect the child so that
"after a full moon, it [the fetus] vanishes again to practically nothing." Agnes
was told to venerate the dead king, Henry VI, through whose spiritual merits a safe birth would result. From that time, the child grew in Agnes's womb
until the birth took place as and when predicted, to the happiness of both
parents. The child was normal, without (says the scribe) the monstrous
deformity that one might have expected from so curious a gestation.

A more typical problem was reported of Eymeniarda of Narbonne,
pregnant for seven and one-half months, who was attacked by a painful,
constant fever that lasted about two weeks. Three well-known doctors
agreed that nothing could be done, so communion and the last rites were
administered. Eymeniarda's mother, her brother John, and Stephen (another

kinsman) gathered round the dying woman. Grief-stricken at the impend-
ing loss of his sister, John vowed a barefoot pilgrimage to Louis's tomb in
Marseilles, promising to take his sister there and to offer one pound of wax
and some cloth, should Louis restore her health and release her from the
pregnancy. That evening she was relieved of her fever and of a male child
who was baptized, even though, as the record notes, she should have continued to carry him another six weeks. When asked the usual follow-up
interrogatories by the papal commissioners, Eymeniarda was vague about
when the vow was made and who was present, since she had been feverish
at the time, but her brother and Stephen, who also testified, cleared up these
points. Apparently the child, although baptized, did not survive his premature birth.[31] A happier conclusion was recorded in England where a nobleman's wife, coming to the end of her pregnancy, was afflicted with "dropsy,"
an imprecise term that suggests turgidity or edema. Her friends, realizing
that this would complicate delivery, were in despair. Sure enough, when she
gave birth the child seemed dead and she herself was in great danger. Even
so, she had sufficient presence of mind to ask her husband to leave, not
wanting him to see his son. Meanwhile some of the women prayed to Simon
de Montfort, who died in 1265 battling English royal forces, and they suggested measuring her body for a candle for the "martyr." After the midwives
carried out this suggestion, the woman's condition improved. Her husband
returned to her side, asking about the child, and, despite attempts to spare
his feelings, eventually he found the *abortivum*. After he bent a penny over
the infant while vowing the coin to Montfort, the child opened its eyes and
began crying.[32]

In the preceding century Becket was called upon in a similar case. Aliza
of Middleton, pregnant, was afflicted with dropsy—a horrible swelling,
the monk wrote, which complicated her already dangerous state. Whenever
she shifted position in bed, she heard a rush of water in her womb.
Medicines, herbs, and potions were administered, without effect. Aliza then
turned to celestial doctors *(medici)*, making vows to saints such as Leonard,
Margaret, and Edmund (the first was patron of pregnant women; the second, a protector from childbirth's dangers), but the saints seemed to ignore
her. She grew desperate, begging for her uterus to be cut open *(uterum . . .
aperiri)* and the infant extracted and baptized so that, even if it should die,
it would be reborn in the Lord.[33] No one, however, would agree to carry out
this operation, this "pious impiety," as the twelfth-century Canterbury monk
called it. After five days of labor her midwives advised her to call on Becket,
which she did, vowing to visit his tomb if first she felt herself visited by *him*.
As soon as these words were out of her mouth, throughout the whole house

everyone heard a bursting sound, and a great deal of water flowed from her womb. The midwives could not assist because of the heat of the waters. Aliza thought that she was producing twins; her mother agreed that there was more to come from her womb, as even more water gushed out. At last, having expelled what (in the monk's words) had blocked egress, she gave birth to a healthy boy. Aliza's behavior was typical of medieval sufferers from afflictions of all kinds: earthly medicaments were tried, then the spiritual or celestial. Her case is perhaps less typical in the number of attendant midwives: seven, along with her mother.[34]

Women's preexisting complications or ailments, then, and illnesses contracted after conception threatened both mother and fetus. There was yet another source of danger: no matter how careful they were, some expectant women suffered trauma. Sometimes these physical shocks were deliberately inflicted. In November of 1255, for instance, "Robert le Cordwaner beat Sarah wife of Henry the Tailor so that she gave birth to a female child"; about the same time it was claimed that "Richard Scharp wool-merchant beat his wife Emma so that she gave birth to a still-born boy" after which he was arrested for homicide; and in the 1270s an accusation was brought against a certain William, alleging "that he beat his wife Alice so that she gave birth to a still-born boy," although he was acquitted because "the suspicion is slight."[35] These are hardly isolated cases: similar beatings followed by miscarriages were reported elsewhere — Devon in the 1230s, for example.[36] Other traumas were truly "accidents." When Christiana, Richard Tayler's wife, seven months pregnant, fell down some steps from the solar (upper floor) of her house in Surrey, the result was painful labor followed by the expulsion of a tiny female fetus of meager, deformed shape, "a monstrous imitation" of a child. Her thighs were twisted and badly joined at the hips, there were horrendous concavities on her back, and her digestive powers were so weak that anything given for nourishment was vomited up. Nevertheless, while nearly wasting away, she survived for nine months in this lamentable condition. At that point her parents invoked Henry VI's help and took her measure — as is the custom, the commentator remarks. The child, named Ysodia or Ysydora, began improving, mending from that day forward.[37] Historians examining abandonment and infanticide in medieval and renaissance Europe might find this an interesting case study. This very unhealthy female infant would seem to have been a prime candidate for immediate rejection; yet through parental care, Isadora Taylor survived — at least through this dangerous phase of early childhood.

Accidents also happened because animals were part of nearly every facet of medieval life. In a case that also emphasizes the importance of baptism, Master Thomas Bartholucius, thirty-six, testified that some nine-teen years earlier (another example of early marriage) he had a wife called Thomassucia. They lived in her father's house in Montolmo, some twelve miles from Tolentino, Thomas's birthplace. On Good Friday in 1306 he was taking his pregnant wife to Tolentino, perhaps to join his kin in celebrating Easter in his home town. It had rained the previous day, the roads were muddy, and about halfway through the journey his wife's horse slipped and Thomassucia, near term, fell off. The horse began trampling the woman's feet, its hooves twisted in her clothing. After the animal calmed down, Thomassucia was helped back on, and they completed their journey. About a week later she gave birth to a boy, but the women, believing that it was doomed, performed a makeshift baptism. Then the infant seemed to die. Thomas, meanwhile, vowed a wax image to Nicholas. Noting signs of life in the child, the women called to the grieving father, who was walking about his house. Finding the infant reanimated, Thomas made arrangements for its "proper" baptism. It was carried to church, baptized, and named John. Two days later John was dead. The mother told the papal commissioners that, as was usual for women who had just given birth, she was resting, although she could hear people discussing the child. Another witness to John's birth, fifty-year-old Margarita, was sworn in. For whatever reasons, the papal notaries did not in this instance summarize the testimony as they usually did, but recorded it in detail. While her testimony contains some discrepancies when compared with the father's version of events, this does not necessar-ily discredit her.

> Were you present when a son was born of the wife named
> Thomassia de Monteulmi [Montolmo], and her husband
> master Thomas de Tolentino? *Yes, in the husband's house.*
> Was the child born alive? *Yes.*
> When did the birth of this son occur? *It was not more than eighteen
> years ago.*
> What month was it? *April.*
> What day was it? *Thursday after Easter.*
> Who was present? *The mother of master Thomas, a woman named
> Grana, who no longer lives.*
> Was the birth prior to the death of brother Nicholas? *Yes.* [This
> differs from the father's statement.]
> Was the infant immediately baptized because of necessity, in the
> paternal home, by the women there on account of mortal
> danger? *Yes.*
> Could the infant have been carried to the parish church without
> mortal danger to it? *No, as far as it seemed to me.*

Was the infant placed alive in a container of water, with the intention of baptizing it, in the house of its father? *Yes.*

Was the infant, when taken from the container of water, alive or dead? *Dead; it had all the signs of death in its eyes, hands, mouth, and whole body.*

Did anyone make vows and prayers to God that, through the life, merits and prayers of brother Nicholas, God would resuscitate him from death to life, so that he could be baptized according to ecclesiastical form and his soul not be lost? *Yes.*

Who made these vows and prayers? *The mother of Thomas called Lady Grana.*

With what words were the prayers made? *That God should resuscitate the boy through the prayers and merits of the said brother Nicholas; she asked brother Nicholas to ask God that the child could be baptized in ecclesiastical form, lest he lose his soul; in return she would fast on bread and water every Friday for the rest of her life in reverence for God and brother Nicholas.*

Were you present when these prayers were made? *Yes.*

After the prayers, did viability appear in the newborn? *Yes.*

Was there a delay between death and resurrection? *Yes, a good hour.*

Was the infant carried to the church to be baptized on the same day? *Yes.*

What church was the baptismal church? *The church of the Blessed Mary.*

Were you present at the baptism? *Yes.*

What name was given to the child? *John.*

How long afterwards did the child live? *For two days.*[38]

LABOR PAINS AND PROLONGED LABOR

Medieval recorders of miracles, no doubt with the words of Genesis clearly in mind—"I shall give you great pain in childbearing; with labor you will bear children"—acknowledged the excruciating and violent suffering that many women underwent, which they themselves could only imagine. Margarita of Camerino told the commissioners that one of her neighbors, Sanctucia, was in such difficult labor that death seemed better to her than life. The women thought that she was, in fact, about to die. But Margarita prayed to Nicholas that if he helped the woman, "I shall come to the church where thy body lies buried, barefoot and with my hands bound." At once Sanctucia began speaking and was freed from her labor. Although many women were there, Margarita noted, she could not remember their names since it was a long time ago, and in any event, she never thought that she would be testifying about the incident.[39] The pain of childbirth was not easily forgotten: it was so feared by a French tavernkeeper's wife who had already experienced it that, although on the verge of giving birth, she went to Louis's tomb to beg for freedom from that torture. That very night she produced a girl, painlessly, for which she offered the saint a candle.[40] In several instances in medieval collections, when reference is made to the pains of illness or accident, an explicit comparison is made with the pangs of childbirth. Henry VI's miracle chronicler, seeking for words to describe the agony experienced by Alice Smith, who suffered from a kidney or bladder stone, noted that her pain seemed greater and sharper than that of childbirth.[41] In another case, from southern France, a woman's afflicted eyes tormented her for three weeks during which she cried out as if in labor; she had never felt such torture, she claimed, even in childbirth.[42] In one of Urban's miracles, a nobleman was suffering so badly from stone that he howled day and night "like a woman giving birth."[43] Conversely, the absence of screams, tears, and shrieks could seem ominous to the women hovering round a parturient. As Oudeburgis labored, the pains were so sharp that she lost the use of her tongue and seemed as insensible as an image.[44] After the midwives vowed, she produced a son, although, as the record notes, the birth was contrary to the usual manner: his back was twisted round to where his front should have been, and his little body was bent; his head and feet were touching together—perhaps a frank breech presentation. In such a state, as the collector of the miracles wrote, the little globular body was taken without harm from the mother's womb. While actually giving birth, however, the mother emitted not one sound, no cry or groan, which seemed unnatural (innaturaliter) to the midwives, for whom labor screams seem to have been a "necessary" part of the birth ritual.[45] Sometimes, however, the extreme pain of a parturient, as in a Pomeranian case, drove the attendant women themselves into great distress.[46]

Perhaps even more than the sharp pains of delivery, women feared prolonged, exhausting labor. In medieval as in modern times, lengthy, difficult labor was a matter of grave concern, affecting both mother and infant.[47] One of the best-known literary expressions of this comes from the memoirs of the twelfth-century abbot Guibert de Nogent, who described his own birth and how his mother suffered "pains long-endured, . . . her tortures increasing as her hour drew near. . . ."[48] There are many examples in the miracle records of labor lasting two, three, five, or eight and more days. Before his death in 1305, Nicholas of Tolentino was involved in one such case, which centered on Flordalisia, in labor—as she testified some twenty-five years later—for about eight days. Because of the faith she had in the holy man, she sent for him to confess her sins, believing that she was about to die. He arrived, prayed that God should release the woman from her labor, and within two hours of this she was freed. There is no mention of the infant's survival.[49] An English woman was nearly deranged from labor pains she endured for fifteen days.[50] It was feared that she might become violent and do away with the child but, after drinking Becket water and falling asleep—during which time she dreamed that a hand gently touched her womb—on waking up she discovered herself near birth. Onlookers considered it marvelous that her next hour—usually (the monk writes) the most dangerous period for those giving birth—was passed without pain. She produced a son. This case is typical of many miracles in which the suffering woman's labor is relieved, and the child is well and healthy, or, if "dead," resuscitated after appeals to a saint. However, some births ended tragically even in these reports, as recounted in a Becket miracle involving a Lisieux woman.[51] According to William of Canterbury, her breasts swelled with milk, her womb began to open, and the fetus moved with a stronger pulse, but—by God's will—the parturition was changed to grief, the swelling of her body into the fear of death.[52] Powerless to expel the fetus, she lay screaming and weeping for more than two months. Following a vow to Becket, the fetus seemed to disappear and she recovered. At least this French woman did not have to experience the horror of an English knight's wife, who went into labor but was unable to effect birth. As our Canterbury monk put it, she was destined to be not mother but sepulcher for her baby. Fifteen days later she was measured to Becket, after which she produced something that looked "like meat boiled in a pot."[53]

An even more unhappy case was noted by William of Canterbury, who opened his account by reflecting that the "life of the continent is peaceful; the life of the married, laborious."[54] After expending a few more lines on such commonplaces, he began his report: Margaret from the village of Hameldon was pregnant. One winter night, because of an imbalance (of the humors, presumably) in her body, she got a nosebleed that lasted for hours. The menstrual blood reserved for the nutriment of the fetus, William wrote, was thus exhausted. (William and many of his contemporaries believed, on ancient authority, that at conception a woman's menses became placental food for the child and, after birth, the blood was converted into milk for the baby.[55]) As a result, according to William, Margaret bore a dead child in her womb—"not womb but tomb" (a well-worn phrase, *non utero sed tumulo*), "not a son but a corpse" *(non filius sed funus)*, from December to February. She went into labor but the fetus would not be expelled. What, William asks rhetorically, was the unhappy woman to do? Eventually, part of the fetus came out: the head remained within, and for three days the miserable woman was tortured by this sad burden. The midwife was unable to help. At last Margaret called her husband, described her unimaginable pain, and asked him to put her affairs in order since she would soon die. Perhaps as a final attempt to escape death, she begged him to vow a pilgrimage to Becket's tomb. After this was done, Margaret expelled an infant with decaying nose and ears, "stinking and of scarcely human form."[56]

MIDWIVES AND BIRTH COMPLICATIONS

In the late twelfth century, when William of Canterbury was writing, midwives, usually older women, assisted at births in exchange for small gifts or often simply out of Christian charity. By the later Middle Ages, in some towns at least, they were paid (and regulated) by secular authorities.[57] The expectation that such women would attend those in travail was emphasized by one husband who, hearing that his wife would allow no one but her own daughter to assist her, claimed that this seemed abnormal.[58] Midwives (*obstetrices*), while applying their medical skills and *materia medica,* undoubtedly brought physical care, experience, and sympathetic comfort to the suffering, frightened women they visited and helped. And, as Löhmer notes, in the Middle Ages trained doctors were probably no better able to deal with difficult births than midwives.[59] Often a midwife's job was not an easy one, nor particularly well remunerated, and she might fall under suspicion if anything went wrong. Midwives were linked with witchcraft in the late-medieval *Malleus Maleficarum* or "Witch-Hammer," a baroque heresy hunter's compendium concocted, among other things, of ecclesiastical fear of women and male anxieties about sex, sin, and guilt. However, the assumption that midwives were frequently, or widely, accused as witches has been vigorously challenged recently.[60]

It was not uncommon for several midwives to attend what was feared might be a difficult or unusual birth. The iconography of medieval childbirth indicates that two, three, or even four midwives and servants might gather at the birthplace at one time; in a case presented earlier, as many as seven midwives were mentioned.[61] The status of these women is not always ascertainable, since some "midwives" were no doubt merely helpful neighbors, such as Lucy, Esther, Christina, and Helen, who assisted Katerina (recorded in a Swedish case from 1408), denoted as "highly trustworthy matrons."[62] Sometimes midwives took shifts or, if one gave up the case as hopeless, another might replace her. Although their training was rudimentary and traditional, these women had a vast repertoire of techniques and skills. In France, when Hersent finally began to give birth after difficult labor, the infant's arm lay across the birth canal "against the natural order," as the scribe noted. The midwives averred that out of "a thousand" women in such a situation, scarcely one could escape death.[63] Nevertheless, after continued manipulation and prayers by the midwives, Hersent recovered from her peril and give birth in a normal fashion. Many medieval medical books contain illustrations of acrobatic fetuses in a variety of positions, with instructions for midwives: in a Bodleian manuscript, for instance, one of the drawings is accompanied by a caption reading "If it [should] try to come out knee-first, push it back in and draw it forth by the feet."[64]

From time to time medieval midwives encountered the unexpected, the doomed, the gruesome cases, as their modern counterparts still do, for which there was little help from the medical manuals that most midwives probably never even saw.[65] We have already noted occasions when their job was anything but pleasant. In the south of France, Alaracia, about seventeen, was pregnant with twins, but after she fell from the animal she was riding, one of them died in her womb. Six weeks later the midwives extracted the dead, putrefied fetus by removing it in pieces from her body.[66] Alaracia managed to survive in spite of this horrendous experience — she provided this testimony nine years after the events — and the surviving twin was baptized and lived for several months. Although Alaracia seems to have escaped significant damage as a result of this exercise in surgical midwifery, many a mother — as medieval texts warned — was brought to grief through lack of a good midwife.[67] A striking example of this is the case of Dulceta, from Marseilles.[68] About 1297 Dulceta, age seventeen, realized that something was dreadfully wrong with her pregnancy, her first, which had gone the full nine months. After three or four days in labor it was clear that the fetus was crosswise in her womb, and dead. She carried it four more days, until her husband Michael, then about twenty-two or three, realizing that her life was at risk, called for assistance. Various midwives arrived but gave up when she was unable to expel the child. At this point another midwife named Guillelma, who called herself a *bayle* or *obstetrix*, entered the picture. She testified that she assisted as midwife "for God's sake" since Dulceta was a pauper. She extracted the dead, stinking fetus with her hands.[69] Dulceta collapsed after the operation, and Guillelma made the sign of the cross over her, as for the dead. Although Dulceta regained consciousness, her life was completely changed. As she later testified, in the process of extracting the fetus the midwife injured her: a bone, or what Dulceta assumed to be a bone, became lodged in her reproductive passage *(in natura sua)* where it pressed and pierced her so frightfully that for two years she was unable to rest, stand, or lie normally in bed. She could not cover herself unless she drew the bedclothes toward her with her teeth. When she did manage to walk, she was quite hunched over; often she had to lie down "like a dog" to eat. She became so disabled that eventually she had to do everything in bed, including the necessities of evacuation. As a result, worms bred in the accumulated filth around her legs and buttocks and gnawed holes in her flesh.[70] The bedridden Dulceta stank so badly that scarcely anyone could stand to be near her, according to a certain Hugua, who, when about twenty-one, had watched as the dead fetus was extracted.

At last, since nothing relieved her pain, and thinking that it would be better to risk death than to live in such abject distress, in 1299 Dulceta, by then about nineteen, asked a surgeon to extract the fragment that had caused her such long, constant, and irremediable affliction. Perhaps her poverty had as much to do with this delay as her fear of surgery. The surgeon agreed to carry out the operation, stipulating however that he would not touch her unless her husband or someone else of her blood *(de sanguine suo)* was present. Dulceta told him that she would arrange for her husband to be there and asked the surgeon to return in the morning, since she could not go out to him.[71] Presumably she told her husband about this arrangement, for that very day Michael suggested that she vow to Louis, who was working miracles. Dulceta, who had begun to fear the next day's operation (as well she might), promised Louis that if the "bone" were miraculously expelled and her infirmity cured, she would take a wax image to his tomb. In addition, she promised that every Saturday for as long as she lived, with the Franciscans' permission she would clean and sweep out the church housing Louis's tomb. Having made this vow she fell asleep, facedown in her filthy bed. When she awoke she felt herself freed of pain in her back and legs; as she raised herself up, an object fell from her body painlessly. She dressed and went to the surgeon to cancel the operation and then, even before breakfast, visited Louis's tomb. Since she was a poor woman (the record emphasizes this, describing her as *pauperrima mulier,* a very poor woman) who could not afford a wax image, she begged pennies in the church to purchase one to offer at the tomb. When Michael came home, having been out working "because he was poor," he found his wife standing at St. Martin's fountain. She held out for his inspection the object that had tormented her for two years. He testified that it was as big as a nut, while another witness (Hugua) claimed that it was half a palm wide, and Dulceta herself stated that it was three fingers wide. Eventually the Marseilles Franciscans obtained the "bone"—whatever it may have been—expelled from her body and kept it in their church as evidence of Louis's powers. Dulceta concluded her testimony with a candid observation that was probably true of many such vows and good intentions uttered by desperate women and men. Although she cleaned and swept the church on certain days as promised, eventually she found it too much of a burden: the church was large, and besides this, being so poor, she had to work elsewhere to "earn her daily bread with her hands," as she testified. Nevertheless, she claimed, she did what she could whenever possible, and proposed to go on doing so.

Sometimes midwives were confronted not merely with dead or rotting fetuses but with disfigured or monstrous neonates, as in the case of Isabel's son, who did not even seem human at birth: his head, shoulders, and limbs appeared to be a single mass.[72] There were wounds on his head and the neck was stretched as if by violence. After a vow by the child's father (to go on pilgrimage while consuming only bread and water), the child revived and lived. Sometimes subterfuges were used to hide these deformities from parents, at least until the mother had recovered from the birth trauma. For instance, when Margareta produced a son whose right arm was bent backward, the nurse hid the child for as long as she could, so as not to cause anguish to the mother or household. Finally Margareta commanded the nurse to present it; seeing the deformity, the mother and her relatives were engulfed by grief. However, when measured (for a candle to de Montfort,) the onlookers claimed that the infant immediately raised and nimbly flexed his right arm.[73] Usually, however, birth deformities were not so easily removed. The experience of a thirteenth-century French mother epitomizes the anguish caused by children's deformities. Ever since birth, her child's hand and arm hung useless at his side, as if dead. He could not raise his arm to feed himself. His despairing mother frequently cried out "Why did I conceive such progeny in my womb, and why did I create an offspring of degenerate nature; oh God, why was he not carried from my womb to the tomb. . . ." In words like these, the manuscript continues, with sobs and tears she often lamented her son's wretchedness.[74]

HUSBANDS AND FATHERS

In a few of these examples we have glimpsed the husband playing a part in the birth process. The records reveal that often men were emotionally and physically involved in even the very first stages of childhood, but, although probably expected to be nearby, normally men do not seem to have witnessed their children's births. Sometimes the husband's concern for his wife is obvious. In 1404 Peter Wolff told papal commissioners that some nine years earlier, when he was about thirty-one, his wife fared so badly in childbirth that the midwife went to him, saying "Most dear friend, don't be upset, [but] your wife is dead." Peter, however, was far from calm: he urged her to return and touch his wife carefully between the breasts near the heart, to see whether she could find "any warmth or spirit of life." It is interesting that even though Peter obviously was worried, he himself did not venture into the birth chamber to examine his wife. The woman did as he asked but still found no signs of life. Peter, believing his wife dead, wept bitterly and, on the midwife's advice, sent for friends and relatives to organize the funeral. At that point, a young man of the household recommended that Peter invoke the blessed Dorothy. The grieving husband vowed that if his wife were restored to him, he would not have intercourse with her until after he had walked barefoot to Dorothy's tomb in simple attire.[75] His wife revived and lived in good health for three more years. Since there was no mention of an infant, it probably did not survive childbirth.[76]

A husband's "place" at his child's birth, and an idea of the physical surroundings are evident in another Pomeranian case, in which Paul, a knight, described his experiences of May 1397. He began by admitting to the papal commissioners that he had doubted the miracles ascribed to Dorothy of Montau, on one occasion saying that he would not believe that she was a saint "unless I see some sign or revelation, by her, done for me." Some days after these words were spoken, his wife, Anna, went into labor. The women came to minister to her in a separate room, while he awaited the "good news" about his wife and child outside the chamber.[77] About midday he noticed a woman unknown to him going in and out of the birth room. Though he could not see her face, he knew that none of the village women had that particular kind of sky-blue garment. Later on he asked his household servants and retainers about the woman dressed in a blue tunic and red cloak; they claimed to have seen no such person, naming everyone who had been present. Paul then interrogated the women who had assisted his wife, but they denied any knowledge of the stranger. He named one particular village woman as a possibility: "Was it not so-and-so?" but the women responded "Hardly!" Even his wife remembered no such individual in the birth chamber. Four days later Anna fell seriously ill and asked her husband to send for the Eucharist. After the priest arrived, Paul, ruminating on the unknown woman, concluded that she must have been Dorothy herself, whose holiness he had doubted. He went to his wife, told her this, and vowed a pilgrimage to Dorothy's tomb. Then going into a secluded place (men often did their praying "secretly," as we shall see), he begged Dorothy to restore his wife to health. Within a short time Anna recovered. No surviving infant is mentioned. Some men, then, exhibited traits that constituted a stereotype until recent times, when more and more husbands go into the delivery room, videocameras at the ready. Before this trend, they and their medieval precursors usually waited outside, in varying states of anxiety, until word was brought that—as they hoped—all was well with both wife and child. But sometimes the news was anything but good.

In one instance of prolonged and painful labor, even though a midwife was present the husband also played a role, of sorts, in the birth. About 1297 Bertrand of Marseilles came home from foreign parts to find his wife in labor, which continued for five or six days. Bertrand testified (in 1308) that, being unable to remain in bed because of the pain, she got up and began leaning on a storage chest. P. A. Sigal suggested that this account proved, "indirectly," that women gave birth while lying in bed, since that is where Bertrand first saw her.[78] It is also possible, however, that Bertrand misinterpreted her actions and was in fact witnessing the traditional birthing posture adopted by women of the region, not her reactions to pain.[79] Bertrand's wife was screaming and crying out "The child is coming: get it!" At this, Bertrand shouted for the many women "who were outside the room," thus emphasizing that he was alone with his wife, without a midwife in attendance. In the same instant he saw the infant fall to the floor and remain there, silent. The midwife came in with the others, picked it up, and told Bertrand that both body and soul were lost. Given the inert silence of the infant and its coldness and bluish color, the father could only agree. The midwife handed the child over to Bertrand's sister-in-law Beatrice, who caught it up in her mantle. Stupefied at first, she began weeping and imploring the help of St. Louis, to whom they had commended the child before its birth. At the same time, the father asked her to put down the boy and take care of his wife. With the mention of the dead saint, however, the child began whimpering. They put him into warm water—the usual treatment for newborns—which brought him to full recovery. The delighted father visited Louis's tomb that very day, where he offered a candle of the child's length, and next day he took the happy news to his own mother, who had not been present at the birth. The boy, quickly baptized and named John, was taken every year to Louis's tomb, with an offering of a candle. When the mother testified, she remarked that she had been so big that people thought that twins were due. Her labor was long and painful, she claimed, and as the time of delivery approached she became increasingly anxious, calling repeatedly upon St. Louis for herself and for the *creatura* in her womb. She related the events of the birth, adding that through all the commotion she had not actually seen her son, but could hear the conversation between her husband and sister and truly believed that John had been born dead.

POSTPARTUM DANGERS

Birth complications described in these records had wide-ranging consequences for the mothers, from short-term discomfort to death. Some women
were very seriously damaged in the process: the case of Dulceta, bedridden
for two years, was related earlier. Flore Nicole was another whose birth
trauma had long-term repercussions. Unable to rest day or night for three
years because of a prolapsed womb, and finding in her agony that doctors
and medicines seemed more harmful than helpful, she wanted to have her
exposed womb removed surgically. At her mother's suggestion, and in her
own daughter's presence, she made a vow to St. Clare. One night in her
chamber (where she always had a light burning), the saint visited her in a
vision and told her not to have the surgery. When Flore objected, "I can no
longer bear it," Clare replied, "Bear it, for within three days I shall free you."
The promised cure took place within the specified time. When the papal
examiners asked her to describe this nocturnal visitation, Flore said that
Clare looked just like her painting at her tomb, except that in the vision she
was dressed all in white.[80] A late-medieval text, under the condition it calls
"precipitation of the uterus," suggests that "the uterus falls out because of the
illness that a woman has in bearing a child." As usual, after diagnosis treatment is prescribed: "if the uterus fall out underneath at the privy member
after childbirth, let the midwife put it in again with her hand." After this procedure the midwife is to burn a stinking substance beneath the affected area,
while having the patient "smell fragrant things. . . ."[81] These directions
made sense in a physiological system in which the uterus or womb was
thought of as a moving, semi-independent creature that, repelled by or
attracted to smells, could be forced to relocate itself in its proper position.
Even though as early as the second century A.D. Soranus challenged the idea
that the uterus behaved "like a wild animal [issuing] from the lair, delighted
by fragrant odors and fleeing bad odors," the belief continued throughout
the medieval period. As the bombastic Paracelsus claimed in the early sixteenth century, women were mere containers for that mysterious creature,
the womb: "The health and good condition [of women] depends on the con-
tentment and healthy state of that animal."[82] Such an anatomical model, postulated by men, allowed them to "explain" women's reputedly irrational
behavior as a failure of the weak vessel to control the demands of this
aggressive, unpredictable animal within; hence female lasciviousness, for
instance, arising from the appetite of the womb itself.

Occasionally subtext clues about clerical attitudes toward sex, pregnancy, and childbirth turn up in the records' details. This seems to happen

less often in canonization inquests, and more often in other hagiographical materials, such as lists collected at saints' tombs by the monks, canons, or friars who cared for shrines. Whereas later-medieval papal canonization inquisitions were occasions for gathering what was, for the times, "objective" testimony, the less formal collections also could be used for didactic purposes. From time to time an element of sermonizing enters these records, even a censorious attitude, generally absent from the testimony recorded at papal hearings. For example, there is an illustration of the so-called Magdalene theme among the twelfth-century miracles attributed to Oxford's patron saint, Frideswide. In this compilation we encounter Mabilia of Shifford, evidently an unmarried woman whose postpartum anguish was narrated by Philip, prior of the Austin canons in whose church Frideswide's bones rested. He recorded how Mabilia's womb began to swell after a "sinful encounter" and how, during the autumn, she gave birth with the greatest pain and torment. Worse followed: her limbs grew crippled, her spine curved, so that "by the time her purification should have taken place," as he writes, she could barely drag herself along the ground.[83] Philip stresses pain as punishment for fornication, which in turn prevented Mabilia from achieving "purification." In medieval England this rite of purification was also known as the "churching" of recently delivered mothers, a ceremony marking the termination of the period following childbirth during which women were not allowed into holy places. Although percipient or sympathetic medieval clergy such as Pope Gregory I (d. 604) softened the harsh rules of Leviticus (Lev. 12.1-8) that barred women from holy ground for thirty-three days following the birth of a boy or sixty-six days for a girl, and required an expiatory offering on the woman's part, even after A.D. 1500 in England it was expected, at least by some clerics, that a woman would enter church only after a suitable time had elapsed since childbirth (often forty days). During the rite she received "absolution" from the priest.[84]

Mabilia—to continue Prior Philip's story—having heard about the miracles of Frideswide, and learning of a procession in which a chest containing the saint's bones was to be carried through the city, had herself taken to a place near the church. She hoped that she would be cured as the relics passed over her while she lay on the ground, like the woman with the flow of blood in the Bible, Philip adds. With this reference Philip emphasizes the clerical fear of pollution of holy places as well as something more fundamental, though certainly not true of all men: the male horror of women's blood.[85] Even a drop of blood falling from a recently delivered woman's womb to the floor of a church was powerful enough to pollute the entire building, bringing divine services to a temporary halt. Hence the exclusion of such women until a time when this was unlikely to happen. As for Mabilia, a downpour squelched the Oxford procession. Afraid of being crushed by the milling crowd in the church, she remained in prayer outside the church doors, where she was cured (and purified?). Thereafter she walked into the building to offer a candle at the saint's shrine; she went home a few days later.[86]

Another postpartum complication that attracted the interest of the Hippocratic school was in a sense the opposite of the prolapsed womb, the retention of the afterbirth, or the "secundine." Herbert Felton's wife, for instance, fell victim to this, having ejected only part of the afterbirth.[87] Becket's twelfth-century miracle recorder, attempting to provide a "medical" explanation, claimed that as a result, the affected humors ascended, causing illness in her inner parts and chest. Writers in the later medieval period recommended that the afterbirth should be carefully removed: "The midwife should anoint her hands and with her nails pull out the secundine if she can. . . ."[88] Certainly the victim described by the Canterbury monk was troubled: she was afflicted with insomnia, which led in turn to a wasting of her body even though, by day, she still attended to her regular chores, always holding her hand on her groin. For two years she did this, sometimes having good days when she felt better, although she was never free of discomfort. Finally, two days after drinking some water from Becket's shrine, she was cured. There is no way to determine how common this affliction was, although Soranus claimed, ominously, that the arfterbirth was "often" left behind.[89] In spite of such complications and life-threatening debilities associated with childbirth, medieval women were willing to risk all for the sake of their infants.

NEONATES

For the infants who survived their first treacherous moments of entry into a new world, a standard routine was followed, which included a bath in warm water and perhaps a rubbing down with oil or other materials. Löhmer notes that this ritual at the side of the exhausted mother came to be a common motif in late-medieval woodcuts and drawings of childbirth.[90] Even these apparently salubrious activities could lead to tragedy, however, as the wife of Hugh Blundel in northern France discovered. She had given birth, and, "as the custom is," the infant was bathed. The water was so hot, however, that the boy "died."[91] Hugh had gone to hear a sermon and, in the midst of it, someone shouted that he should go home since his son had died. Running home, he took up the boy and carried him to Laurence's tomb. After lying inert for the space of a three-mile walk, the infant revived and lived for six years. Another ritual, well documented in word and image, was the swaddling of the newborn child from head to toe.[92] Contemporaries claimed that swaddling helped to keep the child warm and that the constriction assisted in "forming" the limbs; but the most obvious benefit to busy mothers was the child's immobility.[93] Hence, in theory, the infant was unable to hurt itself even if left alone. Swaddling bands were not supposed to be wrapped too tightly, but the fact that Mabilia of Vauchères in southern France, whose hands had been injured, was able drag her son to herself for breast feeding by gripping his swaddling bands with her teeth suggests that, in some cases, the cloth casing was well secured.[94] An example from England, taking place during August 1490 in the village of Brackley, not far from Oxford, illustrates the sort of calamity that could result from insufficient attention to the swaddling bands. The narrator introduces the case with his usual moralizing: "Where anything negligent is done regarding infants, much adverse fortune will follow; permitting an infant to have its freedom so often turns laughter into tears, joy into grief, clapping the hands into beating the breast, jesting into weeping."[95] He then summarizes the story of George, six-month-old son of Thomas, who was put by his mother Oliva into his cradle for the night. He was not swaddled as usual but simply rolled up in some cloth. Oliva merely tied on the cloth with a linen belt "such as women usually wear." The cradle was suspended above the floor. While Oliva lay sleeping alone in bed (I don't know why, the narrator interjects, her husband was absent), the little one wriggled about, got out of his wrappings, and was strangled by the belt as he fell from the cradle. At length Oliva awoke and prepared to offer George the breast, as usual. When her groping, extended hand touched the naked little body (corpusculum), her heart began to pound. Feeling about more carefully, she found her son hanging from the cradle, the linen belt around his neck. She could not tell how long he had been hanging, but he was cold and rigid. Stupefied and grief-stricken beyond all description, Oliva got up and undid the knot, at which the boy fell like a lump of clay. She picked him up and carried him out of the bedchamber to an inner part of the house. In tears she cried out incessantly to King Henry to help her "dear son." Kissing the child, she longed for her husband. At one point, tempted by the Corruptor, says the narrator, she considered throwing the child aside and fleeing; but some neighbors, awakened by her cries, arrived and began consoling her. On her knees, with palms heavenward, she continued to cry out to the dead King Henry. After saying the Lord's Prayer and bending a silver penny over the boy in honor of the saint, when she put her finger into the child's mouth she discovered signs of breathing; with a belch he vomited a great deal of bloody gore and then, put to the breast, he revived.

Besides, or perhaps in addition to, being swaddled, sometimes children were tied into their cradles.[96] That seems to have been the cause of the horror, also recorded in England, experienced by Sibilla about 1289. Sibilla negligently (the scribe writes) left three-month-old Margery in her cradle in the care of another infant and went off to her sheep-shearing early one May morning.[97] In the mother's absence Margery loosened her bands and fell out of the cradle; she remained hanging upside-down from pre dawn until daylight. Evidently this cradle, as in the previous case, must have been suspended above the cottage floor. When the mother returned and found her infant "dead," many neighbors congregated at hearing her screams. This was the sort of tragedy against which an early-fourteenth handbook for parish priests, the *Oculus Sacerdotis*, had warned: priests were to admonish their parishioners against rashly tying young children into their cradles and leaving them unattended by day or night.[98]

Aside from seeing to the bathing, swaddling, and physical comfort of the neonate, assistants supplied nourishment to both mother and child. The records suggest how common it was for mothers to nurse their own children, a practice that churchmen and medical writers tended to support; the nursing Mary became a familiar icon among the many manifestations of late-medieval mariolatry.[99] Nevertheless, the hiring of wet nurses was traditional in some regions such as Italy, where the practice seems to have been associated with more affluent townsfolk. In thirteenth-century England, it may have been customary among those who could afford it. After Agatha of Salisbury gave birth, the chronicler notes that *since* she was poor she could not keep a nurse in her house.[100] This became serious when her milk failed and, for seven days, she had to sustain her son on beer. Afraid of losing him, Agatha went to Osmund's tomb, where she prayed for help. Even before leaving the cathedral her breasts began swelling with milk, which she showed to her husband and friends.

The employment of wet nurses has attracted the interest of historians, especially those dealing with renaissance Italy, which has provided abundant records about wet nursing in diaries and contracts.[101] Miracle collections are another source of information about this phenomenon. For instance, in 1325 papal commissioners heard Romanella, wife of Melanzolus of Perugia, testify that a few years earlier Joanna of Perugia gave birth to a son named Benvenuto.[102] Joanna asked Romanella to find a wet nurse *(baila)* for the child. This was somewhat unusual if, as has been suggested, in renaissance Italy the husband usually selected the wet nurse.[103] In any case, Romanella did so, bringing the nurse to the house, then returning with Benvenuto and the nurse to the latter's place in the Perugian countryside. There the two women remained for two days, during which time the child became extremely ill. Especially anxious since she had been the one who had found the wet nurse, Romanella prayed to Nicholas of Tolentino, which resulted in the child's revival.

Occasionally the records reveal aspects of the emotional ties that developed in the triad, mother-child-wet nurse. Although there are examples of infants dying while in the "care" of seemingly negligent or indifferent nurses, bonds of real affection could be established between surrogate mother and infant, a topos in medieval literature.[104] According to the mid-thirteenth-century encyclopedist Bartholomew the Englishman, wet nurses were accustomed to hug and kiss their charges, to sing and whistle them to sleep, even to chew their food for them, before placing it in the toothless infants' mouths.[105] Permutations of this relationship appear in mystical writings—for example, in the visions of St. Lidwina in Holland (d. 1433), who imagined that her breasts "swell with milk on Christmas day" as she thought of nursing the infant Jesus; and in theological fancies about Jesus himself as nurse, from whose breasts we suck "the milk of sweetness," as Aelred of Rievaulx wrote.[106] The canonization records, on a more mundane level to be sure, also shed some light on the existence and strength of the bond between child and nurse. When Joanna gave birth to James in Marseilles, his feet and legs were extremely deformed, so that he walked on the sides of his feet. Guarssias, from Aix, became his wet nurse when he was about age one. (There is no indication of who had been nursing him up to that time.)[107] She nursed him for three years, often watching him put his feet and legs around his neck when she bathed him. This saddened her greatly. Eventually, some two years after Guarssias left the household, while she was in Aix she learned from Joanna that James had been cured through a vow to St. Louis; this made Guarssias extremely happy. After returning to Marseilles, for three more years (until his death at age eight or nine) she saw James almost every day, well and fit. Joanna's testimony, incidentally, emphasizes the resilience and adaptability of even severely handicapped children. Joanna had heard about Louis's miracles in a sermon at the church where the saint was buried. When she returned home, she sat down at the table where she and her husband discussed vows to Louis, with James himself taking part in their conversation. Joanna asked the boy to "say the *Ave Maria* in honor of the blessed Louis, so that he might pray for you." She told the papal examiners that she believed that he did say this prayer, although she did not actually hear it, since at that moment the child went down into the street with the other boys. Upon returning from play, he showed himself cured before all the company, some twenty people, still sitting at the table.

DEATH AND BAPTISM

When casting his memory back over his own life, the brilliant Edward Gibbon, archetype of genteel pomposity, had much to say in his *Autobiography* about the work that made him famous, the *Decline and Fall of the Roman Empire*. Amid his musings, he dropped a few comments that emphasize, for us, the precariousness of infancy even in eighteenth-century England, in the bosom of a relatively well-off family blessed by Enlightenment physic. He was, he informs us, the firstborn of the children, to be succeeded by five brothers and one sister, all of whom "were snatched away in their infancy." He continues, "The death of a new-born child before that of its parents may seem an unnatural, but it is strictly a probable event . . ."[108] Archaeology has confirmed this grim probability: of 364 graves examined in Sweden, dating to ca. 1100-1350, 183 (50 percent) were of children age seven and younger; of these 183, 113, or 62 percent, were infants less than twelve months old.[109] Some historians have asserted that in view of a high infant mortality rate, medieval parents were emotionally calloused when faced with the prospect or the reality of their infants' deaths. Although this may have been true in some cases, many examples considered in this book and in the works of other investigators of medieval childhood, suggest that this is not a valid generalization. On the contrary, the death of a newborn could cause the greatest anxiety and sorrow, especially since Christian doctrine held that if an infant died without baptism, it was eternally doomed. Conciliar legislation repeatedly directed bishops and priests to emphasize to their congregations the importance of baptism.[110] The universality of this concern is illustrated in two northern European examples. In a miracle attributed to Birgitta (Bridget) of Sweden, extreme grief was felt for a stillborn infant *"especially* because it had died without baptism."[111] In a passage from the *Legenda* of St. Hedwig of Silesia (d. 1243), the point is made even more clearly: after the birth of a dead girl, "the whole household gathered and plaintive cries arose, not for the death of the little girl but because she had died without the sacrament of baptism."[112]

This fear of eternal damnation accounts for much of the violent anxiety displayed by mothers, even as they were still recovering, when they realized that their infants were stillborn or had died immediately after birth. Clerical reporters of these tragedies might be expected to emphasize the need for this fundamental sacrament, administered, preferably, by the clergy. Ordinary lay people seem to have shared clerical anxiety about baptism well before the end of the Middle Ages. In Pomerania on May 3, 1405, for example, Katherina, a thirty-six-year-old miller's wife, testified that during 1396, after five days of labor, she produced a stillborn son. Being told that she had labored in vain since her son was dead, she begged the women to pray to St. Dorothy that the boy receive baptism and "take on a soul."[113] They did so, after which he began howling; he lived for another two and one-half years. On the other side of Europe, in the south of France, Sancia prematurely gave birth to a dead daughter.[114] She herself, as the doctors believed, had been in danger. When the midwives told her that the infant was dead, she cried out, "St. Louis, will my daughter die without baptism and be damned? St. Louis, help me and her; show your virtues in her." At once the infant began crying, and the midwives bathed and baptized her. Sancia, however, not content with that baptism, begged St. Louis to prolong the baby's life "until she's been baptized by a priest." And what she requested—writes the chronicler—she obtained: the girl was baptized by a priest and then, "returning her spirit to God," died. This example illustrates several aspects of contemporary childbirth. First, the presence of doctors indicates that Sancia's family may have been relatively well-off and that she may have suffered medical complications during her pregnancy. Second, it suggests that Sancia had already made vows to Louis of Toulouse. An expectant mother in another French case illustrates this common custom. Mary, the pregnant wife of an Auxerre leather worker, went to the gates at Pontigny to commend herself and her fetus to God and St. Edmund.[115] When the time came for delivery, she went into extremely difficult labor, eventually producing a son who appeared to be dead. Hoping to spare the mother's feelings, the midwives agreed to keep his death from her (until they thought that she had recovered, presumably), but she ordered them to bring the infant to her. "Stricken to her innards with the stings of sadness," in her grief she cried out, "St. Edmund, what did I do to you, or what commit, that I should have a dead fetus after I so devoutly commended myself, and it, to your grace at the abbey gate?" Several of the medieval cases mention visits by pregnant women to the shrines of saints.

Sancia's outburst also illustrates parental grief arising from the belief that the unbaptized were forever barred from heaven. A few medieval reports even suggest that some parents believed that baptism "created" the infant's soul, contrary to theological teachings. For instance, in 1374 the husband of a French victim of bubonic plague who was five months pregnant feared that if the infant died in his wife's womb, it could not be baptized "and have a soul in its body." In another, less convincing instance from the same region, the mother of a newborn who was not breathing prayed that he return to life "to receive baptism and have a Christian soul."[116] Sancia's case emphasizes not only that baptism was essential but also that a priest, although preferred, was not necessary for its administration. Parents themselves, or midwives or neighbors, could do it. In an English pastoral manual written ca. 1400, for instance, parish priests are directed to tell midwives to memorize the baptismal phrases, in proper order, in case of need.[117] Long before 1400, however, lay administration of baptism in an emergency was well established. Going back no farther than the thirteenth century, in his tract on the seven sacraments (ca. 1241) the Spanish prelate Peter of Albalat, for instance, wrote that "priests should admonish the laity that if necessary, when they feared for the lives of children, they could baptize them." If the child did not die as anticipated, the parents could take it to church, where ancillary rites could be performed by the priest, who first interrogated the parents to find out what baptismal words had been used. If their phrases were acceptable, then all was well. In doubtful cases, the priest could baptize the child, but in a conditional form: "If you are baptized, I do not baptize you; if you are not baptized, I baptize you in the name of the Father. . . ."[118] While the physical well-being of their children was important, these examples suggest that, for many medieval parents, the spiritual health of their child was an even more serious matter, which might require emergency baptism.

Alternatively or in addition, it was not unusual for very ill, dying, or even dead neonates to be brought into a church and placed near or on the altar or upon the tomb of a purported saint, into whose care the fearful parents commended them. Christian parents had been doing this since at least the time of St. Augustine.[119] Any subsequent movement that was detected in the infant's body was taken as a sign of life that allowed baptism to follow.[120] By the fifteenth century, church conciliar decrees, such as those promulgated at Langres (1452), prohibited such behavior, which was open to abuse—the natural physiological changes taking place within dead bodies, it was recognized, could easily be mistaken for signs of life.[121] In such cases a corpse might be baptized, which was contrary to the canons. In addition, perhaps the local clergy would then unjustly claim a "miracle" for their saint.[122] In spite of canonical restrictions, however, these shrine-side activities remained commonplace throughout Europe. Apparently, some parents were not reassured by the late-medieval doctrine of a *limbus puerorum*—limbo—a place reserved for the souls of unbaptized children. Although they were not supposed to suffer physical torments, nevertheless the children in limbo were eternally deprived of the presence of God. Many parents could not accept this: in 1440, for instance, in the diocese of Exeter, people ran *(cucurrerunt)* to nearby churches with their newly born infants to have them baptized when they believed their lives to be in danger.[123] Such paraliturgical rites, and recourse to special sites where infant "revivals" occurred, continued long after the Middle Ages had ended.[124] Silvano Cavazza has shown how widespread the rites were in seventeenth- and eighteenth-century Europe, while in nineteenth-century France, as Judith Devlin writes, the "momentary resuscitation of dead babies seems to have been a surprisingly popular kind of miracle. . . ."[125] These rituals were condemned in the Limoges countryside as recently as 1912.[126] In medieval, as in modern, France, parental anxieties outweighed clerical mandates. Even the clergy were susceptible to sentiment. When, in Marseilles, Massilia and Peter's newborn was raised from the ground, his body was blue-black and his neck bent like a dead child's.[127] Since she was so afflicted with pain and weakness, Massilia could not discern whether her son had actually died. After learning that he was dead, she begged St. Louis to revive the child so that he could be baptized. At the mother's request, the child was carried into the church where, while the priest was saying the words of the sacrament, he began whimpering and was brought back, crying, to his happy mother. He lived for another three and one-half months. In this case the local priest followed his charitable inclinations rather than canon law, since the church taught that the dead were not to be baptized. Nor were infants who died unbaptized to be buried in hallowed ground.[128] Uncertainty about the church burial of unbaptized neonates is reflected in a report from Berard, the notary of Tolentino. In 1325 he testified that, more than twenty years earlier, after difficult and especially painful labor, his wife produced a stillborn son.[129] A little pit was dug in the house *(in domo)* for its burial but, since some of the women thought they saw it move, they baptized it.[130] Next morning, as they were about to bury the infant in the house, Nicholas the holy man of Tolentino sent a message: he had had a vision during the night that convinced him that the infant's soul had been saved. Consequently the mother, "who seemed sadder about the loss of the soul of her son than the death of [his] body," was able to send the corpse to church for burial.

Although parents were conscious of the spiritual dangers of unbaptized death, they were also well aware of what could happen to the tiny body itself, when circumstances prevented its burial in consecrated ground. Silleta, nearing term, suddenly began bleeding from her nose; when she pinched it to restrict the flow, blood came out of her mouth. The doctors and their medicines were useless and, in this condition, half dead from loss of blood, she gave birth to a dead boy. The midwives and other women prepared to bury the unbaptized infant's body outside the cemetery, but after Silleta made a vow the child revived and outlived its infancy.[131] In two cases noted earlier in this chapter, both reported in the first quarter of the fourteenth century from different parts of southern Europe, the unpleasant circumstances of non-ecclesiastical disposal were graphically presented.[132] In one instance from southern France, Alaracia gave birth to dead twins; one was extracted in rotting bits, the other, thought to be dead, was removed whole. The midwives placed the second twin amid the dung in the stable next to the pieces of the decomposed fetus. This apparently callous treatment of infants' remains also occurred in the Italian case of Thomas and his wife, Thomassucia, who fell from her horse and subsequently produced an apparently dead infant. After giving it an impromptu baptism, Thomas ordered it to be placed on the dungheap in his stable. Thomas must have had some misgivings about the efficacy of the baptism (perhaps the infant seemed dead before being baptized?), for he promised St. Nicholas a wax image if his son revived so that he could be baptized in church "lest his soul perish." Canonical prohibitions against burying an unbaptized infant in consecrated ground also meant that it was sometimes necessary, when both mother and child died in birth, to cut the child out of the woman and bury it beyond the sacred boundaries. Although canonists debated whether the mother in such cases could rest within the churchyard, the general opinion was favorable.[133]

Stable burial, in any event, accorded with canon law: since these infants could not be buried as Christians, their physical fate was immaterial. The canonists even pondered the question whether it was proper to baptize a dismembered infant. The second fetus produced by Alaracia was, at least in appearance, normal.[134] The grandmother, therefore, invoked the help of St. Louis on behalf of this fetus, although not on behalf of the first, because, according to Alaricia's testimony, it had come out in bits and pieces.[135] Having made her vow, the grandmother saw the "fetus or [grand]daughter" *(fetum seu filiam)*, who was in the stable lying in the dung, begin to tremble. The baby was rescued and baptized, living another seven months. As a prelude to this short existence, however, both of the young parents (Alaracia was seventeen, her husband John about twenty-one) had seen the remains of their twins lying in the stable. As John put it, when he came home from work in the vineyards that day, he found several women in his house and, out in the stable, amid the dung and straw, a fetus that seemed quite dead.[136] Surely baptism was sought, whenever possible and however performed, in order to avoid such brutal disposal as well as to save an infantile soul.[137]

INFANTICIDE

There is a special category of child death, however, in which baptism might seem far from a parent's mind: infanticide. In fact, it is evident that parents sometimes performed primitive baptisms on the newly born infants they were planning to kill or abandon. In 1457 fourteen-year-old Denisette, impregnated by her stepfather, took her newborn in one arm and, with her other hand, cast water on its head while saying "My child, I baptize you in the name of the Father and the Son and the Holy Spirit"; she kissed it, commended it to God, and threw it into a sewer. Jeanne Hardouyn baptized her infant before smashing its head on the ground; about 1399 Berthomée Noyon, lacking water, baptized her infant with her own saliva before killing it. The killing of an unbaptized child was judged a heinous crime: sixteen-year-old Hannette was burned to death for having done so.[138]

The characteristics and frequency of medieval infanticide are currently under review, with an extensive bibliography on the subject being generated in the process. Historians are debating the pervasiveness of medieval infanticide, motives or intent, methods, and its manifestations in secular and canon law.[139] A major hindrance to productive discussion of this issue is the absence of reliable data for an act easily disguised as accidental or natural death. Scholars rarely avail themselves of language as trenchant as the following: "We are stating unequivocally . . . that the evidence for child abuse and infanticide being widespread phenomena [in early medieval Europe], by any reasonable understanding of such phraseology, is utterly lacking."[140] In spite of occasional bursts of such directness, the twists and turns of this historians' debate continue: Barbara Hanawalt, who found few references to infanticide in English coroners' records, tends to dismiss evidence of "widespread" infanticide in England. Writing in 1986, she was particularly critical of psychohistorians who "have delighted in making medieval peasants great practitioners of infanticide."[141] Whatever its incidence in Hanawalt's England, in 1972 Brissaud wrote that for late-medieval France infanticide was a "sad reality" although he cautiously added that it is practically impossible to establish statistics.[142] In 1989 Sylvie Laurent, after reviewing much of the same data as Brissaud, concluded that infanticides were not uncommon in certain regions of late-medieval France.[143] Using other sorts of data for another area of Europe, in 1973 Richard Trexler wrote that in renaissance Florence "infanticide against one's own and against other children was common." Although, like Brissaud, Trexler believes that statistical results are beyond reach, he concluded that "the evidence of extensive infanticide cannot be gainsaid. . . ."[144] Given contemporary socioeconomic and familial hardship on the one hand, and multiple anxieties arising from guilt, sin, and the fear of being publicly shamed on the other, it is likely that infanticide occurred regularly in England as in the rest of Europe, although its extent cannot be determined at present.[145] As suggested by the French examples, a young girl's fear of being "shamed" was a powerful incentive for infanticide. Desperation arising from poverty was another strong motive. When in the early 1290s some Herefordshire villagers, in the midst of their Sunday frolicking, discovered a child's body in a fishpond, they immediately assumed that it was the daughter of a certain Christina de Grenewey, a pauper who lived by begging in their village while accompanied by the "poor little girl" (parvula) and a small son. The villagers thought that Christina had thrown her child into the pond "because of poverty and misery." Their attitude toward an assumed infanticide of a pauper child is indicated by their deciding to remove the corpse from the pond that night and fling it into a nearby river so that someone else would "find" it and bear the appropriate responsibility; having made this plan, they returned to their bucolic recreations.[146] Apart from deliberate infanticide, parents might attain the same result by choosing to attend with greater or less assiduity to the nurturing of their children or to the assuaging of their illnesses, as is suggested in chapter 3.

A custom often referred to in the miracles was the calling together of neighbors when a child was thought to have died. Differing from the shouting and cries that went up when a dead child (or adult) was discovered—the "hue and cry"—this was a deliberate "display" to neighbors, with parents sometimes carrying the bodies out of their cottages and into the public gaze. In one of Becket's reports, a woman snatched her "dead" child from its bath and cast him onto the road outside her house, before shouting for the neighbors.[147] In some cases this behavior may have been an involuntary panic reaction. In other instances, however, it seems to have been a deliberate invitation to neighbors to witness, as far as was possible, that no "foul play" had been involved. There are also hints that when blame was about to be directed at parents, one of them might deflect guilt by implicating the other, as in the Pomeranian case of a mother who handed her "dead" child to her husband, whom she believed responsible for the near drowning.[148] This sort of activity may have been motivated by the desire to avoid suspicion of infanticide. One circumstance in particular was often linked with purported infanticide: in medieval Europe it appears that the intentional or accidental killing of children was routinely associated with sleeping arrangements.

Parish priests warned, with good reason, as we shall see when considering children's accidents, against parents letting their young play near water or fire. They also often admonished them against "overlaying," the suffocation or smothering of children taken into parents' or nurses' beds. In many cultures smothering by a midwife or either parent is said to have been a common mode of child killing, as in nineteenth-century Europe, where "overlying" may have been "a covert form of infanticide."[149] Although a modern historian suggests that sudden infant death syndrome played an unrecognized part in child mortality, medieval churchmen, who would have read in the Book of Kings about the woman whose "child died because she lay on it" during the night (1 Kings 3:19), interpreted the deaths in their own fashion.[150] Thirteenth-century church councils repeatedly incorporated warnings against parents sharing their beds with their infants and young children. The same sentiment was expressed in the fourteenth century, for instance in the English guide for parish priests called *Oculus Sacerdotis* of about 1320, which admonished parishioners against having their children in bed with them, and in Florentine synodal decrees of 1327.[151] While such warnings were being made as early as the ninth century,[152] it has been claimed that overlaying was still a significant cause of infant death in the fifteenth-century province of Canterbury.[153] It is interesting, when considering the elements of deliberation and motivation in such cases, that penances assigned to the women held to be responsible for such deaths tended to be lighter if they were poor.[154]

In England, as in France and Italy, mothers reportedly woke up to find their children "dead" beneath or beside their own bodies. One case adds the detail that the child, when removed from the mother, bled profusely from nose and mouth.[155] A noteworthy aspect of the English cases reported in the Cantilupe data is that in three instances children were said to have been "smothered" not by their mothers but by sleeping nurses, probably live-in family retainers. It is likely that these were unintended tragedies, since wet nurses throughout Europe had a vested interest in the health and life of children in their care; however, the picture grows more complex when dealing with "institutional" wet nurses employed by late-medieval and renaissance cities. Like infanticide, the rise of orphanages has attracted growing interest among scholars. Related to the history of orphanages is the custom of abandonment, which some contemporaries may have viewed as an alternative to infanticide. This topic also has become increasingly visible in writings on social history, especially after the 1988 publication of *The Kindness of Strangers* by John Boswell, examining abandonment particularly in medieval and renaissance Europe. Not all scholars agree with the book's arguments. Regarding Boswell's views on the altruism of strangers who saved abandoned children, one historian doubts that the author "really cared whether or not his representation had any correspondence to what actually could have been going on."[156] Although these are important topics that should be mentioned in any study of medieval childhood, the miracles do not provide much information on infanticide and abandonment: about a half-dozen "suffocations" of infants were reported among the 110 birth and early infancy accounts, and three or four were included in the 156 accident cases; in a Becket miracle, Queen Eleanor is said to have cared for a foundling abandoned in the road.[157]

Some of the miracles do, nevertheless, present interesting perspectives on "overlaying." The potentially tragic consequences of what seems to have been a truly accidental smothering are evident, for instance, in the French case of Ersand, who was breast-feeding her year-old daughter Bertula one night as she lay in her cradle at the foot of the bed.[158] Sleepily stretching her arms over the child as it sucked, Ersand lapsed into a deep sleep. In another room Ersand's mother, Ysabella, realized that she could no longer hear the usual noises of the suckling infant or the mother's voice as she tended her child. Horrified by this silence, according to the monastic scribe who reconstructed the events, Ysabella frantically leapt from her bed, saw Ersand lying on the little girl, and began screaming "Get up, daughter, get up! Look—you have suffocated your child!" Ersand awoke to find herself crushing her daughter, who seemed dead. The two women removed the little wrappings (*panniculis*) that swaddled her and intently examined the infant. They found the body cold, the limbs rigid. Ersand snatched up the child, crushing her to her breast to make her suck. Nothing happened. She cast her down, began running back and forth, tearfully screaming, then two more times she picked up Bertula and tried to suckle her. Finally, in her grief, shame, and disgrace she contemplated suicide, "adding sin upon sin at the instigation of the Enemy," writes the narrator. Her mother restrained her, and after the two women calmed down somewhat, Ysabella suggested that they commend Bertula to St. Edmund, enshrined at Pontigny. Collapsing on the ground by the corpse, they began threatening Edmund: "If you do not return this girl to life, we will kill ourselves." Bertula finally revived, after which Ysabella and Ersand took her to Pontigny, praising God and St. Edmund. Aside from revealing the violent emotions accompanying her misfortune, Ersand's experience also suggests something about contemporary breast-feeding: rather than take the child into bed with her, she suckled her as the infant lay in its cradle near the bed. Toward the end of the Middle Ages some cradles were made with bars across the top, possibly to prevent mothers or nurses from leaning over, and perhaps upon, the child they suckled.[159] The frequency of cases like Ersand's may have stimulated such improvements.

The fear of disgrace and shame mentioned by Ersand, sometimes attributed to parents whose children were endangered because of adults' carelessness, is also seen in an Italian case recorded in 1325.[160] According to her own testimony, one August night when Ceccha of Tolentino was about twenty-two she was in bed with her children, Clarucia, her small daughter, and her son, Vannucio. She was holding her son at her right side, gently stroking him to keep him from crying, since he wanted to breast-feed. On her left she had little Clarucia, whom she was suckling. After holding her children like this for about an hour, she fell asleep. Upon waking up and calling out for someone to bring a light, she saw the pallor of death on Clarucia. Fearing to be blamed for smothering her daughter, she began imploring Nicholas of Tolentino to free Clarucia from death and to free herself from infamy. Some parents suffered the uncertainty of not knowing whether they were guilty of negligence, as in the case of Isabel, whose daughter was born in 1371 in Avignon. Three days after the birth, while the two were in bed, Isabel, wishing to hold her child, found her "dead": her mouth was open, her eyes upturned, and her face and limbs black and limp. Stricken to the heart, as she testified before the papal commissioners, Isabel cried bitterly, not knowing whether she herself had caused her daughter's death while sleeping, "even though," she stated, the two "had been lying far apart."[161] The wet nurse Perreta and the godmother Johanneta came in, and all three women prayed, Isabel making a vow to Urban V. After about half an hour Isabel told the nurse to take the infant "to the fire for warmth, and put your breast into her mouth so she can suck, for I believe that Urban will revive her." Both Perreta and Johanneta responded that this was useless since the infant was dead; at this Isabel shouted "Do what I said! Take her to the fire!"[162] They carried her to the warmth, the nurse squeezed milk into the infant's mouth, and at last the child opened her eyes and began to drink. In summing up their materials, the papal notaries referred to this case as an "accident" *(axidentus)*, miraculously remedied.

SOME GENERALIZATIONS

It is worth recalling one of P.A. Sigal's caveats, that "miraculous" testimonials about children saved from death or difficult births inform us only about the unusual cases, not the ordinary ones.[163] This chapter analyzed 110 cases of this nature. The sources can be divided into two groups, those pertaining to northern Europe (England, northern France, and Pomerania, 59 cases) and to southern Europe (51 Italian and southern French examples). Findings based on these figures provide tentative indicators of paths into future research. For instance, when difficult or unusual births occurred, or when newborns apparently died and returned to life, both northern and southern parents, in roughly the same proportions, tended to call together several members of their family and kin. In both North and South, again, about the same proportion of cases explicitly indicate that midwives were present (although they can be assumed to be in the background in most deliveries). In only 5 out of 110 cases were doctors called in to assist in difficult births; but of these, 4 were mentioned in southern European records and only 1 for the North. We shall return to this issue of recourse to *medici* or physicians in later chapters.

Given medieval European cultural assumptions and social expectations, it is probable that endangered male infants would have attracted a greater investment of parental time, emotion, and effort than afflicted female infants. If so, one might assume that parents would have made greater efforts on behalf of affected boys than girls by, for example, taking more trouble to appeal to saints and to promise offerings, or carrying the infants to shrines, or going to a papal hearing, sometimes years later, to describe their child's successful encounter with the miraculous. The sample of cases dealing with infants tends to bear this out: overall, male neonates were the objects of parental concern more than three times as frequently as female. In 110 instances, the gender was indicated for 72 children; of these, 56 (78 percent) were boys, 16 (22 percent) girls. This disparity suggests that parents, midwives, or attendant neighbor women may have been more attentive or tenacious where male offspring were concerned than they were for infant girls. In the case of Alaracia, for instance, her infant daughter was already lying in the stable amid the dung when some trembling of the tiny form was noticed; was such peremptory disposal the fate of others born seemingly lifeless and female? On the other hand, the example of Isadora Taylor, who was born severely malformed yet was cared for tenderly by her parents, emphasizes the dangers of generalizing from a limited sample. In the next two chapters on illnesses and accidents, similar questions will be asked regarding the children's age, gender, and family involvement.

Finally, although the neonates' well-being was the center of interest in most of the miracles, saints were also called upon to assist in the mother's travail: in nearly a third of the cases (32 out of 110), reference was made to prolonged or unusually painful labor. Even more significant, perhaps, is the mention of debilities that tormented many mothers following birth. Eighteen out of 110 women were afflicted by the trauma of birth for varying periods, from days to years, and in varying degrees of severity. Often, in these cases, maternal healing, and not the birth or the neonate itself, was the point of the miraculous report. These supernatural interventions lead one to consider the many unfortunate medieval women who were injured or impaired —in some cases for life —but whose prayers to saints, vows of pilgrimage, and visits to shrines brought no relief at all.

3

MEDIEVAL FAMILIES AND
CHILDREN'S ILLNESSES

....

The child who survived birth and the first year of infancy still faced many dangers: in the Middle Ages, as today, childhood accidents claimed many lives. Then as now, an unexpected death, often in the midst of carefree play, was particularly devastating to parents. We shall examine several of these sudden, unforeseen deaths in the next chapter. It might be argued, however, that acute and especially chronic illnesses, because they deeply involved the families—sometimes for months or years—were even more emotionally taxing to adults. Although practically all the illnesses recorded in saints' lives ended with a "cure," until that happened shrine-side records and canonization testimony emphasize the anxiety, fear, and stress suffered by parents, kin, and neighbors. The following examples, selected from 334 instances provided by the miracle lists and depositions, illustrate the variety of family reactions when children became ill. The cases are grouped by categories that reflect medieval concepts of illness and disability. They are, therefore, culturally interpreted experiences employing a variety of "vocabularies of discomfort," linked to contemporary beliefs about the body and its well-being.[1] The categories, in other words, tell us more about subjective expressions of illness as understood by the families and their children than about objectively defined medieval diseases.[2] Only rarely do the miracles present sufficient details for retrospective diagnoses by modern medical historians, such as the one convincingly propounded by Dr. Eleanora C. Gordon.[3] Nevertheless, we can attain a general overview of the range of medieval illnesses by following the descriptions given by parents and others involved in the alleviation of children's distress.

CATEGORIES OF CHILDREN'S ILLNESSES
AND DISABILITIES: EXAMPLES FROM 334 CASES

Children with Afflicted Limbs

Apart from what it tells us about children and parental care, a case investigated by papal agents in 1308 illustrates the variable perspectives provided by witnesses as, in turn, they made their sworn statements. Beatrice, about nine, claimed that she had been so crippled for four years that she could neither walk nor feed herself.[4] Her mother, Cecilia, commended her to St. Louis and carried Beatrice on her back to his tomb in Marseilles.[5] Along the way, at first sight of the city, Beatrice asked her mother to put her down "since," she told her, "I think I can walk." After the girl walked a short distance, her mother hoisted her up again and continued on.[6] At the tomb Beatrice was given some bread. For the first time in four years, she testified, she ate without her mother's help, and began walking as well. The papal commissioners had her walk for them and examined her feet and hands, which bore signs of atrophy. Asked to name witnesses to her earlier disability, Beatrice said that there were several, but she could remember only her maternal uncles, Peter and William. Cecilia testified that when Marseilles came into view from "Saint Michael's Plain" on February 24, 1308, her daughter asked to be put down; she took three or four steps by herself.[7] Picking her up again, Cecilia carried her into the city, where they lodged in a neighborhood known as "the Temple." Next morning — Sunday — she carried Beatrice into the Franciscans' church, putting her down at the tomb. After praying for her daughter's health, Cecilia saw Beatrice's legs, hands, and feet straighten out. When food was brought, the girl fed herself, and then she walked about the tomb. When asked who had known of her daughter's disability, Cecilia stated that it was common knowledge back home in Santa Cruce, where her neighbors had seen her carrying Beatrice on her back as they went around begging. She also named her two brothers, John (whom Beatrice referred to as Peter) and William, as well as Bartholomew the bailiff of Santa Cruce priory. Cecilia finished by noting that two women, Ramunda and Rixenda, were present when she made her vow. As suggested earlier, the making of a vow was the crucial link between suppliants and the meritorious dead. The next witness, Cecilia Helziarsse, claimed that she had seen the crippled girl nearly every day, because they were neighbors. In her opinion, "even if her house were on fire" Beatrice could not have escaped. The sight of the mother carrying her daughter on her back or in her arms was familiar in Santa Cruce. Although the witness had not actually heard Cecilia vow to Louis, she thought this likely, since she had frequently heard her make vows to other saints. In addition, Cecilia knew that Beatrice's mother had taken her to various churches for a cure: to a forest chapel of St. Mary and to the churches of Blessed Andrew, St. Bartholomew, and St. Pancracius. Anyone who had known Beatrice before her cure at Louis's tomb, she concluded, would have to admit that the restoration of the use of her limbs was a great miracle, "beyond nature." The final witness touched upon the harsh realities that must have troubled many poor pilgrims. The widow Katherina kept a hospice in Marseilles. She deposed that on the evening of Saturday, February 24, 1308, Cecilia, with her daughter on her back, appeared at her door. Katherina had never seen them before. The mother was crying because, as it was so late, she could not find any lodging; Katherina gave in to Cecilia's begging to take them in "for God's sake." The mother immediately sat Beatrice by the fire and put bread into her mouth. When Katherina asked about this, Cecilia replied that the girl had been crippled for more than four years and that they had come to Marseilles hoping for a cure. Early next morning Cecilia put Beatrice on her back and took her to the church. When they returned around midday, Beatrice was walking by herself, her mother holding her hand. Cecilia, weeping for joy, claimed that St. Louis had miraculously cured her daughter. Cecilia's long ordeal, to say nothing of the child's, is one of many examples of suffering endured by medieval parents for the sake of their offspring. Beatrice, literally a burden, was an aggravation to Cecilia's poverty. In more affluent families such disabilities may have been less onerous, at least physically, for the parents. After Bertrandeta, the ten-year-old daughter of a French *seigneur*, was suddenly paralyzed, her father's squire carried her about until prayers brought relief.[8]

Several of the crippled children seem to have been victims of congenital deformities or afflictions: as one English father put it, his son had been lame from his mother's womb.[9] In another English case, ever since birth a girl's hands were so "contracted" that her fingers were bent into her palms and she had never been able to feed herself until, when she was seven, her father took her on horseback to Becket's shrine.[10] Occasionally such defects were attributed to faulty deliveries. For more than a year after her son had been drawn out of her by both feet, as Alifanda testified in Italy, his toes and feet were abnormal.[11] In France, according to statements recorded in 1282 in the process that led to the canonization of Louis IX (d. 1270, canonized 1297), Herbert, a fifty-year-old dyer who had lived in Paris for some twenty-six years, had a child named Mabileta.[12] Up to about age four and one-half, she had not walked. She could not support herself because her knees seemed to be "dislocated." Whenever Herbert put her on crutches, she fell over "like a lump of wood" as soon as he let go of her. He had tried this, he claimed, "more than a thousand times."[13] Her feet and legs looked typical of girls her age, and there were no lesions; but he noticed that the round bone on her knees moved laterally much more than was normal, as if disconnected. He testified that about eleven years earlier a neighbor, an Englishman named Richard Vaudien, asked him why he did not take his daughter to Louis's tomb, where "they say" miracles occurred. When Herbert replied "I don't know," Vaudien emphasized the goodness of saints, leading Herbert to realize that a spiritual spokesman was necessary with God, as he put it, just as an intermediary was necessary with a royal official. As a result of their visit to the tomb, Mabileta was cured.

Some children, whether congenitally crippled or afflicted after several years of normal development, used crutches. Ceptus, whose feet were so twisted that he walked on the sides rather than the soles of his feet, was such a child.[14] After living as a beggar for several years, he was cured, when between nine and twelve years old (witnesses gave several estimates), by being placed upon Clara of Montefalco's tomb. In his excitement at the miracle, as the people were running toward him and the bells were ringing, Ceptus threw down his crutches and walked away; no doubt they were hung up at the saint's tomb, with the other votives. Besides using crutches, lame children pulled themselves along with wooden hand trestles, as often shown in medieval representations of pilgrims at shrines.[15] Some children were only partially afflicted, which was slender compensation for Bellaflore, for instance, whose right foot was so swollen that for a year she could hardly bear to touch the ground with her big toe; doctors could not help.[16] After her mother promised to dedicate Bellaflore and a wax image at Nicholas's tomb, and to go there with her own hands tied, the girl began walking normally. Although these cases stressed the curative powers of the saints, some crippled children were examined and treated by secular healers as well: in southern France, the child's father called in a certain Master Peter "and other doctors, both physicians and surgeons."[17] Of course, most saints' supporters would claim that mere human remedies were useless.

Neck and Throat Problems; Scrofula

Doctors were also called in to cure children with infected throats. Berardescha told papal inquisitors in Italy that, as a result of such an infection, for two or three days her sister Ceccha's swollen neck was as big as her head.[18] When the doctors wanted to cut into the three-year-old's neck, her mother, Margarita, refused permission. Instead, Margarita and Berardesca, with a family servant carrying Ceccha, went to a local holy man, Nicholas

(subject of the later canonization inquiry). He advised prayer and an offering to St. Blaise.[19] After Margarita's gift of a penny, a candle, and an egg in
St. Blaise's church, Ceccha's ailment subsided. In explaining to the pope's
men her reasons for refusing surgery, Margarita provides us with an interesting perspective on medieval Italian parent-child relationships. When the
medici proposed an operation, Margarita vehemently and tearfully implored
them not to cut her child. Given the dangers of contemporary surgical technique, her violent reaction is understandable. However, it appears that these
risks were not uppermost in the mother's mind: when two of Nicholas's colleagues asked why she was so upset, Margarita told them "The doctors want
to cut into my daughter's throat, but a scar will remain and she will be reviled
for it."[20] Parental anguish over the scarring of their children is to be expected;
but this particular mother's despair, in addition, may have been fueled by
anxiety about her daughter's chances in the frenetic marriage competition
faced by many fourteenth-century Italian parents. The significance of this
competition, for parents, is revealed in another Italian miracle collection,
recorded in 1319 for Thomas Aquinas. Nicholas had a daughter (age not
given) who was *gutturnosa*, perhaps suffering goiter. He claimed that, because
of the swelling on his daughter's throat, he would not be able to marry her
off.[21] Testimony about yet another Italian saint, Clare of Montefalco, is also
suggestive: when Ciolus laid eyes on his little Ventuructia for the first time in
two years (she had been living with a wet nurse), he saw that her throat was
very swollen. His first exclamations are revealing: "We are shamed through
this daughter of ours. . . . I would rather have her dead than alive."[22] Perhaps
Ciolus feared that the disfigurement was or might become permanent, causing problems in later years when he would be hoping to arrange her marriage.
After Ciolus promised to encircle Clare's altar with wax, the child began to
improve and was quite well about two weeks later. Little boys were similarly
stricken, as in the case of Cola, age one. The swelling on his neck ("as big as
an egg") did not vanish, in spite of a doctor's assistance, until the mother and
child went on pilgrimage to Tolentino in 1324.[23]

  In another Italian case in which the mother prayed for a cure of her
daughter's swollen neck without surgery, the infirmity was described as
scrofula *(infirmitate scrufularum)*. It subsided, in the mother's opinion, after a
pilgrimage following which her daughter vomited, "curing" the ailment.[24]
Her contemporaries were not alone in assuming that a swollen neck was a
symptom of scrofula. The Hippocratic *Aphorisms* rated "scrofulous swellings
in the cervical glands" as a common disease of prepubescent children.[25] In the
Middle Ages, it was believed that the royal touch could cure scrofula. When
the knight Roger's fourteen-year-old began to suffer from scrofula or

glandula, which, as the chronicler put it, "they say" can be cured only by contact of the royal hand, he took her to the "most illustrious" King Henry II (d. 1189), whose touch, Roger claimed, caused the swellings to subside.[26] After they returned home, however, Margaret's whole body grew diseased; she could not bear to have anyone touch her legs and feet. She wasted away to the point that her bones seemed to poke through her skin. Taken in a cart to the Oxford shrine of Frideswide, she and her parents prayed through the night; by morning she was so improved that she went home not in the cart but on a horse, "cured." She died soon afterward. Margaret's disease progressed to its mortal end in spite of her parents' solicitude and the temporary relief stimulated by a king's touch and a saint's tomb. Other English parents, 300 years later, were similarly perturbed when the swelling on nine-year-old Agnes's neck did not go away.[27] Although they called in the very best *(expertissimos)* medical help, all that resulted was a diagnosis of "the King's Evil," scrofula. While the parents deliberated how to obtain the royal touch from Richard III, then "in the second year of his usurped reign" as the chronicler put it, they heard of Henry VI's miracles. After their prayers Agnes's swelling burst, with the draining of much fluid; she recovered in four days. "Thus"— the narrator's bias is refreshingly patent—"the dead king's powers exceeded those of the living king." What royal hands could do for scrofula in England, a saint's toes could do in southern France. After about four years of John's suffering scrofulous fistulas oozing "horrible putridity" in his neck and throat, on the evening of November 27, 1360, his mother took him to the church where the Countess of Ariano's body lay in state. While praying for help, she touched John's neck to the dead woman's feet, which was followed by a rapid cure, eventually leaving scars on his neck and under the left ear.[28]

"Gout," Swellings, and "Dropsy"

Although it is tempting to translate *gutta* as "gout," and in some cases a generalized arthritic joint inflammation in children, mimicking some of the symptoms of adult gout, seems to be indicated, *gutta* with modifiers also meant anything from epilepsy to ulcer, stone, or some sort of rash. For instance, Petronilla testified that her nine-year-old daughter, also called Petronilla, suddenly was stricken about four years earlier by what some people called *gutta,* although she herself did not know what the illness was. It affected her child's spine and legs, which became so rigid and afflicted that she could not walk. The mother mentioned in passing that before her daughter became ill, she had been healthy and strong enough to go (or walk) about and work as was fitting to her age (she was then around five years old).[29] It cannot be determined what sort of "work" was envisaged, or the precise meaning of the afterthought "fitting to her age," but this aside throws some fleeting light on the topic of the age at which parents expected their children to begin assisting them with daily chores. The younger Petronilla remained weak and crippled for more than two years. When the mother heard about the miracles attributed to Louis, she commended the child to him and vowed a wax image. Within three days, the mother testified, her daughter began to walk again. In some cases, no doubt, when a child fell ill parental worries were magnified by the loss of the child's labor. At the same time, unmistakable evidence of love for ill or disabled children, which seems to supersede any economic considerations, appears throughout the medieval collections. After thirteen-year-old Joanna developed an ulcerated swelling on her left side, her parents, in addition to calling in doctors and surgeons, tended her carefully, changing her soiled bandages as needed, "since they loved her very much."[30]

Given the state of personal hygiene, water supply, sanitation and sewage disposal, levels of nourishment, living and sleeping arrangements, and medical ignorance prevailing throughout most of Europe before, during, and long after the Middle Ages, for our medieval families almost any ailment could become life-threatening, no matter how trivial or commonplace it might appear to us. These hard facts of life sometimes led to what we might, at first glance, dismiss as overreactions to the ordinary bumps, scrapes, and minor infections of daily life. In these circumstances, therefore, it is understandable that whenever Thomassa looked at the swollen eyelid of her son Vannectus, age three, she burst into tears. She did this for several days as the swelling, at first the size of a bean, grew until the whole eye was shut.[31] By then the doctors—there were three of them—wanted to lance the eyelid, which frightened Thomassa even more. She vowed to take her son to Clare of Montefalco's tomb; she would go barefoot without a cloak and make an offering of some silver. Three days after her vow, pus began flowing from the lesion, and within fifteen days the eyelid seemed normal. The infirmity had lasted, in all, about four months. Many of the children in these records were afflicted with "swelling" in various parts of the body, a symptomatology that could refer to almost anything. Like Vannectus, who was cured after a vow to Clare, little Bellus also benefited from that Umbrian saint's powers. His father claimed that Bellus, when about two months old, suffered for some fifteen days from an abscess on the groin that became so serious that the father feared for his life.[32] Grandmother Massiola said that the swelling looked horrible *(aspectu orribile)*. The boy's mother, Helen, vowed to take the child, with a wax image, to Clare's tomb. While Helen, Bellus, and Massiola were en route to the shrine the swelling burst, leaving nine wounds, which healed within a few days.

The expression "dropsy" conveys as little when applied to children as it does to women about to give birth. As in the women's situation discussed in the last chapter, it seems to indicate some sort of edema, perhaps distinguished, somehow, from the equally general term "swelling." A dropsy case reported from southern France involved Alaracia's son Peter, age ten.[33] He became so "dropsical" and swollen in stomach and legs that he could barely walk; he was afflicted in his liver and spleen (as, presumably, the doctors told Alaracia); he himself complained of stomach problems. Alaracia turned to a good local doctor, who cared for the boy for three months. According to another witness, this was Master John of Provence, who was physician to a pope (possibly Boniface VIII, 1294/5-1303). His treatment included medicines and poultices (or plasters, *emplaustres*), but the child's condition deteriorated and the swelling and pain increased. Seeing this, in about 1298 his mother took Peter to Montpellier because, as she testified, there were many doctors there.[34] In fact, by this time Montpellier had become one of Europe's leading centers of medical studies. Alaracia put her son into the hands (literally—*in manibus*) of an eminent doctor for four months, whose ministrations, however, did not benefit the boy at all. Finally, the doctor decided to have Peter drink a special concoction that he believed would bring relief.[35] As it happens, in Montpellier during the 1290s Master Arnald of Villanova, among others, was elaborating rules about the proportions of components in medicines, particularly the "wonder-drug" theriac.[36] For whatever reasons, the doctor's plan worried Alaracia: seeing that many promised remedies had not helped, she was afraid that this new one would be as useless. Perhaps she feared that it would be dangerous as well; she may have heard of deaths in the region caused by the administration of the wrong drugs, or in improper dosages.[37] Alaracia turned with sadness and devotion to Louis, who had died recently (1297) and to whom miracles were attributed. She vowed that if her son were cured of his dropsy without having to drink the medication, she would take him to Marseilles and offer a cloth and a pound of wax at the saint's tomb. Preparations for the medical treatment went ahead, however, and the night before he was to have the drink, she took her son aside for a quiet talk. The boy remembered this conversation well, as he told the papal examining board ten years later. In the course of their discussion he told her that he felt better: "really, it seems that the pain has lessened, and the swelling too." Peter, taking no more medicines from that point, recovered within fifteen days. Alaracia was very grateful, as she told the papal commissioners, especially considering how her son's illness had worsened: although he had been in doctors' care for so long, he was harmed rather than helped by their efforts.

Hernia, Rupture

According to the late-medieval physician Bagellardus, "There sometimes happens to infants a horrible condition against nature and commonly called rupture . . . or hernia." This was brought on, he suggested,
by "excessive crying or from [a] fall upon the stomach or from flatu-
lence contained in the intestines, although it can happen from excessive
consumption of milk. . . ." A contemporary, Metlinger, suggested that
ruptures appeared in children "from much crying, yelling or hard
coughing."[38] James, son of Countess Matilda and Roger, Earl of Clare
(d. 1173), suffered from a hernia for some forty days following his birth
because of his excessive screaming, the twelfth-century Canterbury
monks suggested, anticipating Bagellardus. His intestines descended
into his scrotum, which swelled and hung down nearly to his knees.
Although Roger offered forty or more silver marks for his cure, no doctor would accept the case unless he could operate on the infant. The
parents, however—apprehensive because of James's tender age—were
unwilling to consent. (One of the monk reporters claimed that the
mother, in particular, was reluctant to allow surgery.) When he was two,
his mother took James to Becket's shrine and washed him with the martyr's water; within three days the infirmity had vanished.[39] A similar
drama was taking place about the same time in northern France. The
miraculous events attributed to Laurence, archbishop of Dublin who
died in Normandy in 1180, include an account of Margaret, a woman of
high estate whose firstborn son suffered from hernia.[40] When the boy,
greatly loved by his parents, was about six, his intestines burst from his
body in the shape and size of two large fists. His grandfather suggested surgery, horrifying Margaret. She said that she would care for
him for the rest of her life rather than expose him to mortal danger; she
would not permit him to be cut.[41] Next day, accompanied by the boy's
nurse, she carried him to St. Laurence's tomb. Placing him upon the
tomb, she prayed: "St. Laurence, I give you my son, and I dedicate him
and myself as your servants. . . . I will only take him away [from the
shrine] dead or cured."[42] The nurse then took him in her arms and they
both fell asleep. Waking up during the celebration of the Mass, the boy
scrambled from the nurse's lap and started running about. When
Margaret saw this she sent the nurse in pursuit, "so he won't hurt himself"; for they kept a sort of pillow between his legs to support his hernia.[43] The boy, however, claimed that he was cured, which the two
women and the shrine custodian found to be the case. In later years he
became a knight.

Fear of the surgeon's knife was universal. Smiralda of Spoleto, anxious about the surgery proposed for her ruptured three-year-old, vowed a candle for St. Clare's tomb if he were cured without being cut. Subsequently her son was cured, as Isabella, a kinswoman living in the same house with Smiralda, testified. Southern European households, as we shall see, often embraced kin beyond the "nuclear family." Margarita, a neighbor who verified Smiralda's story, claimed that her own grandson, who lived with her, suffered a similar infirmity for a year. After the surgeons were called in, Margarita vowed—in the presence of her daughter, who also lived in the house—to take a wax image of the child's loins or buttocks to Clare's tomb if the knife could be avoided.[44]

Parents realized that most children were simply too delicate for surgery, cautery, or phlebotomy.[45] For his part, the wise surgeon would act only after receiving parental permission.[46] After examining John's herniated scrotum Philip, an Italian surgeon, concluded that the child, age five or six months, was too young for the knife. Nevertheless, Philip insisted that surgery was the only thing that could cure him.[47] In the testimony and miracle lists, it is often the mother who resists surgery for this particular ailment: when her husband arrived with a doctor who planned to remove her son's testicle, that was hanging down to his knees, Morindella of San Genesio in Italy would not allow it.[48] Even though parents often appealed to alternative sources of medical opinion and assistance, such as the "knowledgeable women" called in to treat a three-year-old whose viscera protruded from his anus,[49] in some cases reluctant mothers and fathers had to admit that surgery was needed, in spite of the evident dangers. These were very real dangers, as shown in the following example.

Stone, Other Genitourinary Problems

The incident involved a prominent family in late twelfth-century Oxford. Benedict's five-year-old son, Lawrence, had been tormented even from the cradle by bladder pains. Over the years the illness had worsened, until the boy, in great distress, was passing blood.[50] He became emaciated, pale, and short of breath. The doctors asserted that he had a bladder stone requiring surgery. Benedict, who had already spent a good deal on doctors, found a surgeon whom he promised to reward if he cured his son. Blinded by avarice, as the record's compiler put it, the surgeon agreed. The parents, horrified by the prospect of a bloody operation, went away and left the surgeon alone in their home to do his work. Having stretched out the little boy *(puerulum)* on a table and tied him down, which was (the record notes) normal practice, the surgeon cut into him so unskillfully *(inartificiose)* and extracted the stone with such clumsiness that he could not stop the bleeding. The boy, it seemed, died in misery. The agitated surgeon closed the wound, announced that he had forgotten some ointment at home, forbad anyone going into the boy's house until his return, and fled the city. Meanwhile the mother, after two hours of stomach-churning fear and anxiety, began to wonder why the procedure was taking so long.[51] She went into her house and found Lawrence on the table. The recorder of these events, who was related to the boy's father, writes, "[I]t is beyond my powers to describe her sadness at the sight." She became hysterical, but even in such a state she and her husband prayed for supernatural aid, promising to make their son a servant of God and St. Frideswide (later, Oxford's patron saint) if he should revive. Lawrence opened first one eye, then the other, began stirring, and called out to his mother for a bit of food.[52] When Lawrence had recovered, his parents handed him over to the Oxford canons to learn sacred literature and, presumably, to serve in Frideswide's church. The surgeon is not mentioned again. Perhaps his guilt and anxiety led him to the confessional and priestly absolution. The topic of guilt and moral responsibility for death during surgery appears in a thirteenth-century confessor's manual, where an entry reads "A surgeon came and confessed that he often performed lithotomies, and after the operation many of his patients died; but he didn't really know whether he was the cause of their deaths or not."[53]

In spite of crude techniques, insanitary operating conditions, and deaths so frequent that lithotomies appeared in penitential guidebooks, there were successes. For two weeks three-year-old Poncius was in great pain because he could not urinate. The family called in Master John the *medicus*, who examined the child by palpation, then pronounced his ominous verdict: Poncius seemed incurable without surgery. At first John refused to operate, but he agreed after obtaining legal assurances that he would be held blameless should the boy die of the surgery.[54] In addition to making such agreements, some doctors and patients arranged that the full fee would be withheld until the patient recovered (sometimes confirmed by other doctors), or that one fee was due in case of recovery, a lesser amount if the doctor failed or death resulted. Occasionally doctors had notaries record contracts with their patients before treatment or surgery. In one example, the patient agreed to hold the doctor "quit, immune and discharged at law and extrajudicially," including, the parties added hopefully, "before God."[55] Obviously, worries about malpractice suits are hardly an invention of the modern era. In the case of Master John and Poncius, it turned out that the guarantees were a wise precaution on the doctor's part: so much blood came from Poncius that bystanders "believed his soul had flown." The boy's uncle Bernard, seeing this, made a vow to Pope Urban, and in that instant a stone "big as a hen's egg" was taken from the boy's member. Within a few days he was on the way to recovery. The operation by this "doctor surgeon" (*medicus cirurgicus*) was witnessed not only by Uncle Bernard but also by the child's mother "and various others," which, it is easy to imagine, may have had a deleterious effect on John the *medicus*'s surgical performance.

In the ancient world Hippocratic writings recognized that children were particularly susceptible to stone, especially between weaning and puberty. The reason was "the warmth of the whole body and of the region about the bladder in particular. Adult men do not suffer from stone because the body is cool. . . ."[56] Medieval doctors such as Aldobrandinus of Siena warned in 1256 against giving children over seven years of age milk, fruit, and cheese if they were to avoid suffering from stone, while in a late-medieval pediatric manual, first published in 1473, Bartholomew Metlinger issued similar advice not to children but to mothers: "Urine stones come in children because the mother eats much cheese or, according to others, many brown berries, whortleberries or elderberries."[57] At about the same period another specialist, Bagellardus, described the effects of stone on parents as well as suffering children: "Infants are especially troubled when they cannot pass urine, and twist and turn and cry out, while the parents are saddened and the doctors are aroused because they do not know the causes of the infant's pain."[58] Such a child was the subject of a Pomeranian woman's testimony. When Caspar, son of a house servant named Katherina, was stricken with stone at age three, for fifteen days he was unable to emit a drop of urine. His agony was so unbearable that he rolled about on the ground day and night, screaming and crying.[59] A short time after Katherina vowed to visit Dorothy's tomb, she heard a peculiar noise from her son, as if he had burst. Wailing and crying, she ran to him and in his lap found a stone the size of a pea; he was never again troubled by that sort of illness. In another Pomeranian case, after two days and nights of extreme pain and swelling of the abdomen, a two-year-old boy ejected a stone (as his mother testified) the size of an acorn.[60]

The causes of this disease in children are still not firmly established. It is clear, however, that whereas idiopathic bladder stone in children ceased to be a common disease in most of western Europe and America by the end of the nineteenth century, it is still, in the late twentieth century, an endemic disease of children in northwest India, southern China, Thailand, Japan, and other regions of Asia. There seems to be, as ancient and medieval doctors theorized, a link between maternal nutrition and an infant's predisposition to developing a bladder stone. Where the disease is still widespread, it appears more often "in children of the lowest economic class, which is usually agricultural, predominantly in boys before puberty."[61] At a World Health Organization symposium in Bangkok in 1972, attention focused on correlations between the incidence of the disease in children and regional socioeconomic, and therefore nutrition, levels.[62] Why boys should be the most common victims is, again, still not understood, although different rates of urine evacuation in boys and girls has been suggested as a predisposing factor. In any event, it is a boy's affliction: from 1960 through 1962 at a hospital in Thailand, 506 stones were removed from adults, 161 from girls, and 1,113 from boys under nine. The highest incidence occurred at age two and one-half.[63] Five of six cures of "stone" in the present study involved boys. Although modern western parents would not expect to see this particular affliction in their infant boys, their medieval predecessors were not so lucky. For them, stone was just one more entry in an already long list of childhood ailments—as it still is in many parts of the world.

Sometimes the medieval records indicate urinary problems without specifically mentioning "stone," although this may have caused the problem. Whatever the etiology, the symptoms were distressing to parents, who did whatever they could to alleviate their children's pain. In one case, they put warm objects over their child's bladder to encourage urination; others tried relaxing their distressed children in warm baths with, occasionally, beneficial results.[64] Even when the affliction did not produce violent pain, it still caused parental anxiety. A group of men traveling from Tolentino to San Angelo broke their journey on May 2, 1320, and lodged in a hospice in the village of San Flaviano. One of the guests noticed that the landlady's little boy, about five, would go outside and then return as if in great pain, throwing himself into his mother's lap. When the guest asked what upset and hurt the boy so much, she answered, "Oh, he has a very bad kind of illness: he cannot urinate [normally]. I've spent plenty on doctors, with no results; I don't know what I'll do."[65] One of the men told her about Nicholas, the miracle worker of Tolentino, suggesting that she pray to the saint, vow her son to him, and promise a candle of her son's length. She did so, and asked her guests to take the candle back with them to Tolentino. They demurred, however, since they were going in the other direction; however, they agreed to stop on their return, when she could give them a candle to take to the shrine. As soon as she had made her vow, her son got up from her lap and went out. When he came back in, his mother asked what he had done outside. He probably responded, "I peed, and it didn't hurt," although the fastidious papal notaries Latinized this as "I made urine" *(ego feci urinam)*. In fact, one of the visitors saw him outside doing so, seemingly without pain. When the men again lodged with the woman ten days later, on their way home, she told them that the boy could urinate normally. She gave them the candle as promised, and many of her neighbors also gave the men candles for the saint's tomb in Tolentino, because of the cure.

"Fevers" and the Plague

Many children, especially those living in hot, humid, malarial southern Europe, were victims of "fevers." In all, 45 of the 334 cases were fevers, and of these 45, 93 percent were reported in the southern cults. No other illness category showed such a high correlation between type of ailment and region. Long-lasting fevers, sometimes coupled with other problems such as dysentery, could change healthy children into mere "skin and bone" *(ossa et pellis)* or give their usually full features the "sharpness" of death. An inability to eat while feverishly semiconscious left some of the revived children famished: "Father, bring me something to eat," said one, and "I'm starving" another, when their recoveries began.[66] Although modern medicine usually considers fever a symptom, some medieval families seem to have viewed it as a disease in itself. In the case of malaria, or ague, as it was sometimes called, this was not far wrong.[67] There seems little doubt that Isoarda of Apt in southern France was suffering from malaria: the notaries described her fever as "double tertian," referring to its periodicity.[68] The noble Francisca of Apt, thirty-five, swore that her niece Isoarda, who lived with her, was afflicted all through Lent. Her doctors, none of them of much help, included Master Unias, a Jew *(iudeus,* who reappears in these records treating a notary's son for fistula).[69] Finally, on a Sunday in March 1363, Francisca vowed a cloth the length of her niece and a barefoot pilgrimage to Dalphine's tomb. Because the girl was still feverish fifteen days later, Francisca tried another approach and asked her kinswoman Catherine de Podio, who had known Dalphine in life, to lend her any item of the saint's clothing she might have. Catherine gave her some of Dalphine's hair and a bit of her headgear, which Francisca wrapped in a piece of cloth and tied around her niece's throat. By daybreak the fever broke in a sweat, after which Isoarda made slow progress until she was cured. Others present when Francisca tied on the bundle included Huga her *familiaris,* whose surname, she told the commissioners, she did not know.[70] Catherine of Podio, like Francisca a widow about thirty-five, also testified. This noble kinswoman of the young Isoarda noted in passing that the twelve-year-old girl was the wife of Laugerius of Apt, another illustration of early marriages in some families. Catherine mentioned their fear that the fever was of a severe variety, not just some transient discomfort. Isoarda herself testified on June 13, 1363, confirming this information and noting incidentally that one of the cloth relics of Dalphine's was red, the other white.

In Marseilles, about fifty miles south of Apt where Isoarda was cured, five-year-old Peter had been feverish for five or six days.[71] His father, Poncius, called in Master Manentus, a famous doctor. Even though Manentus visited the boy two or three times a day, after curfew one evening Peter seemed about to die, and they held a burning candle before his mouth—customarily done, the record notes, for those nearing death.[72] Finally Manentus told the father that his son was no more alive than those buried in the cemetery. Raymond the priest closed the boy's eyes and mouth and covered his face with a linen cloth; a blessed candle was kept burning nearby, as was usually done for the dead. This was too much for the father, who raised his hands to heaven and berated St. Louis: "[Y]ou have heard my prayers badly, since I often devoted my son to you and begged for his health," and "St. Louis, save my son for me; if you do, he will take his shroud to you." The boy's mother joined in, reminding St. Louis of the many times they had commended Peter to him, and begged the saint to restore his health; but "now we have lost him." Poncius, constantly crying out "St. Louis!" often uncovered his son's face hoping to see signs of life.[73] For a long time they all remained with the corpse, until, about midnight, the priest and doctor left. Poncius, "sad and exhausted," went to bed to regain his strength, leaving the mother and other women with the corpse. Among them was the wet nurse who had suckled the boy. Very sad *(multum dolorosa)* because of his death, she was crying and constantly calling upon St. Louis, another example of a strong emotional bond between child and wet nurse, noted in the previous chapter. When she uncovered Peter's face, as the father had done, it seemed that the lower lip moved a little; she touched and prodded the boy, bringing her face close to his. She called for Poncius, but he found his son as cold and stiff as before. Around sunrise, however, the child's lips opened a little and he began to speak; the doctor and priest were called back to the house. Soon Peter was moving slightly and asking for his mother. She gave him a drink—warm milk, as the father recalled. By nine in the morning the boy was asking to go to Louis's tomb. There Peter offered a candle and cloth (his shroud, presumably). Back at home, he began a recuperation that ended in his recovery three days later. Incidentally, an older son of Poncius provides a glimpse of contemporary living and sleeping arrangements in this southern European family. Marquet, about twelve when his younger brother became ill, testified that although he and Peter ate and slept in their grandfather's house, his feverish brother was cared for in their father's house.[74] One night after the curfew bells, Marquet, in his father's house, heard that his little brother had died. As everyone began to mourn, Poncius told Marquet to go back to his grandfather's house and go to bed, as usual. Having returned, Marquet and his sister wept for a long time, then they got into a bed and slept until morning.[75] When they awoke, they learned that their brother had revived.

Fever also struck down a young boy in central Italy about 1317. As friends and relatives gathered, expecting the worst, Cinctia vowed a wax image of her son Lippulus at Clare's tomb.[76] Although some improvement was noted, a doctor, called in eight days after the vow, told the mother that the illness was not finished with Lippulus. Next day Cinctia took a sample of her son's urine to the doctor. Appearance, odor, and taste of a patient's urine, and the strength and rhythm of the pulse, were two universal diagnostic indicators used by medieval *medici*. Uroscopy is depicted in many manuscript miniatures, which show people bringing flasks of urine for a doctor's inspection. He would make his diagnosis and recommendations for treatment based on this examination, in many cases without ever seeing the patient. Any well-stocked medieval medical library would include at least one manual containing a drawing of perhaps twenty-two flasks of urine, arranged in a color wheel of hues from black to silver—with several shades of yellow and gold in between—each flask accompanied by suggested diagnoses.

In this case, after the doctor looked at Lippulus's urine, he told Cinctia that the boy would die later that morning. On her way home, she stopped at Clare's tomb and commended her son to the saint, begging to "find him well and walking." When she returned she saw that he had improved (*melioratus*, which does not suggest full recovery). Although he wanted to get out of bed, Cinctia would not let him. Meanwhile Grana, a neighbor, claimed that Cinctia had been foolish: "He wasn't cured by any miracle; the ailment ran its course and came to an end." After thinking this over, Cinctia put off taking a wax image to Clare's tomb as promised since, as she explained to the papal examiners, she was a poor woman and anyway, after listening to Grana's explanation, her faith in Clare started to weaken. While the medieval records mention pilgrims begging in order to purchase their promised offerings to the saints, perhaps Cinctia, even though poor, could not envision herself in the mendicant's role. When her son again became feverish, with speech loss, chest pains, and shortness of breath, Cinctia sent for the doctor once more. Upon learning how ill the boy was, he merely instructed the messenger to tell the mother to "make him a tidy bed," as if to say (Cinctia testified) that the boy could escape death no longer.[77] As the mother began mourning her son, Bartholella, another neighbor who was also a kinswoman, advised Cinctia to return to Clare; consequently the mother again commended Lippulus to her, reaffirming her original vow. That night the child improved. When yet another relative arrived in the morning to find the boy much better, he also suggested that Lippulus was cured simply "because the illness has run its course; there is no other reason." Difficult though it must have been for her, as she stood before the papal commissioners, their clerks and their notaries recording her every word, Cinctia admitted that once again she succumbed to this explanation, her faith in the saint again diminishing. Lippulus became feverish and afflicted from head to toe. By evening the boy seemed finished. That night Cinctia, praying fervently to Clare, again promised solemnly to carry out her vow, and the next day the boy was free of his fever, which "never returned." Although Cinctia might seem to us a vacillating creature easily influenced by neighbors or kin, it should be noted in her defense that she lived in the very town in which the corpse of the saint had been entombed for nearly a decade. If Clare's cult developed along lines noted elsewhere in medieval Europe, the first people to lose interest and faith in the "new" saint's thaumaturgic power would have been those, like Cinctia, who lived closest to the shrine itself.[78] Fluctuations in Cinctia's convictions may have been typical of medieval people who had God's chosen few as neighbors. Finally, the case of Cinctia and Lippulus reveals how important kinship networks could be in these domestic dramas.

The bubonic plague, which repeatedly scourged Europe from 1347 on, was also accompanied by fever. Some outbreaks of the disease were thought to have been especially serious among infants and youths, as claimed in one southern French case.[79] The description of ten-year-old Bernardetus, stricken in the 1370s, recalls some of the vivid symptomatology summarized by Boccaccio in the first pages of the *Decameron*, written some twenty years earlier. The boy fell ill of plague and developed a carbuncle, as well as seven swellings in various parts of his body. After lying helpless for three weeks, unable to eat, he had become nothing but "skin and bones"; as far as the doctors and neighbors were concerned, he was finished. One evening while his mother was preparing a meal, alone in her kitchen, she broke down and began weeping and praying to Pope Urban. Upon returning to her son's room, she found him much improved, asking for fresh plums and some bread.[80]

Neighbors or kin hovering around sick children, in addition to making promises to saints, sometimes "signed" them with the sign of the cross, a custom noted in several plague cases.[81] However, as suggested in chapter 1, in most children's illnesses (and other miracles) it was the vow, above all else, that seemed the essential promoter of recovery. Some assumptions about vows surface in two widely separated plague cases. In one, reported in 1417 in Sweden, when a seven-year-old plague victim (an only son) seemed near death, instead of making a vow herself his mother went to a "devout matron" to ask her to vow on her son's behalf, illustrating the belief that a request directed to God and the saints that came from someone of elevated spiritual character was the most effective.[82] In southern France a different approach was taken. When a venerable judge who had lost all but one of his children to the plague saw his only surviving son, William, come down with the disease, he called in two doctors; they pronounced the boy incurable. The judge, praying through the night, promised to make the child a monk at Marseilles if he should survive. When the eight-year-old woke up about dawn the father, joining his son's hands together, said, "My son, say these words in this way: 'I, William, vow to you, holy Pope Urban, to visit your tomb as soon as I can, and with God's help, I will be your son among the number of your monks at Marseilles.'"[83] In this way the judge confirmed and, as it were, expanded his own vow, in nearly identical words, through the mouth of his son. As a jurist the father, presumably, would have been more sensitive than most parents to the legalities of oaths and promises. On the other hand, medieval canon lawyers could pass many an hour debating the binding force of an eight-year-old's vow.

Sometimes the vow was made not a moment too soon. A butcher living in Nice saw his daughter Mondeta, age one, fall victim to the pestilence. The girl was being sewn into her shroud by her mother and godmother when the butcher, crying and lamenting, made a vow that "resulted" in her recovery.[84] Just as timely vows might be rewarded, however, unfulfilled vows could bring retribution, as to the family of a ten-year-old who, like Mondeta, contracted plague.[85] The girl relapsed after her parents kept putting off the journey they had vowed to take to Urban's tomb. She took to her bed, chastising her father for his broken promise and predicting that he would be punished ("You will see"). Then she turned to the wall and died.[86]

Mental Afflictions: Dementia, Demoniacs, Epilepsy

Although several of the preceding reports contain dramatic elements, cases of "possession" were often highly dramatic. This affliction, entailing acute psychological and physiological dysfunction expressed in what appear to be culturally formulated behavior patterns, was well established in the medieval Christian mentality. Raving victims were trussed up and left at saints' shrines for hours, days, or weeks to struggle with their invasive spirits. Usually there was no explanation—why a particular individual suddenly was targeted by invisible, malign forces. Only occasionally are underlying assumptions, in the following example probably arising from beliefs about "haunting," visible beneath the surface of the medieval text. In fifteenth-century London, one evening as young Agnes Alyn walked home through the cemetery of St. Dunstan's church, she was attacked by evil spirits and rapt into a terrified frenzy.[87] It was obvious to those who saw her that she had lost her mind. Back home, Agnes was beaten and put to bed. Here, what might appear to be child abuse should be seen in context: demoniacs of all ages and either sex, whether lying at home or tied up at shrines in medieval churches, were sometimes "therapeutically" beaten or whipped by bystanders, parents, or pilgrims. It was believed that demons were unable to possess the soul but could take over the body. Consequently, anything that made their temporary abode uncomfortable for them, such as a beating, would encourage the malevolent forces to depart—a species of exorcism by percussion, as it were. This beating might be pursued energetically enough to draw blood, at least from adult sufferers.[88] These strenuous efforts were no more successful in Agnes's case than they are today, when children are beaten to death by adults who believe them to be possessed.[89] In the middle of the night Agnes began to scream, claw at her limbs, pull out her hair, and rip her clothing. For ten days she was deranged. The doctors were useless, her mother was beside herself with anxiety; finally the parents commended Agnes to Henry VI. The little girl heard their prayers, began chanting "King Henry, King Henry, King Henry," and soon recovered.

French parents were just as convinced as English ones that a beating would soon bring a possessed child back to his or her normal state. When Guillelmina was about ten, just before vespers one day she went crazy or demoniacal, according to her father, John of Marseilles. She uttered strange, foul, and shameful words that normally she never would have said.[90] Besides this indecent shouting, John's testimony continued, Guillelmina clawed at her clothing and face; her family bound her hands to keep her from injuring herself or others. She remained tied up, mad, until the next evening. John made a vow to Louis and took his raving daughter to the tomb, where she was cured. Nineteen-year-old Guillelmina herself appeared before the papal agents to state that she did not remember being mad or demoniacal, because she was young at the time, but she well remembered her hands being tied when she was about nine (not ten, as her father thought). After she had grown up *(adulta facta)*, she testified, her parents told her that they had bound her because she had become frenzied and demoniacal, ripping herself and her clothing and saying very shameful *(turpissima)* and strange words. Guillelmina stated that she believed her parents. The next witness was the mother, a fifty-year-old with the delightful name Splendosa, whose testimony more or less matched her husband's. She added, however, that the "fury" had twice touched her daughter (perhaps on an earlier occasion?), who would bite unless restrained. As a remedy, Splendosa beat Guillelmina with a large stick, although — the mother claimed — her daughter did not feel it.[91] Splendosa also reported that Guillelmina shamelessly *(impuðenter)* uncovered herself. Seeing this (did this motivate him particularly?), her father was moved to devote Guillelmina to the blessed Louis, then take her to the tomb, where the girl fell asleep and awoke sane. A certain Candia, about thirty, narrated a slightly different version of these events. She claimed that some eight years earlier she watched as Guillelmina slashed her face and clothing with her fingernails, totally uncovered herself, screamed furiously, attacked her mother with her teeth, and put filth, dirt, and foul things into her own mouth. Candia also saw the girl's mother beating her with a stick but did not see her tied up. Although she had not heard Guillelmina's father make a vow, she saw him lead her by the hand to Louis's tomb and, on the girl's return, Candia heard her exclaim that she was cured. The final witness was William, about twenty-five, who had seen the girl enraged or frenzied; people claimed that she was a demoniac. Prior to the attack, she was well behaved, as was "fitting to her age."[92] During her fits, however, she rolled her eyes, moved her mouth and head peculiarly, shamelessly uncovered herself, and bared her teeth; once he saw her bite her father's arm. She put filth and dung into her mouth, smashed her father's pots and vases (he was a potter), and said foul, shameful words. After a day and night of this, William saw father and daughter leave for the church. When they returned later that day, Guillelmina was cured.

Guillelmina's shouting rude words, exposing herself, clawing and biting, thrusting dirt and dung into her mouth, breaking things, and attacking her own parents seem to be a horrific inversion of the behavior expected of Christian children: she was supposed, presumably, to be demure, quiet, docile, and modest. Her actions, in stark contrast to this catalog of idealized proprieties, constituted a bizarre pantomime of the Virtues that sometimes featured in contemporary pulpit rhetoric. For example, the possessed Guillelmina's activities suggested, even parodied, the sins of gluttony, lust, anger, and perhaps even pride in attacking her natural superiors, her parents. It is unfortunate that we are not given more details; it would have been intriguing to learn what Guillelmina screamed at her parents or the "shameful" comments she hurled at the world in general. Young men presented similar patterns when possessed, in their frenzy perhaps unconsciously acting out an inversion of normal, socially approved behavior. Bartholomew, like Guillelmina from southern France, became mentally afflicted when he was around fourteen.[93] The illness attacked suddenly; Bartholomew bit his parents and anyone else who approached, and put twigs, stones, dirt, and whatever else he could seize into his mouth. The boy was out of his senses *(extra sensum)* for a week. (His mother testified that the condition was at its worst during the first three days.) After his father, Raymund, commended him to St. Romanus of Carpentras and to Mary Magdalene with no results—his son remained in *furia*—he made a vow to Louis.[94] With deep emotion Raymund joined his hands together, raised them to God, and prayed that the boy be freed from his infirmity; Bartholomew's mother did the same. Just then the boy, who had been watching his parents, raised his hands and eyes heavenward and quieted down; he was cured, as several neighbors looked on. One of them, Alaracia, testified that after curfew one evening about two years earlier, she heard a clamor coming from Raymund's place. After getting out of bed and going into his house, she saw Bartholomew on his bed. He ripped at his clothing and face, attacked his parents and others with his teeth, uttered strange words, twisted about while moving his eyes and head "like someone mad," and ate stones, earth, and every sort of filth he could snatch up. After commenting that his parents were especially disturbed since he was their only son, Alaracia concluded by noting that when she saw the boy seven days later, he seemed to be free from his madness.

Testimony about both Guillelmina and Bartholomew was presented to the same set of papal canonization inquisitors, and it is appropriate to question whether similarities in the reported behavior of the two children was a result of preconceptions in the minds of the pope's appointees and their notaries, who could have prompted the witnesses. It is possible that these learned men working in early fourteenth-century Marseilles, knowing what things to look for in possession cases, found them. One way to test this is to examine a reported possession emanating from a different milieu. The following was recorded in England about 150 years before the Marseilles testimony. According to the Norwich monk Thomas of Monmouth, one day the son of Richard of Silverun

> was seized by the devil and began to handle himself so roughly that seven men were hardly able to chain him. He remained in this state, bound, for six days, eating nothing, and sleep entirely forsook him. Thus bound he was at last brought by his parents to the . . . tomb; and as he approached it he suddenly yelled with a terrible voice and said "What do you want with me? where are you taking me to? I won't go there! I won't go there!" But as he was being dragged thither . . . he burst his bonds, not by his strength but by that of the evil spirit, and attacking his mother, threw her to the ground and fastened his teeth in her throat. And he would certainly have killed her, had not the people run up and rescued her. Then, gnashing his teeth, and glaring fiercely on the bystanders, he maltreated frightfully all whom he could reach.

After being bound again and placed by the tomb of the so-called child victim of local Jews, William of Norwich (d. 1144), he was cured an hour
later.[95] These resonances between a monk's account from twelfth-century
eastern England and testimony recorded by the sophisticates supervising a
fourteenth-century canonization inquiry in the south of France are interesting but hardly uncommon. Going even farther back, the same elements
appear in a story taken from an early Life of St. Gall, for example, who died
in the seventh century: A young girl "immediately fell to the earth by reason
of the assaults of the horrible demon, and rending herself in a lamentable
fashion, began to utter loud and terrible cries accompanied by the most filthy
words."[96] Whatever the reasons for such similarities, the image of the red-
eyed, shouting, blaspheming, violent biter and scratcher who had to be
restrained was repeated many times in medieval miracle collections: in thirteenth-century Worcester, Henry, age twelve, rolled about on the pavement
next to Wulfstan's tomb shouting "as if quite mad";[97] and in the same century
a frenzied woman who had bitten her mother's nose (or finger) was trussed
up and taken to Hereford cathedral where her blasphemous shouts, echo-
ing throughout the church, disrupted divine services and drove the canons
almost to despair.[98]

Although some possession victims seem to have acted out a culturally
constructed script, possession certainly was not the only sort of mental disturbance suffered by medieval children. For instance, in the later twelfth
century a knight's wife reported that "my little one" (parvulo meo), not yet
seven, suddenly began shouting "Look! They're coming!"[99] The child would
abruptly become quiet, pause, then start up again with "Look! They're
there! They're coming!" The household was in an uproar, the parents begging for Becket's help. William, the child's father, hung a portion of the
saint's clothing (provided by the Canterbury monks) around the boy's neck.
The child immediately rested his head on his father's knee, slept, and awoke
cured. The parents took him into their bedroom, removed the relic, and fell
asleep; soon the boy started shouting again. William and his wife leapt
from bed, ran to him, and put the relic around his neck, while making
solemn vows to Becket; thereafter their son was peaceful. Afterward the
parents, who lived outside Reading, went on pilgrimage to Becket's tomb.
There is no way to judge whether, or to what extent, the boy's behavior was
consciously invented—perhaps merely to gain the attention of his parents—or was the result of genuine but transient mental confusion. The
child simply may have awakened, screaming, from a nightmare.

Nightmares, or visions, featured in another English case, situated not in
the usual familial context of most other reports but in the midst of a surrogate,

monastic "family." Among the inmates of the Cluniac priory at Pontefract was Nicholas, age fourteen.[100] He jumped out of bed one night and began running about the dormitory screaming in horror "Help, Help! They're holding me, choking me; they're going to twist the life out of me! Help, Help!" The other brethren, awakened by the commotion, restrained him, saying "What is it, brother Nicholas? Look, we're here with you, your brothers! Bless yourself with the sign of the cross!" The shouting continued, however, long into the night. The prior, in charge of the house, suggested that perhaps Nicholas "meddled in magic while in the world, wrote [magic] characters or gazed into swords." (This gazing refers to divination by staring into a polished surface (scryomancy), a common mantic technique in medieval Europe, often involving people who were assumed to be closer to the "other" world, that is, children.) The brethren, eventually exasperated and doubtless longing for their beds, asked the prior to move Nicholas into the infirmary; but the "father" (as the Canterbury narrator calls him), considering the noble origins and tender age of his "son," was reluctant to "excommunicate" him.[101] Instead, the prior placed some bits of Becket's clothing around Nicholas's neck, after which the *lemures* left the novice alone.

The late-medieval medical writer Bagellardus propounded theories (derived, generally, from ancient Greek and medieval Arabic ideas) about another neurological condition that attacked children, epilepsy *(morbo caduco)*. Bagellardus described this disease, which some tried to ward off by hanging an emerald around the child's neck, as "the mistress of children" that "restrains the animate members by loss of consciousness and checks movements almost entirely. . . ." It was "due to some fear or noise or the like. Moreover, it happens to infants in earliest life either after birth or at birth." Bagellardus considered parental feelings as well: "[B]ecause such a disease is a great annoyance to the infant, it terrifies both the father and mother and all attendants."[102] While Bagellardus emphasized rigidity in an epileptic seizure, in the Hippocratic writings the disease is described more dynamically: there is "loss of voice, choking, foaming at the mouth, clenching of the teeth and convulsive movements of the hands. . . ."[103] This is the picture usually presented by medieval witnesses, such as Joanna of Spoleto, who testified that her daughter Bionducia had suffered epilepsy for two months: when the fits seized her—once or even twice a day—she collapsed to the ground. It was a wonder, as another witness put it, to watch the girl's hands and feet twisting and trembling while she foamed at the mouth, senseless.[104] After the girl's grandmother (who lived in the same house in Spoleto with the mother and child) made a vow to Clare, Bionducia was cured. The witnesses said that this occurred at Spoleto about 1313 or 1314. In San

Severino some sixty miles away, and within a year or two of Bionduccia's cure, a similar event took place in the home of Bilia and Giliolus. Their son Cicchus often fell to the ground, frothing at his distorted mouth, his eyes rolling, his hands and feet uncontrollably agitated. Sometimes he remained in this state for three days and nights.[105] Fearing that her son might remain permanently mad or impaired, Bilia commended Cicchus to Nicholas, promising to strip her son and offer his clothes at the tomb. This vow, witnessed by several women, resulted in the boy's recovery. The "falling sickness" entailed a variety of dangers for its victims: one of them fell so violently in seizure that he broke his arm.[106]

Seeing and Speaking: Eye Afflictions and Mutism

Miraculous healing of the crippled and the blind were "standard" cures in the New Testament, early saints' lives, and in the records of miracles reported or observed at shrines throughout the Middle Ages. Although cures of the blind seem to have occurred more often among women and members of nonprivileged social echelons, at least in later medieval England and France, victims came from all social categories.[107] Little Mendina's father, for instance, was the "noble" Mallus de Petino. After an attack of what may have been conjunctivitis, for two months Mendina could not see very well.[108] In November 1322, when her maternal grandmother Gentelucia attempted to examine the child's eyes, she could not even see them, presumably because the eyelids were so inflamed. Gentelucia called in one of her daughters, the child's aunt Angelescha, and the two women again tried, unsuccessfully, to examine Mendina's eyes. With many tears they fell to their knees beside the cradle, vowing to leave the girl's clothing and a candle at Nicholas's tomb. Grandmother then went to her other daughter Andriola (Mendina's mother), and explained what had been done; Andriola promised to carry out what Gentelucia had vowed. Next morning, in the bed chamber of the grandmother's house, the child told all three women that she could see. In 1325 the papal examiners agreed that Mendina's eyes were healthy, even beautiful. Although doctors were not mentioned in Mendina's case, occasionally *medici* testified about cures, even of their own children, as did Master James of San Angelo, a forty-year-old *medicus* and kinsman of Nicholas himself.[109] For "days and days" the eyes of his son Montucius, age three, were infected, producing a great deal of blood and pus. After the doctors, presumably James's colleagues, claimed that the condition was incurable, in his wife's presence James, on his knees with his arms extended, promised to take Montucius to Nicholas's tomb, offer a wax candle, strip his son, "and leave his clothes there." That was in May of 1323. The infirmity vanished and, the doctor testified two years later, never returned.

A more dramatic case involving a child's eyes was reported six or seven years earlier, in the same region of Italy. In 1318 or 1319 Peter of Spoleto told the papal commissioners that about ten years before, he had gone to Holy Cross Monastery at Montefalco to see the wonder-working corpse of the holy Clare. (This would have been just after her death, while the cult was most productive of miracles.)[110] While there, he observed a boy whose eyes had "come out of their sockets and were hanging down on his cheeks as far as his nose."[111] Peter watched the parents hoist the boy up to lie on Clare's tomb. After about an hour, the boy's mother picked him up, and as she did so it was evident that the child's eyes had returned to normal; the boy responded appropriately when various objects were shown to him. The extent to which witnesses might exaggerate a child's infirmities, as in this testimony, comes out even more obviously in a case from 1325, when Lord Franciscus testified about his son, Zuccius.[112] Some twenty years earlier, while Zuccius was still an infant in his cradle, one day his mother, Thomassia, found him squalling mightily. Because of the gushing tears she could not see his eyes, which upset her so much that she too began crying. After promising Zuccius's weight in wax at Nicholas's tomb, the child became quiet, opened his eyes, and seemed healthy as ever. Franciscus was an eyewitness, as was his own mother, Sophia (who had since died). His statements suggest an excitable mother's overreaction, perhaps heightened by the presence of her husband and mother-in-law. A trivial event. Thomassia's fuller testimony takes us a little farther into the bosom of this central Italian family. She claimed that her son Zuccius, still at the breast — whom her husband had described as still in the cradle — one day appeared to have gone blind. At first she did not consider appealing for help from Nicholas of Tolentino, the local holy man who had recently died, because she had little faith in him. She assumed, she confessed to the papal interrogators, that the brothers at St. Augustine's church stirred up devotion to Nicholas merely for profit, by attracting attention and offerings by ringing their bells whenever miracles were claimed and by having people place images on his tomb. However, as she looked at her "afflicted" child, she realized that her disbelief had brought on the infirmity. Crying intensely in her fear that her son would lose his eyesight, she made a vow to Nicholas; within an hour Zuccius could see. This happened in front of many people in "her, or (notarial reportage indicates that she seems to have corrected herself) her husband's," house.[113] A neighbor's comments, finally, raise the events to the realms of fantasy. The widow Nina swore that on a Wednesday in August of 1306, she was visiting her next-door neighbors Franciscus and Thomassia, who had her son Zuccius on her lap. He was not quite a year old. When, in the midst of their conversation, they heard the bells of the Augustinians' church, Franciscus said, "What are those foolish hermit brethren doing! They put images on Brother Nicholas's tomb, they claim that he performs miracles, they ring their bells—and it isn't true!" Thomassia agreed: "They put images there, though Brother Nicholas does no miracles." At that moment, Nina averred—drawing, no doubt, on the embellished memories of twenty years—Zuccius's eyes went "pop" and dangled down on his cheeks.[114] At this horrendous sight the mother began screaming "Help me, Saint Nicholas," while Franciscus, the grandmother Sophia, and Nina herself started wailing. They sent for Master Thomas, a doctor, who declared (according to Nina) that only God could help the child, since "his eyes, being outside his head *(extra caput)*, are lost." The grieving parents, ashamed of their disbelief, promised Nicholas an offering of wax equal to the weight of the child, his cradle, and his clothing, and Thomassia vowed never again to wear trimmings of gold, silver, or silk. At once, Nina claimed, the boy's eyes became normal.

It is impossible, as well as pointless, even to begin to guess what may "actually" have occurred on that Wednesday in August. Certainly the folkloric motif of eyes popping out as supernatural punishment was well established in medieval hagiography. At best, this case provides a fleeting view into an Italian family's home, in which a squalling child held on his mother's lap in the company of his father and grandmother caused exaggerated maternal anxiety, while coincidentally a neighbor visited and the conversation turned to the newly operative local saint—with rather unusual results. In testifying, the father said nothing of his own lugubrious reaction, which according to neighbor Nina was as impassioned as the mother's; and although Nina claimed that both parents expressed skepticism about Nicholas, only the mother—not the father—admitted this to the papal commissioners. Whether these omissions were prompted by Franciscus's masculine pride or embarrassment, by his having forgotten the details, or by Nina's tendency to embellish her testimony are issues beyond resolution. These miracle collections often particularized the general belief that saints punished their detractors. For example, in medieval Wales an angry woman brought her blind daughter home after lingering for three days at Wulfstan's tomb in Worcester, complaining "If the things they say about Wulfstan were true, he would have cured her."[115] As far as she was concerned, she would never believe in the saint again. Suddenly one of her twelve-year-old son's eyes shut; it was closed so firmly that the parents could not open it.

Before or after their cures, some children were "tested" to determine the reality or extent of their debilities or subsequent physical improvements. This was easily done, it was thought, in cases of blindness. Thus Peter, about thirteen, said that he could not see a glass container held in front of him after closing his "good eye."[116] Mutism was another commonly challenged, since easily feigned, affliction. If the child—as in the following report—was also a beggar, suspicions of fraud were strengthened. The example provides material for reflection on the treatment of indigent children who, in this case, lacked even the minimal protection of a parent or other relatives.[117] Nine witnesses provided extensive testimony, much of it repetitious, about John, from a village outside Ludlow on the Welsh border; the child grew up knowing nothing about his parents. From at least age nine John, a mute, begged among the citizens of Ludlow, who were accustomed to see him eating by pushing food down his throat with two fingers, as he lacked a tongue. By 1287 or 1288, when he was about sixteen, one or more of the Ludlow women who had heard of Cantilupe's miracles persuaded him to go to the saint's tomb at Hereford, some twenty miles to the south. He did so, remaining in the cathedral city for about six months. While there, the only apparent change was the growth of a stump where his tongue should have been. Some, but certainly not all, of the Hereford people interpreted this as miraculous. Several sympathetic Hereford citizens were supportive of the young beggar: Roger Tailor, for instance, fed the boy on over a hundred occasions, even putting him up now and then. Others in the city, however, were less accommodating: often John was forced to open his mouth for inspection before any alms or food would be given to him. More seriously, John was often beaten, as four of the witnesses testified, to see whether he was faking the mutism. He bayed like a dog, two witnesses recalled, as mutes "usually did when beaten." A Hereford underbailiff once ordered other beggars to beat John with his own stick; on other, frequent occasions, he was beaten in the houses of the cathedral canons and elsewhere in the city. Even Gilbert, the Hereford canon who guarded Cantilupe's tomb and witnessed the eventual "cure" of the boy, had beaten him. At last, having had enough of this Hereford hospitality, the boy returned to Ludlow. With his stump of a tongue he had to repeat things three or four times before being understood; some thought the "poor little one" *(parvulus)* was speaking Welsh, others claimed that his utterances were unlike any language. In Ludlow, the mouth inspections continued: one Sunday, for instance, he had to open wide for several town matrons who cornered him in the porch of St. Lawrence's church. About this time (early May, probably 1288) his story came to the attention of Hugh of Brompton, warden of the Hereford Franciscans, then in Ludlow as a guest of the respected Margery de Aylrithe. Hugh, who harbored some doubts about Cantilupe's miraculous talents, examined John, then took him back to Hereford. Although he told the boy that they were going to try for a better tongue,[118] Hugh may have hoped to debunk claims about the dead bishop's healing powers, perhaps expecting that John's condition would not improve. After spending the night with the Hereford Franciscans, in the morning John went to the tomb. There, on May 7, 1288, he was apparently cured. Hugh came quickly *(festinanter)*, looked into the boy's mouth, had him speak, and then, after ordering a bell ringing and a procession, preached a sermon on the miracle. After staying near the shrine and cathedral for a week or two, John went back to Ludlow "to publicize the miracle," then returned to Hereford where, according to some witnesses, he took the cross (became a crusader), left town, and never was seen again.[119] Perhaps he did actually go off to battle the Muslims; however, one of the witnesses claimed to have seen him in Ludlow a few months after the cure, speaking both Welsh and English—as he continued to do "for many years."

In some of these cases, as in the childhood accidents to be examined in the next chapter, it is unclear whether we are encountering adult careless-ness, neglect, or child abuse; or whether we are dealing with a societal norm, however harsh, cruel, or inappropriate it may seem centuries later. For example, we have seen that medieval expectations and assumptions led to the beating of demoniacs, tied up and stretched out helplessly at shrines. As for the "Welsh" mute, the motives of those who beat him can be inter-preted in various ways. Presumably, just as demons could be removed by force, the truth could be thumped out of malingerers and frauds, who were then sent on their way. This was important, because no matter how seriously they took their commitment to Christian charity, individuals, towns, cities, royal and episcopal almoners, and monasteries had to set limits to the num-bers of the ill, disabled, and poor they could attempt to support.[120] Apart from that, "foreigners"—in medieval terms anyone from the next village and beyond, who might become a burden to indigenous inhabitants through poverty or illness—would very likely be discouraged from staying in any given location, at least for more than a few days. Wayfarers and pilgrims could expect some charitable assistance, but even in their case, this was only—as it were—in passing. But for beggars who were not only outsiders but also, possibly, faking their disabilities, officially sanctioned beating was an effective deterrent to extended visits. John did, after all, leave Hereford and return to Ludlow. Moreover, the fact that *continued* beatings were inflicted on John during his stay in Hereford suggests that some citizens there may have taken sadistic pleasure in the process—the underbailiff, for example, under the guise of "duty"; and unchristian motives may have prompted some of the beatings that occurred privately, in the cathedral canons' houses. An illiterate, mute, poor, orphaned child must have been among the most vulnerable of human beings medieval society could have produced, an object whose daily existence was marked by charitable pity, cold indifference, and deliberate abuse. However, for every miracle report that reveals the dark side of human nature, there are many more that indicate the opposite tendencies, as in another mutism case.

Martin, en route to his Pomeranian village, began thinking about his six-year-old son, Laurence, who had never said a word in his life: "He turned over in his mind his son's affliction," as the papal notaries put it.[121] Recalling Dorothy's holy deeds, Martin fell to his knees in the road to beg her spiritual largess for his son. Later that day, as he approached his house, Laurence ran up to him with the words "Good father!" Martin testified that the boy continued to speak normally ever since his cure, five years earlier. The father's strong emotional attachment to the boy is understandable given the fact that, as Martin stated, Laurence was his only child; in addition, it turns out that Laurence was born when his father was about forty-nine years old. Perhaps Martin feared that he would have no other sons.

Miscellaneous Ailments

Although life could be cruel to physically disabled children and their parents, nondisabling deformities also brought misery to medieval families. William testified that when his daughter Catherine was about eighteen months old, she developed a fleshy growth at the end of her nose.[122] This thing, which looked like a little horn, nearly touched her upper lip. On one occasion some seven months after the growth had appeared, while William was holding Catherine on his lap and looking at his only child, he began to weep. One of William's co-workers, obviously an insensitive boor, joked about the girl's face, chiding the father with "What a daughter you've got!" This moved William to call upon Louis, promising to take the girl to his tomb and present a wax nose; just after this vow — in the time it took to say an *Ave Maria* — Catherine, while wiping her nose, found that the growth had vanished. They looked everywhere, but the bit of flesh had disappeared; nor was any mark left on her nose. Both parents were involved in these events, as was one of William's nieces. In 1308 when the papal agents examined the child, then about nine, they saw that she had a normal, well-formed nose. When they asked William who else had known of the girl's disfigurement, he responded that only he, his wife Dulcia, and a few others knew about it since he had not allowed her out *in publico* because of the deformity.

Presumably this was meant to guard the family from shame or, put another way, to maintain family "honor." The girl's mother, Dulcia, about twenty-two at the time of the cure, testified that the child had been three years — not eighteen months — old when the growth began; such chronological discrepancies, occasionally encountered in these records, reflect an insouciance typical of the era. Dulcia also testified that she did not know what such a deformity was called, nor had she heard it named.

Although Dulcia was unable to identify her daughter's affliction, witnesses in another case brought before the same canonization hearing in 1308 were quite sure of what ailed six-year-old Sanchia (Xanctia): it was St. Anthony's Fire (ignis beati Anthonii). This affliction may have resulted from eating grain infected with Claviceps purpurea, a fungus causing ergot poisoning that manifests itself in several ways, including gangrene.[123] St. Anthony's Fire also has been associated with erysipelas, usually a streptococcal infection that results in reddening of the skin, sometimes with blistering, abscesses, or septicemia. Sanchia, the sixteen-year-old daughter of Hugua and Peter of Marseilles, swore before the papal commissioners that at age six she had been afflicted with St. Anthony's Fire. The affliction "burned" a patch of flesh around her genitalia about a palm in width, nearly to her navel.[124] She was taken to a hospice in Marseilles where sufferers from the Fire went to stay, an example of a medieval family availing themselves of secular, before turning to spiritual, assistance.[125] While there, the burning sensation stopped and the already-burned, black flesh (gangrenous, presumably) was sloughed off, but her genitalia were left damaged and closed up, with only a small perforation through which she urinated.[126] Consequently, as Sanchia told the pope's representatives, she could not have a man; she was still a virgin.[127] Hugua concurred, having seen and felt the damaged place many times. Not only that, but the area healed so imperfectly that after leaving the hospice Sanchia could barely walk. Sanchia remembered this immobility well, having endured it for six months. About the time that miracles began to be claimed at Louis's tomb, one Saturday Sanchia's mother carried her outside their house and set her down so that the girl could attend to the necessities of nature. When Hugua re-entered the house alone she knelt and tearfully prayed to Louis. She then got up and began making her daughter's bed; as she was busy spreading out the bedclothes, Sanchia walked in, claiming to be cured. Next day, accompanied by many men and women, they went to Louis's shrine in Marseilles where Sanchia, walking normally, offered a one-pound wax image at the tomb. In 1308 Hugua testified that the only other person to witness the cure was her own mother-in-law, who had since died; but as to Sanchia's inability to walk, and her cure, Sanchia's father Peter knew about it, as did their neighbors. When giving his testimony, Peter, adverting to Sanchia's inability to walk properly for about six months after her stay in the hospice, claimed that he learned the reason for this from his wife, his wife's mother, his own mother, and other women: they told him that the flesh between Sanchia's legs remained tightly joined. It may have been thought inappropriate for the father himself to examine the six-year-old girl, or perhaps he simply was not interested in doing so; in any event, he took his information about her condition from the women. Peter concluded by observing that his daughter and wife went to Louis's tomb "with many other women," which suggests that he himself did not go and indeed gives the impression that this was a women-only group, even though his wife had claimed that men and women had accompanied her and Sanchia. Whatever the circumstances in this particular instance, the details of many medieval cases of miraculous healing suggest that, as in caring for mothers and infants at birth and in preparing corpses after death, women seem to have preempted men (other than doctors) in dealing with children's illnesses, although this was by no means universally true. Many cases illustrate women's predominance as care-givers: a boy with respiratory complications and fever was looked after by "several neighborhood women,"[128] while another infant, unable to urinate, was attended by "many women" who witnessed his cure.[129] Along these lines, it is interesting to find a thirteenth-century Franciscan friar recommending that older girls acquire a basic medical knowledge.[130]

It seems that modesty, guarded by a circle of women, excluded Sanchia's own father from intimate knowledge of her plight. In another case from an earlier period, the child victim herself, about fifteen, seems to have hidden her affliction from both parents. Between December 1170 and January of 1174 Cecilia, the daughter of Jordan of Plumstead in Norfolk , was stricken with what the miracle report denoted as cancer.[131] "In her virginal modesty," the Canterbury monk wrote, "she would have preferred pain rather than revealing anything shameful." Presumably the "shame" was linked to the site of the cancer, which affected her thighs and buttocks. These areas were eaten away, exposing ligaments, joints, and bones. Finally her parents, alarmed by the paleness of Cecilia's face, insisted that she tell them what was wrong. She showed them, to their dismay and disgust: such revolting odors came from a foot-long ulcer that even her mother was said to have wished her dead; her family spurned her and the neighbors too were horrified.[132] Nevertheless, her bandages were changed hourly. Cecilia, unable to sit up or lie down, had to kneel and bend forward, the least uncomfortable position she could tolerate. She was incapacitated like this from late summer to

early March in the following year, when death seemed imminent. On a
Tuesday she stopped eating and drinking, remaining in bed huddled next to
the wall, her eyes wide in a fixed stare, her knees drawn up, unmoving. She
seemed neither alive nor dead.[133] On Friday evening a neighbor woman, seeing Cecilia in that state and believing that she was nearly dead, berated the
household: "How badly you are behaving, permitting this girl to die in her
bed. Why is she not set out on a hair shirt, as is the proper custom for dying
Christians?" The visitor was referring to the custom, of monastic origins, in
which the dying were placed on the ground.[134] Accordingly, the girl was carried outside her house and put down in an open area, her body cold, her
knees bent and her eyes still staring. They could not straighten out her legs.
A linen cloth was put over her and candles were lit, as if at a funeral. After
appeals to Becket, eventually the girl moved her hand and tried to speak, but
nothing intelligible came out. Next day she took food and drink, and by the
third day, the lesions on her cancerous thighs began to clear up; within three
weeks her skin was restored. Her father related these events to the bishop
of Norwich (William Turbe, d. January 16, 1174), who directed his priest
William to look into the affair, with the assistance of two trustworthy
matrons who examined the girl. After reviewing the findings of their diligent
investigation *(inquisitio)*, the bishop sent a confirmatory letter to Canterbury,
which Jordan carried on his thanksgiving pilgrimage. The horrendous
nature of cancerous disfigurement is also evident in the case of an eleven-
year-old English boy who suffered cancer of the mouth for about five years.
Eventually, he could barely eat: whenever he tried, his food was ejected
through his nostrils.[135]

A different medieval scourge, prevalent even now in the less-developed
countries of the world, struck another English child, twelve-year-old
William, son of Agnes of Oxford. William, whose dysentery led him to
death's door, began passing blood that, the monastic commentator notes,
was of the sort that normally comes from the veins.[136] Everything was
arranged for William's funeral, when the application of some Becket water
led to his recovery. However, during his convalescence he seems to have
been attacked by yet another illness: he developed a deathlike pallor and
emaciation, ulcers appeared on his face, and his nose became swollen. It
seemed to be leprosy, which the Canterbury monk also called elephantia-
sis.[137] Any number of afflictions could transform a child's face into a monstrous mask, as was made clear from southern French testimony of 1363.
About three years before Countess Dalphine's death in 1360, a woman
from Sens diocese traveled south to beg her assistance. The woman brought
her daughter, about twelve, who was afflicted with the illness commonly

called—as the notaries expressed it—*Noli me Tangere*; her face had become so horrible that it nauseated anyone who looked at her.[138] In modern medical dictionaries the phrase *Noli me tangere* refers to a cancerous ulcer, usually of the face, which destroys bone and soft tissue; it is also known, less pleasantly, as rodent ulcer. In this French case, the girl's mother had undertaken her journey with her daughter after dreaming that the girl would be cured by Dalphine's touch. Unfortunately for the woman and her disfigured daughter, Dalphine's attendants, knowing that the countess was depressed by such things, kept these importunate folk away from their mistress. Although forced to stay outside, the woman refused to leave; for four days she begged to see the countess. Finally, as a compromise the attendants brought out some water in which Dalphine had washed her hands. This was applied to the girl's face with positive results, as the mother believed, and with no medical intervention.

As we have seen, doctors were called in to treat some of these cases. Occasionally parents claimed to be more successful in caring for their ailing children than the doctors they hired. Monaldisca of Tolentino reported to papal commissioners that nearly fourteen years earlier her fifteen-month-old son Cischus had a fistula in his lower right eyelid, creating a wound deeper than half the length of her finger.[139] When the doctor inserted a probe, the child's eye rolled about and a great quantity of putrid liquid flowed out. For five weeks her son was "in the doctor's hands," without any improvement. In fact, the doctor-surgeon *(medicus ciroicus)*, Master Francis of Tolentino, refused to charge for his services because he believed that Cischus would lose the eye. When Monaldisca was told this, she went sadly to Nicholas's tomb one November evening and, holding her son in her arms, prayed for his cure, promising the boy's weight in grain as an offering. At home the next evening, she removed a spike of grain (apparently the cause of the infection) from the child's eye, and in that instant foul matter poured out. Within eight days, without any medications—nothing was put into the wound by the mother, doctor, or any other person, she claimed—the eye and eyelid healed. The boy, when about fifteen, was examined by the papal commissioners. Swearing that he believed that his cure had been wrought through Nicholas, Cischus added that because "he was a child" at the time (he was not yet two), he could not recall the events about which his mother had testified. Monaldisca, then, succeeded where her son's doctor failed. But even when (or especially when?) a child patient was the daughter or son of a doctor, the point was made that mundane medical knowledge was often powerless when compared with miraculous interventions. For instance, Nicholas of Spoleto, a doctor *(medicus,* also denoted *fisicus)*, was evidently unable to assist his ailing son Bernard, who fell ill about 1318.[140] He had been attacked suddenly one night by pain so fierce that he was unable to speak, and this debilitation lasted until midmorning of the following day; no one knew what was causing the pain. In her anxiety, his mother, Clara, made a vow to Clare of Montefalco. In the time it would take to say six or eight *Pater Nosters*, Bernard began speaking and regaining strength and memory, until he seemed quite recovered. The pain ceased and he was able to walk by himself, but "to watch him better" his mother would not let him out of the house, since he was still somewhat weak.[141] Mannuctia, another woman who was there that day, claimed that Bernard had been so stupefied with pain that he seemed near death, *in articulo mortis*; she also observed that his mother, who could not bear to see him in such pain, sometimes left her son's side. All this happened, according to Mannuctia, in the presence of "many ladies" who had gathered when Clara became frightened about her son.[142] Another person at the scene was the boy's father, Master Nicholas, the doctor. He testified that a grave physical ailment had suddenly overcome his son, who was beside himself with pain and unable to respond to his mother, although she called to him for a full hour. When asked what the illness was, the father/doctor replied that "they were pains brought about by a flux *(fluxus)*." The expression "flux" was relatively nonspecific, but as mentioned earlier, often refers to dysentery.

Medieval children were victims not only of bacterial and viral infections but of parasites as well. A London infant was said to have been infested in his face and mouth, while a four-year-old Italian boy spewed worms from mouth and anus.[143] Three-year-old Poncius began vomiting worms and seemed near death, until he returned to health after vows were made to Pope Urban.[144] Another disease indicated in some of the reports may have been smallpox, as in the case of Robert, about four, who suffered "the pestilence of pustules" *(peste pustularum)* that turned his skin and face into a repellent mass of fetid sores, so that he became a scarcely tolerable burden.[145] His parents were especially sorrowful and anxious since he had been such a pretty little child.[146] Eventually the boy claimed that King Henry had called him (in a dream?) to his shrine: as Robert informed his mother, "He told me to come to him with you, riding on a horse, but not a wooden horse"; that is, the narrator breaks in to explain, not riding on a stick, as children usually do in their games.[147] In a less detailed report, a moneyer of southern France told papal commissioners how his five-year-old daughter, Petronilla, became feverish and developed pox or variola. She weakened daily until, by the eighth day, she could hardly open her eyes or eat.[148] Another infirmity was specific in name only, since the identity of the disease known in England as "the sweating sickness" is still a matter of contention.[149] During 1491 Anna, a fourteen-year-old servant of William Belfeld in Surrey, a girl who—writes the chronicler—had reached puberty, was a victim of the sweating sickness that had killed several people at that time.[150] She fell ill while her mistress was away tending to a neighbor's funeral; she was alone in the house when stricken. Someone found Anna and told the mistress, who anxiously hurried home, followed by some of her neighbors. She and the other women found the girl lying on the ground, senseless. Believing that nothing could be done, they decided to prepare her for burial. The mistress told some of her women to sew the body into a shroud while she, in her husband's absence, went to the church to arrange for the girl's burial. As the women began to prepare the linen shroud, they noticed a movement of the small breast; drawing back in amazement, they fell to their knees and prayed to God and Henry.[151] Anna recovered as if from a heavy sleep, afterward going to Henry's tomb with her mistress and a crowd of her girlfriends *(amicarum)*.

Unspecified Illness

The revival of children as they were being sewn into shrouds was trivial in comparison with the macabre experience of a southern French couple whose son "died" of some unspecified illness.[152] Just after the six-year-old was buried, his frenzied *(quasi furiosa)* mother threw herself upon the tomb, where she remained for two hours, crying out to Urban V for help. When she and the bystanders heard a scream, they raised the lid of the tomb and found the child alive. While most resuscitations "from death" were not as spectacular as this one, they often reveal the depths of parental emotion and grief, as in the case of Jordan, a Yorkshire knight who had known Becket. Late one summer his household was suddenly afflicted with a malady that killed his son's nurse; about ten days later Jordan's ten-year-old son, William, was nearly dead from the same illness.[153] While a priest performed the last rites, Jordan kept vigil over his son. One of the two Canterbury monks recording these events commented that he preferred to pass silently over the extreme grief of the parents that, he believed, even the simplest reader could imagine. When a group of about twenty Canterbury pilgrims arrived, Jordan suppressed his grief long enough to provide them hospitality for the night. Next morning, as they prepared to leave, he offered them breakfast. Meanwhile, the priest returned to take William to the church for burial, but the father refused to release the body. Taking some of the Becket water carried by the pilgrims, Jordan told the priest to put it into the boy's mouth. The priest, although wondering about Jordan's mental state (the Canterbury monks claimed), did as he was asked. Nothing happened, but

Jordan continued to watch and wait. In the afternoon, when the priest again tried to take the body away for burial, remarking that the boy had been dead for two days, Jordan once more refused, commanding that more Becket-water be brought. Jordan uncovered William's face, propped up his head, separated his clenched teeth with his knife, and poured some of the water into his open mouth. When the left side of the boy's face showed some color, Jordan poured more water down his throat. The child, opening one eye and seeing his parents in tears, said a few words, then fell silent. Jordan asked someone to bring him four silver coins, quickly; he bent two of these for himself and his wife and the other two for the child's resuscitation, placed one of them at William's left side, the other at his right, and promised to go to Canterbury at mid-Lent to offer the child to the martyr.[154] Then the parents sat and waited, their perseverance being rewarded that evening when the boy revived. In spite of his son's recovery and Becket's reminders conveyed in visions to a local leper, Jordan put off his promised pilgrimage. Another of his sons fell ill, and the next day Jordan himself and his wife also collapsed into bed, ill and in despair. Meanwhile their son, who was older than William, worsened and died. This increased the parents' distress, particularly Jordan's, who loved the child dearly, "especially since his own face seemed reflected in his son's."[155] Jordan now acknowledged the effects of his broken vows and set out on pilgrimage to Canterbury. After great hardship, the barefoot parents finally arrived at Becket's tomb with their son William, where they described their miraculous escape from illness and the recovery of one of their two sons.

The reluctance of a parent to accept a child's death and to part with the body is illustrated in another of Becket's miracles. The affected child was James, the son of Roger earl of Clare (d. 1173).[156] In mid-Lent James (not yet two) was attacked by an illness and "gave up the ghost" while Matilda his mother was at church. No one wanted to tell her of her son's death. But, as the Canterbury narrator reminded his readers, no child knows how to keep a secret, a sentiment echoed next century in the writings of Bartholomew the Englishman, who tells us that children "keep no secrets, but repeat everything they see and hear."[157] Sure enough, the dead child's brother ran to church, where he tearfully conveyed the bad news. Matilda hurried home to find that the infant had been carried from her bedroom into an outer hall and laid out on the floor.[158] Presumably, the household felt that although James was too young for formal last rites (usually administered only from age seven), the infant should die as a Christian, on the ground and not in bed. In any case, Matilda found James open-mouthed, cold and rigid, barely breathing (although already reputed "dead"), his tongue and lips drawn back, only the whites of his eyes visible. Snatching him up, she reportedly cried out "St. Thomas, restore my son to me: you cured his hernia [referring to an earlier occasion, noted above]; now restore life, holy martyr, to the dead!" With the child still in her arms she rushed to a chest, took out some of Becket's relics, poured some Becket water into the boy's mouth, then thrust a little portion of Becket's hair shirt down his throat, incessantly crying out to the "holy martyr." Although the knights present, as well as the Countess of Warwick and other women, chided her to be silent *(ut taceret)*, with her bare knees on the floor she continued crying out, even more strenuously, to Becket. Finally, her aged chaplain, Lambert, is said to have exclaimed "What's got into you, my lady? You're behaving foolishly; you're being silly, even mad to carry on and speak thus. Is it not for the Creator to do what he wishes concerning his creation? Stop this: put down the child and treat it as a dead infant; it's great foolishness to want the impossible." In William of Canterbury's version Lambert concluded, "Don't irritate the Divine Clemency with such fatuous talk." Everyone else said the same sort of thing. Matilda refused to moderate her outbursts, however, carrying on for another two hours. Eventually the color returned to the child's face and soon he was rolling his eyes and wailing. Afterward, the countess went barefoot to Canterbury with her son, accompanied by the Countess of Warwick and many other women, as well as the chaplain, Lambert, and several knights, all of whom testified as to what they thought had happened.

Life in noble households seems to have been influenced by rules of propriety and a set of expectations that included avoidance of overtly sentimental behavior, which could, in some circumstances, be considered "shameful." We shall return to this topic in the conclusion. In the two English examples just given, the knight Jordan and the Countess of Clare came under disapprobation because their reactions seemed, to some, to violate "proper" ways of behaving. What the historian Heinrich Fichtenau noted for an earlier medieval period—that "immoderate cries of sorrow were more suitable for the lower ranks of society" than the upper—seems to have been as true of the twelfth century and later.[159] As emerges from the details of a miracle reported in early fourteenth-century Italy, families as well as individuals of elevated status were expected to project a certain image. Paulucia, the daughter of Lord Francis of Tolentino, a nun in the convent of St. John at Santo Genesio, stated in 1325 that some twenty years earlier, in March, she was in her brother Manfred's house in the village of Santa Lucia about three miles outside Tolentino.[160] It was evening, about complines, and her brother's wife, Ymillia, was breast-feeding her daughter Sennucia. Besides the two parents and Paulucia, a sister of Paulucia and a nursemaid were there. Suddenly the child trembled and apparently died in her mother's arms. Everyone in the room began wailing, crying, and begging: they implored Nicholas to restore life to the child lest they incur distress and shame, especially since Manfred and Ymillia were important *nobiles persone* of the area. The parents grieved not only for their child but also because, according to custom, anyone dying outside Tolentino could not be brought back inside the city walls but was to be buried at the gate.[161] Their prayers for Sennucia continued, and sometime around the middle of the night she revived. That Manfred of Tolentino, his wife, sisters, and household were in a country village at the time of this event suggests that he held property — perhaps several properties — outside his town residence, as did many town dwellers of *trecento* and *quattrocento* Italy. Normally very close political, administrative, social, and economic connections existed between the renaissance Italian city and the villages of its surrounding *contado*. There would have been nothing unusual in a member of the urban nobility visiting his country estates. Manfred's anxiety stemmed from the possible denial of solemn burial for his daughter along with the ceremonious publicity due the urban nobility. This example is notable for the presence of a wet nurse *(bayla* or *balia)*, whose role, particularly in medieval and renaissance Italy, has been the subject of much research, as suggested in the previous chapter.[162] That evening in 1305, the mother was nursing her own child even though a wet nurse was present.

Parental sorrow and an inability to accept the threatened loss of a child can be observed, of course, at all levels of medieval society. In 1363 Huga, the twenty-year-old wife of Master Stephen, a notary of Provence, swore on the Bible to tell the truth to papal officials. Speaking her "Romance" language *(in romancio)*, Provençal, she claimed that earlier that year her son Albert, age one, stopped breast-feeding for a week, taking only a little milk from a spoon; even then he barely opened his mouth.[163] On the eighth day, however, after vomiting whatever was given him, from nightfall to about midnight he seemed dead. He was cold and stiff, bearing the signs of death, as Huga and others believed. As was customary, candles were lit around the dead child. When her friends and kin wanted to wrap his body in a shroud and take it away, Huga begged them not to do so. She continued praying to Dalphine, vowing to go, every year for as long as the boy lived, on a barefoot pilgrimage to the tomb with her son, a gift of several measures of grain, and a large candle.[164] After her vow Albert began crying, Huga rushed to offer her breast, and the *parvulus* soon recovered. Aside from the boy's parents, his uncle Rostagnus, about thirty-five, was there too. His perspective on these events differed slightly from Huga's, as is only to be expected. He testified that after his nephew fell ill, he visited him several times until, on the evening of the eighth day, about the time of the *Ave* bells, when he went to see him he found him dead. As he made the sign of the cross on the corpse, the mother, wailing in her grief, called upon Dalphine. The bystanders took her away from the body to lessen her pain; she went off to stand by a window in the house. When one of the women noted signs of life in the boy, Huga placed her breast in the child's mouth and, when he began sucking, everyone — Uncle Rostagnus included — was overjoyed. He remained in his brother's house for another hour or so, then went home, gladdened. There were several people at the notary's house that evening, including Bertrand, another of the boy's uncles. Around the time of the *Ave* bells, he testified, he went to Huga's house and found his nephew on the brink of death: when he rubbed the child's feet, they felt stiff and cold as marble; even so, the little boy did not seem quite dead to Bertrand although, he testified, there were "some" signs of death. Many of Bertrand's contemporaries, from the Mediterranean to Scandinavia, would have acknowledged finely graduated distinctions between "nearly dead," "dead," even "quite dead."[165] After about an hour, however, Bertrand and others concluded that Albert was, indeed, quite dead. At that point Uncle Bertrand (and his own son) went home, expecting to bury his nephew the next day. Uncle Rostagnus remained by the child, for whatever reason, until the boy recovered. In the morning, Bertrand found the child alive and feeding at his mother's breast. After Easter, the two uncles as well as Huga, Albert, and several others went together on pilgrimage to the countess's tomb, where the mother fulfilled her vow.

Our final example of apparent death from unspecified illness, and further illustration of variety in parental reactions, takes us more than a generation beyond uncles Rostagnus and Bertrand, down another step in the social ladder, and away from sunny Provence to the village of Burgersdorff, some fifty miles south of the Gulf of Danzig on the Baltic. In 1404 the peasant family of John and Elizabeth Oppelyn, "good people" *(honestes)* according to their neighbors, told papal commissioners about their three-year-old, Katherina.[166] The parents testified that one morning before daybreak Elizabeth bathed the child and about an hour later put her to bed. Soranus, an early second-century physician, suggested that women bathed their infants often because "when it has grown weary after the bath it keeps quiet and falls asleep."[167] If that purpose was in Elizabeth's mind when she put Katherina down for an early-morning nap, she was soon disappointed: the child, groaning violently, began vomiting green matter.[168] Elizabeth went to her daughter, presumably cleaned her up, then assumed that, having vomited, she would fall asleep. Apparently the mother was not too concerned. Returning a little later, however, Elizabeth found the child cold as ice, her body stiff. Stung by grief, Elizabeth told her husband, called her neighbors together, showed them her child's body, and anxiously asked what to do. Thinking it likely that Katherina was dead, they placed a candle by the child's hand. Some of the villagers — the "village women," according to one witness — wanted to ascertain more carefully whether Katherina had really died. They dug up some earth from beneath the hearth and put it, still quite hot, on the girl's breast, to see whether she would react. Pustules, swelling, and burned flesh resulted, but Katherina did not stir. She remained motionless for about five hours. Finally everyone knelt and began crying out to Dorothy; the girl's father, on his knees, was also weeping loudly, asking Dorothy's help. Eventually the child's eyes moved and she began breathing and speaking. By the end of the day Katherina was as playful as ever. Later the parents took their child, and bits of her burned flesh, to the cathedral as proof of the dead saint's powers.

Although the children discussed in this chapter eventually were cured — and we have no means of knowing for how long or how effectively — nevertheless, their tribulations make for rather depressing reading. A few examples, however, contained their lighter moments. The boy's condition in one of these cases, admittedly, does not seem to point in that direction: Anthony suffered fever, spinal deformity (with the bone poking through the skin of his back), and an ulcerous swelling, and was sightless, speechless, and replete with the signs of death.[169] His mother, Monna, about twenty-eight, "signed" the boy, who was between three and four, with the sign of the Cross and then turned her sad thoughts to Countess Dalphine. At Dalphine's tomb, Monna vowed that if Anthony lived, she would visit the tomb regularly, barefoot, say seven *Aves* and *Paters* every day for the rest of her life, fast on bread and wine before her pilgrimages, and offer a wax image. Subsequently some of her household servants arrived, announcing that Anthony was calling for her. Overjoyed, Monna hurried home, went to her son and called out, two or three times, "Anthonete." No response. "Anthonete," she called again, "do you hear me?" No response. Finally Monna said "I'm going to [a place nearby]; do you want to go with me?" At this he immediately opened his eyes, which had remained closed for three days, and replied, "Yes! Wait for me!" Within a week he was out of danger. The cure was witnessed by the parents, the boy's grandmother and aunt, and many household servants *(familiares)*. Although Anthony may have recovered from his fever, nothing was said about his other debilities. In England, Becket's miracle chroniclers described how Roger, little son *(filius parvulus)* of the knight Savaric, was very ill with diarrhea.[170] For twenty days he could tolerate only water. Finally his parents made a vow on his behalf to the

English martyr and then sat down to a meal. They received a dish of happiness during the first course, as the Canterbury monk puts it, for while they were eating, the child whom they had left half dead in his chamber got up, put on his clothes, and came in to those at table, playing and twirling in front of them with (singing out, presumably) a *taratantara*, in his light-heartedness. His parents caught up their special table companion, while the rest of the company marvelled at Roger's sudden recovery.

CHILDREN'S ILLNESSES AND DISABILITIES: OVERVIEW AND ANALYSES

Given the reasons for their compilation, nearly all of these reports ended with a revival "from death" or a cure. Sometimes parents went to great trouble and expense for their children, quite apart from their pilgrimages and the offerings they left at tombs. Some also paid for medical assistance, in one English case bringing in not only the most famous London doctors but also many from outside the city. In another instance, when the son of a man in the archbishop of Canterbury's household fell ill, expert London physicians and surgeons were called in, even the "very famous men" who attended to the archbishop himself.[171] The recovery of an ill child sometimes repaid such expense and concern, but of course the records say nothing about the many children who failed to respond or recover, despite spiritual or earthly therapy. Considering the state of contemporary medical treatment, children were probably just as well off without visits from doctors, no matter how *famosissimi* they might be. In the case just cited, for instance, some of the archbishop of Canterbury's "famous" medicos diagnosed the child's ailment as *gutta*, or paralysis, while others blamed the poisonous effects of an evil spirit.[172]

Who called upon doctors more frequently? Given the more extensive traditions of "secular" studies, of stronger classical and Arabic influences around the Mediterranean and the presence of famous medical schools, it is reasonable to assume that more medical assistance would have been available to the southern European populace in general—gathered in several urban centers, where the professionals were concentrated—than to the northerners. A look at the number of *medici* called in to treat the children mentioned in our records tends to confirm this: of the 334 cases, 54, or 16 percent, explicitly mentioned doctors or surgeons. The frequency with which professional healers were involved in the childhood illnesses differed markedly between northern and southern Europe. About twice as many southern European as northern European cases, proportionally, involved doctors being called in by concerned parents: 13 (10 percent) of the

124 northern cases mentioned doctors, but 41 (20 percent) of the 210 southern cases included one or more *medici* at some point in the curative process.

What types of illnesses did doctors treat, or saints "cure"? Although the
categorization of medieval children's illnesses is often little more than guess-
work, nevertheless, by following the clues and descriptions provided by parents, neighbors, doctors, and sometimes the children themselves, one can
determine which broad classification seems appropriate. Even so, as figure
3.1 shows, the largest class still remains undifferentiated "illness." This figure summarizes reports for 101 girls and 233 boys. Proportionally more
boys suffered stone and other urinary problems and hernias and ruptures
than girls; more boys suffered fever than girls, and more boys, when compared with girls, were said to have been "ill" without further qualification.
Girls were more often afflicted with crippling illnesses or lameness, eye
problems, epilepsy and episodes of overt mental confusion. In no category,
however, was the gender difference more than 10 percent: consequently, it
would be unwise to press these observations further.[173] All that can be said
with certainty is that, in the cases examined, more than twice as many boys
as girls (30.2 percent girls, 69.8 percent boys) were thought to have been so
ill that requests for miraculous intervention seemed appropriate. Does this
reflect a "real" difference in the rate at which boys fell ill when compared
with girls? It is possible, of course, that the figures for gender that turned up
in our accounts of miraculous healings of illness are idiosyncratic. Other
studies of medieval saints' cults, however, tend to confirm this male preponderance among miraculously cured children. In analyzing testimony
recorded as part of the canonization process of Elisabeth of Thuringia
(d. 1231), Jürgen Jansen found that 62 percent of the thirty-four ill but
miraculously cured children were boys and 38 percent, girls.[174] In their
study of sixty-four children who had been the subjects of miraculous cures
in early-medieval European cults, Kroll and Bachrach found that 70 percent
were boys, 30 percent, girls.[175] Even if certain illnesses, such as hernias and
bladder stones, were physiologically associated with boys more commonly
than with girls, the relatively few reported cases of those afflictions could
hardly account for the overall gender imbalance favoring boys. Does it
suggest a different attitude toward boys, perhaps a greater solicitude for
males, a greater emotional and even economic investment in their health,
than for females? These matters are examined in chapter 5, after additional
information about childhood accidents has been reviewed. For the present,
the medieval records suggest that there are apparently a few distinctions in
frequency of ailments associated with either sex and that boys' illnesses were
reported more frequently than girls'.

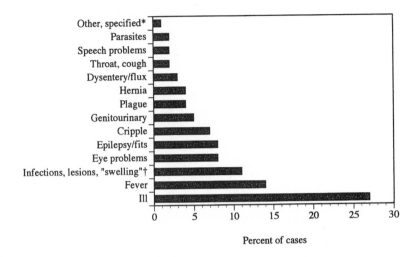

*St. Anthony's Fire (2 cases); cancer (2); sweating sickness (1)

†"Swellings" (18 cases); fistula/ulcer (7); deformities (4); scrofula (4); pustules (2); jaundice (1); leprosy (1)

Figure 3.1 Ailments or afflictions reported in 334 cases, showing percentages of children involved in 14 types

The ages at which children were reported to have fallen ill are shown in figure 3.2. Of the 334 cases of illness, ages were specified for 227 (68 percent) of the children. Apparently, about half of them (48 percent of girls, 56 percent of boys) became ill before reaching the age of four, a pattern that further analysis indicates was the case for both southern and northern Europe. The figures suggest that a child's first few years were indeed the most dangerous period of its life, a fact acknowledged by contemporary medical writers. These harsh facts of medieval existence are emphasized in the first double column in the chart, which shows that children less than a year old constituted the largest single age bracket for reported illnesses. These figures do not include complications at birth or other perinatal difficulties of the kind described in chapter 2. If they did, the percentage of victims younger than one year would rise much higher than shown. Klaus Arnold, reporting on a medieval Thuringian cemetery, noted that of 209 children's burials, 53 were age 6 to 13; for the remaining 156, 54 were under 1 year of age, (i.e., 26 percent of all 209 children.)[176] Figure 3.2 suggests that about 20 percent of our sample (counting boys and girls together) fell within this age bracket.

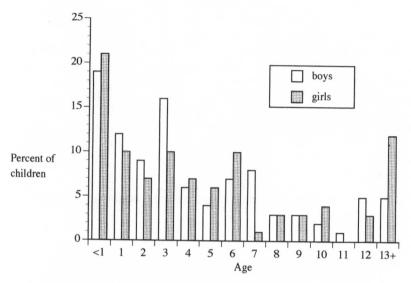

Figure 3.2 Ages at which children became ill (159 boys, 68 girls)

It would seem not only that boys were involved more commonly than girls, but also that they were cured more quickly than girls. What was the average duration of children's illnesses and debilitations? As suggested in figure 3.3, medieval parents endured varying periods of anxiety as their children's illnesses took their course over days, months, and even years. The figure indicates that about two-thirds of male children (65 percent) but only half of the females (51 percent) had been cured within a month of falling ill. In the conclusion, it is suggested that some of the differences noted in these figures may be attributable to parental bias in favor of males. The gender difference is most apparent by the end of the first two weeks of illness: whereas a third of the girls (33 percent) had regained their health, nearly half (46 percent) of the boys had recovered within that time. In the period between two and four weeks after becoming ill, however, both sexes were virtually identical in recovery rate. Thereafter, rising girl and falling boy recovery rates reflect the fact that most of the boys had already been cured. Children of both sexes suffered long-term ailments in about the same proportions. Crippling debilities probably lasted longer than most of the other illnesses that attacked medieval children.

Even if a child somehow managed to pull through, regardless of how long it took, and a saint was credited with a cure later reported to shrine-keepers or papal agents, we are seldom told of the child's subsequent illnesses or attacks. There was no follow-up. Fifteen among the 334 children in the miracle lists had died at some point between their "cures" and the recording of testimony about those cures. We have no information on what might have happened to the others. Nor are we told, except indirectly in a few instances, that after recourse to some shrine or saint's memory the child was not cured; canonization records, for the most part, only include success stories.

Another aspect of the curative ritual that illuminates adult-child interaction centers on the vow — specifically, the person(s) who most frequently vowed for a sick child. Most (95 percent) of the illness reports indicate who pronounced the words, and these individuals are tabulated in figure 3.4. Given the circumstances of most children's illnesses, in which they were cared for by their families, the emphasis on parental, and particularly maternal, vows is not surprising. Nevertheless, it is also obvious that nearly one-third of those making vows for children were the victims' fathers, who, as will be emphasized in later chapters, were as deeply involved emotionally as the mothers.[177] A different configuration appears, as we shall see in the next chapter, when we consider those who made vows for child victims of accidental injuries and near drownings.

A sick child became an increasing burden on parents as an illness worsened over several days, weeks, or months. The records reflect deep, underlying familial affection in many such cases, which occasionally culminated in desperate grief at a child's "death" after a futile regime of care and concern. When children were accidentally injured, however, or were unexpectedly found "dead" by drowning or other mishap, parental reactions were nearly always immediate and explosive in their intensity, as normal family existence seemed instantaneously to have been overturned. The jurist Beaumanoir, recording in the 1280s the customs of the county of Clermont, distinguished between the "natural" death of a nursing child, which distressed the heart of its father, and the "unnatural" death of offspring by suffocation, burning, or drowning, which, Beaumanoir noted, caused a father even greater anxiety.[178]

We turn now to those "unnatural" deaths that, in our sources, were not deaths at all.

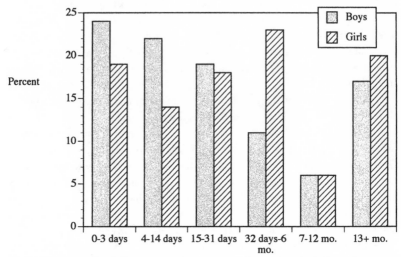

Figure 3.3 Length of illnesses in 242 cases out of 334 providing this information (158 boys, 84 girls)

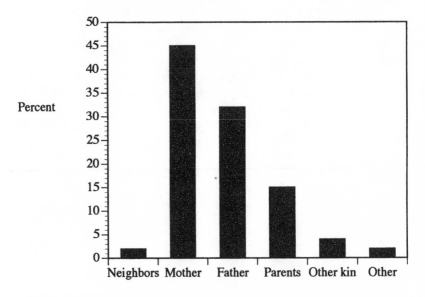

Figure 3.4 Who made the vows for ill children? "Mother" and "Father" refer to vows by one parent only; "Parents" indicates vows made by both for the victim.

4

CHILDHOOD ACCIDENTS

....

When analyzing the causes of children's accidents, today's medical experts usually consider the physical environment, the social and familial milieu, and the ethnicity, gender, age, and developmental levels of the victims.[1] Many of our medieval cases can be approached in a similar fashion, in spite of large gaps in the evidence. For reasons to be considered in the concluding chapter, most of the children's accidents in the selected hagiographical sources were reported from northern, particularly English, villages rather than from cities and towns of southern Europe. The snug villages idealized in the poetry and art of Victorians fearful of industrialization and urban squalor, have finally come into being in our own century, as any gaggle of tourists can affirm after visiting some of the cloyingly "quaint" settlements of England's Cotswold region. In reality, however, life in medieval villages was far from idyllic. In spite of Sunday diversions, holy days and festive occasions, and ale or wine for comfort, for most ordinary inhabitants laboring through the agricultural cycle from one year to the next, village existence was grim, monotonous, and hard. Nor, it seems, were all villages the friendly settlements of popular imagination. As Barbara Hanawalt writes, many English peasant families "had a croft, messuage, or close, as the bit of land surrounding the house was called. It was enclosed by ditches, walls or hedges and was used for garden, house, barn, and perhaps other outbuildings belonging to the family."[2] In some regions, then, a wall surrounded the peasant's cottage and croft, which might be sited on an elevated platform rising above sunken village roads; alternatively, some cottages were located on their individual "islands" reached only by planks thrown across ditches. In short, the nostalgic concept of the open, neighborly village is—at least in England—currently under revision. As Grenville Astill puts it, the need "for the family to be consciously and physically separated from the rest of the community has not received sufficient attention."[3] For children, the village with its outlying fields was a particularly dangerous physical environment. Apart from natural features that attracted them such as lakes, streams, and rivers, and the animals they were too small to control, they were threatened by man-made hazards such as ditches, fishponds, and wells; by old fences and rickety bridges and other shabbily made or poorly maintained structures; and by that ubiquitous, attractive menace, the mill where their parents ground their grain.[4] Mills ranked very high among places of potential hazard for children, especially the entry channels: many unfortunate children were unable to gauge the force of the fast-moving water as it flowed through the millrace just prior to being propelled against the wheel. The deep pools formed on the other side of mill wheels also interested unwary children. When they left this outdoor environment to enter their homes, children often exchanged one set of dangers for another. Given the structure and materials used in most medieval houses, it is not surprising that many children suffered when the wattle-and-daub, thatched cottages went up in flames. In addition, the cottage's open hearth (rather than a fireplace) was an ever-present source of danger, especially for toddlers still coping with the complex process of walking without falling over.

MIRACLES INVOLVING CHILDREN'S ACCIDENTS: EXAMPLES FROM 156 CASES

Burns and Scalding

The hearth, often uncovered, probably was especially dangerous for children, particularly in northern regions during the winter. In Pomerania, for instance, little Margaret fell into the fire and burned her neck and face so badly that the bones were exposed; Barbara, still a nursling, accidentally fell into the fire, burned her face and eyes, and could see nothing for four days; and Vincent, eighteen months old, also suffered facial burns after he fell into the fire one November day.[5] A little English girl evidently tried to stop herself as she fell into the hearth, since her face and the fingers of one hand were burned.[6] Because the hearth, focus of family life, was used for cooking as well as illumination and warmth, scalding injuries sometimes resulted from childish curiosity or clumsiness. Forty-year-old Angelucia, a doctor's wife, reported to papal commissioners in central Italy that when her Manfred was two, he fell into some boiling water in a cooking pot in her house in San Severino.[7] His right arm was so badly scalded that he could not extend it properly; another Italian child, about three, seriously scalded his jaw, eye, and ear after falling into some boiling water.[8] Whereas the miracles note survivors of such accidents, coroners' records show us the fatalities: two-year-old William died "immediately" after falling into a cauldron of boiling water, as did Thomas, also two, while Cecilia, age three, died in a pot of green peas, and little John died after falling into a vat of hot mash, a necessary fixture in English homes where ale was made and sold.[9] In some cases children died after the scalding contents were accidentally tipped on them, although Ralph the smith was outlawed for (deliberately?) pouring a bowl of hot water onto a three-year-old boy, "[k]illing him instantly."[10] The ambience of Devon cottage life leaps from the pages of a coroner's report describing how Henry was "scalded to death when a piglet knocked a pot full of vegetables onto him."[11]

Drownings

While burns and scalds endangered young children, drownings constituted most reported children's accidents. In addition, these tended to be the most extensive and detailed cases examined by papal commissioners or reported informally in collections of *miracula*.[12] Many children drowned in streams or ponds; some fell into wells. Man-made village wells or private wells standing in a family's close were, as Hanawalt reminds us, "treacherous, for often they were simply pits in the ground without a superstructure over them. It was easy for a child to fall in and easy also for the weight of a filled pitcher or bucket to pull in an adult, since the ground around the well would be muddy and slippery. The wells were deep and narrow, making them difficult to get out of. . . ."[13] A calamity perfectly illustrating these words occurred one mid-June day in the late fifteenth century, when Margery sent her six-year-old housemaid ("little maid," *ancillula*) to draw some water from the nearby well.[14] As the girl threw the wooden bucket into the water, she lost her footing and fell in, sinking, in the imagination of the miracle recorder, "like a lump of lead." After a while, Margery began wondering why the child was taking so long. When she got to the well and saw the floating bucket, the old woman, too weak to do anything by herself, hurried back to call her other domestic servants, in particular young Thomas Stokes. After running to the well, Thomas saw that the girl had fallen in. He leapt into the well, stood in water up to his chest, and grasped her feet and pulled her out. Since they thought that she had been submerged for about half an hour, everyone anticipated the little girl's funeral. Young Thomas (who may have been related to the girl) vowed that if she survived, he would eat no meat or fish until he could go to King Henry's tomb; he and the bystanders got down on their knees to pray. About "an

hour later" the girl began breathing again. Seven days later the young
man arrived with his stepfather at the king's tomb in Windsor, where their
story was added to the record. This drowning case contains elements common to many others: the child was alone, there was uncertainty about the
duration of submersion, and recovery was not instantaneous.

All over medieval Europe, the fountain, spring, or well, apart from the
obvious function, was a popular venue for neighborly meetings and gossip.
In rural Brittany even in the twentieth century, for example, "two of the traditional foci for social interaction among women neighbors [were] the well
and the *lavoir,* or washing pool."[15] However, whenever feasible it was much
more convenient to keep a water butt in or near a dwelling. Unfortunately,
these objects were attractive hazards to inquisitive medieval children. In
1307 Katerina, wife of John Tailor of London, told papal commissioners
that recently, as she was walking by the house of Ralph the goldsmith, her
neighbor, she happened to hear a commotion and lamentation inside.[16]
Going in, she found the mistress of the house, Alice, holding her son Gilbert
and weeping bitterly, saying "Alas, alas, my infant is dead."[17] It seems that
about 3 P.M. on Monday, July 3, 1307, the women of Ralph's household
were working in a ground-floor room of their house near the Franciscans'
church (Greyfriars, off Newgate Street). Alice, more than thirty years old,
was in perhaps her last trimester of pregnancy. When the papal commissioners wanted to hear her testimony on August 3, 1307, they took her deposition in her garden since she was so large that she was unable even to go
down the road to nearby St. Paul's, where they were holding their investigation.[18] Others present at the accident included Alice's daughter, Joanna;
her son John, about seven; Gilbert's nurse *(nutrix),* Beatrice, about fifteen; and the housemaid, Matilda. As they chatted and worked, Gilbert,
about eighteen months old, wandered unnoticed to the front door, where a
water butt stood on a platform just outside to collect runoff from the eaves.[19]
The container could not be seen from inside the house. Shortly afterward,[20]
John went out and discovered his brother's feet sticking up over the lip of
the water butt. He could also see a bit of his tunic. John began shouting *(cla-
mans et vociferans)* that his brother was drowned, at which Matilda, who happened to be closest to the door, ran up, pulled out the infant, and placed him
in his mother's arms. They carried him upstairs—presumably to the "solar,"
or living quarters above the ground-floor shops of medieval towns—where
they prayed and measured Gilbert to Thomas Cantilupe. The mother vowed
to go to the Hereford shrine or, if she were unable, to send someone in her
place. This must have been about the time that their neighbor Katerina came
in. They felt Gilbert move slightly, at which Joanna held his mouth open

while the nurse Beatrice, squeezing her breast, squirted in some milk.[21] As Beatrice testified, instead of swallowing, the child spewed out milk and water. Eventually, however, he recovered and was put to bed, although he did not regain his normal color for another eight days.

Slippery ground at the lip of a well threatened a little serving girl; a water butt almost finished off a London boy; and a dilapidated bridge nearly caused the death of William at Donington, a place now known as Downton Farm just inside the Welsh border. Although the stream in which the child "drowned" was altered long ago, testimony offered to canonization investigators in 1307 indicates that the Somergeld, now called Summergil Brook, could be crossed at Donington by a wooden bridge—from which William (age two and one-half years) fell one Sunday morning in mid-September of 1305.[22] Hugh of Atforton was standing in a field with his cattle about sunrise that day when he noticed that Alice, William's mother, had just crossed the bridge, which the villagers usually used when the water was too deep to ford. At that time, the depth under the bridge was about four feet, although it could increase to as much as ten feet, reaching the bridge itself. Because Hugh often fished near the bridge, he knew that it was unsafe—it had no railings and was in disrepair: at one point villagers had to walk an uneven plank no more than two feet wide across a large gap in the structure. That is why, when he saw William following his mother, toddling about thirty feet behind her, Hugh shouted to Alice to make William go back since the bridge and water were dangerous.[23] Alice turned and told her son, about to cross the bridge, to go home; when he did nothing, she broke off a willow switch and moved toward William, who, crying, began to return home. At that point Hugh collected his livestock and moved on. Another villager, Thomas le Frayns, witnessed Alice follow her son home, leave him in the close or sheepfold of her husband's house, and order her housemaid, Matilda de Harpeton, age about eleven, to watch him.[24] Alice testified that no one else was at home except her one-year-old daughter, also named Matilda. Alice returned to the bridge, crossed it, and continued her journey. She and her husband John de Lorimer had been invited by the lord of a place called Burwor (also spelled Borwore, Borwor) in Old Radnor, about a mile and a half distant, to a special meal with friends that evening. Alice, about twenty-six or seven at the time of the accident, explained to the commissioners that she was disabled, which was why she had set out for Burwor so early that Sunday—in fact, just after dawn. Presumably she was planning, or expected, to assist in the preparations for the evening's activities. Her husband, meanwhile, had gone to church in New Radnor about a mile away (like Downton Farm, just inside the border of modern Wales).

While Alice was slowly walking toward Burwor and John was at church, their son William ended up in the stream. Witnesses later assumed that he had toddled away from the house and, like any infant *(infantuli more)*, once again tried to follow his mother, in the process falling from the dangerous bridge. The maid Matilda claimed that she was unaware that William had slipped out. After she learned of the drowning, in fact, she fled from the house; the parents never again employed her. However the accident happened, the body was found by Thomas, son of William of Donington. About fourteen at the time, Thomas had been sent out by his grandfather at around nine that morning with instructions to collect some wild apples for a sauce. As he started to ford the Somergeld about seventy feet downstream from the bridge, Thomas saw some red clothing in the water in the middle of the stream to his right. Thinking at first that it was some woman's washing gone astray,[25] he took a closer look: he saw a small, recently shaved head, then recognized the body of John de Lorimer's son William, his own cousin.[26] The water, about a foot deep at that point, was flowing over the child's upturned face. Thomas judged that the stream had carried the body down from the bridge until the current was too weak to propel him any farther. He dragged the boy to the bank and raised the hue and cry (following the custom of the region, the papal notaries added). The villagers drawn to this shouting found the child's limbs rigid and his body "stone cold."[27] Hugh of Atforton, the man who earlier that morning had warned Alice that William was toddling after her, carried the child to a clearing closer to the village, where he put him down. The victim, apart from being cold and stiff, lay with clenched teeth and staring eyes, which were veiled with a film. Hugh suggested that the bystanders pray to Thomas of Hereford and measure the child. Someone gave him a thread with which he carried out the operation, as everyone (some in tears) knelt to pray as best they could. Hugh forced a piece of wood into the boy's mouth and upended him, causing a great quantity of water to gush out. The child's wet clothing was removed and Hugh held him in his lap, for perhaps half an hour, before carrying him into William of Donington's house, not far from the stream, where they made a fire. They turned first one side of the little body *(corpusculum)* and then the other toward the heat, hoping to warm the child evenly.

When John Hoke, about eighteen, ran from his mother's house toward the sound of the hue and cry, he saw Hugh in the clearing, holding the boy next to him. The child seemed lifeless, which prompted some of the village women to suggest that his hands and feet should be bound in preparation for burial, a suggestion that was not carried out.[28] After John Hoke had prayed by the body, he went to fetch the child's father, John de Lorimer, a man of about thirty-three. Hoke found him around 9 A.M., returning from New Radnor church (Donington's parish church), where he had just heard Mass. He was with his brother-in-law and another villager, Adam Panay. When given the news, John de Lorimer rode at full speed back to his village, where he found the boy in William of Donington's house.[29] Hugh was holding him in his lap; John found his son's body cold and inert, the piece of wood still in the boy's mouth. John remained at his son's side, as other villagers crowded into the house to kneel and pray. Just past midday, lacking hope of resuscitation and—as he testified—being unable to bear the sadness,[30] John de Lorimer left his son's body and went to join his wife at Lord William of Burwor's dinner, even as more villagers were entering the house.

This apparently callous behavior can be interpreted in various ways: as the result of bewilderment and shock; as a way, as John himself suggested, to assuage his grief; or as the behavior of a man resigned to the death of what would appear to have been his only son. It is also possible that even in grief John believed that important social obligations must be fulfilled. He may have been under obligation to Lord William of Burwor, although he held his lands of Lady Margaret de Mortimer.[31] Whatever his motive for going, John de Lorimer remained at the dinner until nightfall. His wife Alice, of course, had been at Lord William's all day. She testified that in the evening, while still at the dinner, she was told that her son had fallen into the water and had been miraculously revived. Presumably she and her husband were both given this happy news.[32] When they returned home after vespers, they found their son in bed, alive.

After the father had gone off to attend the dinner, Hugh, evidently very concerned, remained with the boy until the early afternoon (as long after midday as it would take a man to walk about three miles), when he put his finger into William's mouth and felt him bite down; Hugh then felt the heart beating. Others, including an "outsider" from New Radnor, also touched and felt the boy for signs of life. The child groaned weakly, looked about him, and screamed violently, which some thought to be a final death cry. This suggests that some of the onlookers believed that his death from drowning was a gradual process, culminating in this "final" event. In fact, as modern health professionals know, death from drowning can occur hours, even days, after a victim has been pulled from the water and "resuscitated." One witness thought that William glared savagely as if deranged, another claimed that he moved his eyes around as if terrified by something.[33] Hugh held on to the child, who eventually fell asleep in his lap. When he again opened his eyes about an hour later, he seemed more composed. Hugh asked if he wanted anything: yes, William said, some bread and cheese. This was given him, as well as some "toast" (*tosta*, which the notaries described as bread roasted at the fire) put into beer to warm it.[34] After the beer-toast had been administered, William recognized bystanders and responded to them. Later in the week the parents and villagers took the boy to the cathedral, where the Hereford canons celebrated yet another miraculous sign from "their" saint, Thomas Cantilupe.

Apart from wells and bridges, other man-made temptations surrounding village children were the ditches, pits, and ponds dug for a variety of purposes. One of these ponds nearly claimed a young victim in the hamlet of Little Marcle near Hereford one afternoon in early May of 1304, while twenty-six-year old Edith Drake was cleaning her cottage.[35] In the midst of her chores Edith noticed that John, eighteen months old, was not in the house. She assumed that her son had awakened from his nap and gone outside to play with the other village children, perhaps in the road or along the public way.[36] Edith continued her spring cleaning for another thirty minutes, removing accumulated rubbish. She finally stopped to go out and look for her son, whom she expected to see playing with the other little ones (*parvulis*) somewhere near her house. She did not see him or any other village children. Two neighbors whom she encountered had not seen John; the three searched through the village for about half an hour, when Edith thought of the watering pit for livestock near her house. After running to the site, she found little John floating facedown in the water. Fully clothed, Edith leapt into the water, which came up almost to her shoulders, dragged John out, and put him down in the road.

Not far away but out of sight of his own house, the boy's father, fifty-seven-year-old William Drake, was digging a ditch between his lands and the public road when, from somewhere near his cottage, he heard his wife's crying and wailing. He ran toward the screams and found his son lying on the ground. Bystanders said that John's body was cold and rigid, but William could not bear to touch the boy, as he testified in 1307, because of his grief. As more villagers, hearing the shouts "usually made when a dead body was found" (i.e., the hue and cry), gathered round the body, someone held the boy upside-down and another examined him for signs of life. The grandmother, Edith's mother, Cecilia (about forty-seven, making her younger than her son-in-law), hearing the shouting near her daughter's place, rushed from her own house to find her grandson lying in his father's close (*clausuram*). Her lamentations joined those of the villagers and John's parents. Two knights who happened to be traveling along the main road were drawn to this pitiable outpouring of grief. One of them measured the child for a candle to be offered to Cantilupe. Along with about twenty vil-

lagers, some in tears, the knights knelt there in the road for about thirty minutes, everyone saying the *Pater, Ave,* and *Credo*. While these kindly knights
were absorbed in prayer, unluckily for them one or both of their mounts ran
off. Consequently, the strangers' vigil ended abruptly as they went chasing
after their horses. Edith, meanwhile, saw one of her son's eyes open. After
a pause during which one could say the *Pater* twice, the other one opened as
well; then John opened his mouth. The flow of time *(fluxo . . . tempore)*
between opening the eyes and the mouth, Edith estimated, was about the
same as the time a man usually remained at table having a meal. Edith
pressed milk from her breast into her son's mouth several times and, eventually, he vomited water mixed with milk. She held him upside-down and a
great quantity of water gushed from his mouth and nose. Just before sunset, Edith placed her breast in John's mouth, again, and finally he began
sucking, having "returned" to life. Two days later he was babbling as usual,
but he could not walk properly until Saturday, when he was taken to
Hereford cathedral and placed on Cantilupe's tomb. Full recovery took
some three weeks.[37]

Animals and Work-Related Accidents

Animals constituted another environmental danger underlying many childhood accidents. During the Middle Ages most domesticated "farm" animals
except pigs were valued more for their muscle power and as sources of com-
modities, such as wool and leather, than as food. The cattle tended to be
spindly and about six inches shorter than modern livestock.[38] Fish, birds,
and wild game helped to make up for the poor nutritional quality of the
domestic stock. Regardless, animals evidently had more than a utility value
in contemporary consciousness: animal motifs pervaded medieval art, from
the curiously carved figures in cloisters that sent Bernard of Clairvaux into
high indignation, to miniatures and decorated margins in manuscripts that
teem with mythical and real beasts occasionally dressed as humans (foxy
bishops perhaps), to version after version of bestiaries, to imaginative and
didactic literature such as *Gesta Romanorum,* which featured Aesopian tales
with a Christian twist. Apart from these indications (and there are many
others), the stories of Hubert converted by a crucifix between a stag's
antlers, Francis preaching to the animals, Cuthbert using seals or otters as
foot warmers, and wild beasts gathering at Godric's Finchale hermitage are
folkloric and hagiographic medieval motifs reflecting the prelapsarian epoch
when man and beast, so it was imagined, lived in harmony.[39] The reality,
however, was often far from harmonious. When a messenger was spotted by
friends as he rode through a place near Durham, they invited him in for a

drink and a meal.[40] After tying his horse to a post, he passed a five-year-old girl sitting on a bench outside the door as he entered. About six in the evening the messenger came out, mounted, and spurred his horse, which suddenly kicked, striking the little girl and knocking her to the ground. A crowd of men and women gathered, shouting and wailing.[41] Some cradled her in their arms, others caressed her, trying to determine whether she was alive. Her head seemed horribly crushed; nearly half her face was gone. The girl's grandmother, holding her, called upon the Virgin and King Henry. They took her into a church, hoping that their tearful prayers would be more effective in front of the crucifix or the sacrament of the altar; the girl's mother threw herself to the pavement, overwhelmed by grief. About eleven that night, while they were still in the church, a drop of fluid ran from the girl's right eye into her mouth, which onlookers took as a positive sign. Eventually the child recovered, and her face and left eye, which had been almost knocked out, regained their normal appearance.

In an earlier era and a different setting, another English child encountered an even more violent animal. William of Oxford, about twelve, had been taken to London by his mother. Near their lodgings in a leather dresser's place, a crowd gathered to enjoy some bull-baiting, a popular sport with twelfth-century Londoners.[42] Having been savaged for some time, the bull broke away from the dogs and began charging about, scattering the crowd. Attracted by the shouts and barking, William went to the doorway to investigate. Unlucky boy: before he could jump back in, the bull, just outside the door, hooked him with its horns, threw him to the ground, and trampled him. William's mother ran out and pulled her crumpled child from under the beast, shouting for help from Thomas Becket. At this, the Canterbury monk writes, the bull became docile, even letting people touch it, and the dogs also fell silent, apparently immobilized by Becket's name. Eventually William recovered from his injuries. This case reminds us that children's confrontations with animals occurred in towns and cities as well as in the countryside. An infant's death from a sow's bite may seem, at first, somewhat unusual for urban London, until one recalls that the rural atmosphere of even the largest European cities was maintained, with local variations, until demographic shifts beginning about 1500 brought an end to the fields and open spaces within city walls.[43] And, of course, flocks and herds often were driven through city streets to market. During the late fourteenth century, five-year-old Britoneta became a victim of one of these urban cattle drives, in Marseilles.[44] She was gored while playing with other children, the horn entering her head below the ear. The animal carried the girl through the entire "Triparia" quarter of the city, with local inhabitants in pursuit. Finally

Britoneta was tossed into the air, landing behind the animal, where she lay as if dead. Only the whites of her eyes could be seen, she was motionless, and her body had turned quite "black."[45] When her aunt saw Britoneta like this, she commended her to Pope Urban, promising a wax head at the pontiff's tomb. The girl began speaking and a little later had recovered.

What may have been a more typical child-animal accident occurred in a village about ten miles from Exeter, where John Berow lived and farmed. He had an eight-year-old stepson whose youth and physique unsuited him for rustic labor; nevertheless, the narrator claimed, the boy obeyed his stepfather as a real father, cheerfully doing whatever he was told.[46] One day in May the boy was helping his stepfather with the plowing. While prodding the ox, the boy accidentally went too close: suddenly the animal turned, gored him in the neck, and threw him to the ground. The stepfather, aghast with anguish and helplessness, tearfully prayed to King Henry. After the flow of blood stopped, John took the boy home, and within a few days the child had recovered. This case not only illustrates an apparently congenial working relationship between child and adult but also, in emphasizing the stepfather's grief, provides a counterweight to the medieval literary theme of coolness or even hatred between parents and their stepchildren.[47] The injury to John's stepson, a "work-related" event, was linked not only to the physical environment but also to the contemporary social environment. The lives and safety of some children, such as the six-year-old housemaid who fell into a well while fetching water for her mistress, were threatened while, and because, they were engaged in some sort of work or chores for their elders. The age at which medieval children were considered significant augmentations to the labor force, and socially "valued" for this reason, is contested. The miracle records provide some information on this topic. Apart from the two examples just mentioned, we have encountered another instance of child labor in the case of the eleven-year-old housemaid (*ancilla*) who fled after her charge, the infant William, toddled into the stream at Donington and, in the last chapter, the "work" that Petronilla's five-year-old might have performed but for her illness. Obviously, children carried out a variety of economic tasks; one case describes a nine-year-old who was spinning as she walked along the road, but fell and accidentally ran the sharp spindle into her left eye.[48]

Some of the child labor mentioned in these records was no more than casual errand running. In one instance, it is clear that some parents, like their modern counterparts, were not surprised when the errands did not get done or done well. In the hamlet of How Caple very early one Saturday morning, John the fisherman, about fifty, told his son Nicholas, eight, to take the cow with the white star on its head to a pasture near the local lord's field.[49] About midmorning the boy brought back the cow and went inside for some bread and milk. To make sure that the cow did not wander into the lord's field, John told his son to go to the river to fetch some supple branches (probably willow) lying in his boat, so that hobbles could be made for the cow. Nicholas—his mother testified that he usually obeyed his father—did as he was told. As the boy approached the boat, which was moored to the bank with an iron chain, the ground gave way and he slipped into the river. The last thing that Nicholas could remember, as he later deposed, was being in the water under the boat. The only witness was a girl named Margery, who lived on the other side of the river in the hamlet of Ingestone. She saw the boy go under but could do nothing: the river was wide at that point, no boat was available, the nearest bridge was six miles away, and no one across the river could hear her cries for help, although she shouted many times. How Caple is a few hundred yards from the Wye, its fields sloping sharply down to the river; as Margery claimed, it is unlikely that anyone in the village could have heard her shouting down on the flats on the opposite bank. The fact that she could not tell even the victim's father what she had seen until the next day, when he was fishing and his boat came within earshot, emphasizes the communication problems in this hilly section of Herefordshire.[50]

At the time of the accident, the boy's father, John, and his mother, Lucia, were inside their cottage. Although Nicholas did not return when expected, his parents were not alarmed: John assumed that he was playing with his "age mates," while the mother also thought that Nicholas was dallying in "youthful frivolity."[51] His parents were unconcerned, even though it was late afternoon, and the boy had been gone since before midday; after all, it was spring (late May-early June), the weather was warmer, the days longer. Around five o'clock a little boy, about four according to John (other witnesses gave his age as seven and ten), the son of a poor woman who begged in the village, came to the cottage saying that Nicholas had drowned. John ran to the river, followed by his anxious wife, who was unable to keep up with him. He went to his boat, saw marks in the riverbank where someone had slipped into the water, then hurried along looking for Nicholas. In a bend of the river about forty feet away he saw something white in the water. Since his son had been dressed in linen, John knew that it must be Nicholas.[52] He snagged him with a long hook (possibly taken from his boat) and was dragging him to the bank as Lucia arrived. When the parents looked down at their son's body, they were "shaken to the core" and collapsed to the ground, senseless.[53] Cristina, a neighbor whose house was opposite John and Lucia's (she had come running with Lucia), finished pulling Nicholas from the river, then revived the parents by throwing water in their faces. Another person who ran to the scene was the preteen Felicia Morker, Lucia's sister, who lived in the family's house. When the parents came to, they, Felicia, and Cristina all tried to resuscitate Nicholas, the father hanging him upside-down while the three women massaged his body. Milk, water, and (according to his mother) blood came from his mouth. The mother took a thread from her purse and measured her son to Cantilupe, while the others knelt and prayed. The parents carried him home and put him into their bed where he lay unmoving, the color of lead, his eyes veiled with a film. John, thinking it improper to bury his son with his eyes still open, decided to close them: when he touched the eyelids, however, the boy screamed "Help, Lord; help, St. Thomas!" three or four times, and recovered. Some nine years later, Nicholas told the papal examiners that he remembered falling into the water, then waking up in his father's bed about the time that the chickens roosted for the night. Nicholas also remembered his father holding up one hand and asking if he could see: "*Sic*—yes, your hand." He then moved his fingers, asking Nicholas the same thing: "moving your fingers" was the reply. The joyful parents then went out to tell their neighbors of the miraculous recovery. Later, by candlelight, Lucia tried several times to give Nicholas some warm milk with a wooden spoon; after finally succeeding, she saw him fall asleep. When he awoke at cockcrow to announce that he was hungry, his father fed him some semolina pudding, after which the boy slept again. Later in the day, Nicholas dressed himself and asked when they would visit Cantilupe's tomb. On Tuesday the whole village went to the cathedral, the story was told, and the canons celebrated with a procession and *Te Deum*, as young Nicholas was displayed and pointed out to everyone.[54] The family vowed an annual pilgrimage to Hereford for the rest of their lives. The victim, about seventeen when he testified, claimed that every morning he said ten *Paters* and *Aves*, repeating these prayers several times a day in thanks for his resuscitation.

Children injured while working or running errands usually were old enough to take care of themselves, but often parents took infants and toddlers with them to work, or at least allowed them to tag along. Since the most common peasant pursuit was farming, this created a potentially dangerous context, with not altogether surprising results. For example, a twelfth-century peasant in Norwich diocese was heaping straw when, taking a break, he threw aside his two-pronged fork, unaware that his daughter, nearly two, was playing beneath the straw. One of the prongs pierced the top of her head, the other grazed her back.[55] She began writhing on the ground and foaming at the mouth. The peasant's lord, a knight, hearing of the incident, ran to the scene, removed the prong that the confused rustic (*rusticus . . . stupidus*) had left in the girl's head, and sent for a doctor, who declared, however, that recovery was hopeless. At this point the knight's wife urged her husband, about to go on pilgrimage to Canterbury, to make an offering to Becket for the girl's recovery. On his return, the knight found the child playing. Shortly afterward she was taken to Becket's shrine, where her neighbors provided testimony, handing over a letter from the knight setting out the details. A similar incident was reported from Pomerania in 1404 by Hannis Vogeler, about forty. Hannis, who called himself a peasant, told canonization commissioners of an accident that happened about six years earlier while his wife, Katherina, was loading a cart with dung that she intended to spread over the fields.[56] When the cart was full she threw her iron fork toward the heap of dung, but it somehow accidentally struck her three-year-old son John in the head. The fork entered near his ear, and John collapsed to the ground as if dead. Katherina tearfully vowed to take the child and a silver offering to Dorothy's tomb. Within eight days John had regained his health. English coroners' records once again provide mirror images of these tragedies, but without the circumstantial detail or the happy outcome: "Gilbert le Batur stood on a hayrick with an iron fork in his hand, and by misadventure the fork fell on the head of Michael son of Hugh, so that he died three days later. Gilbert fled. . . ."[57]

When combined with parents' carelessness, the custom of allowing children to accompany them left many grief-stricken: a terrified miller in Pomerania, fearing that his son had drowned in the mill waters, did eventually find him submerged and "lifeless";[58] one August day in 1481 in England Richard of Westwell, another miller, took his four-year-old grandson, whom he loved dearly, to work with him. After sending the boy off to play as usual, he went about his business.[59] Later, when he called the boy and got no response, he began running about anxiously searching for him. He found him in the mill pond. Unable to reach him, in his anguish Richard broke into loud cries, which attracted a crowd. Eventually the boy was recovered, and after prayers by the neighbors and his grief-stricken grandfather and parents, he revived. Other children suffered similar fates as a result of accompanying their mothers or fathers to work: a two-year-old girl nearly drowned at the seaside while her father was refitting a boat.[60] Before Joanna started threshing grain, she put down her year-old daughter where she could watch her. Unfortunately, she overlooked her child's tendency to put things into her mouth—in this case a spike of grain that, lodged in the infant's throat, incapacitated her for more than ten weeks. As the narrator explained, "Infants, without a jot of sense, put into their mouths whatever they can grasp."[61] Even the most innocuous kind of parental "work" might prove dangerous to children, one way or another: in the Little Marcle case examined earlier, an infant toddled out of the house and into a pit of water while his mother was preoccupied with her spring cleaning; similarly, while her mother was busy with housework, a three-year-old girl wandered into another part of the house and managed to hang herself from some cloth loops used to close the cellar door;[62] and in the short time it took for a woman to go outside to fetch her wimple bleaching in the sun, return to her chamber, and put it on, her Edmund—an *infantulus* not yet two—fell into the household cess-pit.[63] When Theobald, seven, asked his mother if he could go with her to bathe in the river while she washed the clothes, she thought nothing of it until, straightening up from her work, she looked around and could not see him. Terrified, she threw aside her washing and began screaming and shouting. Theobald was found cold and stiff, without any vital signs.[64]

Although children who merely accompanied their parents to work were sometimes put at risk, it was riskier to leave a child at home alone when a sitter, sibling, or other relative was unavailable. The potential danger in such cases is self-evident and will be considered in a later section of this chapter, on parental negligence. For the present, a single example will suffice. Agnes, age two, was sleeping one day when her mother slipped out to do some gleaning at Stoneley near Coventry.[65] While she was working, a fire started in the village and her little cottage (*domuncula*) began to burn. Seeing the sparks and smoke, everyone rushed from the fields back to Stoneley. The woman ran through thick fumes and confused shouting to her burning house. Almost deranged, the narrator reports, she screamed "Oh my sweet child! the fruit of my womb dying in the flames! it's unbearable!"[66] Suddenly, from the midst of the fire, bystanders heard a voice repeatedly crying "Mamme, Mamme." When the mother heard her child, ignoring the danger she ran into the flaming cottage, snatched up Agnes, and brought her out unharmed. Hanawalt has shown from English coroners' records that babies left at home were at greater risk during the busiest season in the agricultural year (May through August), when parents spent more time in the fields.[67]

The Dangers of "Play"

Although some children were injured or nearly drowned while working or running errands, or suffered as a result of their parents' work routines, many medieval children, like their modern counterparts, were in the midst of careless play when they became endangered. Bernard de Gordon, a Montpellier physician writing in the early fourteenth century, defined the period from about age seven to fourteen as "the age of concussion" since, during those years, children "begin to run and jump and to hit each other."[68] Less violent play, by the sides of streams or ponds—or in one case a water-filled iron mine—might easily result in tragedy.[69] The records also describe children putting themselves at risk while running in a garden collecting nuts (and falling on a knife), hunting for birds' nests (and falling from the top of the tree), or playing about in a skiff on the river Thames (and nearly drowning).[70] Some were doubly "innocent" victims in the sense that, unlike the children just described, they were passive onlookers at public entertainments or contests. During the early fifteenth century a carpenter, Richard Wodewell, testified that while he and some friends in a hamlet near Salisbury were throwing stones and lumps of iron at a target, several local youths were watching the game.[71] Cristina Cerlee, nine, was sitting about twelve feet beyond the target. After making several attempts without reaching the mark, Richard threw his iron—weighing about a pound—which accidentally overshot and smashed into the back of Cristina's head. One witness stated that Richard rushed into the local church seeking asylum, saying that he had killed a girl.[72] Cristina lay gravely wounded on the ground for an hour and a half but eventually recovered; several days later she went with friends and her parents to Osmund's tomb where, with profuse thanks and prayers, they left the iron weight as an offering.[73] Two other latemedieval English cases emphasize the dangers of archery for unwary children who happened to be in the wrong place at the wrong time. Thomas, about four, was watching some Kentish boys practicing archery when he was struck in the right eye.[74] When the arrow was withdrawn, blood flowed heavily from his mouth and nose as well as the eye. A similar incident occurred in Rutland where, on April 24, 1491, the villagers surged into the springtime fields for archery practice, shooting at distant, small targets.[75] Since some of the archers were irresponsible or unskilled, their arrows fell among some nearby willows. Reginald, a little boy *(puerulus)* watching the event while standing among the trees, was struck in the chest near the heart. When he crumpled to the ground, everyone—archers and onlookers—ran up, ending the game in grief, the miracle recorder noted rhetorically, as clapping turned to breastbeating and laughter became tears.[76] By common agreement, the body was snatched up and hurried into the church, where many sorrowing villagers gathered. After they commended the boy to the Virgin and King Henry, he eventually recovered. A more unusual example of a passive child injured in the midst of play, of sorts, involved little Petirka. In Pomerania during 1394 or 1395, Elizabeth took her son, about two, to a Christmas party of the kind the villagers "usually had" at that season. Toward evening she put the child down to sleep on a bench, covered him with a cloth, and rejoined the revellers.[77] Soon afterward however, one of the drunken male *(inebriatus)* partygoers sat on the boy. Elizabeth began screaming "You're crushing him!" Terrified *(maxime perterrita)*, she examined her child and found him "dead," but after his grandmother, mother, and other guests (probably sobered by then) prayed and vowed to Dorothy, he revived about cockcrow.

Play also set the scene for a tragedy examined, in great detail, by the Cantilupe canonization commission. Giving evidence in Hereford between the fifteenth and the twenty-fifth of September, 1307, ten individuals testified at length about the incident, their accounts taking up eighteen folios of the Vatican manuscript.[78] This case is probably the single most extensively reported "miracle" attributed to any saint in medieval England. (See the appendix for a translation of the testimony). The events took place in Wisteston (referred to by its inhabitants as merely a "place," *locus,* not a village), a hamlet in Marden parish some six miles outside Hereford. There is nothing left of Wisteston but a pile of rubble marking the place where Wisteston Court, or House, once stood, and the foundations of a nearby chapel. It is likely that this medieval accident occurred somewhere between Wisteston House and the chapel, which are separated by a few hundred yards of rich field and meadow, perhaps on property now known as Brick House Farm.[79]

Sundays were days of rest and relaxation, freedom from the weekly routine; and Sunday April 18, 1288, was also, perhaps, one of the first days when the signs hinted that winter was truly over and spring very near—the kind of April day that Chaucer may have envisaged when he wrote of folk anxious to go on pilgrimage.[80] In Wisteston, about three in the afternoon, groups of people began making their way from their cottages to the local beer-tavern *(taverna servicie)* or pub, in the home of Walter and Joan de la Wyle. It was said that as many as 100 people gathered, among them Adam and his wife, Cecilia. As they were walking, the couple saw their daughter, Joanna, nearly five, following them. Since they knew that other children would be at the pub, they did not mind her tagging along. On arrival, Cecilia began chatting with her friend Joan Wase, who was little Joanna's godmother, while husband Adam, presumably, went off with the other men.[81] As one might expect, Joanna and the other children grew bored; she went out into the tavern garden with her friend John, about nine months younger, the son of her godmother, Joan Wase, and Thomas Schonk. The two children crossed the garden and went up to the embanked fishpond owned by the tavern-keeper. John, Joanna, and two other children began throwing stones into the water.

The pond was large, some sixty by twenty-four feet, and about six or more feet deep; the surface of the water was four to six feet below the bank. According to Joanna's testimony given some nineteen years after the event, while playing *(luderet)*, John, acting "childishly," bumped against her and knocked her down the embankment toward the water.[82] Sliding on the sand and clay, she clutched at weeds growing along the sloping bank, uprooting them. John could not help her. Screaming, she went into the water. Then, as her parents later told her, she drowned.

Back at the pub, the younger people, after having a drink or two, formed a dance line, as was their custom, the witnesses said, and went out through the garden. Led by Thomas Schonk, age about twenty, the dancers seem to have followed a circuit past the fishpond and back by the same route to the pub; then from there out to the public way, returning finally to the pub. On their first "pass" *(transitu)* by the fishpond, about four of the dancers spotted some cloth in the water. Thomas, the dance leader, said that it was probably left there from some woman's washing, which they would investigate on their return. When they did come back to the pond, to their fear and stupefaction Thomas Schonk and three or four others discovered that the bit of cloth was part of the clothing of a little child, possibly the daughter of a local beggar woman.[83] The leaders decided that it was "not expedient"—to use Schonk's own words—for anyone else in the dance line to see this discovery.[84] It is not clear, incidentally, why everyone in the group could not see what the dance leaders saw. In any case, they decided to retrieve the corpse from the pond that night and throw it into the local river.[85] Although one of the group wanted to report the matter to Walter de la Wyle, the pub and pond owner, he was silenced because his fellow dancers (especially Thomas Schonk) did not want to risk the potential inconvenience, expense, and even prosecution that often followed the discovery of a dead body. Having made their decision to dispose of the remains under cover of darkness, Schonk and his cronies led the dancing villagers back to the pub, from which their dance line would set out for the public road. For a few of them, no doubt, their dancing may suddenly have become less enjoyable: quite apart from their illegal intentions regarding the corpse, they had already broken the law by not raising the hue and cry at once.

During the thirteenth century, it had become established at English common law that anyone who discovered a corpse was to raise the alarm immediately—the hue and cry—then report the find to the local authority, often a hundredal bailiff (a "hundred" was an administrative division of a shire, or county). These officers in turn informed the nearest coroner; there were usually four coroners in each county, but probably only three in

Herefordshire at the time of this event. Meanwhile, the body was not to be moved until the coroner arrived, examined it, took evidence from the local people, and noted his findings, which were later recopied into the official coroners' rolls. These rolls were presented as needed later on—for example, in the county court. In addition—and this is why no one at the pondside in Wisteston wanted to be "first finder" of the little girl's corpse—the coroner "attached" (obligated) the first finder(s) to be present at the next shire court, where the death would be formally examined. Not only that, but the normal practice was for coroners to attach, besides the finder(s), neighbors living near the place of the body's discovery, and then to take pledges or sureties from two additional people for each person attached, who became guarantors—roughly, bail bondsmen—that everyone involved would show up in court. By the time the coroner had come and gone, at least fifteen local people might find themselves involved, with some of them required to travel to the next court session. When they got there, the chances were good that the coroner's rolls would reveal irregularities in their actions—for instance, that they had not raised the hue and cry immediately, or had moved the body—which made them, or their whole village, or even the entire hundred or town liable for a fine.[86] The village could also be fined if any of the attached individuals failed to appear in court. Their sureties, too, would be liable to pay up. And finally, if a particular object had caused the death, it was forfeited (as a "deodand"). In the case of wells and ponds, they were filled in by the coroner's orders. One can perhaps sympathize with the frightened villagers peering down at the little corpse in the pond in Walter de la Wyle's field.

Meanwhile, Thomas Schonk's son John, the playmate who had bumped Joanna into the water, went into the pub to tell his mother, Joan, the victim's godmother, about the accident. He found her talking with Cristina, the victim's mother, and Ralph Tailor. In her testimony of 1307, John's mother claimed that when her son said that Joanna had drowned, they thought he was just prattling "childish words."[87] Moreover, because Ralph was telling them something, Cristina and Joan took no notice of the boy's comments.[88] However, on this point the testimony is inconsistent. John's father, Thomas Schonk, leader of the dancers, told the papal commissioners that while he was dancing (during the first return to the pub?) his wife Joan came out to tell him that their son had said something about a drowning, although the victim's mother had not understood John's words. It is possible that only John's mother could have understood some of the four-year-old's phrases, to which Cecilia was not paying much attention anyway. In any event, Schonk testified that after his wife told him this, he went to the pub, snatched his son by the ear *(per aurem)* and took him home, warning Alice, his sister-in-law who was also the housemaid, not to let him out. Schonk, presumably, returned to his dancing. The possibility of collusion between husband and wife is particularly interesting because it was the wife, the victim's godmother, who eventually pulled the girl from the water. Perhaps her hand was forced, as the next developments suggest.

John somehow got out of his house and returned to the pub, where he found Cecilia and his mother still talking to Ralph. Plucking at his mother's clothing (was she deliberately ignoring him?) he said—plainly enough, this time—"Joanna is all drowned in the fishpond" *(tota submersa est)*. The two women and Ralph ran to the pond. John pointed to where the girl had gone under. Throwing off her cloak, Joan waded in at the shallow, discharge end. Even though she could not swim, her clothing billowed out and buoyed her up as she struggled toward the middle of the pond. With the water up to her armpits, she saw the hem of the child's clothing under her. She hooked the hem with her foot and reached down with her right hand, momentarily submerging her head as she retrieved the girl. Dragging Joanna behind her, she made for the edge of the pond; when she was near enough, she heaved her godchild up onto the bank "like a lump of wood." As Ralph Tailor helped Joan to climb out, Cecilia rolled the body about on the ground, trying to determine whether it really was her daughter, since mud and disfigurement made identification difficult. When Cecilia recognized the red laces on the shoes she had bought only the day before, she collapsed in grief. The dancers, out on the second loop of their "circuit," saw the commotion and rushed to the pond, as did the crowd from the pub, including the girl's father. With everyone gathered around the unmoving body, someone suggested raising the hue and cry. Adam, the victim's father, however, said that instead of shouting, they should pray to Cantilupe. Everyone—around forty men and women—began to say the *Ave* and *Pater* and other prayers. Meanwhile they cut away the belt from around the girl's bloated stomach, tried to push her swollen tongue back through her rigid jaws, and held her upside-down to drain out the water; but nothing seemed to restore life and breath. While the mother cradled her child's body at the water's edge, Walter, worried about coroners filling in his fishpond—and he should have worried, given that no hue and cry had been raised and the "corpse" had been interfered with—suggested pretending that Joanna had not died in the water; so the body was carried into his pub. There they continued attempting to revive the child, without effect. By evening Walter, evidently convinced that resuscitation was impossible and afraid of the consequences of a child's death in his tavern, asked Adam and Cecilia to take the girl home, which they did.

Although Cecilia was pregnant (she gave birth about a month later), she insisted upon keeping Joanna's cold body next to her. Fearing for the mother's health, the group made her get into bed, still holding the girl. They also built a fire, more for the mother's sake than for her "dead" daughter's. At dawn the mother felt Joanna move, followed by the child's vomiting and moaning. When Cecilia asked Joanna how she had ended up in the water, the reply was "John pushed me."

With great happiness her family took her to the parish church at Marden, where the bells were rung, as they were in the chapel at Wisteston; she was placed upon the altar while thanksgiving prayers were offered. Although the villagers objected, being worried about her fragile condition, Adam carried Joanna on horseback, with a pillow as saddle, and made for Hereford, being joined en route by inhabitants of three or four surrounding villages. Having grown to about thirty people, some barefoot, the group entered the cathedral and placed Joanna on Cantilupe's tomb. The canons satisfied themselves as to the "miracle," the bells were rung, a sermon was preached, the *Te Deum* was intoned, and everyone thanked God and Thomas. Next Sunday, Adam returned with a wax image of Joanna, which was hung up by Cantilupe's tomb. There it remained, he testified, until it fell apart from age.[89] Even if this votive disintegrated, the memory of the event was constantly renewed in Joanna's family by their pilgrimages to Hereford cathedral once or twice each year, which, as they swore before the papal board in 1307, they intended to repeat for the rest of their lives.

A "Trip and Fall" Case

Children, particularly younger ones, were liable to injury as a result of tripping and colliding with solid objects, falling from bridges into streams, stumbling into hearth fires, and toddling into ponds. The long-term consequences of children's problems with balance, coupled with a disregard of where they were going, are brought out in a case involving an English girl about the same age as Joanna of Wisteston, who had to wait for some ten years before receiving her miraculous relief. Alice's father, William of Lonsdale, waited too, coping year after year with his child's accidentally caused disability. Papal commissioners visited William on August 9, 1307, as he lay very ill in his house in St. Giles Parish outside Cripplegate in London. Next day they talked to other witnesses, including his nineteen-year-old daughter, Alice.[90]

About 1293 William set off from Lonsdale in northern England on a pilgrimage to the Spanish shrine of St. James of Compostella. There was nothing unusual about a Yorkshireman wishing to go to one of Europe's

most frequently visited pilgrimage centers.[91] He took along his daughter
Alice, about five, leaving his wife Idonea behind. As they followed one of the
main routes south, near Stamford, Alice—carelessly, as she admitted years
later—stumbled in the road and fell. William carried her on his back to
London. Stamford, about eighty miles from London as the crow flies, was
over 160 miles from Lonsdale. Possibly William did not take his injured
daughter home because he hoped that her condition would improve as they
continued their pilgrimage. However, when they reached London perhaps
a week or so later, things were worse. They spent their first night in the city
at Southwark where Alice, a poor little one *(paupercula)* as she later
described herself, slept between two doorways. In the morning she had no
strength in her foot, arm, and left side of her body. Soon her swollen foot
became infected and began to suppurate. Putrid matter flowed from various
fistulas, including one was so big that William could stick his finger into it,
he claimed, and so deep that he could see her ankle bones. One night, as
they rested by the fountain at the church of St. Clement Danes, Alice,
screaming and crying out to her father, bathed her foot in the fountain to
soothe the pain. Eventually Alice was treated as a charity case by Gilbert,
a London surgeon, who twice put plasters on the foot. After examining her
a third time, however, he told William that he could do nothing more. For
ten years Alice and William lived by begging in London. Sometimes she
dragged herself along on the ground after her father, sometimes he carried
her on his back. On one occasion, a certain Amicia and other women
noticed Alice begging outside the church of Saint Martin in the Fields during Sunday Mass. To see whether she was faking, they lifted up Alice's
clothing and examined and touched her legs and hips. They found that the
joints were indeed crippled, that the girl could not walk, and that putrid matter flowed from her foot.

Somehow, William heard of miracles attributed to Cantilupe. Although
the Hereford wonders began in 1287, they do not seem to have come to
William's notice until 1303.[92] He measured Alice for a candle and vowed to
visit the bishop's tomb in Hereford. He also made a vow to St. Giles, just in
case Thomas failed to heal his daughter. Alice testified that her father [fol-
lowing "the English custom," the notaries wrote] invoked the saint while
bending a penny held over her head. He may have performed both procedures, measuring as well as coin bending. William then began collecting
alms for his daughter's transport. Eventually he saved enough for a wheelbarrow, put his daughter into it, and trundled her off to Hereford.[93] They
arrived in mid-May 1303, when she would have been about fifteen. Alice
testified that for three days she and her blind stepmother, Leticia (apparently

her father had remarried in London), prayed at the bishop's shrine. On the third night during the first bell for matins, as she believed, while sleeping Alice saw an old man with lily-white hair approach. He was dressed in white except for a black cap, part of which was hanging below his neck like the amice worn in church by chaplains; he wore, she recalled, a ring with four precious stones. He was carrying a little pyx.[94] Like the vision's hair and clothing, the liquid in the pyx was white.[95] The vision-figure anointed Alice with the "milk," starting between her breasts and moving down to her navel; then with both hands he anointed her left side, her knee and the afflicted foot. When he had finished, Alice — still in her vision state — raised her hands to heaven and shouted "Lord Saint Thomas, Lord Saint Thomas, have mercy on me!" The old man, smiling somewhat, made the sign of the cross on her face and forehead, although he did not actually touch her, and vanished. At that point Alice began stirring in her stepmother's lap. When Leticia asked why she was moving about, the girl replied that she could walk. She got up but fell down, then got up again and remained standing, although she could not walk without a stick. According to her father, after the cure was verified "certain individuals" — very likely some Hereford canons who appreciated the publicity — convinced them to remain in the cathedral for another week as proof of Cantilupe's miraculous powers. At last, leaving their wheelbarrow behind, probably as an offering, they returned to London; on the way Alice sometimes used her staff, sometimes not. Upon arrival, father and daughter thanked everyone who had helped to fund their pilgrimage.

Apart from providing a case study in William's devotion to his daughter, this testimony yields additional glimpses of English society and the life into which poverty had forced Alice. Parent and child had supported themselves on London charity for some ten years. The places where these indigents did their begging constituted, presumably, part of a circuit followed by other unfortunates. It included, according to the manuscript, the churches of St. Giles outside Cripplegate, St. Clement Danes, Saint Martin in the Fields, All Saints at the Haymarket, and "other London churches." As in many parts of the Catholic world today, the poor congregated around their holy places. Another aspect of life illuminated by this account has to do with the pilgrims who went to Hereford. The variety among the fictional pilgrims of the *Canterbury Tales*, embracing "types" from all ranks of contemporary society, is at least partially reflected in the small band of pilgrims who left London for Cantilupe's tomb about a generation before Chaucer's birth: in addition to the beggar girl Alice, her father William and stepmother Leticia, there was William Prior, perpetual chaplain of All Saints Haymarket;

Thomas de Gisors and Lady Margery Gisors (probably, given this title, "Lady," of elevated society); Gervase and Margery de Moulers (again, probably a married couple); and William of Oxford, who testified that he earned his living by manual labor, hauling casks of wine from ships and cellars with ropes and other devices. There are other parallels here between medieval art and life: just as William and Alice had rested in Southwark on their first night in London, Chaucer's band of pilgrims spent their last night in London "In Southwerk at the Tabard" before setting out next day, "The holy blisful martir for to seke. . . ."

Parental Negligence

The anguish and pain of parents as they witnessed, or were told about, their children's mishaps is evident in many accident cases. These instances weaken the postulate, which one hears less and less often, that medieval parents in general were uncaring or indifferent to the injuries, illnesses, or deaths of their sons and daughters. On the other hand, some parents were careless, or very casual, when dealing with their young offspring. Perhaps simple ignorance of children's limitations lies behind some of the medieval cases of parental "negligence," as it sometimes does in modern examples. In medieval Pomerania, was it negligence or mere inexperience that led a young mother (age eighteen) to give her nine-month-old child a small bone from a suckling pig to chew on—with the result that the child nearly choked to death?[96] On the other hand, in some instances clearly we are confronted with very serious lapses. This has been noted in other studies: basing his analysis on Scandinavian miracle records, Christian Krötzl, after documenting many examples of parental love and care, considers it "astonishing" that on occasion "small children were left without supervision even for relatively lengthy periods at night and during winter." He illustrates this in the case of a two-year-old Swedish boy left alone in bed on a cold night while his parents attended to affairs elsewhere. The child got out of bed in the darkness and wandered into the forest. The parents and neighbors found him the next day, still alive. Another infant, left alone one November evening, nearly froze to death after climbing out from under the bedding.[97] Parental neglect is explicitly mentioned in a Pomeranian case involving Elizabeth and her seven-month-old daughter, Margaret.[98] One night, as she took the baby from the cradle, it seemed to Elizabeth that the infant had died. She and her husband became greatly distressed, not only because of the girl's condition but also because they once had a little boy who, "because of their negligence," died after falling into some boiling water. They feared the recurrence of infamy, when people might say "Look! Coming from a party, again they neglected *(neglexerunt)* their child."[99] The parents were especially concerned since they had, in fact, again been at a party the evening that Margaret seemed to have died. The implication seems to be that when they came home to bed, they were still feeling the effects of the conviviality. Drunkenness (in the mother) was also hinted at in a case to be described, concerning Roger of Conway.

An English case in which negligence was an important factor began just before six on a Wednesday morning in the spring, around 1304, when Robert and Letitia were at work in their fields near Tewkesbury.[100] Part of their house had recently burned down, and they were plowing up the ground in the area where their hall used to be, perhaps to clear ground for new building, or even for spring planting. Robert was at the left, guiding the four oxen drawing a two-wheeled plow, Letitia was on the right. Their son Geoffrey, about eighteen months old, was lying asleep on the ground.[101] After several passes back and forth across the area, suddenly Letitia saw that the right wheel, which was of wood, without an iron rim, was only a few feet from her son's head. Robert, on the other side of the plow and animals, heard his wife's screams as the wheel crushed the infant's head. Stopping the animals, Robert examined his son, who had been sleeping on his stomach. The wheel had passed over Geoffrey's ear and temple; on picking him up, Robert saw that a stone the size of a large nut had been pressed into the ear next to the earth, drawing blood. It seemed to Robert that the soft skull had become elongated. After attempting to squeeze the boy's head back into shape, they concluded that he had died. The parents, as they later testified, were in a quandary, afraid to report the incident and risk the expense of going before the royal court, perhaps being jailed, and seeing their animals, plow, and other goods confiscated.[102] Robert told Letitia to say nothing to anyone; they even considered running away. They put the infant into their bed in a corner of the house that had survived the fire and, from morning to afternoon, they called and shook the child, whose body grew cold and rigid. Toward late afternoon Robert, recalling the wonders reported of Cantilupe, measured the child; on their knees the parents tearfully begged for the restoration of their boy, saying the *Pater, Credo* and *Ave* several times. By nightfall they were still huddled in the corner of their burned-out house in the midst of the darkened fields, watching over Geoffrey by the light of a few candles. As they continued to pray through the night, at one point Letitia felt Geoffrey take a breath. Finally, at dawn their son began to babble. Holding a candle nearer his face, they saw that his eyes were moving. After Letitia fed him, by midmorning he was out of danger. By the third day he seemed nearly normal, except for swelling and bruising on the head; even three months afterward, there was still some discoloration and swelling above the eyebrows. The family had gone to Cantilupe's tomb every year since the accident in 1304, and on this occasion, in 1307, they happened to arrive in Hereford while the commissioners were taking evidence.

No doubt modern notions of parental negligence are out of place when examining some of these medieval events, and it is a cliché that the "negligent" parents of one culture are the "normal" parents of another.[103] However, contemporary awareness of parental negligence was indicated in several examples already provided, and even more clearly in the following case. The distinguished Sir John of St. John, Lieutenant of Aquitaine and household knight of King Edward I (d. 1307), died on Thursday, September 6, 1302.[104] A year later at Conway, on the Welsh border, the lord bishop of Bangor and other ecclesiastical and secular dignitaries were observing the anniversary of Sir John's death by offering a Mass in his honor on September 7, in the church of the Blessed Mary. Unexpectedly, a group of townspeople burst into the church, interrupting this staid ecclesiastical business, to announce the miraculous resuscitation of a child who had fallen into the dry ditch around the castle. Conway was a "planned" settlement, a bastion of English presence and power in Wales; the town walls were actually an extension of the castle. The ditch into which the child fell had been excavated during the construction of the castle, completed in 1292. The miracle of resuscitation was attributed to Cantilupe, once a member of the king's circle of advisors, whose name would have been known to the notables present in the church. After the excitement had subsided, on that very day they composed a letter commemorating the wonderful event and sent this, bearing their pendant seals, to the bishop's Hereford shrine. Four years later the papal canonization investigators summoned several of the original witnesses to Hereford, to provide *viva voce* evidence. The letter of 1303 and the testimony of 1307 provide detailed information about the accidental death and recovery of Roger of Conway.[105] The essence of the letter, dated September 7, 1303, was as follows: On the night of September 6, 1303 Roger, age two years and three months, son of Dionysia and a servant of Conway Castle named Gervase, fell into the ditch (twenty-eight feet deep) around the castle, where he lay "naked and dead" until discovered early next morning. The town coroners arrived to inquire into the death, but a townsman made the sign of the cross over the boy with a penny that he dedicated to Thomas Cantilupe, and "in the twinkling of an eye" the child revived.[106] He was carried to his mother, who breast-fed him and then, accompanied by a crowd, took him into the church, where Sir John's anniversary services were under way. There, as the child fully revived, a *Te Deum* was sung in the presence of the notables, who then sent a letter about these events to Hereford.

Four years later several witnesses provided fuller testimony on the matter. Dionysia and Gervase, who was a cook for Lord William de Cycons, knight, constable of Conway Castle, were characterized as poor people *(pauperes)* who lived in a house "a stone's throw" from the castle.[107] On the evening of September 6, Gervase left the house where his wife lived and went to a vigil in the church of the Blessed Mary for two deceased castle servants. Dionysia did not accompany her husband, remaining at home with another castle servant, Wenthliana. Gervase last saw his son Roger tied in his cradle "as infants are [usually] bound."[108] He also left his daughters Agnes, then about three, and Isolda, about five, in the house with their mother. Later that evening, Dionysia and Wenthliana left the house to go to the vigils, putting the two girls into one bed and leaving Roger asleep in his cradle. They closed but did not lock the door: it could not be barred from the inside, Dionysia explained, since the girls were asleep. The two women then went to the church, some five hundred feet from the site of the castle drawbridge; their house was probably somewhere between the church and the bridge. Roger awoke later on that night. It was afterward surmised that — as infants do *(infantile more)*, the record notes — because he wished to go to the castle, having gone there with his father on other occasions, Roger got up naked, left the house, and made for the castle bridge. In the darkness, not realizing that the bridge had been raised, he fell into the ditch. A castle guest testified that he heard a child cry out, early that night, but hearing nothing else, he paid it no further attention. Meanwhile, Roger's parents were in church. Gervase, for reasons he does not disclose, began to worry about his son. Returning home by candlelight, he found the door open, his two daughters asleep, but no Roger: the swaddling clothes were in the cradle along with the child's other clothing. Gervase woke up some neighbors, but they knew nothing. Assuming that someone had taken Roger into their home, Gervase returned to church and reported to Dionysia that their son was missing. She later claimed that she too assumed that a neighbor had taken in the toddler. In contrast to his wife's somewhat sang-froid attitude, Gervase testified that the longer he remained in church, the more disturbed *(turbatus)* he became. Again he returned to look for Roger with a light, as before; and, again, his son was nowhere to be found. Since it was very late (vigils lasted all night), Gervase did not rouse his neighbors a second time. He returned to the church, where he remained until the vigils were over.

At dawn, castle personnel spotted Roger lying in the ditch. The constable ordered John de Griffin (castle gatekeeper) to examine the boy, who had frozen spittle on his mouth and was lying with his feet pointing toward the town, his head toward the castle. De Griffin — who later testified that when he heard that a child had been found in the ditch, he feared that it might be his own son, whom he kept with him in the castle — picked up Roger, saying that he was dead; he wanted to take him from the ditch, but John de Boys, seneschal of the castle, ordered him to leave the boy as found and to fetch the coroners. The child's parents, meanwhile, returned home just before dawn. Although her son was still missing, Dionysia fell asleep because, as she later testified, of her great anxiety (about Roger, presumably) and her exhaustion after the all-night vigils. Gervase was about to return to work in the castle when the constable, Lord William, ran up to ask where he had been that night. Rather than first telling him about the accident, the constable asked Gervase about his own whereabouts: was this an imputation of blame or indication of suspicion? When the father responded that he had been in church at a vigil, the constable replied that he had vigiled badly *(male vigilaverat)*, because his son had been found dead in the castle ditch. At the site of the accident, Gervase asked whether he might recover his child, but the constable refused to allow anyone to move the body until the coroners arrived. Gervase testified that when his wife heard what had happened, she rushed to the bridge, where neighbors had to restrain her from throwing herself into the ditch with her son. Seeing Dionysia in this state, Gervase clambered up to the bridge to console her, at which point the coroners appeared. According to her own testimony, however, Dionysia learned of her son's accident from the gatekeeper John de Griffin, who came to her house to ask where her son was, an approach similar to the constable's approach to the husband; one of the witnesses had heard that Dionysia had been drunk that evening. When she replied to Griffin that she did not know her son's whereabouts, John told her that he was lying dead in the castle ditch. At this, she collapsed to the ground, nearly out of her senses. Her neighbors tied her up to keep her from leaving the house.[109] The commissioners did not probe further into these discrepant statements; did she escape from her house and rush to the bridge?

Whatever that particular sequence of events may have been, the coroners Stephen de Gaimowe and William of Nottingham, with William their scribe, arrived along with a jury of twelve townsmen. Having taken sureties from Griffin as "first finder" of the body, they all went into the ditch and examined the boy, "as pertained to their office," the record notes, to see whether he had any wounds, and the length, breadth, and depth of these, which would be recorded in writing and turned over to the coroners' superiors.[110] Having physically examined the body, the coroners and jury withdrew near the bridge to write their report. They had determined that the boy was dead, being "as stiff as wood and cold as stone."[111] Meanwhile, John

Seward, a townsman, ignorant of, or ignoring, the prohibition about dis-
turbing the body, went to Roger, still lying in the ditch. John had visited
Cantilupe's tomb and was aware of the miracles reported there. He bent a
penny, made the sign of the cross on the child, and vowed to take the coin
and child to the Hereford shrine. He then hung the coin around Roger's
neck with a piece of string. After opening the boy's mouth and seeing the
tongue move, he called to the coroners and other bystanders. William, the
coroners' scribe, had just set pen to parchment to begin recording the
inquiry into the child's death, when John shouted.[112] The jury and coroners
hurried back down into the ditch. The coroners ordered John, then holding
the child in his arms, to put Roger down. After some movement was seen in
the body, the boy was carried into Richard le Mercer's house nearby, then
taken to his mother's home. He seemed dead—Dionysia could sense no
breath in him, even though she placed her tongue in his mouth, which was
so cold that it pained her. She then cut open her blouse down to her belt and
put Roger next to her skin to warm him. Another witness claimed that the
boy was also wrapped in moistened linen and warmed. Everyone—coroners, jurymen, and bystanders—followed Dionysia, still carrying Roger
next to her flesh, into the sacred ambience of the church, where services, as
it happened, were being held for Sir John of St. John. Once inside,
Dionysia sat with Roger before the cross. Over 200 people, Dionysia
believed, were there. The bishop of Bangor, celebrating Mass, came to her
and made the sign of the cross with his thumb on the boy's forehead.
Dionysia then felt him move and his heart beat; at this marvel a *Te Deum* was
sung and the notables' letter was drawn up. Before day's end Roger could
stand up unaided and was also feeding at his mother's breast.

The testimony indicates, *inter alia,* how variable were contemporary perceptions of life and "death": the coroners released the body as "alive" thanks
to Cantilupe's miraculous help, but the mother, receiving it, seems to have
believed that her son was still "dead"; he does not appear to have been fully
resuscitated until inside the church and after the bishop had touched the
body—without reference to Cantilupe.[113] The Conway case also presents an
opportunity to observe a shift from one type of historical record with one set
of underlying purposes (a coroners' report) to another type with its own purposes (a canonization process). Normally, by the time that England's county
coroners had arrived on the scene, victims usually were, and had been for
some time, well and truly dead. This example is unusual in the speed with
which coroners, their jury, and William their scribe began the inquest.

Toward the conclusion of the parents' testimony in 1307, when the
papal commissioners asked Gervase how he thought the accident had

occurred, he responded by suggesting that Roger had unwrapped himself in the cradle. He was not certain whether his son usually did this, since sometimes he lived with his wife in the house, sometimes in the castle where he worked. Gervase assumed that, when his son awoke to find only his sleeping sisters in the house, he opened the door and made for the castle, where he often had gone with his father. Since it was dark and the bridge had been raised, Roger fell into the ditch. Finally the boy's father testified (in French) that neither he nor his wife had been drunk that night. Dionysia added her own concluding comments, testifying—in English since, as she admitted, she knew neither French nor Latin—that she and her husband were poor but led a good life.[114] While pregnant with Roger,[115] she continued, she and Gervase had gone on pilgrimage to Thomas's tomb at Hereford, some eighty-five miles distant. Dionysia went barefoot; her husband, shod. She had asked the dead bishop to be her personal "helper" *(adiutor)* and the helper of the child in her womb. Within three weeks of the miracle, she claimed, she and her husband had taken Roger to Cantilupe's tomb, accompanied by Lord William the castle constable; John de Havering, knight; the clerics Thomas of Cambridge and Hugh of Leominster; and many others.[116] After telling their story to the Hereford canons and handing over their sealed letter, the party remained in the city for a week. During their return to Conway in early October 1303, before they were forty miles from Hereford, Roger's swelling and scabs were gone.[117]

Three important elements—surroundings that predisposed to accidents, children's physical limitations, and parental negligence—that contributed to the Conway incident also came together in a late fifteenth-century example. After prefacing one of his narrations with a moralizing warning about careless parents who endangered their children, the recorder of Henry VI's miracles presented the case of John Hargrave and his son, also John, about fifteen months old. On a religious feast day in November, the parents went to the village church for vespers, leaving the boy at home—quite negligently, the commentator adds, for they must have been aware of his helplessness; at his age, the infant could barely get around with the help of benches or stools, usually crawling rather than walking.[118] As John was wandering alone about the cottage *(domuncula)* he fell into the hearth, where a fire had been set for his comfort (evilly so, remarks the commentator). He could not move, and no one was there to help him. Meanwhile the church service concluded. As the boy's parents walked home with some neighbors, they could smell something burning; no one could imagine where the stench was coming from. As John's parents approached their own house, their anxiety grew; when the mother and a friend, Joan Sherman, ran into the cottage, they burst into tears at what they saw. The father came in, followed by the crowd. They found that the skin and hair of the child's head were burned away, his face grotesquely swollen; an eye and ear were badly disfigured. About an hour after the parents, godparents, and neighbors began praying to King Henry, the child began recovering. By the beginning of spring, five months later, the burned skin had sloughed off and new flesh had appeared. When the father visited the king's shrine at Windsor in early May to fulfill his vow, he presented part of the child's burned scalp, which was suspended above the tomb—and is still there, concluded the commentator, to this very day *(usque hodie)*. Perhaps John's parents, on the evening of the tragedy, had underestimated their son's curiosity or his mobility; perhaps they assumed that he would have recognized the obvious dangers of fire. Regardless, it was patently negligent to have left a toddler alone with an open fire. Some adults who were careless about children and fire endangered themselves as well, as in a southern French case. A two-year-old, sleeping with or near her parents, knocked over a candle and set alight the straw mattress and the hangings around the bed.[119] Fortunately, the parents awoke in time to control the fire, saving themselves and their child.

Responses to Accidents: Physical Remedies

Even though a child might have been thought "dead" after being suffocated or pulled out of the water, there were resuscitation attempts, which took many forms. Rather than immediately dropping to their knees in prayer, villagers, kin, even strangers carried out all sorts of physical operations, trying to force life back into the inert form. In miracle records, though not in coroners' rolls, these efforts were successful. As suggested at the outset of this study, when dealing with what purports to have been a miraculous recovery from death, speculation about what "really" happened is, for the most part, a fruitless exercise. Professor Kelly's injunction that readers should be "spared the trite reductionism of 'explaining' the miraculous" deserves approbation.[120] Given the vagueness of medieval notions about time generally, and specifically times of submersion, discovery, resuscitation, and recovery; and given equally vague estimates of just when (and which) signs of death were to be identified in the victims, this cloud of uncertainty must inevitably vitiate attempts to discover "the truth" about these cases. For instance, the body of five-year-old John, being taken from a pond in which he had drowned, was kept at home for two days "lest perchance any sign of life might appear in him."[121] Nevertheless, at the risk of skirting the Kelly precept and toppling into a reductionist abyss, it may be illuminating to review some modern instances of child drownings followed by resuscitation. To begin with, twentieth-century children have survived after being submerged for more than one hour; usually, in such cases, the water was very cold.[122] In commenting on how hypothermia may aid children's survival under water, one team of specialists noted that some victims "could be revived long after recovery from the water. . . . For this reason it is sensible to continue resuscitatory aid as long as several hours after a body has been recovered," especially in fresh-water drownings.[123] On the other hand, children have died up to two days after their apparently successful resuscitation from near-drowning.[124] Sophisticated equipment and care greatly facilitates the resuscitation of today's drowning victims, but it still includes immersion in warm water, wrapping in heated blankets, and the drinking of warm fluids.[125] In the rescue of Joanna of Marden/Wisteston, the child's body was warmed by a fire and the mother's body; in a French case two women placed the infant in warm water while attempting to revive him; little William, drowned in Summergil Brook, was stripped and placed by a fire, his body being turned so as to be heated evenly; a child pulled from a well at Salisbury was taken home senseless but, being wrapped and warmed at a fire, recovered; another child victim of drowning, in Scandinavia, was given warm beer.[126] In addition, "drowned" children were agitated by being upended—a French commentator claimed that this was "the usual remedy in such cases"—rolled about on the ground, beaten on the soles of the feet, and fondled and massaged by parents, kin and onlookers.[127] Here it may be apposite to note that James P. Orlowski, a Cleveland physician specializing in pediatric intensive care, in a 1988 editorial about drowning in the normally reserved *Journal of the American Medical Association,* used the terms "miraculous recovery" and "miraculous recoveries" to describe resuscitations after unusually long intervals of time.[128] This is by no means an unfavorable reflection on Orlowski's credibility or the utility of his article, but merely an example of how easy it is, even for today's medical professionals, to slip into such language.

Nonsupernatural responses were activated in all sorts of cases, not just drownings. In several examples, bystanders—kin, neighbors, or even strangers—applied physical manipulation, making contact with the affected children through touching, caressing, prodding, shaking, hugging, feeling for a pulse, for breath, for motion of the heart. When everything seemed to fail, the group eventually lost hope and stopped trying physical means, turning instead to supernatural assistance. This was a common progression of events in most of the "miracles." Doctors' efforts, as we have seen, were another nonsupernatural response. Although mentioned more often in cases of children's illness, medical specialists make an appearance in the accident records as well; recall, for instance, the London surgeon who donated his expertise in attempting to help Alice, the young beggar who had injured her foot while en route to Compostella. Given the purpose of these records, however, it is unlikely that any successful medical intervention would be acknowledged, whether in treating illness or in assisting accident victims. Three Italian cases illustrate this. After a boy suffered a compound fracture of his left leg while climbing a wall, infection set in. For two days the child lay as if dead; indeed the doctors gave him up for dead *(pro mortuo)*, saying that no medical help in the world could save him.[129] In the second example, even though Angelucia's husband was a doctor *(medicus)*, when their son scalded himself badly, his father's medical expertise was of no use at all.[130] In a third incident, while a mother was carrying her daughter to a doctor for treatment of a head injury, she stopped off at a saint's shrine. This action, as it turned out, obviated the need for mundane medical help.[131] In the accident in which a Norfolk peasant accidentally struck his daughter with a pitch-fork, the doctor summoned by the peasant's lord despaired of her life, believing that her brain had been injured.[132] In all of these cases, saintly assistance alone was credited with success in restoring the health or life of affected children. Of course, as in the case of illness, the reputed efficacy of other remedies was linked to a different level of the supernatural world: charms, philters, talismans and tokens, stones, herbs, potions and salves, administered by those who claimed to possess special knowledge and powers.[133] As noted, these were rarely mentioned in the miracle records, although canonization witnesses were routinely asked whether they thought a cure or resuscitation could have been effected through incantations, sortilege, superstitions, or the power of words or deeds, or through any medicinal, artificial, or natural remedies.[134] When the lame Alice of Lonsdale was testifying, she made a point of saying that she washed her injured foot in the fountain of St. Clement Danes not from any sense of devotion to the fountain or stream but because she had no other means of treating the wound.[135] Even more sinister were the implications behind the papal representatives' asking Gervase of Conway whether there were any magic-practicing women in Conway, by whose evil machinations his son Roger could have been transported into the castle ditch.[136] Obviously, the spectrum of medieval healing techniques and practitioners was extremely broad. A final example of yet another type of specialist comes from an Italian case reported in 1325: after Cicchus fell from a ladder and broke his hip, he was immobilized for seven weeks. It was believed by "those who know how to set bones" that he was doomed to permanent disability.[137] These "persons," neither surgeons nor *medici*, are akin to individuals known in France, for instance, as *rebouteux*, whose skills in the healing arts were still respected in the early twentieth century.[138] Although they specialized in caring for fractures, sprains, and neck and backaches, their repertoire extended to alleviating pain in various parts of the body, often by laying their hands on the afflicted area.

Responses to Accidents: Anger and Shame

Whatever the particular circumstances, and whether in the countryside or in town, as parents and neighbors gathered around a recently discovered victim, the outpouring of grief began. This very natural response is examined in the next chapter. Another emotion that surfaces occasionally in the records is anger. In a few cases, parents or other relatives set off in violent pursuit of the negligent or the careless who were thought to have injured their children. For example, around eleven one morning Thomas Plott's year-old daughter, Anna, playing "like any infant" by the public road in Sheppey, Kent, was run over by a loaded dung cart.[139] As the miracle recorder puts it, her tender little body ended up rather like a flat cake (or, in Eleanora Gordon's more vivid translation, "flat as a pancake").[140] The blood was flowing from Anna's eyes, nose, and mouth as her screaming mother gathered her up in her arms. Thinking that she was already dead, she put Anna down and began pursuing the peasant carter, shouting bitter accusations. Although Anna recovered, her arms were still bruised a week later. In contrast to this mundane English traffic accident, a French child was injured in the midst of festive celebrations, which may have made the child's apparent death even more distressing. In May around 1300, the people of Carpentras were enjoying their annual two-week merriment before Pentecost, decorating their houses, streets and squares with their best cloth hangings. There were games, processions, and feasts.[141] In one of the squares a crowd of dancing and singing revelers and trumpeters paused to unfurl a banner.[142] As a youth named Bernard rode up, his horse became skittish at the noise. Whether attempting to control the animal, to turn back, or simply to show off, gathering "as much force as he could muster," with a great shout Bernard spurred his horse, which—whatever the rider's intentions—charged into the crowd. As a result, five-year-old Raymundeta was crushed by the horse's hooves. The girl's twenty-eight-year-old kinsman James, who loved her very much, began chasing the rider with his drawn sword. He wanted to kill him, as he confessed to the papal tribunal some eight years later; but Bernard escaped. Someone picked up the trampled girl, whose head dangled "as with the dead," took her into a nearby house and put her on a mattress, while people gathered around her. Meanwhile, while fleeing his pursuer, Bernard happened to encounter his victim's mother, Rixendis, who, hearing some sort of commotion, had come out of her house to investigate. She knew Bernard—they were neighbors—and could see that he was terrified and pale; she said "Hey [*sic*] Bernard, what's going on with you? Come into my house and relax."[143] But Bernard curtly replied "Lady, let me go" and went off as quickly as possible, in great fear.[144] Rixendis continued walking toward the disturbance, when James came up with the terrible news. She rushed screaming to the square. Raymundeta's skin was bluish in color, her mouth full of froth. Although there were no detectable signs of life when Rixendis first examined her injured daughter, the child recovered within a few weeks.

As we have seen, the emotional gamut run by adults, especially parents, sometimes included, besides grief and anger, feelings of remorse, guilt, shame, or dishonor. When a child's injury or death was thought to be a result of parental negligence, these were perfectly understandable reactions. One September morning, as Mary was busily preparing her flour for the day's baking, her daughter Margery, five, went up to her as usual. As Margery approached, however, her mother shouted "Get away! Your hands are dirty!" The girl ran to wash in a nearby mill stream but was pulled in by the force of the water.[145] The mother was prostrated by grief, which probably was enhanced due to self-reproach. In an almost identical accident, a mother openly accused herself of the guilt of her child's "death." In this instance, after a five-year-old had helped her father slaughter a pig, he told her to wash off the blood in a pit of water. While doing so, she fell in. When the girl was recovered, the mother cried out to her neighbors that, if anyone was "guilty of this accident," she alone bore the blame, since (according to the Canterbury monk) she "should have provided someone to watch her, but I was blind."[146] Weeping copiously and calling on Becket, the mother continued to heap guilt upon herself, an interesting reaction since it was the father who actually sent the child into potential danger. Fear of dishonor was also noted in some cases, sometimes linked with anxiety about legal liability. When the villagers were discussing what to do with Joanna in the fishpond at Wisteston, one of them wanted to raise the hue and cry, but, as we have seen, the victim's own father asked him not to do so. The reason? According to the girl's rescuer, Adam was worried that they might "fall into ill repute." In another detailed English case, the drowning at How Caple, a witness told the papal commissioners that they turned first to spiritual assistance because they wished to avoid the "scandal" associated with raising the hue and cry. In a Pomeranian case, a similar fear of dishonor was perhaps behind a husband's threats to his wife when he came home to find that their daughter had injured herself with a knife. He warned that if she died, his wife would never again have a day's peace.[147]

Long-Term Effects on Children's Lives

When children died as the result of illness or injury, no doubt parents and kin were emotionally touched, whether for a short period or the rest of their lives. Similarly, when children came through their harrowing experiences successfully, afterward not only their families but they themselves probably were affected, transiently or permanently. Occasionally the records show the extent to which "miracles" were life-altering experiences: an encounter with the supernatural must have left its mark on many adults and their children. Joanna of Marden was one such child. In April 1288, after her rescue from the fishpond in the pub garden, her parents took her to Hereford and placed her on Cantilupe's tomb. Eyewitnesses claimed that she seemed especially radiant and lovely on that day. Everyone's gaze focused on her: the admiring bystanders included Wisteston and Marden villagers, people from other villages, and the inhabitants of Hereford itself, who had run out to touch and kiss the little girl as the procession approached the city. We lose sight of Joanna for several years after her miraculous rescue from "death," until September of 1307, when she appeared in Hereford before Cantilupe's canonization commission. She was then in her early twenties. Some nineteen years had passed since the day she sat atop the bishop's tomb, beaming at her well-wishers. Her testimony uncovers aspects of her life during the intervening years. To begin with, since the miracle, she and her family (by 1307 Adam and Cecilia had produced five sons and three daughters) had gone on pilgrimage to Cantilupe's shrine at least once, sometimes several times, each year. Since the distance was only about six miles across flat countryside, this was no great accomplishment, although they claimed to make the trek barefoot. Her father noted that they did this especially on the feast day (May 20) of Ethelbert, patron saint of the cathedral; in 1307 Cantilupe, not yet an officially recognized saint, had no feast day of his own. Each year, as Joanna prayed before the tomb, she probably relived that wonderful day when, because of saintly intervention, she was the center of all attention. In fact, she testified that she — and her mother, interestingly — frequently dreamed about going to the tomb and praying there.[148] Whenever Joanna and her family went into the city on pilgrimage, year after year, others in the cathedral must have recognized and congratulated them once again for their great fortune. Indeed, apparently Joanna was something of a local celebrity: according to her father, many noble folk *(nobiles)* from distant places still, after some nineteen years, came to see her because of the miracle.[149] The villagers continued to call her "Adam's daughter whom St. Thomas had saved"; she was also known in her village, Joanna testified, as "St. Thomas's virgin," a claim substantiated under oath by one of her neighbors.[150] This expression was more than a mere manner of speaking, for it seems that Joanna really did see herself as the saint's "virgin": she testified that because of her devotion to Thomas, "up until the present time [she] was unwilling to marry, though she had been urged by her parents and others to accept a suitable man."[151] As a result of her spiritual encounter, Joanna seems to have dedicated herself to lifelong virginity. Celibacy was an option for many lay women, even within marriage — as in the case of the unforgettable Margery Kempe (d. 1439) of Norfolk. Joanna's father's testimony shows that he was proud of her status; her mother, however, seems to have said little or nothing about Joanna's virginity or refusal to marry.[152] For us, Joanna's story does not end when the 1307 commission finished its work, dismissed the witnesses, and sent its report to the papal curia. Between August 1318 and March 1320, when a committee of cardinals scrutinized twenty-six of Cantilupe's miracles, the first one considered and debated was Joanna's.[153] In April 1320 Cantilupe was officially canonized, and Joanna's was the first to be mentioned among the miracles referred to in the papal bull. It is pleasant to imagine Joanna, who would have been about thirty-seven, standing, probably in a place of honor, in Hereford Cathedral on that day in 1320 when the papal bull canonizing Cantilupe was read to the assembled crowd. Whether she was there or not, or even among the living in 1320, Joanna's miracle was celebrated annually at Hereford and other churches on Cantilupe's feast day (October 2) when the liturgical offices and Mass of St. Thomas of Hereford were intoned. Every year until the Reformation, at a certain point in the liturgy one of the readings began, *Quedam namque puella etatis annorum quinque* . . . , "And a certain girl five years of age lay drowned in a deep pit for a long time, dead. . . ."[154]

Someone else who might have been given a place of honor in Hereford Cathedral when Cantilupe's canonization was announced was Roger, who had fallen into the ditch at Conway castle. His miracle also was mentioned in the pope's bull. As in Joanna's case, there are indications that his miraculous encounter with death had long-term effects, although of a different nature from St. Thomas's virgin. In 1311, when Roger would have been about ten, Ralph Baldock, bishop of London, wrote to the abbot and convent of St. Osyth in Essex. Baldock reminded the abbot and canons of their agreement to pay an annual pension of six marks toward Roger's education. Subsequent to the conclusion of the Cantilupe canonization inquiry in 1307, Baldock, one of the papal commissioners, had turned Roger over to Thomas, one of his own London canons, to be educated;[155] now he was reminding the abbot of his promise of financial assistance in the venture. Baldock also expressed the hope that eventually, after Roger had completed his education, he himself or the abbot could provide the young man with a clerical position.[156] Apparently, as Baldock sat with his colleagues in 1307 listening to testimony about Cantilupe's miracles, he was particularly struck by the incident involving little Roger and his parents, who called themselves "poor people." For whatever reasons, he took upon himself the responsibility for Roger's future. Since Baldock died in 1313 and no more is heard of Roger, we can say only that, at least during his early years, the boy's life continued to be affected by his miraculous resurrection. One can only speculate about the extent to which other children's lives were similarly changed, over the longer term, by their near-death encounters. In a late-twelfth-century French case, a toddler's escape from death was physically memorialized in the midst of the village itself: Ernulph, about eighteen months of age, fell into the village well. Although his parents, paralyzed with grief, were unable to pull him out, a neighbor woman and her daughter took him from the well and tried to revive him, with no effect. After being wrapped up and carried to St. Laurence's tomb, he recovered that evening. Those reporting this miracle claimed that people still pointed out the site of the event, saying "Here is the well where Ernulph drowned." When the villagers made this report, Ernulph was about forty years old.[157]

Another example of how children's miracles affected them as adults is provided in the case of five-year-old Mary, who fell into a well on August 4, 1244. Upon being discovered next morning, she was pulled from the water and put on the altar of St. Gertrude (seventh-century abbess of Nivelle in Brabant), where everyone prayed for her. After her revival the bells were rung and the miracle celebrated. The bishop ordered a procession and Mass in St. Gertrude's memory every anniversary of the miracle, with a forty-day indulgence for those attending; on those days, Mary's miracle was to be recited before all the people. Meanwhile, Mary grew up *(adoleverat)* and, after returning from a pilgrimage to Rome, she humbly served in the same church where she had miraculously recovered. Every year until her death, presumably, she and the congregation would have heard the story of her own wonderful resuscitation.[158] The same sort of effect is suggested in the case of Agnes, the fourteen-year-old child of John and Joan Bromley of Salisbury. Her decision to become a nun may well have been influenced by her recovery from a serious injury. One December day as she was going down to the lower level of her house—down steps, perhaps, or a ladder—she fell onto a sharp spit, hot from the fire, which had been propped with its point upward. The spit entered under her navel and emerged between her shoulders.[159] Her mother rushed up and pulled out the spit as Agnes lay on the ground, while her father and other neighbors knelt to pray tearfully, vowing a pilgrimage to Osmund's shrine.[160] Agnes revived: within two days she was out of bed and walking about the house; after ten days she had recovered completely, and a few days later she went with friends and parents to give thanks at Osmund's tomb in Salisbury. A short time afterward she relinquished the world to become a nun at Amesbury, about eight miles to the north. When testimony about Osmund's miracles was being collected, Agnes, then sixteen, was summoned from her convent. She corroborated the statements of her parents and a neighbor, in the midst of her testimony mentioning something that suggests why, perhaps, she had shifted her life from the secular to the religious plane: after she had fallen on the spit and miraculously recovered, she stated, she "well remembered" her mother telling her how she had died.[161]

A variety of aftereffects marked the minds and bodies of other children "miraculously" saved from the consequences of their accidents. William of Donington's mother, testifying two years after the near drowning of her toddler, told the papal examiners that her son was still terrified of bridges and water. It is likely that other medieval children saved from drowning did not escape wholly unscathed. A modern specialist suggests that for every child who dies by drowning, 500 or 600 others experience near-drowning accidents, some of them so serious that the victims require resuscitation. This is significant since up to one-third of resuscitated children are "moderately to severely neurologically damaged" as a result of their near-drowning experiences.[162] Sometimes, in the Middle Ages as in modern cases, the lingering consequences were physical as well as spiritual or psychological. When Nicholas of How Caple testified about his own rescue from the river some eight years earlier, he looked "somewhat listless" to the commissioners. He claimed, when they asked if he had fully recovered, that ever since the incident he often felt a heaviness in his body, especially near his heart.[163] Other child survivors carried the physical marks of their encounters for a long time afterward: during the four years that had elapsed between Alice of Lonsdale's Hereford cure and her appearance before the papal commissioners on August 10, 1307, several people had seen her walking about London with a stick or cane. The commissioners had her walk with her stick and without it; she could walk unaided, they noted, though somewhat lamely *(claudicando)* because of her damaged ligaments. The pope's men also observed scars and concavities on her leg. Ever since John of Little Marcle had been rescued from the watering hole, his mother testified, there were marks *(intersigna)* in his eyes and nose, and some of his skin was discolored, a mixed yellow-green. When John was brought before the examining board, they agreed that these indications were still visible. In the case of the infant run over by his parents while plowing near their burned-down house, when the notaries and commissioners examined him at age five, they discovered that though he had no scars above his ear where the wheel passed, his head seemed rather pointed.

Aside from bent bodies, roughened hands, sunburned skin — in a famous passage, Froissart refers to peasants as "small and dark" — and the other effects of a life spent mainly out of doors, many peasants and their children would have had scars and badly knit limbs, the results of the daily hazards and accidents of an agrarian routine. But the signs borne by the children and adults who appeared before canonization commissions were scars of honor, almost of sanctity. These marks of a saint's concern, incorporated into the bodies of the fortunates rescued by heavenly largesse, were for rustics and other nonprivileged groups their own stigmata, analogues of the honorable battle wounds that were a prerogative of the fighting classes and of the visible, bloody marks that a few living holy men and women exhibited during the later Middle Ages.[164] The scars of the miraculously saved signified not ignominy or mere accident but grace, the primary exemplar being Christ himself: on the walls of many medieval parish churches the Christ figure was not only crucified but gruesomely attacked by innumerable instruments of daily life used by craftsmen who, in ignoring their religious duties, thereby continued to "wound" Christ. Toward the end of the medieval period, ordinary parishioners would have been aware — in some areas at least — of a growing dedication to the five wounds of Christ; in the sixteenth-century English Pilgrimage of Grace the mainly rustic participants demonstrating against Henrician policies carried a banner of the Five Wounds. Tangible signs of their saintly salvation, therefore, must have enhanced the spiritual repute of miraculously rescued children in the eyes of their neighbors and in their own as well. Finally, these scars, portable and visible proofs of saintly powers, reinforced enthusiasm for a curative cult just as much as sermons and bell-ringing and official pronouncements by priests, bishops and even popes.

The citizens of Hereford, flocking to little Joanna of Marden as she was being brought to Cantilupe's shrine, hoping to kiss, touch, or just to see her, show how well recognized was this "separated" state, even in the absence of scars or other physical indicators. Some children carried with them an awareness of their own special status for a good portion, or for all, of their lives. However, as in the case of "miraculously" revived infants or of sick children made well, some of these lucky accident victims' lives were cut short from other causes: in one case, only six months later; in another a year after the miracle (six years before a papal commission heard testimony); in a third instance, a girl died two years after her miraculous rescue.[165]

CHILDHOOD ACCIDENTS: OVERVIEW AND ANALYSES

It is relatively easy to establish which of the two sexes was involved most often in these medieval accidents. Of the 156 victims described in our miracle records, 101 were boys (65 percent) and 55 were girls (35 percent). Among 127 medieval child victims of accidents whose sex was specified in the miracle accounts she reviewed, Eleanora Gordon found that 64 percent were boys, 36 percent girls.[166] Barbara Hanawalt, examining medieval Northamptonshire coroners' rolls — where no reputedly saintly interventions preserved the lives of the children — discovered a similar ratio: "the percentage of accidental deaths of boys under twelve was much higher than girls — 63 percent of all accidental deaths among children were male."[167] In discussing this imbalance, Hanawalt suggested that medieval infant boys tended to toddle "farther afield observing their father's work."[168] Since this work normally took place away from hearth and home, the risks arising from lower levels of supervision and a potentially dangerous environment were greater. We have seen little Roger tumbling into the castle ditch at Conway as he retraced the path he had "often" taken while accompanying his father, the castle baker, to work. Girls trailing their mothers around the cottage presumably would have been "safer," although the case of the toddler who hanged herself while her mother worked in another room reminds us that this was not always so. From one point of view, then, gender differences in the children who became accident victims were, at least in part, related to medieval cultural traditions.

From another viewpoint, however, the fact that figures for modern child victims of accidental injury and death are so similar to medieval ones raises questions that admit of no simple answers. Although there are manifest dangers in applying modern findings to medieval circumstances and one cannot press medieval-modern comparisons very far, especially when dealing with medieval cases that spanned four centuries, nevertheless the data do suggest some interesting correlations. The ratio of 65 percent male to 35 percent female victims that appears in the medieval accident reports still holds true today: studies of twentieth-century accident victims indicate that globally, in developed as well as in developing countries, the ratio of boys to girls (excluding firearms and automobiles as causes) is about two to one.[169] In the face of these statistics, a legitimate question is why, in medieval Europe as in the modern world, more boys than girls were and are accident and drowning victims. What — to many parents — may seem an "ordinary" fact of life, that boys "naturally" get themselves into mischief more readily than girls, is far easier to observe than to explain. Modern researchers have provided abundant evidence to indicate that, between birth and about nine months to one year of age, the period during which children are wholly dependent on older caregivers, accident rates for both sexes are about the same. From about age one, however, when infants begin to develop greater mobility, curiosity, and independence, boys begin to overtake girls as accident victims. As Avery and Jackson point out, for some twentieth-century observers, this difference may be related to a tendency to expose boys to risks more often, or more readily, than girls. For others it is viewed not as a result of cultural traditions but of genetics, in which purported higher levels of generalized physical activity and aggression among boys is biological. The disputes continue: the extent to which these factors are "genetically determined or culturally imbued by parents' and society's expectations of boyish vigor remains open to debate."[170] In an article published in 1987, it was noted that "Consistently over the past thirty years, 64 percent of all accidental fatalities of children in Canada involved boys. This figure is similar to that of other studies [references supplied], but few explanations for this sex difference have been offered."[171] Whatever the reasons may be, they seem to have been operative in medieval Europe just as they continue to be today.

The incidence of children's accidents tended to vary with age as well as gender. Of the 156 medieval accident cases, 105 included information on the ages of the child victims, producing a configuration as shown in figure 4.1. Confirmation of this trend is again supplied in Hanawalt's coroners' rolls, in which she found that "the number of accidents dropped dramatically for both boys and girls after they reached the age of four."[172] Gordon's figures also bear this out: "Forty-seven (58 per cent) of the children whose ages are known had an accidental injury before their fourth birthday."[173] As with gender, modern statistics about victims' ages bear similarities to medieval ones: in our study, 58 percent of girls and 61 percent of boys who were accident victims were four or younger, a pattern often repeated in modern reports. For instance, in a sample of 39,949 nonfatal home accidents recorded in the United Kingdom for 1988, 58 percent of the victims (both sexes) up to age fourteen were four or younger.[174] The same age configuration was discovered for victims of burns and drowning, in a survey of childhood accidents from fifty-eight countries in 1971 and 1981.[175] In two obvious respects, modern statistics differ from medieval ones: today automobile accidents cause more deaths and injuries to older children and teenagers than other causes, and drowning (the second most common cause of accidental death among modern children older than age five) has, in the words of one researcher, "become an accident of affluence" in developed countries, where recreational habits and the proliferation of swimming pools have had the expected effects on children's deaths from this cause.[176] Nevertheless, for children under ten, in modern drowning cases, as in medieval, the first through the fourth years are the most dangerous.[177] As a result of increasing affluence and the use of auto-mobiles, accidental death rates for twentieth-century children tend to increase from about age nine rather than to decrease. In the Middle Ages, however, if a child survived beyond about the fifth year, death before reaching adulthood probably would be caused not by accident but by illness.

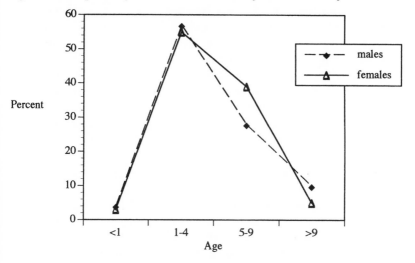

Figure 4.1 Age ranges of all accident victims for whom specific ages were reported (105 cases out of 156)

Any exploration of the relationships between age and gender in medieval children's accidents also must take account of the types of mishap suffered. The categories are shown in figure 4.2, which indicates that near drowning was the most common cause of children's accidental "deaths" reported in the miracle lists and canonization testimony. It accounted for 79 of the 156 cases, or 51 percent, in which the ratio of boys to girls was two to one (67 percent to 33 percent), which is similar to modern figures for this particular accident.[178] Throughout medieval Europe, especially from the thirteenth century on, church councils and synods drew attention to these threats to children's lives and typically directed priests to warn their parishioners to guard their offspring from the dangers of "fire and water." This warning was found in other writings as well: as Philip of Novara wrote, about 1250, "People usually say that children should be kept from fire and water until their seventh year; one could just as well say the tenth year...."[179] Analysis of the circumstances of the most common medieval mishap, drowning, provides some suggestions about the effects of age and gender in this recurring tragedy.

Some drownings occurred in domestic contexts—while bathing, or in vats, water butts, or nearby wells. Others took place outside the immediate vicinity of the home, in ponds, streams, rivers, pits—although some of these might be near the victim's house—and mills, which were particularly dangerous for little boys. Figure 4.3 illustrates the relationship that existed between gender and the circumstances of drowning; drowned girls were found in locations tending to reflect domestic circumstances, whereas proportionally nearly twice as many boys as girls were said to have drowned in water courses found outside the neighborhood of the home, close, or manse. Although these few examples suggest that medieval boys were more aggressive, inquisitive, and physically active, with perhaps greater freedom of movement than girls, no explanation of these differences is available. Very few preambulatory medieval infants were claimed to have been in danger of drowning. Quite often, when infants were near-drowning victims, the mishap took place at bathtime. Even here there are interesting resonances between medieval and modern experiences. Some of these cases provide examples of parental negligence, which, as in our own time, is sometimes difficult to distinguish from child abuse.[180] As recently as the 1980s, a medical study of bathtub drownings in California indicated that parents tended to overestimate the ability of children older than nine months of age to care for themselves.[181] While there is much truth in the modern stereotype of unwashed medieval masses, this indifference to hygiene may not have included infants; from the day of birth, they were expected to be bathed with some regularity. In the later fifteenth century an Augsburg physician, Bartholomew Metlinger (d. 1491/2), wrote that in its first six months of life "the child should be bathed daily, a daughter with warmer water than a son."[182] Here, as was usually the case with medieval medical writers, Metlinger was passing on ideas about child care derived ultimately from Hippocrates, Galen, and early Arabic and Christian commentators. Testimony in a fourteenth-century Italian case, however, indicates that in some regions infants actually were bathed every evening.[183] Whatever its frequency, the bathing of children by inattentive parents sometimes led to tragedy. In 1398 in Pomerania John's mother was washing him in a child's tub when, having other things to do, she left the eighteen-month-old in the care of his father, Nicolaus. While Nicolaus was preoccupied with something, however, his son slipped beneath the water and nearly drowned.[184] A study published in 1993 suggested that modern bathtub drownings of children are more likely when a father is left in charge, as in this Pomeranian case, or when the child is "being looked after by an older sibling."[185] The latter occurred when, in England, little Gilbert was left in the bath with his older brother, age three, who was supposed to be looking after him while their mother went out

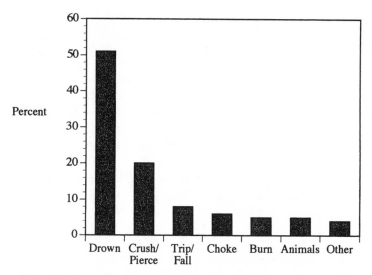

Figure 4.2 Distribution of accident types among 156 medieval children

Figure 4.3 Characteristics of "drowned" children (26 girls, 53 boys)

to do some winnowing. As a result, Gilbert found himself being resuscitated from "the dead" a few hours later.[186]

Philip of Novara commented on dangers from fire as well as water. Apart from risks incurred while crawling or toddling near the hearth, infants and very young children were especially susceptible to danger from house fires, whereas a four- or five-year-old probably would have appreciated imminent peril and run out of a burning building. Hanawalt also noticed this phenomenon in her investigations of medieval coroners' rolls; she found that among the child victims of fires and other forms of accidental death, older children tended to be injured and accidentally killed while away from their homes, whereas younger ones and infants were endangered most often in a domestic setting.[187] Didier Lett's more recent work in medieval miracle records confirms this correlation between age and site of accident.[188] The same pattern is found in the miracle records used in this study. Out of a total of 156 accident cases, 105 indicated both the age of the victim and the site. Figure 4.4 provides correlations between children's ages and places where their accidents or injuries occurred. Modern child-accident studies confirm that the site of an injury or accidental death very often is related to the age of the children involved; younger ones come to

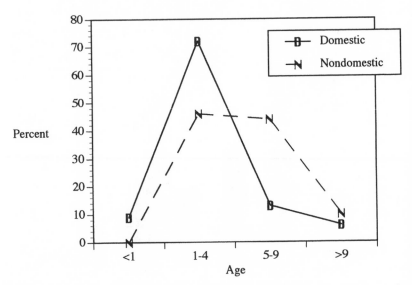

Figure 4.4 Domestic and nondomestic injury and "drowning" sites (105 cases)

harm more often in the domestic environment, whereas older children —
because of their greater independence of movement, higher level of curiosity, and more advanced physical development — usually injure themselves or
are killed accidentally while away from their homes.[189] Similar circumstances surrounded many children's accidents in medieval Europe. However
children came to be injured or nearly drowned — whether at "work" or
playing by themselves or with neighborhood children, or "safely" kept at
home — the discovery of their maimed or nearly dead bodies ("lifeless," as
many medieval witnesses claimed) was the necessary first step toward
recovery. Unlike the onset and course of an illness, in which the child usually was cared for in the midst of a group of people including parents, perhaps aunts, uncles, godparents, and neighbors, and possibly a doctor as well,
young accident victims usually were found alone, often by neighbors who
unknowingly stumbled upon the diminutive "corpse." Sometimes, it is true,
playmates ran screaming from the victim's side to report the calamity, or
mothers would see the sight they feared as they searched for a missing
child. Normally, however, accident victims were found outside the protec-
tive embrace of their kin.[190] This is emphasized in figure 4.5, which indicates
who were the "first finders" of the children. Neighbors were finders as

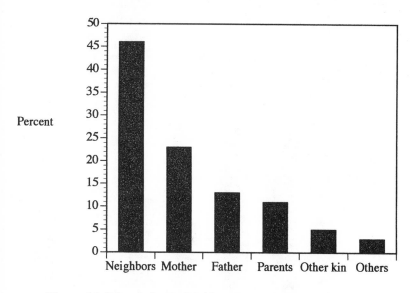

Figure 4.5 "First finders" of child victims of accidents (128 cases)

often as parents; about half the victims were discovered by chance, normally at sites away from home. Neighbors, even strangers, usually responded to a child who had become endangered or injured by immediately attempting to rescue or resuscitate it. Christian Krötzl, examining miracles reported by medieval Scandinavian villagers, sees evidence that they shared in the concern for unsupervised children, regardless of whose children they were; they were village children, and that sufficed.[191] When child victims of mishaps were discovered, many times they were immediately recognized by neighbors who knew which parents had to be told the bad news. Even if they were not among the first finders, neighbors gathered quickly when tragedy occurred. After having left her two young children in the bath together, a mother found one of them "dead"; she snatched it from the water and began shouting and wailing. The women of her English village ran up since, the chronicler suggests, nearly all the men were fishing or reaping.[192] In France the woman who found a five-year-old in a well "broke out in the great shouting typical of women," at which the boy's mother and many other villagers ran up and pulled him out of danger.[193] In Italy Milucia reported that after her son fell and injured himself in her house, many of her neighbors hastened to her.[194]

It was widely recognized that vows, an essential part of spiritual healing, must be discharged unless parents wanted to risk an even worse calamity as

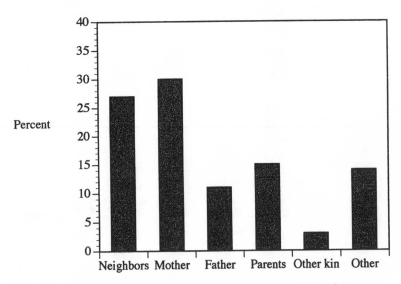

Figure 4.6 Identity of those who made vows for accident and "death" victims (148 cases)

punishment. Given the fact that so many accidentally injured or near-drowned children were found by neighbors, one might expect that these would have been the people who most often vowed pilgrimage and offerings. But, as figure 4.6 suggests, the records do not indicate this. Even though most children were discovered by neighbors, apparently the victims' mothers most often made solemn promises to the saints. For instance, after rescuing a young boy from a well, Elisabeth of Stangendorf in Pomerania carried him to his mother, whom she persuaded to make a vow to the blessed Dorothy for his resuscitation. This she did, as did Elisabeth and several other women.[195]

Although they provide an overview of one aspect of the lives of medieval children, such figures hardly convey the richness of the reports. The miracle records, through the testimony of victims, kin, and neighbors, allow us glimpses of the children themselves: their shaved heads or fair, flowing hair; their colorful garments and their undyed, baggy tunics; and their new shoes with red laces.[196] The records also let us glimpse something of adults' attitudes toward these children, particularly in cases of accidents, in most of which the child's own actions are both described and commented upon. Whereas in birth and illness records usually the victim was passive, in accidents often the child contributed in great part to her or his own misfortune.

5

CONCLUSIONS
....

We have reached the end of our analyses of the 600 "core" cases involving childbirth and the complications of neonatal existence, illnesses, and accidents involving children between the twelfth and fifteenth centuries. It now remains to examine these analyses comparatively, in order to determine, in addition to overall attributes, what the differences were, if any, between northern and southern Europe in children's and adults' experiences of such crises. We begin, however, with some examples of grief, the emotion that accompanied children's endangerment.

PARENTAL GRIEF

In her highly praised book on the daily lives of medieval English peasants, based on coroners' rolls, one topic that Barbara Hanawalt explores is the issue of parental affection. Hanawalt expects that "emotional outpourings from parents upon finding a dead child" would be sufficient evidence of sentimentality. "Unfortunately," she continues, coroners' rolls recording the accidental deaths of children "stop short of the parent's lament."[1] And so they do. Fortunately, it is precisely at this point that miracle records take up the lament: medieval canonization investigations and lists of miracles overflow with parental anguish, profound depression and grief, and physical and mental incapacity and collapse suffered by parents in their shock at a child's injury, illness or assumed death. The tones of anguish and grief are too pervasive to ignore.[2] Canonization testimony and related records carry us deeply into medieval emotionalism, which coroners' records were never intended to penetrate. Although the two types of historical source are complementary, miracle records provide much more information on parental grief.

Even in the violent emotion of grief engendered by a child's death, often medieval men and women seem to have recognized certain norms of decorum. This sense of propriety and constraint was also articulated in the ancient world; for example, Cicero discussed it in one of his letters of about 46 B.C. Plutarch's consoling words to his wife after the death of their two-year-old, in addition to the touching comment that "our daughter was the sweetest thing in the world to hug and watch and listen to . . ." included the admonition "that while reacting emotionally you make sure that both of us—me as well as you—remain in a stable state." He criticized the usual mourning rituals, with crowds of wailing women whose behavior was prompted "by pointless social customs."[3] Plutarch's words do not quite disguise his grief, even though his letter was cast in the tradition of consolatory literature that was commonplace in the ancient world. He disdained the wailing and howling of grief, a contemptible indulgence that was beneath his and his wife's dignity. The consciousness of *dignitas* and duty, controlled by a monitoring intelligence, was intricately enmeshed with the state of manhood itself. In the late Roman empire, as Peter Brown writes, "each man trembled forever on the brink of becoming 'womanish.' . . . It was never enough to be a male: a man had to strive to remain 'virile.' He had to learn to exclude from his character and from the poise and temper of his body all telltale traces of 'softness.' . . ."[4]

Early Christian men shared this attitude, fearing to display inordinate emotion whether in anger, in lust or in grief, which could be seen not only as womanish but also as contrary to Christianity's teachings. Whether virtuous men, respected matrons, or baptized children had died recently, a more appropriate Christian response to their deaths was the satisfaction of believing that they were now better off, sleeping in the bosom of Abraham until Judgment Day, or already enjoying the celestial bliss of heaven. By the late fourth century St. Augustine was condemning excessive parental grief and Basil of Caesarea (d. 379) was writing that neither "men nor women should be permitted too much lamentation and mourning. They should show moderate distress in their affliction, with only a few tears, shed quietly and without moaning, wailing, tearing of clothes and grovelling in the dust, or committing any other indecency commonly practised by the ungodly."[5]

In the central Middle Ages, excessive emotional love for children, dead or alive, was condemned by Philip of Novara, for instance, and the Knight de la Tour Landry, as well as by Etienne de Fougères and Nicholas Bozon. It was not love that was condemned; *showing* children love, it was feared, would make them too proud. In medieval literature, as in classical, husbands often reproached wives for displaying too much love for sons and daughters, as in a line from *Les Narbonnais*: "Madam, Countess, you are hardly wise in bothering yourself so much about your children."[6] Similarly, the emotional behavior of Matilda, Countess of Clare, evoked the same sort of chiding remarks from her own chaplain and peers, described in chapter 3, on children's illnesses.[7] Nevertheless, clerical writers were well aware of the depths of parental grief. The "bitter death" *(acerba mors)* of children, discussed by Julian, seventh-century bishop of Toledo, was reexamined by the English Aelfric, abbot of Eynsham, who died in the early eleventh century: "That is called the bitter death which occurs to children; the premature death, to young men; and the natural [that] which happens to the old."[8] The profundity of a grieving parent's sorrow, a literary topos, is evident in many contemporary sources: the jurist Beaumanoir even allowed that negligent parents should escape the law's penalties because of their grief: "When someone has killed his child, for example by fire or water, or because he was smothered in his sleep, or because he was not watched, the father and mother should not be prosecuted, for their great distress should exempt them from civil prosecution. . . ."[9]

In spite of the fact that society might prescribe moderation in their "great distress," some medieval parents violently lamented the deaths of their children. Extreme grief took many forms. At its most direct, it burst from neighbors and kin as weeping: after a child was dragged from the Thames, wailing and lamentation "resounded on all sides."[10] Some parents fell into temporary bewilderment when confronted by a child's injury: when Katherina realized that her pitchfork had pierced her son's head, at first she was dumbfounded — *stupefacta est.*[11] This stupor could easily slide into denial: after a child fell from the upper floor of a house and the neighbors wanted to bury him, the grief-stricken mother kept the body in her house for five days, refusing to allow burial; some thought her mad.[12] Sometimes concentration on the endangered child shut out all other sensations: at Little Marcle, John's grandmother could not describe the clothing or the horses of the knights who rode up to assist because of her bitterness and sadness, as she said, at the child's "death."[13] Joanna of Marden's mother, Cecilia, testified that she was uncertain how many people ran to the fishpond, since she was suffering great grief at the time. Sometimes there was a stunned incapacity to act: to return to the case from Little Marcle, John's father could not touch his son's body because of his sadness.[14] Some parents crumpled in shock, as Roger of Conway's mother did after she learned of his accident;[15] as noted in chapter 4, after Nicholas was pulled out of the river at How Caple, his parents collapsed on the riverbank, and were brought round after water was thrown in their faces.[16] On the other hand, some parents were stimulated into immediate action. Being told of her child's mishap, a

Pomeranian mother sitting at home leapt up so violently that her head struck a roof beam, which knocked her to the ground, while in another case, in Italy, a father, overwhelmed at hearing of his child's accident, began beating his head against a wall until a neighbor woman reprimanded him.[17] Presumably the neighbor believed that his reactions were inappropriate. Would she have criticized similar behavior in the child's mother?

In her study of renaissance humanists' reactions to what most of them considered Jacopo Marcello's inappropriate grief for his dead son, Valerio, Margaret King cited a work on seventeenth-century England, and another on twentieth-century grief, as the basis for the following: "In pre-modern Europe, the great majority of the parents who grieved were mothers."[18] Some (male) medieval commentators would have agreed that public grief was more appropriate to women generally, mothers particularly: many people were grieving around the drowned body of William of Donington, but according to one witness only the women had tears in their eyes,[19] and in France the mother of a drowned girl turned pale and shed copious tears "in maternal fashion," as the compiler put it.[20] In England, the people tending an afflicted child were described as "womanishly-weeping bystanders."[21] The Canterbury monk who recorded one of Becket's miracles believed that although both parents of a dying child were lamenting, the mother grieved more deeply since she "loved him more dearly" than the father.[22] The records amply confirm the strength of the maternal bond: in France, a woman's neighbors and friends led the greatly distressed mother away from her dying son, age six, so that she would not see the end.[23] Sometimes motherly love drove women to the verge of insanity when they believed that their children were seriously threatened. An English mother was deranged by grief when her only daughter, whom she dearly loved, fell seriously ill; the woman could recognize no one, not even her husband. She was tied up and kept overnight at Wulfstan's tomb in Worcester, after which she recovered her sanity.[24] In a more extreme case from France, when her three-day-old son was thought to have died, Odeardis entered a state of inconsolable grief: "Rapt into a savage fury, she shunned the company of mankind and fled to hiding places in the woods," where she remained with the wild animals, eating oak leaves, for four days.[25] Another French mother, learning that her daughter had fallen into a well, was overwhelmed, and—as the narrator put it—"as women do," she broke out wailing, crying and screaming to her neighbors, "Come! My daughter has drowned!" She tried to throw herself into the well, joining the child in death.[26] The grief of the women of an Italian family is all too evident in an incident that took place on a Saturday in June about 1316, when Joanna and her three children — Puccius, a boy of four or five, and his older sisters, Bellaflora and Servadea—made their way to a mill near their hometown, San Genesio.[27] Joanna went inside the mill, Servadea wandered off, and Puccius and Bellaflora began to play. Puccius picked up a wicker scoop and went to the millrace. As he bent down and dipped the scoop into the water, the force of the current swept him away and toward the mill wheel. Bellaflora tried but failed to rescue her little brother, who was carried headfirst along the rushing stream until be became wedged into the channel, causing the mill wheel to stop turning. Bellaflora began ripping her clothes and screaming for her mother. When Joanna ran from the mill house and saw her son in the water, in her violent grief she too began screaming, ripping at her clothing and clawing at her face.[28]

Fathers also were deeply affected, although in several cases they tended to manifest this rather differently from women. The records suggest that in the Middle Ages, a public form of grief was paralleled by private anguish: just as they were not expected to witness the birth of their children, in several cases men withdrew into privacy to express their grief. Before looking at some paternal reactions to children's purported deaths, notice should be taken again of Margaret King's study. King admits that the elegant consolatory letters composed for Valerio's grieving father tell us little about "parental feeling for those who died young." One cannot but agree. Since these were literary exercises imitating an ancient tradition, they elucidate contemporary humanistic fashions rather than a father's anguish. It is less easy to agree with another of King's statements, however. She seems to suggest that parental and especially fatherly grief was relatively rarely recorded in Italy before the fourteenth century, and even then appeared only in "rarified [*sic*] circles"; she states that disconsolate fathers "can be found" north of the Alps in the sixteenth century, mentioning Luther and the Englishman Brownlow as examples.[29] However, there is no lack of documentation of paternal grief in medieval Europe; this study has provided many accounts of disconsolate fathers, from all social circles, both north and south of the Alps. True, some of the narrators of these medieval incidents seem to have disdained the men who wept for their children. In an English case, when the midwives cried out that a newborn was dead, the infant's father—"his manhood forgotten,"as the Canterbury monk put it—"wailed womanishly," vowed himself and the boy to Becket, then launched into a rhetorical complaint: "Why was life denied the newborn, for whom the time of birth was attained?" And so on: why was the happiness of conception and then hope dashed; why did the mother carry him live so many months, only to give birth to him dead? The father went on like this for a long time.[30] In this instance the monk attributed to the father a form of lament that Doris

Berkvam found to be typical of literary laments of *women* whose children had died.[31] Was the twelfth-century Canterbury monk familiar with this tradition, and did he purposely invert it here, in order to emphasize the father's "womanish" grief? In another Becket miracle, after a Sussex knight learned that his wife had given birth to a dead son, "knightly though he was," the commentator noted, he burst out with "What do we do? What do we do?"[32]

In many of the miracles, however, grieving fathers are treated sympathetically. Among the posthumous wonders attributed to Simon de Montfort, one involved the infant son of constable William Child. The boy was nearly dead from some unstated illness and the father, oppressed by grief, suffered great anxiety and pain. After the *infans* seemed to die, "behold," the commentator exclaims, "sadness upon sadness!" as William threw himself on his bed, where eventually he fell asleep, exhausted.[33] Some fathers refused to leave their endangered children, as in the case of Adam, whose sick three-year-old son was on the point of death. Indeed love is so impatient, the recorder of this event interjected, that one cannot part from the beloved.[34] In several instances, however, fathers drew themselves away from their dying or "dead" children, preferring to express their grief in private. When his son died in 1461, Jacopo Marcello "fled from the light into darkness to grieve" alone.[35] In Pomerania, after the parents of an infant awoke to find her "dead," the father went outside by himself, fell on his knees in tears, and devoutly invoked Dorothy.[36] In another case from the same region, a grieving father described how he went into his room, alone, to pray for his son's recovery.[37] In southern France during the 1370s, while working in his vineyards one evening, a father went down on his knees and begged the dead Pope Urban to intercede on his sick son's behalf,[38] while another French father, anticipating the death of his three-year-old, went out to the stables, fell to his knees, and began weeping for his son.[39] In an English case, with their sick child on the verge of death, the parents fled screaming and crying—the mother to call the neighbors together, the father to weep secretly in his garden.[40] In Normandy, when his feverish son seemed about to die, William withdrew into a small bedchamber *(cubiculum)* and shut the door, grieving for his child and saying to himself "I will not look at my dying boy."[41] Jordan's daughter, who seemed to be dying from cancer, was laid out as if for her funeral.[42] When Jordan, who had thrown himself down on his bed exhausted by sadness, woke up abruptly, shouting "My daughter can't be dead!" his wife replied, "Yes, she is." Jordan called out to Becket for nearly half the night, until he could barely speak. Although there must always have been fathers who behaved this way, these examples suggest a strengthening undercurrent of affective emotionalism in which men's behavior took on some of the tones traditionally associated with the feminine persona, a transformation under way since at least the twelfth century when, as Carolyn Bynum reminds us, feminine traits accumulated around the figure of Jesus.[43]

Some fathers' grief, then, was deeply felt, although sometimes less publicly expressed than that of the mothers. Even though the fiction that men were not supposed to grieve, particularly over children, had been part of Western tradition for centuries, these examples illustrate how the classic paradigm of fatherly stoicism often was disregarded in medieval Europe. Certainly the façade of "manly" behavior was of no concern to a merchant of southern France who, seeing his feverish son near death, "hugging him in his arms, grieved greatly, and was tortured by enormous sadness . . ." as the father himself described his feelings.[44] Sometimes this sadness was unbearable: in 1468, after an accident carried off both his children, a Nürnberg butcher killed himself.[45]

Obviously, grief was a shared sentiment, afflicting both of the parents of dying, injured, or "dead" children. A spectacular example of this comes from the Wulfstan miracles. Hugh and Emma's son John was three years old.[46] The boy fell ill, and progressively his condition worsened until he became mere skin and bones. About noon some eight days after being stricken, John seemed to die. His parents were gripped by deep anguish, especially since he had been their only child.[47] Neighbors drawn to the scene of such unusual grief, moved by compassion, also began weeping. When eventually they suggested preparing for the boy's funeral, the father, "as if struck with a hammer," madly snatched up the body and ran outside the house with "unmanly," prancing gait, glaring with fiery eyes and frightening spectators with his horrible screams.[48] Emma furiously pursued her husband, arms outstretched, face distorted by her screams. Quickly catching up to her husband, she flung her arms around the boy, trying to wrestle him from Hugh. "By what right, man," she said, "do you hurry. . . .[49] How can you cruelly carry off my flesh and blood? Are you going to throw yourself into the river so that the Severn becomes a tomb for both of you? Is it not enough to have lost my son; must I also lose my husband?" As the parents struggled over John, they pulled him about cruelly, even savagely.[50] The limp child looked like a dancer, the narrator claimed, as his parents dragged him this way and that: at one time he seemed to be walking on his hands, then his head jerked up and he seemed to be walking upright, with his arms dangling. The astounded crowd followed this grotesque scene, many of the onlookers in tears. After wrenching John from Emma's grip, Hugh leapt into a nearby cemetery, then ran into the cathedral and deposited his burden at Wulfstan's tomb. The custodians came up. "Look," Hugh told them, "I've brought my son to Lord Wulfstan for resuscitation. I'm not moving him until he's revived." After Hugh had prayed at the tomb for a while, at the suggestion of some of the bystanders he forced open the boy's mouth and poured in some water that had touched Wulfstan's relics. Finally, about the time the bells roused the cathedral clergy from their midday naps, the boy began to move. John eventually recovered his health.[51]

It has been suggested that indications of parental affection for their children grow stronger during the later Middle Ages and that it is "clearer among the peasants than among the townsmen or the nobility."[52] One way to verify this would be to note whether more "emotional" or "uncontrolled" reactions to children's deaths are encountered as the social ladder is descended; whether, as nobles are left behind, so too is the *gravitas* thought to be appropriate to their status. However, several examples described in the preceding chapters, taken from all social levels, suggest that this approach may be too simplistic. Although the principle seems to hold good in some cases, it is not found in others where it might be expected. Such correlations that may exist, linking social status with specific attitudes toward children's illnesses, injuries, or purported deaths, seem to require a more complex explanatory model. The miracles, on the whole, do not suggest that displays of grief (whatever their intensity) varied with social status. On the other hand, the examples suggest that in medieval grief for children, overtly emotional behavior by women was expected or at least tolerated; among men, displays of grief were less expected, and, in fact, may have been felt to be inappropriate for them.

CHARACTERISTICS OF THE CHILDREN'S ILLNESSES AND ACCIDENTS: AN OVERVIEW

In the twentieth century, tremendous advances in the treatment of children's illnesses have occurred in the developed countries. The proportion of children's deaths attributed to accidents, mainly automobile accidents, has risen, relative to their deaths from disease.[53] In medieval Europe, however, as in many developing regions today, illnesses seem to have claimed more child victims than accidental injuries and drowning. In the present study, 32 percent of the recorded incidents involving medieval children in northern and southern Europe were accidents, while 68 percent were associated with illnesses (excluding childbirth cases). Similar findings come from a study of four southeastern German/western Austrian cults, in which miracles were recorded between 1466 and 1600. Among 251 children, Schuh reports

37 percent accidents and 63 percent illnesses.[54] The ratios seem to be close enough to suggest that results for west-central Europe are similar, at least in this regard, to those uncovered in our analysis of northern and southern European cases.

Between the twelfth and thirteenth centuries, and the fourteenth and fifteenth centuries, there seems to have been no noticeable change in proportion of boys (65 percent) to girls (35 percent) in the 156 accident reports analyzed in the present study. In both periods about a third of the accidents involved girls. This suggests that throughout the later medieval centuries, few significant alterations occurred in the physical or social environment, such as expectations concerning gender-specific behavior at play or at work, or in levels of adult supervision. In the 334 illness cases, however, the proportion of boys to girls reported during the earlier period (4.3 to 1) changed noticeably in the later period (1.9 to 1). Expressed another way, miracles concerning sick girls in the sample rose from about 19 percent in the earlier to about 35 percent in the later medieval centuries. Assuming that the incidence of illness among boys and girls remained relatively unchanged between about A.D. 1100 and 1500, is it possible that these variations reflect increased concern for girls, or for their health, in the later medieval period? Some historians claim that females had become less marginalized, in general, during the closing centuries of the medieval period. The debate, however, continues: André Vauchez draws attention to the need to view evidence that there were more female saints in the later period with great care when evaluating the position of late-medieval women, and Bennett has questioned the usual arguments about women's improved socioeconomic status in late-medieval England.[55] There also may have been a higher incidence of children as subjects of miraculous cures generally in the later medieval centuries than in the earlier. Although in this study the major collections were not examined for this shift, it seems a likely hypothesis in view of what Vauchez has written about the changing locus of miracles. Vauchez has suggested that, as belief in the efficacy of the vow grew stronger in the later Middle Ages, more miracles tended to be reported from sites that were increasingly distant from saints' shrines, since immediate contact with holy bones was imagined to be less necessary. Because many cases of cured or resuscitated stillborns and suffocated or drowned children would have occurred far from shrines, an increase in their incidence in the records may be assumed.[56] Another change was suggested by Herlihy and Klapisch-Zuber, in their monumental study of the 1427 census in Tuscany: "If the thirteenth century had kindled an interest in the child's education and a sentimental assessment of its innocence and simplicity, the closing Middle

Ages [in Tuscany] contributed a growing concern for its physical welfare" expressed as an increase in facilities for the care of orphans and foundlings.[57] Such a "growing concern" also may have resulted in increasing numbers of children being taken to holy shrines in search of, or in thanks for, their "miraculous" cures, which were recorded by shrine guardians. Only further comparative research, involving large numbers of cases from different centuries, can elucidate this matter.

In chapter 3 it was found that, among the children involved in 334 illness cases, 69.8 percent were boys, with 30.2 percent of the cured patients girls. The same two-to-one ratio operative in accidents, therefore, seems to have been characteristic of the children affected by illness. This presents a problem: when dealing with children's accidents, medieval or modern, it seems somewhat easier to accept the finding that more aggressive, adventuresome boys were victims than girls; but how does one explain a similar imbalance in the miraculous alleviation of illness? Even if certain illnesses, such as hernias and bladder stones, were physiologically associated with boys more commonly than with girls, the relatively few reported cases of those afflictions could hardly account for the overall gender imbalance favoring boys, a result perhaps of what Philip Gavitt calls a "cultural preference for males."[58] It would seem, too, that little boys were cured more quickly than girls. Figure 3.3, indicating how long children's illnesses had lasted, suggests that girls languished in their illnesses longer than boys. Of the children whose illnesses lasted between one and six months, 23 percent were girls, while only 11 percent boys. As for what appear to have been chronic afflictions, however, boys (17 percent) and girls (20 percent) suffered in roughly equal proportions. In short, in the case of illnesses, our medieval parents seem to have invested more care and effort in their sons; in addition, they seem to have done so more quickly than for their daughters —as far as illness was concerned. Moving from illnesses only, and considering both healing and accident miracles together, Barbara Schuh's analysis of 274 children indicates that 66.3 percent were boys, 33.7 percent girls. As she puts it, clearly girls were in the background.[59] For Schuh, since the demographic situation alone cannot account for this phenomenon, the possibility arises that, to medieval parents, the recovery or convalescence of their sons was of more consequence than of their daughters. In the present study about 70 percent of all children involved in both cures and accidents were boys. Sigal found a similar male preponderance for French cults.[60] In the postmedieval cult he examined, Cousin discovered that, among 109 children, there was a three-to-two bias of boys over girls. He concluded that concern for the health of children was "more inclined toward that of sons than that of daughters."[61] In her 1986 article, "Child Health in the Middle Ages," the pediatrician and historian Eleanora Gordon also discovered that the miracles centered on boys far more frequently than girls. (Her figures indicate 74 percent boys, 26 percent girls). In her words, "the significance of the greater number of boys described in these records is unclear."[62]

The reason for the male bias found in northern and southern European reports of both accidents (perhaps not unexpected) and illnesses (more inexplicable), is probably the most obvious one: in medieval Europe, parents and kin considered boys more important than girls; in a profoundly male-dominated society, male children were valued more highly than female offspring. The greater care of boys could be seen as a passive, indirect, or attenuated form of female infanticide, or "selective neglect."[63] Our data suggest that this male bias seems to have begun at birth. In chapter 2, of 110 cases involving birth and early-infancy miracles, the gender was indicated for 72 children; of these, 56 (78 percent) were boys, 16 (22 percent) girls. This disparity suggests (even taking into account an initially slight numerical predominance of male over female births, about 105 to 100)[64] that mothers, midwives, or helpful neighbor women, and sometimes husbands, may have been more attentive or tenacious when male offspring were concerned than they were for females. According to Sigal, who discovered a similar preference in the birth miracles he examined (twenty-eight boys, or 72 percent, over eleven girls, 28 percent), "the [parental] vow concerns boys more than girls . . ."[65]

Another way, therefore, to examine the question of possible parental bias is to determine who made vows for the recovery of a child most frequently. Figures 3.4 and 4.6 illustrated this information; in figure 5.1, these are combined. Evidently, the type of vower differed according to the type of distress: in accidents, more than 25 percent of the vowers were neighbors, but in illnesses, a mere 4 percent came from this group. These percentages reflect the differing contexts in which the events occurred: whereas injury victims often were discovered away from their homes, illnesses began and ended at the center of the family. In accidents, 57 percent of all those who made vows were mothers, fathers, and the two parents together; in illnesses, this figure rose to 92 percent. Fewer neighbors or strangers were involved in children's illnesses than they were in their accidents. As for the cumulative differences between mothers and fathers, in 377 cases of both illness and accidents, about 50 percent of the vows were made by mothers only; about 32 percent by fathers only; and in 19 percent, both parents vowed together. (Birth and neonatal cases are not included in these estimates; in addition, these figures exclude all other vowers and combinations of vowers in order to isolate only

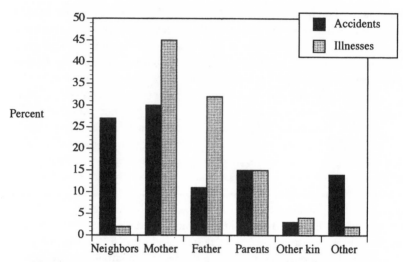

Figure 5.1 Comparison of vowers, accidents versus illnesses (*n* = 465)

the parental ratios.) In his investigation of a seventeenth-century French healing cult, Cousin found that mothers alone vowed for their children in 70 percent of the cases, whereas the father vowing alone showed up in only 30 percent of the recorded miracles.[66] In our data, mothers vowed on their own on behalf of their daughters in 32 percent of the instances but for their sons, in 68 percent of the cases. For fathers, the comparable figures are 27 percent and 73 percent. Little boys were the primary objects of vows by each parent, although fathers tended to commit themselves to their sons' causes slightly more often than mothers did.[67] These findings merely add to the weight of evidence collected in many other studies that conclude that the favored sex was male.[68] Cited often as an example of contemporary expectations regarding boys and girls (at least in thirteenth-century Italy), Salimbene's outburst is worth another glance:

> My mother used to tell me that during the time of this great earthquake [in Parma, 1222] I lay in my crib [he would have been one year two months old then], and that she grabbed up my two sisters, one under each arm—for they were small—and, with me left in the cradle, she ran to her family's home. . . . And because of this, I could never afterward love her as much as before, *because she ought to have been more careful of me, the male of the family, than of the daughters.*[69]

Perhaps Salimbene was right to be indignant, since our data suggest that most mothers would have sought safety with their sons rather than their daughters, if given a choice. To recapitulate: for 562 cases in which gender is indicated in this study, for birth problems, 78 percent of the subjects were boys, 22 percent were girls; for accidents, 65 percent were boys, 35 percent were girls; and for illnesses, the records indicate that 70 percent of the cured patients were boys, 30 percent were girls.

NORTHERN AND SOUTHERN EUROPEAN MIRACLES; POSSIBLE IMPLICATIONS FOR FAMILY STRUCTURES

One of the questions posed at the beginning of this study was whether the miracles might reveal differences between northern and southern Europe in children's illnesses and accidents, and adults' reactions to these crises. The question can be approached, first of all, by asking whether the types of miracle differed according to region. Figure 5.2 suggests that they did. Overall, northern and southern Europe contributed about the same number of cases; 52 percent (311) came from the north, 48 percent (289) from the south. Birth problems (110) were reported from both regions in about the same proportions. With illness (334), however, a disparity appears; southern Europe reported about 1.7 times more cases than northern Europe. The greatest difference, however, is seen in children's accidents (156): northern

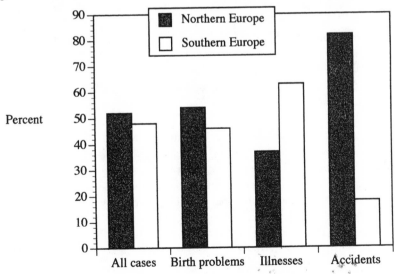

Figure 5.2 Distribution of birth, illness, and accident cases among the 600 children's miracles in northern and southern Europe

miracle collections contain about 4.5 times more accident cases than do southern ones.

Demonstrating these differences is far easier than attempting to account for them. The disparities may derive from chance; perhaps the northern miracle collections selected for examination just happened to contain relatively more accidents, and the southern collections more illnesses. On the other hand, at least two ways can postulated to make sense of these differences. In the first place, as far as illness is concerned, southern Europe (southern France and Italy) was more densely populated, with more urban centers, than the north; and the study as well as the practice of medicine was a long-standing tradition of southern European life and learning. In such circumstances, with a relatively higher incidence of medical professionals available, southern parents perhaps were more sensitive to the state of their children's health, more accustomed than northerners to turn to the medical professions — as indicated in chapter 3, southern parents called in doctors twice as frequently as northern parents — and then to appeal to their saints when professional assistance failed. In the second place, climatic differences between North and South must have affected children's health, provoking some types of ailment (malarial fevers, for instance) while reducing others. As Herlihy and Klapisch-Zuber noted for Tuscany, "The newborn disappear in greatest numbers in the hot months," a trend probably characteristic of northern Europe as well, though perhaps to a lesser degree.[70] On the other hand, given the dismal state of health in the general population throughout medieval Europe, regional differences in specific types of illness probably were relatively unimportant.[71]

As for accidental injuries, another approach is possible, one that more directly addresses the North-South disparity that was, in this area, far more marked than among the illness miracles. When witnesses recalled events before, during, and after children's accidents or illnesses, they re-created the familial contexts of these domestic dramas. It is possible, therefore, to determine which family members (if any) were present, or involved, when the child was affected and subsequently cured or resuscitated. This, in turn, invites us into the treacherous marsh of controversy over conjugal versus extended households and which model is appropriate for various regions and periods. Bennett, for example, believes that early fourteenth-century English households were small or conjugal, with the three-generation household a rarity; in this she agrees with Hanawalt, who, however, points out the perils of comparing rural English with Italian models.[72] For parts of fourteenth- and fifteenth-century Italy, Klapisch-Zuber sees an increase in extended families corresponding with a decline in conjugal families; Herlihy tends to support this, with judicious qualifications, and concludes that "several types of households (at the very least two) existed simultaneously in medieval society. . . ."[73] As Tamara Hareven pointed out in 1991, questions about family structures in northern and southern Europe are very complex.[74] Therefore, it is with some trepidation that we turn to the canonization testimony from northern and southern Europe. The data tentatively suggest that familial structures were, evidently, different in the two regions. In our own times, E. M. Forster summed up the difference well, through a fictional encounter between some Italians and the Englishman, Philip, who was seeking directions:

> "I'll show you!" cried a little girl, springing out of the ground as
>   Italian children will.
> "She will show you," said the *dogana* men, nodding reassuringly.
>   "Follow her always, always, and you will come to no
>   harm.
> She is a trustworthy guide. She is my
>   daughter."
>   cousin."
>   sister."
> Philip knew these relatives well; they ramify, if need be, all over
>   the peninsula.[75]

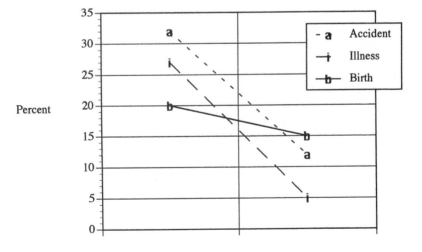

Figure 5.3 Differences in kinship involvement in European regions ("kin" includes godparents and family members beyond the victims' parents)

Figure 5.3 suggests that, indeed, Italian (and southern French) kin seem to ramify more deeply and widely than their northern counterparts: more kin were involved in all categories (births, accidents, illnesses) in southern Europe than in the north. Among the 156 child victims of accidents, only 28 cases were reported from southern Europe. This is a narrow basis for comparison, but it is striking that kin (apart from parents) were explicitly referred to in 9 of the 28 instances, or in 32 percent of the southern cases. Northern Europe provided 128 examples of child accidents, but here nonparental kin were mentioned in only 15 cases, or 12 percent of the sample. Even though, in accidents, often a neighbor or stranger discovered the child's body rather than a kinsman, whenever kin *were* involved, they were more than twice as likely to show up in southern cases than in northern. As for birth complications, the gap in kin participation between North and South is narrowed to 15 percent and 20 percent respectively. Given the circumstances, it is likely that relatives would be involved in childbirth wherever it occurred; but even here, once again kin involvement seems to have been slightly more common in southern than in northern Europe. Among the 334 illnesses, 62 reports (19 percent) included an explicit reference to kin beyond the nuclear family; usually these were grandparents, and then aunts and uncles. Sometimes these relatives, rather than the parents, called on saints, vowed pilgrimages and made offerings at shrines. Of 124 cases reported from the North, kin were mentioned in 6 instances (5 percent of cases); but in southern Europe, out of 210 illnesses, kin were present in 56 cases (27 percent). In short, nonparental kin seem to have "participated" in children's illnesses five times more frequently in southern than in northern Europe. It is just possible that these differences reflect a distinction between the conjugal northern, and extended southern, family models and perhaps indirectly support Hanawalt's conclusions concerning late-medieval English peasants: their familial lives, she contends, were marked by an "indifference toward extended kin." In another passage, she observes that "neighbors and friends, rather than extended kin, played a significant role in daily life" among the English peasantry.[76] On the other hand, for Tuscany, once again Herlihy and Klapisch-Zuber's findings are apposite: "[T]he network of relatives surrounding each individual retained, in this society, a fundamental importance and exerted an almost daily influence"; this network included, in addition, neighbors and friends.[77]

If, as some scholars seem to suppose and as figure 5.3 tends to show, the extended family was more characteristic of southern than of northern Europe in the later Middle Ages, then, to take the theorizing a step further, the findings of a modern study of Asian and West Indian children are suggestive. Large or extended families among these ethnic groups "can be a help in preventing accidents as the young children are likely to benefit from more than one carer at any given time."[78] By analogy, in the Middle Ages a more extensive "safety net" among extended southern European families might account, at least partially, for the relatively low accident rate in the south.

Geography also may have contributed to differential accident rates in the two regions. Drowning (the most common accident type) may have been more prevalent in rural environments with their dispersed populations and concomitant likelihood of low adult supervision. Examination of the drownings reported from the two regions tends to bear this out. Whereas in the South, 14 percent of the children's accidents were near-drowning incidents, in the north of Europe this calamity was recorded four times more frequently (60 percent of cases). Unfortunately, the very low number of accidents reported from southern Europe (twenty-eight cases in all) deprives this hypothesis of much of its force, although similar results are seen in modern findings.[79] An additional, equally hypothetical, explanation for different accident rates in northern and southern medieval Europe is suggested by another modern study, of children's deaths from falls. An investigation into this accident type shows that death rates for Korean children age one to four are seven times higher than they are in the United States, which suggested to the researchers the possible presence, in Korean society relative to American, of a "cultural difference in the perception of falls as a threat to children's lives."[80] If such differences exist relative to falls, perhaps they also exist for the perception of streams and ponds as potential hazards for children. Although the idea is admittedly beyond the range of demonstration, and the dangers of thrusting modern anthropological concepts into medieval contexts are well known, the possibility is worth contemplating, that cultural differences in the perception of potential risk might have played a role in producing different accident rates for the children of northern and southern Europe in the later Middle Ages.

As in many developing countries today, the children reported in our miracles seem to have been at greater risk from illness than accident. The circumstances in which accidents occurred, however, were in part affected by the familial nexus and the environment in which children were raised: in the presence of a network of laterally extended families, particularly in an urban setting, the accident rate was lower than in regions where so-called nuclear families and rural settlements were the norm. When the modern effects of the use of automobiles and firearms are removed from the equation, young children in the Middle Ages and those in today's America, for instance, seem to fall victim to the same types of accidental injury, with boys as victims at a significantly higher rate than girls.

Reports of miraculously cured illnesses suggest that environmental differences between northern and southern Europe may have had a limited effect on the incidence of certain types of infirmity. In addition, our analysis of the reported gender imbalance, durations of illnesses and the identities of those who made vows for sick children suggests that boys were favored in both northern and southern medieval Europe, by mothers as well as by fathers. It is evident that most medieval parents involved in these crises (most of them in their twenties and thirties) expressed profound grief when their children, of either sex, were at risk of death from injuries, drowning or illness, and that although there may have been some resistance to exhibiting grief among adults, especially among men, this reluctance was far from universal. Finally, various cases from among our sources suggest that some adults were well aware of the peculiar psychological and emotional attributes of young children.

Hagiographical materials such as those used in this study might be employed to explore other aspects of medieval childhood not considered in the present work. For instance, the miracle records could be used to examine the effects of rural and urban poverty on children, and adult behavior that passes beyond neglect to undeniable child abuse.[81] In addition, a comparative approach would be feasible regarding medieval childhood among Jewish and Muslim communities, using contemporary treatises such as the 1214 work of Ibn-al-'Adîm, who warns against loving children too much.[82] There is no doubt that, as Barbara Schuh has written, miracle collections provide a particularly interesting overview of the place of the child within the medieval family and of the emotional bonds uniting parents and children.[83] While one of the main goals of this book has been the elucidation of such information, another has been the stimulation of interest in a subject, and in hagiographical sources, that may lead to further revelations about European childhood during the Middle Ages. Medieval miracles, rich in circumstantial minutiae, constitute a treasury of details of contemporary life. Their judicious examination can provide ample rewards for historians interested in medieval children and in many other facets of medieval society and culture. Thousands of cases are waiting to be investigated.

APPENDIX

The Miracle of Joanna of Marden/Wisteston
from MS *Vat. Lat. 4015*, fols. 123r.–140r.

In London, on July 13, 1307, the papal committee of inquisition[1] recorded the agreed-upon procedures for interrogating witnesses in Thomas's canonization hearing. Their questions, or interrogatories, would involve four general topics: (1) Thomas's origins and how he had lived his life, especially as bishop, and his spirituality and virtues; (2) public opinion about Thomas's sanctity; (3) his miracles; and (4) the devotion of the people toward Thomas as a saint. Each of these four main headings was subdivided into several specific questions; for example, under (3), his miracles, questions were asked regarding the age and social status of the person affected, how long he or she had been ill, when, where and in whose presence the miracle occurred, and so on. The proctor of the Hereford cathedral chapter, Henry Schorne, declined to present his own set of interrogatories, although he was invited by the papal board to do so. The three commissioners, realizing that not all of their questions would be applicable to each witness, agreed that only pertinent interrogatories would be asked, so that they would "not waste time in vain, and fill up pages uselessly."[2]

Three or four notaries recorded the proceedings of the papal examining board, and two London priests acted as interpreters for witnesses speaking in English. When the commissioners moved proceedings to Hereford (adjourning in London on August 12 and restarting in Hereford on August 28), they found the local dialect even more opaque, and recruited two Hereford Franciscans to assist the notaries in translating testimony.[3]

The witnesses in London and Hereford had been gathered by the proctor of the Hereford chapter, although some were called by the inquisitors themselves, *ex officio*. After swearing on the Bible to tell the truth, witnesses responded to the questions put by the commissioners. Either at the start of the questioning or at its conclusion, they were asked to describe themselves, their age, origins, social status, and relationship to Thomas or the cathedral if any. The responses, then, tend to follow a set format, although the inquisitors sometimes altered the order or way of expressing the question. The papal commissioners often cross-examined witnesses as to particular points of testimony, and occasionally witnesses offered additional unsolicited testimony.

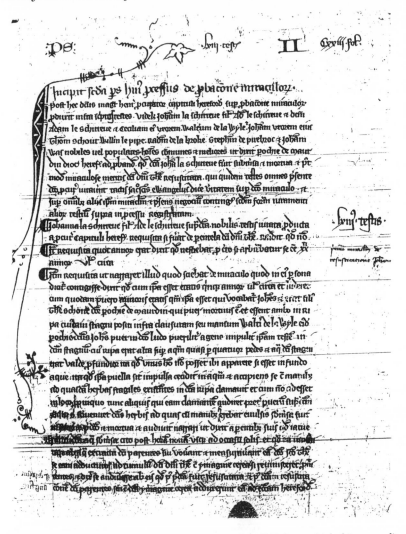

Fig. A.1 Sample page (folio 123r) from MS *Vat. Lat. 4015*, from which this appendix was translated.

By the fourteenth century, canonization inquisitors were well aware that miracles could be faked or attributed to inappropriate agencies: in the Cantilupe process, witnesses were asked whether "any herbs, stones or any other natural or medicinal things were applied, and whether incantations or superstitions, or any fraud, occurred in the operation of the miracle." The ecclesiastical administrators of the period, as much at home in courtrooms as in churches, were also well aware that inappropriate prompting or even subornation might occur: in our manuscript, witnesses routinely were asked "whether they testified out of fear or hatred, request or admonition, love or money; or profits given or promised, obtained or to be obtained; and whether they had been instructed or coached to testify, or had agreed with other witnesses, to testify" in a particular way. This was common form in canonization inquiries of the period.[4]

In what follows, a literal translation of the first few folios of the process provides a sampling of inquisitorial prose common to later-medieval canonization reports. However, from a point in Joanna's testimony, noted below, I have taken the liberty of translating the inquisitors' questions, and witness responses, as direct testimony. (The notaries recorded everything in the third person). This obviates many pleonastic constructions, while at the same time, as far as possible, it restores some life to the deponents' voices.

(fol. 123 r.)

The second part of this process begins, on the proof of miracles

[M]aster Henry, proctor of the Hereford chapter, [on Friday, September 15, 1307] presented the below-written witnesses concerning proof of the miracles, *viz.*:

Joanna la Schirreve, daughter of Adam le Schirreve
Adam le Schirreve
Cecilia his wife
Walter de la Wyle
Joan his wife
Thomas Schonk [variations of spelling recur in text, e.g., Schont]
William le Pipere
Ralph de la Broke
Stephen de Pirebroc
Joan Wase [*alt.* Was; wife of Thomas Schonk],

well-born and ordinary people, the common and the better folk, as the proctor said, of the parish of Marden, diocese of Hereford, for proving that

Joanna la Schirreve had been drowned and dead, and afterward miraculously resuscitated, through the merits of Lord Thomas; all the witnesses, in the proctor's presence, swearing on the Holy Bible to tell the truth about the miracle and all other matters touching the present business, according to the procedural form of the other sworn witnesses [earlier in the process] above.

The first miracle, on the resuscitation of Joanna

Sixty-third Witness [Joanna la Schirreve]

Joanna la Schirreve, daughter of Adam le Schirreve, well-known, witness sworn and presented by the proctor of the Hereford chapter, was asked if she were kin to the Lord Thomas,
    she replied, no.

Asked how old she was,
    she said that she did not know for certain, but she judged herself to be twenty years old or thereabouts.

Asked to tell what she knew about the miracle that was said to have affected her own person, she said that,
    when she was about five, she was playing with a younger boy, now dead, called John, son of Thomas Schonk of Marden parish. While they were on the bank of a pond in the close or manse of Walter de la Wyle of Marden, John, behaving childishly in their play, pushed her into the pond. The bank was some four feet above the water, which was so deep that a person in the depths could not be seen.
    Being bumped, as she fell she clutched at whatever vegetation was growing along the sides of the pond, screaming; but as there was no one nearby, besides John, to hear her screams and come to her assistance, uprooting the plants to which she was clinging she drowned in the pond. She heard it said by her parents that she lay drowned in the water from the afternoon until sunset. Being found and removed from the water, she heard that her parents vowed and measured her to the Lord St. Thomas, promising to take her to his tomb with a wax image if she should revive. And she said that she had heard that after this, she revived. Afterward, her parents, with a wax image, took her to the Hereford church [the cathedral].
(fol. 123 v.)
    The miracle was made public on a Sunday about the feast of the blessed George [April 23], all the girl's neighbors going barefoot in a great procession with offerings to the Hereford church, where the bells were rung,

both in the church and city, on account of the miracle. As for the year, month and day of the miracle and of the placing of her wax image in the church, she replied that she could not remember.

Asked whether she could remember seeing, hearing or feeling anything while she was under the water and while she was dead,
    she replied, no.
Asked whether before or after her resuscitation she had had any visions or revelations concerning the Lord Thomas,
    she replied that she frequently had seen herself, in dreams, near his tomb, praying or going on pilgrimage to him, or [doing] some other devotions around him. Neither Lord Thomas himself, however, nor angel nor other saint appeared to her in dreams or otherwise, that she knew of or discerned.

From this point, the indirect speech of the manuscript is translated as direct questions and responses.

Q. What kind of life do your father and mother lead?
    A. A good and honest life, living by their lands, possessions and animals, giving alms whenever possible; they frequently go to hear divine offices at churches, and they have five sons and three daughters.

Q. As a result of the miracle, were you, your parents and neighbors made more devout, and because of it, do they praise and glorify God and Lord Thomas?
    A. Yes, my father, mother and I come twice a year to the tomb of Lord Thomas, barefoot pilgrims, and we intend to go for as long as we live; and I myself, because of my devotion, up until the present have been unwilling to have a husband, though urged by my kin and others to accept a man appropriate to me.

Q. In your parish, do your neighbors and others say publicly that you had been miraculously resuscitated through the merits of Lord Thomas?
    A. Yes; and commonly and publicly in the parish they call me "the virgin of St. Thomas."

Q. Do you know all the other witnesses who have sworn together and have been presented with you for testifying?
    A. Yes; they are from the parish where I was born, are free and reputed of good faith, and are not of the temporal dominion of the bishop and

chapter of Hereford, but of the dominion of Roger de Mortimer, baron, concerning whose kinship with Thomas I do not know.[5]

Q. Finally, have you testified out of fear or hatred, . . . [etc.; standard question—see above]?
    A. No.

She deposed in English.

DONE in the chapel of St. Katherine in our presence, notaries of this process.
(fol. 124 r.)

Sixty-Fourth Witness [Adam le Schirreve, father of Joanna]

Next day, *viz.,* 16th September, Adam le Schirreve, well-known [or well-born] sworn above, was presented by the proctor of Hereford chapter.

Q. Were you of the household, or are you kin to Lord Thomas?
    A. I was not of the household, but do not know whether I am of kin, since my grandfather had been a sheriff.

Q. How old are you?
    A. In my sixties.

Q. Are you subject to the temporal dominion of the bishop or chapter of Hereford?
    A. No, but to the temporal dominion of the lord king of England.

Q. Describe truthfully the miracle which is said to have involved the person of Joanna your daughter just examined, and the circumstances.
    A. About fifteen years ago and more, about the time the miracles that God was said to have worked for Lord Thomas first began to be publicized, in April, on a Sunday before the feast of the blessed George the martyr, there was a beer tavern in my parish of Maurdin in the house of Walter de la Wile. On that day I and my wife Cecilia went to the tavern after nones [early afternoon], with a good hundred people or so from the parish. When we went to the tavern we left our daughter Joanna at home with her other brothers and sisters.
    However, as we neared the tavern we saw Joanna, then about five, following us. We weren't concerned since many other neighbors' children

were there. Joanna stayed in the tavern for a little while with the other children, then I and several others saw her go out with the children into Walter's garden, where there was a pit or fishpond around six feet deep, some twenty-four feet wide and about sixty feet long; the water was about six feet below the bank. Some sparse vegetation grew around the sides of the pond, which were of mud, sand and dirt.

Joanna went to the pond into which she and John, son of Thomas Schonk, threw little stones. John was about Joanna's age and the son of her godmother. Two other village children were with them, but their names, and whose sons they were, I cannot recall. While they were throwing stones, John bumped into Joanna and she fell into the pond and drowned. I learned of all this afterward.

(fol. 124 v.)

We in the tavern were unaware of this. [Meanwhile,] as was the custom among our younger folk, after having a drink they formed a dance line, and danced through the garden and up near the pond where Joanna was submerged. Some in the dance saw the girl's clothing in the water, and saw her lying in the depths of the pond, unmoving. They assumed that she was the daughter of Cristina de Grenewey of the parish, who begged with her daughter, and that because of her poverty and misery Cristina had thrown her daughter into the pond.

Now the custom in our area and through the whole realm of England, except for the cities, is that whoever is first to find someone killed[6] or drowned ought to cry out and make this public, and everyone hearing the cry ought to follow it up from village to village, as far as the place where there are administrators of the law of the region, before whom the finder announces the killing or drowning. The finder personally is detained unless a suitable warrantor guarantees that [the finder] will be present before the justices of the king as soon as they come to those parts, for submission to judgment before them. Nor is the dead or drowned person to be moved from the place without notifying [those] who, on the king's behalf, inquire into such cases pertaining to the kingdom of England and the royal crown. If the contrary be done, even should the royal agent not come there for three months, [there is] great and serious punishment—[e.g.,] the pit in which anyone is found dead is filled with earth.[7]

On account of this custom, no one among the dancers wanted to make himself the finder of the drowned person, although the villager John de Pirebrok—a servant of Walter de la Wyle who had the pub in his house— wanted to announce the drowning to Walter, which the other dancers did not allow. They thought that, with the coming of nightfall, they would take the girl from the pond and throw her into a river running near the village called the Lugge, concealing publication of the accidental drowning. This was told to me afterward, since I was not in the dance line, but had remained with other adults and older people in the pub. John, Joanna's playmate who had bumped her into the pit, had started to tell this to Joanna's mother, [who was] talking with others. John's father Thomas Schonk (who [*fol. 125 r.*] led the dance line, and who saw, while leading the dance, the drowned girl in the water, being unwilling to publicize the drowning) came in [to the pub, and] seizing John his son, he took him to his wife's house, around one *sta-ðium* [perhaps 100 to 200 yards] away from the pub. He closed him in, lest he reveal the aforesaid. Leaving the house later on, John returned to the pub and finding Cecilia, the girl's mother, he told her about the drowning. The mother, then pregnant—she gave birth within a month—and the girl's god-mother Joan, Thomas Schonk's wife, ran to the pond with Ralph Taylor. [Cecilia] saw her daughter in the pond, and Joan the godmother forcefully threw herself into the water and dragged the girl to the bank.

All this was told to me by others; I did not see the girl in the water, being in the pub engaged with my neighbors. When the girl was taken from the water and put on the land, I was called, and seeing my daughter dead from drowning, with no sign of life, and the girl's mother and many bystanders mourning and crying around her, stirred to my paternal depths I greatly mourned and wept.[8]

I had heard that God worked many miracles for Lord Thomas; on bended knees, with the weeping women, and with great compunction and devotion, I begged Saint Thomas that if it were true that God worked mir-acles for him, he would resuscitate my daughter. And everyone there, about forty men and women, on bended knees tearfully begged for her resuscita-tion; with my belt I measured the girl to Saint Thomas. After the measure-ment, I cut her belt since her stomach was so swollen or bloated that I could barely put my fingers between her belt and her body. Then because I could not open her mouth with my fingers I used my knife, and with my wife's and others' help I tried to put her tongue back into her mouth, for it was stick-ing out, and was black and swollen. When her tongue was forcefully put back in, however, and the fingers holding it in place were removed, at once it thrust out again; her mouth, opening violently, remained thus open throughout the night unless closed by force; but as soon as the force was removed, her mouth (*fol. 125 v.*) opened.

When I had cut her belt and opened her mouth, I and others heard a kind of noise within her body, and one of the bystanders, Walter de Pirebrok, now dead, said, "If there was any breath of life in the girl, she's completely exhaled it," whereas others said that through St. Thomas's merits, God had breathed life into her; hoping from this for her resuscitation, they persisted more fervently in their prayer. However, I did not persevere in this because some said that the breath of life had been sent into the girl through the merits of St. Thomas; on the contrary, I persisted because neither movement, nor breath, nor warmth, nor any other signs of life appeared in the girl until the following dawn [i.e., he prayed not out of thanks but in hope].

Though remaining next to the pond from sunset until the darkness of night persevering in prayer, and though, on account of devotion, all the men had removed their hose so that they could pray, as the women, with their bare knees upon the earth, no signs of life appeared in the girl; from her body about two gallons [*lagenarum*, variable in volume] and more of water came out through her mouth and other natural parts. We brought the mother, who held the girl in her arms and mourned as if she were dead, into the house where the tavern was, and there we remained, persevering in prayer to St. Thomas to resuscitate the girl, until nearly the middle of the night. Since by then no signs of life had appeared, the girl was carried into my house; my neighbors, praying for her resuscitation, followed, remaining in my house all night, hoping and praying that God and Thomas would revive her.

Since the mother did not want to put down the girl, and the bystanders and I were concerned that, on account of her sadness and anguish, the mother might lose her unborn child, we made her get into bed. Because she wished to have her dead daughter with her, the bed was placed near a fire so that the coldness of her dead daughter would not harm the pregnant mother. Though the dead girl remained in the bed with her mother until dawn before any signs of life appeared in her, at dawn the mother felt some movement in her daughter, and said so to the bystanders. We praised and glorified God and St. Thomas with many tears, and the girl at once placed her right hand to her left arm, as it seemed to me. She began vomiting humors and superfluities that had remained in her body because of the drowning, and afterward she spoke. Asked how she had drowned, she said that John had pushed her into the pond. When soon afterward she recovered her strength, about sunrise we carried her to the parish church and put her upon the altar of St. Ethelbert king and martyr, patron of the Hereford church, and the bells were rung there [i.e. in Marden]; and *(fol. 126 r.)* everyone gathered and sang *Te Deum Laudamus*.

Though my neighbors objected, thinking her too weak, I picked her up in my arms and, getting on a horse with a cushion under us, I took her to the church of Hereford [the cathedral]. Many of my neighbors, those who had prayed for her resuscitation as well as others, about thirty in number, came with us, some barefoot; in addition, many from nearby villages, *viz.*, Framington and The Vauld, joined us on the road because of the miracle.[9] Also many from the city of Hereford, from whom I was barely able to protect the girl, wanted to see and kiss her out of devotion for the miracle. And the closer we got to the cathedral as I carried her in that direction, the stronger she became, as the color returned to her face. After I carried her into church and took her to the tomb of Lord Thomas, and a canonical inquisition and proof was made of the miracle, the bells rang through the whole city of Hereford, the people gathered, a huge procession was made, and the miracle was publicized; with tears and great devotion the clergy and people sang *Te Deum Laudamus*, and praise and glory were returned to God and St. Thomas.

Afterward I took Joanna home, and had a wax image made of her, which remained for many years hanging near Thomas's tomb until it was consumed by age. From that time my family and I have come to the tomb of Lord Thomas, sometimes barefoot, at least once a year, as pilgrims with an offering, especially on the feast of St. Ethelbert, patron of Hereford cathedral.

Q. What were the names of those who were in the dance line when they saw the girl drowned in the water?

A. Thomas Schonk, Stephen de Pirebrok (witnesses produced for this miracle [a notarial phrase added to the deposition, presumably]), John de Pirebrok, and many other of my neighbors. What I have testified about the drowning, death and resuscitation of the girl at the invocation of the name of St. Thomas is well known and public [knowledge] to some of my neighbors; in the resuscitation and miracle, there was no fraud, trickery, feigning, artificial contrivance or natural means [employed], but the miracle occurred through the power and virtues of God, at the invocation of the name and through the merits of St. Thomas, which in no way can be doubted; and the girl is still, in our village, called Joanna daughter of Adam le Schereve whom St. Thomas had resuscitated, and many noble folk from distant places still come, in attestation of the miracle, to see *(fol. 126 v.)* her.

Q. Before the drowning and resuscitation of the girl, were you and your wife devoted to St. Thomas?

A. We had been pilgrims to his tomb with other neighbors, and as soon as I saw that she had died, I began to invoke the name of St. Thomas, and all present began in the same way to invoke his name unanimously, with tears, having great faith that God, through the merits of St. Thomas, would revive her. After the resuscitation, however, my wife, daughter and I had no vision or other spiritual [event] that I know or heard about concerning Lord Thomas [which contradicts his wife Cecilia's testimony, q.v. below]

Q. After your daughter's resuscitation, did she say that she had seen anything during the time that she was drowned and dead?
   A. No.

Q. Before the miracle, did you and your wife lead a more spiritual life than your neighbors?
   A. We were faithful and devoted to God and the church, hearing divine services on feast days, supporting ourselves, giving alms as far as was possible, loving our neighbor in charity, and beloved by him, and after the miracle, made more devout, we continued in these things.

Q. Do you know the witnesses who have been presented with you concerning the miracle?
   A. Yes; they are free, and reputed of good opinion and truthfulness in my parish.

Q. Finally, have you testified out of fear or hatred, . . . [etc.; standard question — see above]?
   A. No.

DONE in the chapel of St. Katherine in our presence, notaries of this process. The witness deposed in English; note that on the third day when asked again, he changed [his reply]: he had [at first] said that they asked St. Thomas to resuscitate the girl, and in the repetition he said that they asked St. Thomas to ask God to resuscitate the girl.

After this, next day, *viz.*, the 17th of September [1307], Cecilia wife of Adam le Schirreve, well-known, mother of Joanna sworn above, was presented by the cathedral proctor.

Sixty-Fifth Witness [Cecilia, mother of Joanna]

Q. Are you related to Lord Thomas?
   A. I don't know.

Q. How old are you?
   A. More than fifty.

Q. Describe the miracle said to have happened to Joanna your daughter, *(fol. 127 r.)* and the circumstances.

A. On a Sunday before the feast of blessed George in April eighteen years ago, it seems to me, Adam my husband and I, with many of our neighbors, went to a beer tavern in Walter de la Wile's house in Marden village. When we left the house we left behind Joanna our daughter, then not yet five years old. Joanna, however, followed us to the pub, where she found John, then slightly younger than herself, the son of Thomas Schonk and Joan, who had raised Joanna from the font [i.e., was Joanna's godmother]. As I watched, John and Joanna left the pub together and went into a garden or clearing by the pub, and I did not see what they did there. This all happened soon after nones [early afternoon].

While my husband and I, and several others, were in the pub, John came back in—it seems to me that the time was about midway between nones and sunset—and told me something I could not understand, since I was talking with Joan, Joanna's godmother, and with Ralph Tailor [lit. Ralph cutter of cloth, *cissor pannorum*] of the village, who was telling us something. However, Thomas Schonk, John's father, came in, got his son and led him to the home of his wife Joan. At that time, I did not know why he took him away.

But afterward, when my daughter had been resuscitated, I was told that Thomas [Schonk] knew that his son John, playing with my daughter Joanna in the garden, had bumped or pushed her into a pit or fishpond. Thomas, leaving the pub with many others in a dance line, had led them past the pond where he, with many others in the dance line, saw Joanna drowned. And though Thomas and other dancers saw the drowned Joanna, and a pub servant named John de Pirebrok—who is still alive—wanted to reveal the drowning to the pub owner, they did not permit this, lest they lose their peace of mind[10] and because they believed that the victim was the little daughter of Cristine de Greneweye, a pauper and beggar woman *(fol. 127 v.)* of the parish who went about begging with the little girl and with a young son. In addition [they wanted to keep it quiet] on account of the custom in the realm of England, according to which a drowned or dead person, after a cry was raised by the finder, was not to be moved from the place where found drowned or dead until raised up in the presence of ministers of the king, deputed to such matters touching the royal crown. Thomas and the other dancers planned to take the drowned girl out of the pond that night and throw her into a nearby river called the Lugge, so that the victim would not come to the notice of the royal ministers, and the pub owner and the dancers and others would not suffer expense or loss before the royal court.

On that day, John, son of Thomas Schonk, leaving his mother's house where his father had put him so that he would not reveal the drowning, again returning to the pub after sunset and finding me there talking with Joan his mother, said to me "Cecilia your daughter Joanna has been drowned for a long time now in the fishpond."[11] Then Joan and I quickly got up and, followed by Ralph Tailor, we went to the pond and looked around for Joanna. At first I saw nothing. Joan, her godmother, looking around more keenly, told me that she saw something submerged deep in the middle of the pond. Removing none of her clothing, Joan quickly entered the pond. Her clothing was supported by the water as she swam to the place where the girl lay submerged; putting her head and body under water, she picked up the drowned girl, I don't know how, and coming to the bank threw her like a log up onto the dry land.

I examined the girl to see whether she was my daughter, but could not recognize her face because of the disfigurement and mud, and because her tongue was sticking out, clamped between her teeth; and her clothes were so muddied that I could not recognize them. Looking at her shoes, however, I knew that she was my daughter, because I recognized the new shoes I had bought for her the day before, with red tie-strings around their upper parts. I began mourning for my dead daughter. Ralph Tailor went for my husband, who was (*fol. 128 r.*) still in the pub, and my husband, arriving with many others, and seeing his daughter dead, immediately began to cry out, telling the bystanders that at Hereford there was a saint called St. Thomas, for whom God was said to work miracles, and [my husband] persuaded them to ask him to restore life to her. He measured the girl to St. Thomas with his belt, and cut the cord with which she was cinched, since on account of the swelling of her stomach with water, they could in no other way remove it. When the cord was cut, her belly swelled even more, and the bystanders and I heard a loud noise from her body. We [or possibly, excluding the mother, "they"] thought that the noise was the spirit of life in the girl on account of the invocation of St. Thomas and the measurement, and from that hoped more strongly that our prayers would be granted. But apart from the noise we had no other sign of life in the girl, bodily warmth or anything else, until daybreak.

I think that more than twenty men and women were there [at the pond] — I cannot recall the number well because of my great grief — on bare, bended knees upon the earth, begging with tears and devotion that St. Thomas ask God to resuscitate the girl. We said the *Pater Noster* and *Ave Maria*, and other prayers that we knew. While we were praying, Joanna's father and Ralph Tailor opened her mouth with a knife, and I wanted to put her tongue back into her mouth and close it, but could not, since as soon as

I put her tongue back in, it popped out again and her teeth [also] returned to the state they were in when she was taken from the water. Her tongue remained like that until she revived. Water, as much as her little body could possibly hold, came out of her lower parts as from a vase full of liquid.

After we had been at the pondside until nightfall, we took the dead girl into the house where the pub was, remaining there for the length of time it would take for a man to go about two miles at average pace. Then, being uncertain whether, in that place, the hue and cry might be raised by the drowned girl's finder [Joan the godmother] and others, so that, according to the English custom, the girl would be kept there, I left the pub with my dead daughter, and went to my own house, with my husband and others who continued praying that God would restore the girl through St. Thomas's merits. *(fol. 128 v.)*

After my husband and I were in the house awhile, since I was pregnant and near term — I gave birth in the same month — I got into my bed, put near the fire, since I was weak and oppressed with sadness, and since I hoped, as did the others who were praying there, that God, through the merits of St. Thomas, would resuscitate my daughter.

DONE on the 17 day of the month of September [1307], in the chapel of St. Katherine, in our presence, notaries of this process.

Afterward, next day, *viz.*, the 18th of September, Cecilia returned to the same place before the lords bishop-commissaries and continued her deposition.

Q. Why was a fire made near your bed?

A. Because some said that if it were not done, because I was pregnant I would be imperiled by the coldness of my dead daughter, whom I kept with me in bed next to my bare flesh. I held her in bed and felt no breath of life in her until the dawn, when she first began to move her right foot, as it seemed to me. Afterward there was a quaking throughout her whole body, and I put my mouth to her mouth and sensed her breath, then heard her make a low groan in discomfort, though not expressing any meaning; the groaning continued for as long as it usually takes to say the *Pater Noster* without the chant. I then put my mouth to her ear and asked her what she was doing in the water and she replied that John had pushed her.

At this, I immediately told my husband, and others praying there, about her resuscitation, and I showed her to them; and they, seeing her alive, praised and glorified God and St. Thomas, and they told this [news] to the lady of the village, Margery Wafre, who came with her household to see the girl. About sunrise, Joanna was carried by the lady and a multitude of villagers to the parish church, and she was placed upon the altar of St. Ethelbert king and martyr, patron of the [village of Marden] church and of the church of Hereford [i.e., the cathedral]. From there the girl was taken by her father, astride a cushion on a horse, to the tomb of Lord Thomas in the cathedral; and on the way many from neighboring villages and from the city of Hereford hastened to meet them.

After they were (*fol. 129 r.*) in the cathedral and the girl had lain for a while upon the tomb of Thomas, she restlessly raised her head, and then an inquiry was canonically made into the truth of the miracle, I believe. While I was sitting in the midst of the church with my daughter, a procession was made about us and the bells were rung and the people tearfully sang something, I don't know what. There was a great crowd there and everyone praised God and St. Thomas on account of the miracle.

Q. Because of the miracle, have you and your husband become more devout and firmer in your faith?

A. Yes, and from that time once, and sometimes twice or three times a year, with Joanna and our other children, we have come as barefoot pilgrims to the tomb of Lord Thomas, and we intend to continue as long as we live.

Q. Before or after the miracle, have you, your husband or your daughter had any vision or revelation about Lord Thomas?

A. Frequently thereafter my daughter and I dreamed that we visited the tomb of Lord Thomas, where we would pray and then return [home; but see the father's testimony on this point, above].[12]

Cecilia [at her own prompting, apparently] also said

When our son John wished to take holy orders, the bishop of Hereford was unwilling to ordain him without a true and sufficient title. Adam wanted to give his inheritance as a title to John, but he refused to accept it since the father intended, after the ordination, to take back the inheritance.[13] Thus, because of a defect in title, my son was unable to be promoted to the desired orders. I measured John to St. Thomas and took him to his tomb, asking Thomas to procure through the grace of God the promotion of my son to holy orders. Some years later, when I told the knight Robert Stormy [Stormi] that my son couldn't be ordained because of lack of title, he presented John to a chapel of which he was patron, and thus John was moved forward [lit., *promotus*], and I count this a miracle, through the merits of St. Thomas.

DONE in the chapel of St. Katherine the 18th day of the month of September in our presence, notaries of this process, and the religious brethren Walter de Risebury and John de Brompton, Franciscans of the Hereford convent. The lords commissaries wished [the two friars] to be present at the examination of this witness and of some of the others, for a more satisfactory interpretation and comprehension of the English tongue which, as far as certain words were concerned, was different in the diocese of Hereford from many other dioceses of the English kingdom; and also on account of acquaintance with the people presented, and to be presented, as witnesses by the proctor of the Hereford chapter.[14] Received as witnesses, they [Walter and John the Franciscans] swore *(fol. 129 v.)* touching the Bible in the presence of Master Henry, the Hereford chapter's proctor, truthfully and faithfully to listen to the meaning, to understand, and to translate [the words] of those witnesses who deposed in English, in their presence; and to reveal none of the attestations of the witnesses until they were published. The full deposition of Cecilia, and part of Adam's testimony, was read [for the friars] in the separate presence of Cecilia and Adam.

Next day, Cecilia returned before the lords commissioners.

Q. Before the miracle happened, did you or your husband have any spirituality in your lives beyond your neighbors?
    A. Along with many of our neighbors, we had gone as pilgrims to Thomas's tomb; we are faithful Catholics devoted to the church, supporting ourselves, diligently distributing alms as far as we can to our neighbors, and we are liked by them.

Q. Did any superstitious words, or natural or medicinal means, intervene in the operation of the miracle?
    A. No, but rather by great divine power, the miracle took place through St. Thomas's merits.

Q. Finally, have you testified out of fear or hatred, . . . [etc.; standard question—see above]?
    A. No.

She deposed in English.

Sixty-Sixth Witness [Ralph de la Brok]

Q. How old are you?
    A. I believe I'm in my sixties.

Q. Are you related to Lord Thomas?
    A. No.

Q. Are you under the temporal jurisdiction of the bishop or chapter of Hereford?
    A. No.

Q. Tell what you know about the miracle.
    A. More than sixteen years ago, it seems to me, on a Sunday, though I cannot remember the date or month, I was in the village of Wisteston in the parish of Marden, Hereford diocese, when I heard at sunset that Joanna daughter of Adam le Scherrive of the same village and parish had been taken out, drowned and dead, from a fishpond in the village in the garden of Walter de la Wile. She was taken out by the wife of Thomas Schonk of the parish, Joan Wase, who was Joanna's godmother,[15] who threw her up on the bank in the direction of her mother. I saw Joanna on the bank, *(fol. 130 r.)* dead, without movement or breath or any other sign of life. Her black, swollen tongue protruded partially from between her clenched teeth. Her father Adam, coming upon the scene, was moved by sadness at the drowning of his daughter; tearfully, on his knees, he asked St. Thomas, who lay in Hereford, to ask God to give her life. The bystanders [including this witness, presumably], crying and on their knees, asked the same, saying the *Pater* and *Ave Maria.*
    After the prayers and invocation of St. Thomas, the girl was measured to Thomas, but I don't recall with what the measuring was done, or by whom, though I'm certain it was either the mother or the father. After that, the girl's belt was cut by the mother or father and her mouth forced open with a knife, I don't recall by whom, nor can I clearly recall whether the cutting of the belt preceded the opening of her mouth, or the other way round. However, her mouth being opened, they tried to replace her tongue inside, but as soon as the fingers were removed, the tongue returned to the state it was when she was thrown up on the bank. Before they tried to put the tongue back, they held the girl upside-down and water flowed from her mouth, though I couldn't say for how long she was suspended, or how much water came out.

After all of that, while the mother held the girl, who was about five years old, in her lap, sitting at the side of the pond, we heard some sort of noise from the girl's throat, and we all said and believed that God had infused breath into the girl through St. Thomas's merits; on our knees we tearfully gave thanks to God and St. Thomas. I believed that God had infused life into the girl, though I did not see movement in any part of her body, nor breath or any other signs of life.

When night fell, we went into the house of Walter de la Wile, where the tavern was, *(fol. 130 v.)* and remained there for as long as it would take a person to walk, at a normal pace, about five miles. I left the tavern earlier than Joanna's parents, by about as much time as a person could go for two miles; up to that point I had seen no signs of life in the girl. Next morning I left the village and went into Wales, and when I returned three weeks later, I found the girl as I had known her before the drowning, and everyone in the village and nearby said that the girl, who was still living [in 1307], had been miraculously resuscitated at the invocation, and through the merits, of St. Thomas, and they still say and believe this, and they still call her "Joanna, the handmaiden of St. Thomas of Hereford."[16]

Q. How, and when, did the girl drown, and for how many hours did she remain submerged in the water?

A. I don't know, except through common report; but usually people said that Joanna was playing near the fishpond with her age mate *[coetaneo suo]* of the same parish, John, son of Thomas Schonk, and that John bumped her into the water some time about midway between nones and sunset, and that she remained submerged until sunset.

Q. Was the fishpond deep?

A. Yes, I estimate about six feet; and it was about four feet from the bank of the pond to the water. The fishpond, on level ground, was as deep at the sides as it was in the middle, and measured, I would estimate, about twenty-four feet across and around sixty feet in length.

Q. How did Joan, Thomas Schonk's wife, enter such a deep pond, and pull Joanna from the depths of the pond?

A. [At the pond's drainage outlet] one could enter from the bank without jumping into the water. The water was not as deep there, as it was where the girl was drowned. She went into the pond in that way, and went to the place where the girl was, the water buoying up her clothing while she swam,[17] and when the lower edge (or hem) of the girl's clothing appeared in the water, Joan dragged her by the hem to the land, as they said.

Q. Do you know, or have you heard it said, whether Joan, who took the girl from the water, immersed her head and her whole body below the water when she first began to drag out the girl or her clothing?

A. At the time it was said that Joan had thrust her arm up to her shoulder beneath the water, and with her hand dragged the girl out by her clothing. (*fol. 131 r.*) I did not hear that Joan had submerged her head under the water.

Q. Did you hear whether the girl was in the depths of the fishpond when she was plucked out by Joan, or that she was lying or swimming[18] in between the depths and the surface of the pond?

A. I heard that the girl's face was deep in the water, but I don't know whether in the depths of the pond or in what part of the water.

Q. Who was there when she was measured, and when she made that noise, and when she was carried into Walter de la Wyle's house?

A. Her parents, Thomas Schonk and Joan his wife, Walter de la Wyle and Joan his wife; Stephen de Pirebrok and William le Pipere, [all of whom are] witnesses sworn in this case, and many others, whose names I don't remember; I would estimate about twenty people.

Q. On that day, after nones, were you among the dance line led by the men and women of the village near the fishpond?

A. No, although there were many dancers. I heard from Thomas Schonk and Stephen de Pirebrok that, while they were in the dance line, they saw the drowned girl in their first pass by the place; after her discovery they told me this on the same day and in the same place.

Q. Because of this miracle has your, and your neighbors', faith and devotion increased?

A. Yes, and because of it I am more prone to saying prayers and going on pilgrimage.

Q. Do you believe that after the drowning the girl could have lived by any natural means or other remedy or human help, after being drowned so long in such a way, without a miracle?

A. No.

Q. Were any incantations or other superstitious words or deeds, or any medical or natural remedies applied or brought in, for the resuscitation of the girl, except the invocation of the name of Lord Thomas, the measurement and other things about which you have deposed?

A. No.

Q. Do you know the witnesses presented with you?

A. Yes, and they are trustworthy, of good faith, loving God and venerating the Church.

Q. Have you testified out of fear or hatred, . . . [etc.; standard question — see above]?

A. No.

This witness deposed *(fol. 131 v.)* in English, and said that he is a farmer, making his own living.

DONE in the chapel of St. Katherine the 19th day of September in our presence, notaries of this process; and the above-noted Franciscan friars Walter and John were present in the deposition and examination of this witness.

Sixty-Seventh Witness [Thomas Schonk]

Next day Thomas Schonk, sworn in for proving the miracle of the resuscitation of Joanna daughter of Adam le Schireve [*sic*], was presented by the proctor of the Hereford chapter.

Q. How old are you?

A. Around thirty-nine.

Q. Are you related to Lord Thomas, or subject to the temporal jurisdiction of the bishop or chapter of Hereford?

A. I am not related to Thomas's kin, but do hold my land of the dean and chapter of Hereford, in the village of Marden, and for that land I am their faithful subject, though free.

Q. Tell what you know about the miracle and the circumstances.

A. On a Sunday before the feast of St. George, nineteen years ago it seems, I and many other men and women of Marden parish and our neighbors, after nones by as much time as a man can go at common pace for a mile, went to a beer tavern in Walter da le Wile's house in the village or place called Wisteston, in Marden parish. There were more than sixty [people there]. After drinking and relaxing, for as much time as a man can go at common pace for a mile, the younger people *[iuniores]* in the tavern formed a dance line, and I was the leader of the dance. The dance crossed the tavern and the tavern garden and went into an area next to the garden, where there was a very deep fishpond. On our first pass near the pond I and Stephen de Pirebrok and John de Pirebrok, a servant of Walter de la Wyle, and Robert Mogge (now dead) of the parish saw something submerged in the pond.[19] On this first passage we did not determine exactly whether it was a child or some animal, though we saw the edge of some clothing. I told the others to continue, and that we would consider better what it might be on our return. We continued through the area for a little while and, on returning near the fishpond and carefully looking, we realized that a little boy or girl was drowned there.[20] We assumed that it was the daughter of Cristine de Grenewey, a poor women of the parish who begged with the girl.

(fol. 132 r.) Stephen and John de Pirebrok and Robert Mogge and I decided among ourselves that it would not be expedient *[non expediebat]* that others in the dance line should see this, and therefore we were unwilling to publicize this since no one wanted to be the finder of the drowned one, on account of the danger that could come to them and to the owner of the pond, according to the custom of the English realm. We said among themselves that when darkness came we would take out the little boy or girl and throw [the body] into a river that ran nearby, called the Lugge. Afterward we led the dance line through the middle of the tavern up to the public road. We were in the dance line for as much time as a man could go at normal pace for three or four miles, I think.

Then, however, my wife Joan, coming to me in the dance line, told me that our son John had told her and Cecilia, wife of Adam le Schireve, that Joanna their daughter had drowned. Cecilia had not understood his words. Leaving the dance I went to my son John, who was near his fifth year, seized him by the ear, took him home and shut him in, telling the housemaid Alice not to allow him out; I then went back to the dance, and led it for as much time as a man could go at usual pace for three miles. John, however, got out of the house and, as I watched, went to the tavern and told Cecilia and Joan his mother that Joanna, Cecilia's daughter, had drowned in the fishpond. He said this many times before they understood him. When they did, however, they went with John to the fishpond, and he pointed out to them the place where Joanna had fallen in. At first examination they saw nothing submerged; then looking more carefully, they saw the clothing of a little boy or little girl in the pond. As I and many others watched, my wife

Joan, who had raised Joanna from the holy font [i.e., as godmother], entered the pond from the bank four feet or so above the water, which was thirteen feet at its deepest; with her clothing billowing out on the water, she swam [natavit] to the place where the girl was submerged. She plunged her hand, arm and shoulder into the water, as well as her head, which disappeared from sight except for part of the head-dress that clung to Joan's head. With her hand she grasped the edge of the clothing of **(fol. 132 v.)** Joanna and, dragging her with that hand and swimming with the other up to the side of the pond, she threw the drowned girl onto the bank; the bystanders, extending their hands, helped Joan out of the water. The girl being on the dry land, the parents and the bystanders were mourning for some time when someone, I don't recall who it was, said that God worked many miracles through St. Thomas of Hereford, and that everyone should take off their hose and kneel with bare knees on the earth, devoutly begging St. Thomas that he ask God to give life to the drowned, dead girl. More than forty men and women were saying the Lord's Prayer and the *Ave Maria.*

After we had prayed a little, Adam, the dead girl's father, measured her to St. Thomas with his own belt. Having prayed awhile for the measurement, the father or mother, I don't recall well which one, cut the girl's belt, her mouth having been opened with a knife by Ralph de la Brok of the parish since her black, swollen tongue was partly sticking out through clenched teeth. Nicholas, son of Gilbert of the parish, as I believe, held her upside-down, and water came out of her mouth, nose, and her lower parts as her body was shaken and moved about. After this, about the time it takes a man to walk at normal pace one mile and more, bystanders and I heard a noise coming from her body, but we didn't know whether this was from the water, or what it was from. No breath could be felt when hands were put at her mouth and nose, nor was there any movement or other sign of life in her. We remained there until the shadows of nightfall, persevering in prayers and lamentations.

Afterward we took her and her mother into Walter's house, where the tavern was, and we remained there for about a mile's walk, lamenting and praying for her resuscitation; no sign of life appeared. Then her mother, without the approval of her husband, who wished his dead daughter—on account of [his] fear of the royal court and the customs about those found dead **(fol. 133 r.)** and drowned—to be left in place, carried the girl to her own house. We followed, still praying and hoping for the girl's resuscitation. There a fire was made for warming the body of the dead girl, and her body was placed near the fire. The mother, at the urging of bystanders, was persuaded to get into bed since she was close to giving birth and weakened and oppressed by sadness. When in bed, she wished to have her dead daughter next to her, and a fire [a second fire?] was made lest she be harmed by the coldness of her daughter's body. Around cockcrow, as I heard it said [indicating that the witness may not have been present at this event—see below], the mother felt the girl move her right foot a little, which Cecilia told the bystanders, who prayed more forcefully while asking St. Thomas for the life of the girl. Around the second cockcrow, the mother felt a strong movement in the girl, and also felt her breathing, and showed her, living, to the bystanders. After that, at dawn, since the mother felt the girl to have become strengthened, she said into her ear, "Daughter, what did you want in the water?" The girl replied, "John pushed me into the water." The mother told all of this to the bystanders, who devoutly praised God and St. Thomas. After the first cockcrow and the first sign of life that appeared in the girl in the motion of her foot, I went often to my house, which was nearby [suggesting that Thomas walked back and forth between the houses], and from there returned to Adam's house where these things occurred.

DONE in the chapel of St. Katherine on the 20th of September, in the presence of the friars Walter and John of the Franciscans, and in our presence, notaries of this process.

Afterward, next day the same witness returned before the lords commissioners in order to continue his deposition.

Q. When you and the others in the dance line saw Joanna submerged in the fishpond the first and second time [that you passed the pond], did you see in her any movement, or any sign from which you might have thought that she was still alive?

A. No. If we had thought that she was still alive, we would have taken her out of the pond immediately. But since we firmly believed that she was truly dead, we put off taking her out because of the reasons given [above].

Q. When you in the dance line saw her the first and second times, was the girl in the depths of the water, or was she on the surface?

A. It did not seem to me that she was in the depths, nor on the surface so that she or her clothing could be seen. She was, I estimate, about three feet below the surface, and was in the same place and depth at our first passage, and at our second, and afterward when (fol. 133 v.) she was taken from the fishpond.

Q. At what time was she taken from the pond?

A. She was taken out just at sunset; and I estimate that she was in the water for about a ten-mile walk.

Q. What were the names of those present when she was taken from the water and measured to St. Thomas?

A. I was there when she was taken out, and the girl's mother, my wife Joan, Ralph Atebroke, [and] Emma Caperon, now dead; and in the measuring, the same and the girl's father, as well as several others, forty and more, as I have testified.

Q. Was the miracle publicized in the parish church and the church of Hereford?

A. It was publicized in the parish, and Margery Wafre, the great noble lady of the place, and many from the nearby villages came to see the resuscitated Joanna. And she was carried to the Hereford church, accompanied by many, but I cannot recall whether she was carried to the parish church of Marden.

Q. From this miracle, were you and other people of the parish made more devout and firmer in your faith?

A. Yes. And because of it we more frequently cry out to God, and visit the church and go on pilgrimage to the tomb of Lord Thomas. When the girl was still dead at the bank of the pond, the vicar of the parish of Marden, John de Tydele, now dead, and old clergymen, and widows and children [*parvuli*, possibly "the little ones" in the sense of beggars, but more likely children], were called to pray for the girl's resuscitation, and they came and prayed with the others.

Q. In the doing of the miracle, was there any trickery, sortilege or superstitious words or deeds, or anything natural or artificial [*artificiales*] done so that the girl would be protected from death while in the water, or seem to be resuscitated to life?

A. No, except for the divine power, at the invocation of the name and merits of St. Thomas.

Q. Have you testified out of fear or hatred, . . . [etc.; standard question — see above]?

A. [The notaries write:] "He responded indignantly, 'No.'" [The tenor of Schonk's response is perhaps a reflection of his character. Evidently, he had

managed to brazen out the fact that, of all those involved in Joanna's accident, he had played the most reprehensible part, one that would have made
him particularly liable to royal penalties had circumstances been otherwise. One can only speculate about his relations with other Marden and
Wisteston villagers after that Sunday's events. Perhaps the felicitous results,
coupled with the fact that his own wife was Joanna's godmother and rescuer, softened the hostility that might have been expected from the girl's parents. On the other hand, records in the Hereford Cathedral Archives
suggest that Schonk was something of a "name" in Marden. He is noted as
selling some land to a fellow villager in a Marden manorial court roll of 1302
or 1303; he is again mentioned in a court roll of 1308; and he appears as a
suitor to the manor court, as having been elected to the office of village ale-
taster, and as selling more land in a manorial record of 1314 or 1315; his
name recurs in a roll of 1318-19.[21] Perhaps even in 1288 Schonk was a member of the upper echelons in Marden parish, a personification of that
inequality among peasants now recognized as a common characteristic of
contemporary English rural life. As such, his casual attitude toward
Joanna's fate and what sounds like attempts at bluff self-justification are
perhaps more understandable.]

He testified in English, and lived of his own [i.e., supported himself], as he said.

Sixty-Eighth Witness [Joan Wase, wife of Thomas Schonk]

Joan Wase, a sworn witness, was presented by the proctor of the Hereford
chapter for proof of the miracle of the resuscitation of Joanna, daughter of
Adam le Schireve.

Q. Are you related by kinship to Lord Thomas?
    A. No.
(fol. 134 r.)
Q. Are you subject to the temporal jurisdiction of the bishop or chapter of
Hereford?
    A. No, but to the lord king of England, under whom I have my land
from which I live.

Q. Tell what you know about the miracle [the notarial entry is brief here].
    A. On a Sunday before the feast of St. George about twenty years ago,
Cecilia wife of Adam le Schireve and I, and many other men and women of
the parish of Marden, after nones by about a mile's walk, gathered in the

house of Walter de la Wyle of the village or place of Wisteston of the parish
[of Marden], where a beer tavern was kept. John my son, about four, and
Joanna the daughter of Adam and Cecilia, nine months older than John,
were with us in the tavern when right away John and Joanna went out to
play in Walter's garden by the tavern. After Cecilia and I had been talking
together, and with others, in the tavern for as long as a three-mile walk or so,
John my son came back into the tavern without Joanna, and spoke to me and
Joanna's mother Cecilia, saying that Joanna had drowned; but because they
were childish words, and because Ralph Tailor was talking to me and Cecilia,
we paid no attention. The child then left us and returned to the garden.

Thomas Schonk [Joan does not say "my husband"], the father of
John, who then knew about the drowning accident, suspecting that John
would reveal this, carried him to my house and ordered Alice, my sister,
not to allow him out of the house. A little after sunset, as I estimate, John
returned to the tavern, found me and Cecilia sitting with Ralph, and,
plucking at my clothing, said "Joanna is all drowned in the fishpond."
Hearing this Ralph, Cecilia and I went to the pond, where John pointed
out to us the place where Joanna fell into the water. Ralph and Cecilia
looked around, but could not see the girl. Then John and I looked too,
John pointing to the place, and I saw Joanna submerged near the middle
of the fishpond. *(fol. 134 v.)* Moved by a kind of passion because I had
raised Joanna from the sacred font, forgetting the dangers that would
probably threaten if I entered the pond, I jumped in — shod and wearing
clothing, removing nothing except my hood [or cloak] — from the bank,
about four feet above the water, which was deeper than I was tall, my
clothes being raised and supported on the water. I never swam before this,
nor after I got out of the pond — as she responded, being asked [the form
of the question is not set out in the manuscript, however; perhaps the
notaries are trying to save parchment — from here on, in several instances,
they do not bother to write out the questions]. My body was submerged
up to my armpits, and my clothes were buoyed by the water as I swam to
the place where the girl was. Being asked, the witness replied [again, the
form of the question is not set out in the manuscript], this place was about
ten paces from the bank where I jumped into the pond. Reaching the spot
where she was, I grasped the edge of her clothing with my foot; then dip-
ping the right part of my body and my head under the water, I grasped the
girl's clothing with my right hand. I dragged her up, and swimming, as I
earlier explained, my clothing being supported on the water, I returned to
where I had jumped into the pond, threw her up onto dry land and, with
Ralph's help, got out of the pond.

After she had been on the bank for a while, her parents and others mourning her, one of the bystanders, Ralph Atebrok [another Ralph] — sworn and examined above [the notaries add] — wanted to raise the hue and cry according to the custom of the land that was followed when anyone killed or drowned or accidentally dead was found. Adam, Joanna's father, asked that they refrain from the hue and cry, avoiding a great scandal,[22] and [instead] invoke St. Thomas of Hereford, for whom God worked miracles, asking God to show a miracle in the girl. They invoked St. Thomas, on their knees, and Adam measured Joanna with his belt to St. Thomas. He cut her belt, and Ralph Attebrok with his knife opened her mouth, out of which thrust part of her black, swollen tongue squeezed by her teeth. Nicholas, son of Gilbert of Marden, raised her upside-down, and water flowed from her mouth. After some water had come out, I, who believed and said that the girl was dead *(fol. 135 r.)* when they measured her, went to my house nearby to change my clothes. From that point on, I did not see what was done concerning the drowned Joanna that night, but in the morning I saw her alive.

I went with her to the church at Hereford, and, Joanna having been put on St. Thomas's tomb, she lay there a little while; then she raised her head and arose into a sitting position and looked around at the bystanders. She looked beautiful and healthy to me and the bystanders, and we said among ourselves that we had never seen her look as beautiful and healthy as she was then; nor can I remember her ever looking so healthy since that time; and it seemed the same to others who then and subsequently saw her.[23]

Q. What are the names of those who spoke of her beauty?

A. Her parents, and Margery Wafre and others now dead.

Q. Who was present when you took the girl from the pond?

A. Cecilia the girl's mother and Ralph Tailor; and many others arrived afterward.

Q. In the doing of the miracle, was there any trickery, sortilege or superstitious words or deeds, or anything natural or artificial done regarding the miracle, so that somehow death and resuscitation could be feigned?

A. No. She was truly dead and miraculously revived through the divine power and strength of God operating through the invocation of the name and merits of St. Thomas.

Q. Because of the miracle, are you and your neighbors more devout and more firm in your faith, and do you glorify God and St. Thomas because of it?

A. Yes, and because of it I go on frequent pilgrimages to his tomb, and pray more devoutly and often.

Q. Have you testified out of fear or hatred, . . . [etc.; standard question — see above]?
A. No.

She testified in English.

DONE in the chapel of St. Katherine on the 21st of September, in the presence of friars Walter and John, Franciscans, and of us, notaries of this process.

Sixty-ninth Witness [Walter de la Wyle, tavern owner]

On the next day, Walter de la Wyle, sworn above, was presented by the proctor of the chapter of Hereford for proving the miracle of the resuscitation of Joanna daughter of Adam le Schireve.
(fol. 135 v.)
[Q. How old are you — question assumed in the notarial reportage.]
A. About forty years old.

[Q. Are you related by kinship to Thomas? — assumed question.]
A. I am not of the kin, nor was of the household, of the Lord Thomas, nor subject to the temporal jurisdiction of the bishop or chapter of Hereford, but of the lord king of England, under whose jurisdiction I have my domicile and possessions, on the income of which I live.

Q. Tell what you know about the miracle.
A. In the year in which miracles began to be reported, which God did through St. Thomas, on a Sunday before the feast of blessed George, I was keeping a beer tavern in my house, at which a multitude of people of the parish gathered, about the duration of a mile's walk after the hour of nones. Among them were Adam le Schireve, Cecilia his wife, Thomas Schonk and Joan his wife (witnesses above sworn and examined), and Thomas led a dance line inside and outside the tavern, while I tended to business in and outside the tavern. [Many of today's English country pubs include a garden next to the building; on warm spring and summer days, children are usually much in evidence in these gardens, amusing themselves while their elders are chatting and drinking in the sunshine.]

A little after sunset I heard some lamentation coming from near the fish-pond that I had in the garden. The fishpond is, and then was, over sixty paces in length and twenty-four in width; the water is and was then about thirteen and one-half feet deep. The pond was originally made in such a way that it was as deep at the sides as it was in the middle. Going to the [sounds of] lamentation, I found on the ground next to the pond Joanna, daughter of Adam and Cecilia, about five years old, dead from drowning in the pond. They said that Joan the wife of Thomas Schonk, Joanna's godmother, had taken her out of the pond. I thought, and still think, that the rescuing of the girl by Joan was a great miracle since Joan was not [herself] drowned, considering the disposition of the fishpond, the depth of the water and the way that Joan was said to have done it, jumping in shod and dressed.

While I and other bystanders looked at the girl, drowned and dead, having no more sign of life in her than in dried-up wood, we were very anxious, due to the onerous custom of the English realm in the case of anyone found drowned or killed. Her father Adam told the bystanders that he had heard that God worked many miracles for St. Thomas of Hereford, and that everyone should invoke Thomas to ask God to work a miracle in the girl. The bystanders and I took off our *(fol. 136 r.)* shoes and, on our knees, tearfully and devoutly we begged St. Thomas to intercede with God to work a miracle in the girl and give her life. Adam measured her with his own belt to St. Thomas, and cut the girl's belt. This being done, her mouth was opened by Ralph Attebrok of the parish, with his knife, since [though] she had her mouth shut, part of her tongue, gross and black, was sticking out, clenched in her teeth. After the mouth was opened, I and other bystanders heard a kind of noise in the girl's throat. One of those present, Walter de Pirebrok, now dead, said that if any breath of life remained in the girl she had exhaled it with that noise. She was then turned upside-down, and water came out of her upper and lower parts. The other bystanders and I saw her, without any doubt, dead; nevertheless we prayed that life should be returned.

Among ourselves, many were hesitant because of the possible penalty on account of her drowning and discovery; in order to avoid that risk we agreed to pretend that she was not dead, and, under cover of night, to carry her into my house, so that she would not be found dead next to the fishpond. And so we did it. In the house, a fire was made near the dead girl's body. After we had been there to nearly the middle of the night praying and mourning, no signs of life appearing in the girl, I feared the danger if she should be found dead in my house, and persuaded her parents to carry her to their house. I remained in my house, and did not know, except by what others said, what happened that night concerning the girl's resuscitation, nor did I see her until next day when she was brought back, alive, from the Hereford church. She still lives, and everyone in the parish and round about ascribed, and [still] ascribe, the resuscitation of the girl to a miracle done at the invocation of the name and merits of St. Thomas.

[Q. Was your faith strengthened, etc.]

A. Because of these things, everyone praises and glorifies God and St. Thomas, and they are more devout and firmer in their faith.

Q. While the girl lay dead by the fishpond, who among the bystanders said that they should pretend that she was alive, in order to evade penalties?

A. I was more concerned than the rest [of the bystanders] about the penalties, and afterward, the others [were too].

(fol. 136 v.)

Q. Was the death and resurrection of the girl made up by fraud or trickery, or any other reason; and in the doing of the miracle, was there any sortilege or superstitious words or deeds, or anything natural or artificial done regarding the miracle?

A. No, nothing but the power of God alone.

Q. Have you testified out of fear or hatred, . . . [etc.; standard question — see above]?

A. No.

He deposed in English.

Seventieth Witness [Joan, wife of Walter de la Wyle]

Joan, wife of Walter de la Wyle, witness just examined, being sworn, was presented by the proctor of the Hereford chapter for proof of the miracle of resuscitation of Joanna daughter of Adam le Schireve.

[Q. Age? . . . implied.]

A. I'm in my fifties.

[Q. Kin, etc., of Thomas? . . . implied.]

A. I was not of Thomas's household, nor related by kinship to him, nor [am I] subject to the temporal dominion of the bishop or chapter of Hereford, but to the lord king.

Q. Tell what you know about the miracle.

A. On a Sunday before the feast of blessed George, I don't know in what year, I was in the beer tavern in my and my husband's house where many had gathered. At sunset I heard mourning and lamentation in the garden; Joanna my goddaughter [girls often had more than one godmother; in this case, both godmothers were named Joan] had drowned in the fishpond that was in the garden.[24]

Going up to the mourners, I found them, and Joanna, near the fishpond. Adam her father had cut her belt, and with his own belt had measured her to St. Thomas of Hereford. Ralph Attebrok opened her mouth with a knife since part of her livid, swollen tongue protruded from between clenched teeth. Turned upside-down, water came out of her upper and lower parts. When she was put back on the ground, I and other bystanders heard a noise come from her, because of which I then believed, and still believe, that she was then alive.[25] Some bystanders said that the noise was the girl's last exhalation of life. We prayed there by her until nightfall, then took her into my husband's house. A fire was made by her to warm her body. She remained in the house until the middle of the night, and then was carried to the house of Adam her father. Before she was carried out of my house I touched her and she was cold and motionless, yet it seemed to me, and still seems to me, that *(fol. 137 r.)* she was still alive. I put my hand to her mouth and felt what seemed to be the cold breath of the girl. What happened after she was taken from my house, I knew only from others' statements.

Q. For how long was the girl submerged in the pond?

A. For as long as it would take a person, at a slow pace, to walk from Wisteston to the church in Hereford, which is three and one-half miles away,[26] and to return to Wisteston.

Q. Do you believe that the girl was truly dead before being taken out of the pond?

A. Yes. I don't believe it would have been possible, given human nature, for a small or large man or woman, to have remained for so long under the water as they said Joanna had done, without dying; I believed Joanna was truly dead when she was removed from the water, and a long time afterward, and life was miraculously infused into her through the merits of St. Thomas. [Joan seems to believe that the girl was miraculously revived while still on the bank of the pond.]

Q. In the doing of the miracle, was there any fraud, or sortilege or super-stitious words or deeds, or anything natural or artificial done regarding the miracle so that one could in any way have faked the death or resuscitation?

A. No, she was truly dead and miraculously resuscitated at the invoca-tion of the name, and through the merits, of St. Thomas.

Q. Because of the miracle, did you and your neighbors become more devout and firm in your faith, and glorify God and St. Thomas because of it?

A. Yes; afterward we went frequently as pilgrims to Thomas's tomb.

Q. Have you testified out of fear or hatred, . . . [etc.; standard question — see above]?

A. No.

She deposed in English.

[Being asked, she replied that] she knew the other witnesses, and that they were free and trustworthy.

DONE in the Chapel of St. Katherine the 22d day of September, in the presence of brothers Walter and John, Franciscans, and of us, notaries of this process.

Seventy-first witness [Stephen de Pirebrok]

Next day, Stephen de Pirebrok, sworn above, was presented by the proctor of the Hereford chapter for proving the miracle of the resuscitation of Joanna daughter of Adam le Schireve, drowned.

[Q. Age? . . . implied.]

A. Thirty-eight years old *(fol. 137 v.)* or thereabouts, and not of the household or kinship of Thomas, nor subject to the temporal dominion of the bishop or chapter of Hereford, but I am a tenant of land held of Nicholas de Pirebrok, of which I live.

Q. Tell what you know about the miracle.

A. On a Sunday before the feast of St. George the martyr, how many years ago I don't recall, but I think it was in the first year that they published miracles done through divine power by the merits of St. Thomas de Cantilupe, once bishop of Hereford, I, with many neighbors of the parish of the church of Marden and some others from nearby villages, went to Walter de la Wyle's house, in the place or hamlet *[villula]* of Wisteston in Marden parish, where there was a beer tavern.

Q. At what hour did you go to the house and tavern?

A. After nones, by the time needed for a mile's walk. After we had sat there drinking and enjoying ourselves for the space of a half-mile's walk, I and Thomas Schonk and William le Pipere (above-sworn witnesses) and John de Pirebrok and Robert Mogge, now dead, and several others whose names I can't recall, led a dance in Walter's tavern and adjacent garden and field [*gardino adiacente et viridario*—two different but connected places]. When we passed by a fishpond in the field, we saw in the water the edge of some clothing, and I asked Thomas Schonk, who led the dance, what it was. He said he thought it was some cloth left in the water by a washerwoman. After we led the dance line through the field for about [the duration of] a mile's walk, we returned by the fishpond, and looking more closely into the water we discovered that it was the clothing of some little boy or girl drowned there.

Being stupefied and terrified that the drowning would be imputed to us, in order not be suspected of this, we led the dance through the tavern [and then] to and along the public road; afterward we returned and led the dance in [Walter's] house and garden until sunset. After sunset, when we saw Cecilia, Adam's wife, and Joan Wase and others go out of the tavern toward the fishpond, leaving the dance line I and others followed the women, and we saw Cecilia and Joan looking into the water, and John, son of Thomas Schonk, pointing to the place where Joanna was drowned. *(fol. 138 r.)* Joan Wase, godmother of the drowned girl, at once raised her skirts and jumped into the water. As her clothing spread out around her on the surface, she swam to where the girl was, plunged her right arm and hand beneath the water, grasped the edge of the girl's clothing, and swimming with the other hand to the bank, threw the body onto dry land. One of the bystanders, whose name I don't remember, extended a hand to Joan Wase and dragged her onto the bank.

The girl's mother was rolling her about on the ground, and did not realize that she was her own daughter until she recognized the girl's shoes [or perhaps sandals, *sotulares*], which she had bought the day before; they had red laces on their upper parts. The girl's father, seeing her swollen and full of water above and below her belt that was tightly tied, cut the belt with his knife, and with his [own] belt measured her to St. Thomas, asking him, on his knees, tearfully, that if God ever did any miracle through St. Thomas's merits, he show one then, begging God to revive his daughter. The bystanders, having rolled down their hose toward their feet, some completely removing their shoes and hose, knelt with bare knees on the earth, begging God with tears and devotion that through St. Thomas's merits he show forth a miracle and resuscitate the dead girl; the women did the same. Ralph Attebrok (witness sworn and examined above) seeing the girl's swollen, black tongue sticking from her mouth between clenched teeth, opened her mouth with his knife; she was lifted upside-down, I don't clearly recall by whom, and water flowed from her mouth and other upper and lower openings.

After remaining there until nightfall, praying and tearfully lamenting, hoping still for the showing of a miracle through the merits of St. Thomas, we led Cecilia, carrying her dead daughter, into the house of Walter de la Wyle. After praying there a little while I and others heard a sound in the girl's body; we hoped from this that God had infused life into the girl. Nevertheless, we saw no movement in her. When I put my mouth to the girl's mouth, I could sense no breath of life. Afterward, before the middle of the night the girl was carried by her mother to the house of Adam, the girl's father, the neighbors, men and *(fol. 138 v.)* women, joining them. After we got there Cecilia's bed was prepared, she being pregnant and near term and debilitated from sadness. She got into bed holding her daughter in her arms. Fearing that Cecilia might be harmed from the coldness of her child's body, a fire was made near the bed. At dawn Cecilia felt her daughter move her right foot, as Cecilia then told us; and soon afterward I heard Cecilia speaking with her daughter, thus: "Beloved daughter, praise God and blessed Thomas who have worked a miracle in you; tell me what you wanted in the water." And she replied in our hearing, "John pushed me into the water." The miracle being immediately publicized, the bells rang in the chapel of the Holy Cross of Wisteston, and in the parish church of Marden. Everyone hearing of the miracle glorified God and St. Thomas.

Q. What moved you to stop leading the dance line and to follow the women to the fishpond?

A. Because I assumed that the accident *[casum]* had been revealed to the women by John, son of Thomas Schonk, and that the women had gone to the pond to pull Joanna from it.

Q. How long was it between the time you first saw the edge of the garment in the pond and the removal of the drowned girl from the fishpond?

A. As much time passed as it would take, at usual pace, to walk twelve miles.

Q. The miracle being done and published, because of it was your faith and devotion, and [that of] others to whom notice of it came, increased, and because of this did you praise and glorify God?

A. Yes.

Q. How old was Joanna when she was drowned and removed from the pond?

A. Around five.

Q. In the doing of the miracle, was there any fraud, or superstitious words or deeds, or sortilege, or anything natural or artificial done regarding the miracle so that one could in any way have faked the death or resuscitation?

A. No, Joanna was truly dead and miraculously resuscitated at the invocation of the name of St. Thomas.

Q. Have you testified out of fear or hatred, . . . [etc.; standard question — see above]?

A. No. [He added, being asked,] I know the other witnesses, and they are *(fol. 139 r.)* free and trustworthy.

He deposed in English.

After this, the lords bishops-commissaries, *ex officio*, summoned Roger, perpetual vicar of the parish church of Marden, in whose parish the miracle of the resuscitation of Joanna daughter of Adam le Schireve was said to have happened, and from whose parish the witnesses were said to have been brought in by the proctor of the Hereford chapter for proof of the miracle. The vicar arrived and, in the presence of the Hereford proctor, touching the Holy Bible he swore to tell the truth about the things they would ask him, and about which he would be questioned.

Q. Do you know anything about this miracle?

A. I have been vicar in this place for the past eight years or so, and know about the miracle only through common report; but generally everyone in my parish says that Joanna, though drowned and dead, was miraculously resuscitated at the invocation, and through the merits, of St. Thomas.

Q. Do you know Joanna [who at this time was still living in the village] and the witnesses presented for proving the miracle [their names were read to him]?

A. Yes.

Q. What is their condition?

A. They are free and trustworthy in the parish, and of [good] repute among their neighbors.

He testified in Latin *[literaliter]*.

DONE in St. Katherine's chapel on the 23d of September in the presence of brothers Walter and John, Franciscans, and of us, notaries of this process.

Seventy-Second Witness [William le Pipere]

After this in the year of the Lord 1307, sixth indiction, month of September, the 25th day, William le Pipere, sworn above, was presented by the proctor of the Hereford chapter for proving the miracle of the resuscitation of Joanna, drowned daughter of Adam le Schireve.

[Q. Age, etc., . . . question implied.]

A. More than a hundred years old *[quinquies viginti annorum et amplius]*, not of the kinship or household of Lord Thomas, nor am I subject to the temporal dominion of the bishop or chapter of Hereford, but hold my land of Thomas Wafre, and I am supported by my crops.

Q. Tell what you know of the miracle.

A. On a Sunday before the feast of St. George the Martyr, I don't know how many years ago, I and many neighbors of Marden were together in Walter de la Wyle's house in Wisteston, Marden parish, where there was a beer tavern. I and the others sitting in the tavern saw that many of our neighbors went out into Walter's field. We followed, and saw, next to Walter's fishpond in his field, Adam le Schireve and Cecilia his wife, Thomas Schonk and Joan his wife, and many others looking at the body *(fol. 139 v.)* of the dead Joanna, daughter of Adam and Cecilia, who was said to have drowned in the pond and was taken out of it, but as for how much time she was submerged in the pond I do not know, except for what I have heard.

Then at sunset I saw Adam measure the girl with his own belt to St. Thomas. After that Adam and Cecilia and everyone there, men as well as women, knelt on the ground with bare knees and raising their hands and eyes to heaven devoutly and tearfully begged God that through the merits of St. Thomas he would restore life to the girl. Then Adam and Ralph Attebrok, with Ralph's knife, opened the girl's mouth, and with his own knife her father cut the girl's belt with which she was being squeezed. I do not recall seeing any water coming out of her, or hearing any noise from her. After we prayed and lamented in the field until nightfall, the dead girl was taken into Walter's house, where we tarried until the middle of the night or so. Nor, as I recall, did any sign of life appear in her. The girl was carried to Adam and Cecilia's house, and I went home, and saw nothing further about the girl that night.

Next day about sunrise, the miraculous resuscitation was publicized, the bells of the parish church of Marden were rung, and of other nearby [churches], and of the chapel of the Holy Cross at Wisteston. Many neighbors and I went to Adam's house, where we saw Joanna alive, resuscitated by God through the merits and at the invocation of the name of St. Thomas. Then I went with many others along with Adam, carrying Joanna his daughter, to the cathedral church of Hereford. When she was placed on Thomas's tomb, I saw her raise up and sit there, looking all around, and [she seemed] very healthy. Everyone there thanked God and St. Thomas.

Q. How long did they say that she had been in the water?
A. For as long as it took to walk sixteen miles or so.

[Q. Asked, he replied . . .]
A. I heard Thomas Schonk or Ralph Attebroke or Stephen de Pirebrok of Wisteston, who were in the dance line with many others near the fishpond, say that, while leading the dance, they saw something submerged in the pond, which was the girl, as it appeared afterward.

Q. After the miracle, were people of the parish made more devout and firmer *(fol. 140 r.)* in their faith, and you with them? and did [you and] they thank God and St. Thomas for it?
A. Yes. Because of the miracle, in the village or place of Wisteston the resuscitated Joanna is still called "St. Thomas's Virgin."

Q. Was there any fraud or feigning committed in this miracle, a pretense that she had not died or been resuscitated, or sortilege, incantation, or any superstition of words or deeds, or anything natural or artificial used in the operation of the miracle?
A. No; [rather,] the divine potency and force.

Q. Do you know the witnesses presented and examined in proof of this miracle?
A. Yes.

Q. What is their condition.

A. They are free, considered to be trustworthy and reputable in the parish.

Q. Have you testified out of fear or hatred, . . . [etc.; standard question — see above]?

A. No.

He deposed in English.[27]

ABBREVIATIONS USED IN THE NOTES

AASS　　　*Acta Sanctorum*

Becket　　James Craigie Robertson, ed., *Materials for the History of Thomas Becket, Archbishop of Canterbury, Canonized by Pope Alexander III, A.D. 1173.* Vols. 1-6, Vol. 7 by Robertson and J. Brigstocke Sheppard, 7 vols. [Rolls Series] (London: 1875-85).

Chiara　　Enrico Menestò, ed., *Il processo di canonizzazione di Chiara da Montefalco* (Firenze/Perugia, 1984).

CWHHD　Kenneth F. Kiple, ed., *The Cambridge World History of Human Disease* (Cambridge, 1993).

Dorotheas Richard Stachnik et al., eds., *Die Akten des Kanonisationsprozesses Dorotheas von Montau von 1394 bis 1521* (Köln, 1978).

Henry　　Paul Grosjean, ed., *Henrici VI Angliae Regis Miracula Postuma* [Bollandists], Subsidia Hagiographica 22 (Bruxelles, 1935).

JAMA　　*Journal of the American Medical Association.*

Laurent　Chas. Plummer, ed., "Vie et Miracles de S. Laurent archevêque de Dublin," *Analecta Bollandiana*, vol. 33 (1914), 121-86.

Louis　　*Processus Canonizationis et Legendae Variae Sancti Ludovici O.F.M., Episcopi Tolosani, Analecta Franciscana*, vol. 7 (Quaracchi/Florence, 1951).

Nicholas　Nicola Occhioni, ed., *Il Processo per la Canonizzazione di S. Nicola da Tolentino* (Roma, 1984).

Osmund　A. R. Malden, ed., *The Canonization of St. Osmund*, Wiltshire Record Society, vol. 2 (1901).

Urban　　J.-H. Albanès, ed., *Actes Anciens et Documents concernant le Bienheureux Urbain V Pape* (Paris, 1897).

Wulfstani Reginald R. Darlington, ed., *The Vita Wulfstani of William of Malmesbury ... and the Miracles*, RHS Camden Third Series, vol. 40 (London, 1928).

NOTES

NOTES TO PREFACE

1. Nicola Occhioni, O.S.A., ed., *Il Processo per la Canonizzazione di S. Nicola da Tolentino* (Roma, 1984), 116-30, hereafter *Nicholas*. Berard's general description of events at the tomb are on 123-4.

2. See, for instance, Henri Platelle, "L'enfant et la vie familiale au moyen âge," *Melanges de science religieuse*, 39:2 (June 1982), 67-85 at 77—"indifférence" versus "résignation"; and Marie-France Morel, "Reflections on Some Recent French Literature on the History of Childhood," *Continuity and Change*, 4:2 (1989),323-37 at 329 and, in the same issue, Brigitte Niestroj, "Some Recent German Literature on Socialization and Childhood in Past Times," 345-6.

3. Mary Martin McLaughlin, "Survivors and Surrogates: Children and Parents from the Ninth to the Thirteenth Centuries" in Lloyd de Mause, ed., *The History of Childhood* (London, 1976), 101-81.

4. A more recent overview by Barbara Hanawalt: "Narratives of a Nurturing Culture: Parents and Neighbors in Medieval England," *Essays in Medieval Studies* vol. 12, *Children and the Family in the Middle Ages*, (ed.) Nicole Clifton (1995 Proceeding of the Illinois Medieval Association, www.luc.edu/publication/medieval/emsv12.html), 1996. See also Lorraine C. Attreed, "From *Pearl* maiden to Tower princes: Towards a New History of Medieval Childhood," *Journal of Medieval History*, 9 (1983), 43-58.

5. Shulamith Shahar, *Childhood in the Middle Ages* (London, 1990).

6. James A. Schultz, *The Knowledge of Childhood in the German Middle Ages, 1100-1350* (Philadelphia, 1995).

7. M. Lett informs me that the book will be published by Hachette in the series *La Vie quotidienne*.

8. David Herlihy, *Medieval Households* (Cambridge [MA], 1985), 112.

NOTES TO CHAPTER 1

1. In addition to the classic study by E. W. Kemp, *Canonization and Authority in the Western Church* (London, 1948), see André Vauchez, *La sainteté en occident aux derniers siècles du moyen âge* (Rome, 1981), especially book 1, and Patrick Daly's concise overview in his "The Process of Canonization in the Thirteenth and Early Fourteenth Centuries," in Meryl Jancey, ed., *St. Thomas Cantilupe, Bishop of Hereford: Essays in His Honour* (Hereford, 1982), 125-35. Margaret R.

Toynbee's older work is also useful: *S. Louis of Toulouse and the Process of Canonisation in the Fourteenth Century* (Manchester, 1929).

2. Emmanuel Le Roy Ladurie, *Montaillou*, trans. Barbara Bray (New York, 1980), passim.

3. *Materials for the History of Thomas Becket, Archbishop of Canterbury, Canonized by Pope Alexander III*, A.D. 1173, vols. 1-6, ed., by James Craigie Robertson, vol. 7 by Robertson and J. Brigstocke Sheppard, 7 vols., [Rolls Series] (London, 1875-85), vol. 1, 346-7. Hereafter, *Becket.*

4. This is not to deny the utility of examining "miracles" as manifestations of medieval faith or as modes of collectively expressing and verifying a system of belief. For an overview of the problems of dealing with hagiography as historical source, see, for example, Aviad M. Kleinberg, *Prophets in Their Own Country* (Chicago, 1992), chap. 3, "Wide-Eyed Witnesses and Partial Observers," esp. 59-70.

5. Barbara A. Hanawalt, *Crime and Conflict in English Communities, 1300-1348* (Cambridge, MA, 1979), and, more useful in what it tells us about children, Hanawalt, *The Ties that Bound: Peasant Families in Medieval England* (New York, 1986).

6. Renate Blumenfeld-Kosinski, *Not of Woman Born: Representations of Caesarian Birth in Medieval and Renaissance Culture* (Ithaca, NY, 1990), 14.

7. *AASS,* (I October, 1765 ed.), 610 ff.

8. Professor Susan Ridyard is currently editing the Cantilupe canonization manuscripts.

9. Since the two monks collected their examples independently, comparison of the many duplicated reports sometimes reveals interesting differences in their manner of analyzing or interpreting the same events; cf. R. C. Finucane, *Miracles and Pilgrims: Popular Beliefs in Medieval England* (London, 1977, repr. New York, 1995), 125-6, 162-6.

10. The "dismemberment" and discoveries in the woman's heart are referred to by Vauchez, *La sainteté en occident,* 517; in Enrico Menestò, ed., *Il processo di canonizzazione di Chiara da Montefalco* (Firenze/Perugia, 1984), hereafter *Chiara.* Menestò discusses "I segni prodigiosi trovati nel suo cuore," with illustrations, on clxx-clxxvii.

11. Finucane, *Miracles and Pilgrims,* chap. 4, "Faith-Healing: Medicine and Miracle."

12. Christian Krötzl, "Evidentissima signa mortis. Zu Tod und Todesfeststellung in mittelalterlichen Mirakelberichten," *Symbole des Alltags, Alltag der Symbole: Festschrift für Harry Kühnel zum 65. Geburtstag* (Graz, 1992), 765-75.

13. The monks of Leominster, for example, "failed to ring the bells (provided by the parishioners) at times of service." David M. Smith, "Thomas Cantilupe's Register" in Jancey (ed.), *St. Thomas Cantilupe,* 99.

14. James A. Schultz, "Medieval Adolescence: The Claims of History and the Silence of German Narrative," *Speculum* 66 (1991), 519-539 at 536. On the other hand, other studies have found indications that an adolescent transi-

tional period is identifiable: see Barbara Hanawalt, *Growing up in Medieval London* (New York, 1993), and Kathryn L. Reyerson, "The Adolescent Apprentice/Worker in Medieval Montpellier," *Journal of Family History* 17, no. 4 (1992), 353-70.

15. On the "ages of man" and childhood, see Luke Demaitre, "The Idea of Childhood and Child Care in Medical Writings of the Middle Ages," *Journal of Psychohistory* 4 (1977), 461-90; Michael E. Goodich, "Bartholomaeus Anglicus on Child-Rearing," *History of Childhood Quarterly* 3 (1975), 75-84, and Goodich's *From Birth to Old Age* (New York, 1989), esp. chap. 4, "Infancy and Childhood"; Louis Andrieux, "La Viatique et l'Extrême-Onction des enfants," *Revue Pratique D'Apologétique* 14, no. 158 (15 Avril 1912), 81-100; René Metz, "L'Enfant dans le Droit Canonique medieval" [1976] in *La femme et l'enfant dans le droit canonique médiéval* Variorum Reprints (London, 1985), I:9-96, and Pierre-André Sigal, "Le vocabulaire de l'enfance et de l'adolescence dans les recueils de miracles latins des XIe et XIIe siècles," *L'Enfant au Moyen-Age* (Aix-en-Provence, 1980), 143-60.

16. There are four exceptions out of 600 cases, where the subjects (included because their experiences were particularly revealing) were age 15.

17. Klaus Arnold, *Kind und Gesellschaft in Mittelalter und Renaissance* (Paderborn, 1980), 36-7.

18. H. Platelle, "L'enfant et la vie familiale," 77.

19. Bodleian MS *Fell 2*, fols. 29-30: *pueriliter cónludendo.* "The women" made vows for the child, which were ratified by the parents when they returned home.

20. *modo puerili.*

21. *dissimulaverunt putantes ipsum pueriliter simulare fletum suum.*

22. Richard Stachnik et al.,eds., *Die Akten des Kanonisationsprozesses Dorotheas von Montau von 1394 bis 1521* (Köln, 1978), 78-9; hereafter, *Dorotheas.* The English case involved Joanna of Marden, discussed at length in chapter 4 and set out fully in the appendix.

23. *Becket*, vol. 1, 207; Paul Grosjean, ed., *Henrici VI Angliae Regis Miracula Postuma* [Bollandists] Subsidia Hagiographica 22 (Bruxelles, 1935),17-19; hereafter, *Henry. Becket*, vol. 1, 522.

24. MS *Vat. Lat. 4015*, fols. 64^r-71^v.

25. *Becket*, vol. 1, 200-2, 2, 238-9; *Henry*, 101-3, 141-3, 164-5, 200-3, 205-6, 209-11, 294-5; *Dorotheas*, 176-7; A. R. Malden, ed., *The Canonization of St. Osmund*, Wiltshire Record Society, 2 (1901), 82-3; J.-H. Albanès (ed.), *Actes Anciens et Documents concernant le Bienheureux Urbain V Pape* (Paris, 1897), 453. Expressions used by witnesses were Latinized into constructions such as *sicut pueri libenter facere solent; more ludencium puerorum; juvenili levitate; infantuli more lasciviens; more infancium lustrabat; ut talium moris est; more puerili iocis ac consuetis; more infantili;* and *ut moris est infantium.*

26. *Urban*, 297-8: *quod apperiebatur sibi os suum et dabatur ei lac mulieris.*

27. *Henry*, 247-50. Their effort was Latinized by Henry's miracle recorder as follows:

Rex Henrice, tuum, da, rex Henrice, iuvamen,
Rex bone, rex sancte, rex optime, fer relevamen.
See Edina Bozóky, "Mythic Mediation in Healing Incantations," in *Health, Disease and Healing in Medieval Culture*, eds. Sheila Campbell et al. (New York, 1992), 84-91 for a brief overview.

28. *Becket*, vol. 1, 199-200: *annulis et brevibus.*

29. *Henry*, 103-6: *vulgi videlicet opinionem secuta.*

30. The technique of measuring,while not for the purposes outlined here, is nicely portrayed in Ermanno Olmi's evocation of late nineteenth-century Italian peasant life, *L' albero degli zoccoli*, Produzione Cinema (Milan,1978), available in videotape as *The Tree of Wooden Clogs*, distributed by Fox Lorber (New York) 1990.

31. *Henry*, 286-8: *[V]irgineo fronti tam fortiter impressit, ut ipso tactu inflecteret . . .*, an interesting variation of the custom whereby coins were bent while being held over a victim, which were then sometimes tied on to, or placed round the neck of, the victim until offered at the shrine. It has been suggested by Dr. Eleanora C. Gordon, M.D., that measurement for a candle was peculiar to England: "Measurement for a Votive Candle: A Rite of Healing," *Storia e Medicina Popolare* 7 no. 3 (Rome) (September-December 1989), 3-16. There are, however, many examples of this custom noted in continental miracle collections. If anything, coin bending seems to have been very much an English custom, rather than continental. See also Pierre-Andre Sigal, *L'homme et le miracle dans la France médiévale* (Paris, 1985), 88-9, 96-7. Sigal queries some of my interpretations of the measured-candle ritual.

32. *Chiara*, 379-80, 382, 509-10; *Canonization of St. Osmund*, 42-4, 56-60, 67; Bodleian MS *Fell 2*, fols. 35-6; *Vie et Miracles de S. Laurent archevêque de Dublin*, ed. Chas. Plummer, *Analecta Bollandiana*, 33 (1914), 171; *Becket*, vol. 1, 232-4; *Henry*, 35-7, 193-6, 237-9.

33. MS *Vat. Lat. 4015*, fols. 125^v, 136^r, 138^r, 148^r, 151^r: *flexis et nudis genibus super terram; caligas a genibus suis.*

34. cf. Exod. 3:5 and Acts 7:33.

35. *Processus Canonizationis et Legendae Variae Sancti Ludovici O.F.M., Episcopi Tolosani*, *Analecta Franciscana*, 7 (Quaracchi/Florence, 1951), 314. Hereafter, *Louis.*

36. MS *Vat. Lat. 4015*, fol. 133^v.

37. *Becket*, vol. 2, 227-8.

38. MS *Vat. Lat. 4015*, fol. 139^v.

39. The ritualistic aspect of vowing for positive benefits is mirrored in cursing for evil ones, at least in early-modern England: Keith Thomas mentions a woman who, in 1617, "did curse John Smith, . . . upon Thursday last, . . . kneeling down upon her bare knees and holding up her hands . . . . " *Religion and the Decline of Magic* (Harmondsworth, 1971), 606.

40. *Henry*, 200-203: *Lineis quoque intrinsecus omnino carens.* As the body would not be protected from the roughness of the outer woolen garments, removing inner linens probably would have had the same effect as putting on a hair

shirt, appropriate clothing for a suppliant. In several Italian cases, those making vows specified that they would go to the shrine "without linens."

41. In one English miracle of the fifteenth century (*Henry*, 36), reference was made to the tearful prayers of Samuel's mother, who vowed to give her child to Yahweh (1 Samuel 11-12).

42. Oxford, Bodleian MS *Fell 2*, fols. 35-6: the operative expression was *ego dabo eam tibi*. St. Edmund was Edmund Rich, an English prelate buried at Pontigny in the mid-thirteenth century, canonized in 1246. This child's rescue had been somewhat haphazard: the women's cries attracted a young man from the local tavern, but he was so drunk that he dropped her back into the water during one of his clumsy efforts to bring her up with a rope.

43. Mary Martin McLaughlin, "Survivors and Surrogates: Children and Parents from the Ninth to the Thirteenth Centuries" in Lloyd de Mause, ed., *The History of Childhood* (London, 1976), at 129-32 where McLaughlin deals with oblation. See now Mayke De Jong, *In Samuel's Image: Child Oblation in the Early Medieval West* (New York, 1996), esp. 156-91 for the rituals, and on 176-7 for a note on the relationships between bringing children for cures and offering them to saints through official as well as "uncontrolled and unrecorded ritual performance."

44. Metz, "L'Enfant dans le Droit Canonique medieval," 51; cf. John Boswell, *The Kindness of Strangers: The Abandonment of Children in Western Europe from Late Antiquity to the Renaissance* (New York, 1988), esp. chaps. 8 and 9; De Jong, *In Samuel's Image*, 290-302 for twelfth and thirteenth-century changes in oblation.

45. *Nicholas*, 389-90: *statim cum posset ipse puer nutriri sine matre.*

46. *Nicholas*, 395-6: *si voluerit dictus puer.*

47. Vauchez, *La sainteté en occident*, 535; for his remarks on vows, "temporary oblates" and "sainteurs," those vowed to pay annual acknowledgment of their debt to a saint, see 530-40.

48. *offerre dictum puerum et recolligere eum.*

49. Quoted by James Bruce Ross in "The Middle-Class Child in Urban Italy, Fourteenth to Early Sixteenth Century," in Lloyd de Mause, ed., *The History of Childhood* (London, 1976), 183-228, at 208.

50. This recalls Benedict's *Rule* on the would-be monk who was "stripped of everything of his own that he is wearing and clothed in what belongs to the monastery. The clothing taken from him is to be put away and kept safely in the wardrobe. . . ." T. Fry, et al., eds., *RB 1980: The Rule of St. Benedict in Latin and English with Notes* (Collegeville, MN., 1981), 271. Lanfranc directed the abbot, when accepting a child oblate, to remove the child's outer clothing while saying, somewhat incongruously, "May the Lord strip thee of the old man. . . . "

51. *Nicholas*, 601-2: *et nunquam reportare.*

52. For instance, in *Nicholas*, 308-10, 354-5. Perhaps the sentiments expressed here were similar to those found in a passage from *Germania*, in which Tacitus

writes that no one entered the sacred groves until he had been bound in chains, thus acknowledging the deity's power; cited in V. Flint, *The Rise of Magic in Early Medieval Europe* (Princeton, NJ, 1991), 229.

53. *Louis*, 288. Sometimes the votives seemed to fill the entire church, as reported of Urban's cult at Marseilles, where there was said to have been *infinitae imagines cereae appensae ante sepulchrum et quasi per totam ecclesiam dicti monasterii*. . . . in *Urban*, 49.

54. *Louis*, 319: *illum qui facit ymagines de cera*.

55. On votives, see Barbara Schuh, "Wiltu gesund werden, so pring ain waxen pildt in mein capellen . . . "; *Votivgaben in Mirakelberichten*, in *Symbole des Alltags; Alltag der Symbole: Festschrift für Harry Kühnel zum 65.Geburtstag*, Gertrud Blaschitz et al., eds. (Graz, 1992), 747-64, more generally discussed in Finucane, *Miracles and Pilgrims*, 96-8. That this custom is still very much part of Catholicism today is seen not only in various European shrines but also in Latin American and Brazilian Catholic cult centers: Martha Egan's *Milagros: Votive Offerings from the Americas* (Santa Fe, NM, 1991); further references to European votives in Dom Jacques Dubois and Jean-Loup Lemaitre's *Sources & Méthodes de l'Hagiographie Médiévale* (Paris, 1993), 338-41.

56. *Nicholas*, 124; this was Santo Spirito, rebuilt in the fifteenth century.

NOTES TO CHAPTER 2

1. Klaus Arnold, *Kind und Gesellschaft in Mittelalter und Renaissance* (Paderborn, 1980), 31: "Eine Familie, die ein Kind erwartete, erwartete zugleich die Gefahr des Todes für Mutter und Kind."

2. For these aids to pregnancy, see Christiane Klapisch-Zuber, "Holy Dolls: Play and Piety in Florence in the Quattrocento," chap. 14 of *Women, Family and Ritual in Renaissance Italy*, trans. L. G. Cochrane (Chicago, 1985), 317; Beryl Rowland, ed., trans., *Medieval Woman's Guide to Health: The First English Gynecological Handbook* (Kent, OH, 1981), 147. For a critical discussion of Rowland's edition, which is to be used with caution, see Monica Green, "Women's Medical Practice and Health Care in Medieval Europe," *Signs: Journal of Women in Culture and Society*, 14, no. 2 (1989), 434-73, at 460-8. See also Monica Green, "Obstetrical and Gynecological Texts in Middle English," *Studies in the Age of Chaucer* 14 (1992), 53-88. A useful update on the literature is provided in Green's "Recent Work on Women's Medicine in Medieval Europe," *Society for Ancient Medicine*, Review no. 21 (December 1993), 132-41. I am grateful to Professor Green for sending me copies of these and other articles.

3. James A. Brundage, *Law, Sex and Christian Society in Medieval Europe* (Chicago, 1987), 577.

4. Quoted by Silvana Vecchio in "The Good Wife," chap. 4 of Christiane Klapisch-Zuber (ed.), *Silences of the Middle Ages*, vol. 2 of *A History of Women in the West*, George Duby and Michelle Perrot, General Editors (Cambridge, MA, 1992), 121. Vecchio also draws attention to a preoccupation with female

sterility in writers such as Gilbert of Tournai, John Bromyard, and Francesco of Barberino (122).

5. Sylvie Laurent, *Naître au Moyen Age: De la conception à la naissance, la grossesse et l'accouchement (XIIe-XVe siècle)* (Paris, 1989), 12-16 for discussion and references to medieval works.

6. *Becket*, vol. 1, 264-5.

7. Rowland, ed., *Medieval Woman's Guide to Health*, 169.

8. *Quasi pro obprobrio hoc haberet*, Cantilupe *AASS*, 686 and MS *Exeter College 158*, f. 31ʳ⁻ᵛ.

9. *Urban*, 356-7: *in illa nocte uxor sua concepit filium.*

10. *Nicholas*, 447-8. Christiane Klapisch-Zuber found that in fifteenth-century Florence only a minority of infants were named after saints: "The Name 'Remade'" in *Women, Family, and Ritual in Renaissance Italy*, trans. L. Cochrane (Chicago, 1985), 292-3.

11. *Louis*, 253-4: *non possent habere liberos.*

12. J. R. Hale, *Renaissance Europe 1480-1520* (London, 1971), 16, discussing the palaver in establishing the age of King Louis XII of France (d. 1515).

13. *Nicholas*, 627-8. Her responses were rendered in the following ways: *etatis XXX annorum, ut ipsa dixit; quod dum ipsa stetisset cum dicto suo marito per IV annos, et filios non haberet. . . . iam sunt XVI anni completi . . .* Herlihy and others have discovered that most people—especially women and the poor—seem to have thought of, and expressed, their ages in rounded decades or half decades (at least in fifteenth-century Italy), creating an effect known as "age heaping," which will be discussed more fully: David Herlihy, *Medieval Households* (Cambridge, MA, 1985), 149.

14. P. A. Sigal seems to believe that a girl was not "ready" to consummate her marriage until she had reached puberty: it is likely, he says of a young wife, that "la jeune mariée n'avait pas encore achevé sa puberté et n'était donc pas prête à consommer le mariage." "La grossesse, l'accouchement et l'attitude envers l'enfant mort-né à la fin du moyen âge d'après les récits de miracles," in *Santé, médecine et assistance au Moyen-âge: 110e Congrès national des Sociétés savantes, Montpellier, 1985, Hist. médiévale* vol. 1 (Paris, 1987), 23-41 at 24. Sigal may be referring to the canonists' views on the subject, that consummation of children's marriages *should* await puberty: Nicholas Orme, "Children and the Church in Medieval England," *Journal of Ecclesiastical History* 45, no. 4 (October, 1994), 571. Sigal's words do not suggest this, however.

15. *Soranus' Gynecology*, trans. Owsei Temkin (Baltimore, 1956), 32-3. On Soranus, see Ann Ellis Hanson and Monica H. Green, "Soranus of Ephesus: *Methodicorum princeps*," in *Rise and Decline of the Roman World*, vol. 37.2: *Principate*, Wolfgang Haase and Hildegard Temporini, eds. (New York, 1994), 968-1075. After the twelfth century, Green suggests, the significance of translations of Soranus declined as other gynecological texts became available, e.g., the writings of Trotula, "Soranus," 1057-61. Green is preparing an edition of Trotula. See her article "Trotula" in *Die deutsche Literatur des Mittelalters: Verfasserlexikon* vol. 9, no. 3/4 (New York, 1995), 1083-7.

16. *Urban*, 129, and 219-20: *esset sterilis, licet esset juvenis satis; esset sufficientis etatis ad habendum liberos.*
17. *Becket*, vol. 1, 469-70: *nondum erat ejus aetatis ut mater fieri deberet.*
18. Laurent, *Naître au Moyen Age*, 186, quoting Bernard.
19. "Age heaping" is discussed in David Herlihy and Christiane Klapisch-Zuber, *Tuscans and their Families: A Study of the Florentine Catasto of 1427* (New Haven, 1985), 161-2, 177, and 177-8. Most responding to the catasto (1427) rounded off their ages, ignoring numbers ending in "9" or in "1." There is a similar trend in our much smaller sample: of 141 cases of specified ages (i.e., ignoring ages given as in the "30s" or "40s" etc.), of witnesses and parents, 7 ended in a 9 or a 1, whereas 25 ended in "0."
20. Herlihy and Klapisch-Zuber, *Tuscans and Their Families*, 247-8; it is to be emphasized that these figures are for the city dwellers of Tuscany's capital.
21. Sigal, "La grossesse," 25.
22. *Urban*, 214-5, 348-9: *qui vivere non poterant.*
23. Cantilupe, *AASS*, 666-7, MS *Exeter Coll. 158*, fol. 9r.
24. *Dorotheas*, 37, 293, 463.
25. *Dorotheas*, 405-6; *cui nomen Dorothee imposuit ob reverentiam domine Dorothee.*
26. *Urban*, 338-9: *in tantum quod nesciebat quid facere.*
27. *Soranus' Gynecology*, 45-9, at 48.
28. Cornelia Löhmer, *Die Welt der Kinder im fünfzehnten Jahrhundert* (Weinheim, 1989), 60-9; Ulinka Rublack, "Pregnancy, Childbirth and the Female Body in Early Modern Germany," *Past and Present* 150 (February 1996), 84-110, at 88 and 96; passim for sixteenth and seventeenth centuries.
29. *Cantilupe*, MS *Vat. Latin 4015*, f. 133ʳ; Jacques Cambell, ed., *Enquête pour le procès de canonisation de dauphine de Puimichel contesse d'Ariano* (Torino, 1978), 534, hereafter *Dauphine: pro eo quia erat gravida . . . sive pregnans.*
30. *Henry*, 279-80. As usual, the garrulous chronicler of Henry VI's miracles opens with a flourish including the statement: "Who can have heard without amazement of a fetus carried more than twelve months when it is ordained of all Eve's daughters and held a law common to all pregnant women that nine months fulfils human generation? What can hope to be produced from such a prodigious gestation other than a monstrous thing?" Beaumanoir was quite certain, from his juridical point of view, that "a woman cannot carry a child more than thirty-nine weeks and a day . . ." *The Coutumes de Beauvaisis of Philippe de Beaumanoir*, trans. F. Akehurst (Philadelphia, 1992), 206. The context was Beauvais customary law on illegitimacy.
31. *Louis*, 251-2. There is no doubt about the unhappy outcome in a case involving another French woman, who went to Pontigny to pray for children. Her prayer was granted, and she became pregnant. However, after five months she gave birth to an object smaller than the midwife's hand and of no determinable sex. After prayer to St. Edmund, the object "revived" long enough to be baptized, after which it died. The mother survived in this case even though, the scribe comments, women who abort are usually in danger. Oxford, Bodleian MS *Fell 2*, fol. 43.

32. *The Chronicle of William de Rishanger; The Miracles of Simon de Montfort*, ed., J. O. Halliwell, *Camden Society* vol. 15 (1840), 84, from British Library MS. *Cotton Vespas. A. vi*, a miracle collection with more than the usual number of scribal and chronological inaccuracies.

33. Monica Green (personal communication) notes that the verb *aperire* also can refer in general to "opening" the womb in childbirth, although in this case "cutting" seems indicated by context.

34. *Becket*, vol. 2, 222-3: *obstetrices septem*.

35. Martin Weinbaum, (ed.), *The London Eyre of 1276* (London Record Society, 1976), 18, 23, 61; see also 73-4.

36. Henry Summerson (ed.), *Crown Pleas of the Devon Eyre of 1238* (Devon & Cornwall Record Society, n.s. vol. 28, 1985), 103-5.

37. *Henry*, 223-4.

38. *Nicholas*, 551-8: Margarita's testimony is here translated as direct speech.

39. *Nicholas*, 306-7.

40. *Louis*, 295.

41. *Henry*, 221.

42. *Louis*, 314.

43. *Urban*, 454: *velut mulier parturiens*.

44. Oxford, Bodleian MS *Fell 2*, fol. 41-2: *lingue prorsus destituta officio . . . ymaginem*.

45. For postmedieval European examples, see Jacques Gélis, *History of Childbirth: Fertility, Pregnancy and Birth in Early Modern Europe*, trans. R. Morris (Boston, 1991, first published as *L'arbre et le fruit* in 1984), 120-1, 150-4; also a case from 1711 in Rublack's "Pregnancy, Childbirth and the Female Body," 97, is of interest in this regard.

46. *Dorotheas*, 376. For various means (medical, magical, religious) to assist women in labor, see Laurent, *Naître au Moyen Age*, 186-98.

47. A charm to hasten labor is printed in Fiona Stoertz's "Suffering and Survival in Medieval English Childbirth," in Cathy Itnyre, ed., *Medieval Family Roles* (New York, 1996), 102-20 at 105-6.

48. The autobiography of this medieval precursor of Tristram Shandy (at least as far as birth is concerned) is conveniently found in John F. Benton, ed., *Self and Society in Medieval France: The Memoirs of Abbot Guibert of Nogent* (Toronto, 1984); 41 for quote.

49. *Nicholas*, 523-4; for other examples of prolonged labor (of which there are many), see *Urban*, 305 (three days); and for northern Europe, cf. Tryggve Lundén, ed., *Sankt Nikolaus av Linköping kanonisationsprocess* (Stockholm, 1963), 84 (eight days). Bishop Nikolaus died in 1391.

50. *Becket*, vol. 1, 504-5.

51. *Becket*, vol. 1, 393-4.

52. William's attempt at alliterative reportage is lost in the English: *vertens partum in planctum, tumorem ventris in timorem mortis*.

53. *Becket*, vol. 2, 196.

54. *Becket*, vol. 1, 226-7.

55. Isidore of Seville (d. 630s), for instance, noted this transmutation of blood into milk. In a treatise composed about 1300, *Women's Secrets*, one purported case study dealt with a woman who had "nosebleeds for two days and one night" just before birth; and "the blood she shed was really menstrual blood, which is the sign of the sickness of a fetus." Helen Lemay, ed., *Women's Secrets: A Translation of Pseudo-Albertus Magnus's De Secretis Mulierum with Commentaries* (New York, 1992), 142. William of Canterbury also explained that Margaret's nosebleed took nourishment away from the fetus, taking its life away at the same time. A medieval commentator's disagreement about the deleterious effects of nosebleed is found in *Secrets*, 142.

56. In another Becket case, at the shrine Henry the priest told about one of his parishioners who had gone into difficult labor. Part of an arm and hand appeared, but the midwives could not bring out the rest. In the midst of this the mother threatened to rip out the child in pieces. William the monk claimed that the midwives "challenged the secrets of the womb and vexed the parts that ought to be covered up." Having remained in this affliction day and night, the woman prepared for death. Henry was called to her side. But, in a move that would later have brought down the wrath of Pope Innocent III, for instance, who legislated against such things, Henry turned first to his knowledge of "physic" and suggested cutting off the fetus's arm. Unable to persuade in this matter, he then turned to the salvation of the mother's soul. As it happened, the priest's son had brought along some water from Becket's shrine, which was given to the woman. Within an hour the infant began to turn in her womb, retracted the hand, and was born — dead. *Becket*, vol. 1, 227-8.

57. Myriam Greilsammer, "The Midwife, the Priest and the Physician: The Subjugation of Midwives in the Low Countries at the End of the Middle Ages," *Journal of Medieval and Renaissance Studies* 21, no. 2 (Fall 1991), 285-329 at 296, cites Brussels as the first town in Europe to enact "detailed regulations" of midwives, although they are also mentioned in fourteenth-century city records. On midwives, see also Monica Green, "Documenting Medieval Women's Medical Practice," *Practical Medicine from Salerno to the Black Death*, ed. Luis García-Ballester et al., (Cambridge, 1994), 322-52, esp. 337 ff.

58. *Preter consuetum modum puerperarum nullas ad se ingredi mulierem permittebat . . .* , in *Malleus Maleficarum*, facsimile of the 1487 edition, André Schnyder, ed., (Göppingen, 1991), 138.

59. Löhmer, *Die Welt der Kinder*, 74: for German midwives, it is "sehr zweifelhaft, ob die Ärtze besser mit einer schweren Geburt umgehen konnten als die Hebammen." Laurent (*Naître au Moyen Age*) says much the same as to the relative effectiveness of medieval French midwives and doctors: [as to the latter] "mais faisaient-ils beaucoup mieux?" (173); Löhmer also discusses the secular regulations to which fifteenth-century midwives were subjected, as do Claudia Opitz in "Life in the Late Middle Ages," chap. 9 of Christiane Klapisch-Zuber (ed.), *Silences of the Middle Ages*, vol. 2 of *A History of Women in the West*, Duby and Perrot, eds., 300, and Laurent, *Naître au Moyen Age*, 175-7.

60. David Harley, "Historians as Demonologists: The Myth of the Midwife-witch," *Social History of Medicine* vol. 3, no. 1 (April 1990), 1-26.

61. See, for example, the interesting illustrations in Löhmer, *Die Welt der Kinder* (1989), and Blumenfeld-Kosinski's *Not of Woman Born*, passim.

62. Lundén, *Sankt Nikolaus*, 82, 334-6: *matrone multum honeste*.

63. Oxford, Bodleian MS *Fell 2*, fol. 33-33ᵛ, alt. 34.

64. In MS *Ashmol. 399*, fol. 14; see also, for instance, *Laud Misc. 724*, fol. 97r. Laurent, *Naître au Moyen Age*, 199-204, provides typical examples.

65. Monica Green, discussing the authors and the audiences of medieval medical texts, raises important issues about gender and language in "Women's Medical Practice," esp. 457-73.

66. *Louis*, 134-6: *illa putrefacta prius extracta fuit per frusta de corpore ipsius testis*.

67. E.g., Rowland, ed., *Medieval Woman's Guide to Health*, 165.

68. *Louis*, 165-69, 301. Although the edition of the canonization process (165) indicates that in 1325 she gave her age as about twenty-five years, scribal or editorial error must have intervened; aside from the chronological impossibilities involved (since she clearly stated that the bungled operation occurred in 1297 and the cure two years later, about 1299), her husband's statements would also fit well with the chronology of Louis's developing cult. She probably told the commissioners in 1325 that she was forty-five, not twenty-five; Michael, her husband, testified that he was fifty years old.

69. Is this detail about using the hands included in order to distinguish it from an extraction with instruments (e.g., hooks), which sometimes were employed? The obstetric forceps were not invented until after the Middle Ages. Embryotomy instruments, however, were known (M. Green, personal comm.).

70. *ita quod racione sordium vermes ibi creati in sordibus circa nates et crura corrodebant eam et faciebant foramina plura in carne*, *Louis*, 165-6.

71. The source describes him as *cirugicus* in one place and *medicus* in another, even though often at this time the two terms were used distinctively.

72. *Urban*, 452-3. For theological and medical views on teratology see Laurent, *Naître au Moyen Age*, 228-36.

73. Halliwell, ed., *Miracles of de Montfort*, 107.

74. Oxford, Bodleian MS *Fell 2*, fol. 18ᵛ also as fol. 19 — foliation is variable. In a more extreme case from Sweden in 1414, eighteen-year-old Botilda went into severe labor, nearly dying in the process. Finally she gave birth to a "gross monstrosity" (*edidit monstruosum et grossum nimis*), female twins joined at the umbilicus and stomach, embracing each other. One of the three midwives averred that, even if Botilda had twenty lives, she could not escape death. However, after prayers to Nikolaus, she survived. Botilda's father, sixty-eight at the time of the birth, testified that he heard the story from the midwives and had held the twins, who do not seem to have survived, in his hands. Tryggve, *Sankt Nikolaus*, 78, 318-20.

75. Literally, with no linen garments — that is, with rough wool next to the skin, as in many Italian examples.

76. *Dorotheas*, 365-6. That this Pomeranian husband had reason to fear for his wife's life is indicated in archeological finds from nearly 400 miles to the southwest, in Thuringia. Near Arnstadt, 433 medieval burials, from the tenth to twelfth centuries, have been examined. The ages of ninety-three adult females could be determined. When these are placed alongside the ages of the women in our childbirth miracles, although specific ages are given in only eighteen cases, interesting relationships arise: half of the women involved in our birth miracles were in their twenties, as were half of the Thuringian women. Arnold links these high death rates among women in this age bracket to childbirth and its complications, putting his case with appropriate circumspection when referring to this "sehr hohen Sterblichkeit im frühadulten Alter, die zweifelsohne zu einem grossen Teil auf Todesfälle im Wochenbett (im weitesten Sinne) zurückgeht," *Kind und Gesellschaft*, 37.

77. *Dorotheas*,382-3: the room was a *camera secreta*; as for the "good news," the phrase is *ut sibi de uxore sua et partu bona nuntiarentur.*

78. P. A. Sigal, "La grossesse," 28.

79. *Louis*, 122-6. On the variety of birthing postures in early modern France, see Gélis, *History of Childbirth*, 121-33. Within a year or two of this birth, another Marseilles newborn was described as having been lifeless when "raised from the ground," or earth (*levatus de terra*), which suggests that a standing or squatting (or at least not supine) delivery may have been common in the area about this period: *Louis*, 128-9. When the English chronicler William of Malmesbury described the birth of William, later the Conqueror, he indicated that the infant fell to the ground, where he clutched at the straw—evidently a topos symbolic of great things to come but also perhaps reflecting near-contemporary birthing customs.

80. *Chiara*, 395-6.

81. Rowland, ed., *Medieval Woman's Guide to Health*, 99-101.

82. *Soranus' Gynecology*, 153, 203-4; Paracelsus quote in Gélis, *History of Childbirth*, 60. For other convenient studies of medieval views on women's sexual anatomy and physiology, see Claude Thomasset's "The Nature of Woman," in Klapisch-Zuber (ed.), *Silences of the Middle Ages*; and Clarissa W. Atkinson's *The Oldest Vocation: Christian Motherhood in the Middle Ages* (Ithaca, NY, 1991), "Physiological Motherhood: The Wandering Womb." See also chapter 1 of *Women's Bodies in Classical Greek Science* by Lesley Ann Dean-Jones (Oxford, 1994) for a discussion of classical ideas about female anatomy and physiology, including the "wandering womb," and Helen King, "Once upon a Text: Hysteria from Hippocrates" in *Hysteria Beyond Freud*, ed., Sander L. Gilman et al. (Berkeley, CA, 1993), 3-90.

83. "Miraculae S. Frideswidae," *Acta Sanctorum* (Brussels, 1853), VIII October, 576; with corrections from Oxford, Bodleian MS *Digby 177: Cum enim lubricum pudoris incurrisset, utero tumescente* . . .

84. Gregory's sensible letter on this topic is in Bede's *Ecclesiastical History* I.27. For the customs at late-medieval York and Salisbury, a dated but convenient

source is William Maskell's *Monumenta Ritualia Ecclesiae Anglicanae*, 2d ed. 3 vols. (Oxford, 1882; Gregg reprint 1970), vol. 1, 46-8: *et recipiat absolutionem a sacerdote.*

85. According to a late-medieval commentator on pseudo-Albertus's *Woman's Secrets*, menstrual blood was so poisonous that "if menses touch the twig of a green tree it immediately dries up. . . ." *Women's Secrets*, ed. Lemay, 75. Such ideas were current in Aristotle's day. For an interesting study see Thomas Buckley and Alma Gottlieb (eds.), *Blood Magic: The Anthropology of Menstruation* (Berkeley, 1988). They write in their introduction, "We hypothesize that where the fetus is held to be menstrually constituted, one will find strong menstrual taboos and assertions of pollution" (39). As we have seen, in medieval Europe the fetus was held to be so constituted, and, as noted, pollution taboos were present. On these points, and how the Virgin Mary's menstruation, or lack thereof, exercised medieval men's mentalities, see Charles T. Wood, "The Doctors' Dilemma: Sin, Salvation, and the Menstrual Cycle in Medieval Thought," *Speculum* 56, no. 4 (October 1981), 710-27.

86. For another monkish condemnation of a child born *ex fornicatione* to a couple living in a London wine tavern, with suitably drastic punishment visited upon their infant, see *Becket*, vol. 2, 94.

87. *Becket*, vol. 1, 271-2.

88. E.g., Rowland, ed., *Medieval Woman's Guide*, 147; see *Soranus' Gynecology*, 198, for a similar instruction.

89. Retention of another sort is noted in a French woman who became pregnant and remained so for thirty months; the fetus would not be born. Eventually her stomach opened in the middle (or at the navel) "contrary to nature and beyond mortals' understanding," allowing the infant, dead a long time and putrid, to be taken out in pieces. The woman herself recovered. Arriving at Rocamador church to give thanks to the Virgin Mary, she displayed her wound, still not fully healed. Edmond Albe, *Les miracles de Notre-Dame de Roc-Amadour au XIIe siecle,* (Paris, 1907), 233-5. The miracles were recorded in 1172.

90. Löhmer, *Die Welt der Kinder,* 82-3.

91. Plummer, *Vie et Miracles de S. Laurent,* 170; this prelate died in 1180 and was canonized in 1225.

92. Löhmer, *Die Welt der Kinder,* 114 ff., discusses variations in swaddling techniques. Swaddling continued to be common in America up to about 1800. Charles R. King, *Children's Health in America: A History* (New York, 1993), 19.

93. Shahar does not find this a very convincing reason for swaddling: *Childhood in the Middle Ages,* 87.

94. *Dauphine,* 92, 519.

95. *Nam ubi negligencius aliquid geritur in infantes, adversa plerumque fortuna insequitur, que dum libitum suum habere permittitur, quamsepe in lacrimas risus, in luctus gaudia vertit, in planctum plausus, in lacrimosa iocos,* Henry, 260.

96. Löhmer, *Die Welt der Kinder,* 137-40 for the custom of tying infants into cradles, with illustrations.

97. Cantilupe, *AASS*, 643-5, MS *Exeter Coll. 158*, fol. 11^r, MS *Vat. Lat. 4015*, fol. 244^v.

98. See W. A. Pantin, *The English Church in the Fourteenth Century* (Notre Dame IN, 1962), 199.

99. For nursing iconography in earlier cultures, see, for instance, V. Tran Tam Tinh, *Isis Lactans: Corpus des Monuments Gréco-Romain d'Isis Allaitant Harpocrate* (Leiden, 1973), and Theodora Hadzisteliou Price, *Kourotrophos: Cults and Representations of the Greek Nursing Deities* (Leiden, 1978).

100. *Osmund*, 39-40: *et cum ipsa esset pauper nec haberet unde nutricem teneret in domo sua.*

101. See, for instance, the first few chapters in Valerie Fildes, *Wet Nursing: A History from Antiquity to the Present* (Oxford,1988).

102. *Nicholas*, 180-1.

103. Christiane Klapisch-Zuber, "Blood Parents and Milk Parents: Wet Nursing in Florence, 1300-1530," in *Women, Family and Ritual in Renaissance Italy* (Chicago, 1985), 132-64. In "Women and Childbearing in Medieval Florence," however, Louis Haas suggests that both parents were involved in the choice of wet nurse, *Medieval Family Roles*, 87-99 at 96.

104. Doris Desclais Berkvam, *Enfance et maternité dans la littérature française des XIIe et XIIIe siècles* (Paris, 1981), 49. Berkvam concludes, however, that it is "impossible de déterminer clairement la nature des liens qui se forment entre l'enfant et sa nourrice." Such emotional bonds are probably never "clearly" explicated.

105. Arnold, *Kind und Gesellschaft*, 112-3.

106. On St. Lidwina, see Herlihy, *Medieval Households*, 120 and note; Aelred is quoted in Caroline Walker Bynum's *Jesus as Mother: Studies in the Spirituality of the High Middle Ages* (Berkeley, 1982), 123. Bynum has also noticed Lidwina's interesting behavior.

107. *Louis*, 176-82: *ad lactandum et nutriendum eum.*

108. Edward Gibbon, *Autobiography*, ed. M. M. Reese (London, 1970), 15-17; he rounds off these observations by misquoting Vergil so as to suit his own childhood circumstances: instead of *Primo avulso non deficit alter* (*Aen.* VI. 143), he writes *Uno avulso non deficit alter.*

109. Arnold, *Kind und Gesellschaft*, 35.

110. Sigal, "La grossesse," 33-4.

111. Example from *Acta et processus canonizacionis beate Birgitte*, quoted by Christian Krötzl, *Pilger, Mirakel und Alltag: Formen des Verhaltens im skandinavischen Mittelalter* (Helsinki, 1994), 267: *nimio dolore afflicta, maxime quia infans sine baptismo decesserat.*

112. From *Legenda major sanctae Hedwigis*, in Sigal, "La grossesse," 31.

113. *Dorotheas*, 459-60: *ut animam reciperet et baptizaretur.*

114. *Louis*, 329.

115. MS *Fell 2*, fol. 37.

116. *Urban*, 225-6: *et habere animam in corpore*; 431: *et recipere baptismum et habere animam cristianam.*

117. Judith Shaw, "The Influence of Canonical and Episcopal Reform on Popular Books of Instruction" in Thomas J. Heffernan, ed., *The Popular Literature of Medieval England* (Knoxville, TN, 1985), 53-4.

118. P. H. Linehan "Pedro de Albalat, arzobispo de Tarragona y su '*Summa Septem Sacramentorum*'," *Hispania Sacra 22* (1969), 17; Eudes de Sully's canons in Migne, *Patrologia Latina* vol. 212, column 59. See also Peter H. Linehan's *The Spanish Church and the Papacy in the Thirteenth Century* (Cambridge, 1971), 54-82.

119. Migne, *Patrologia Latina* vol. 38, column 1445, sermons #323-4.

120. Platelle, *L'enfant et la vie familiale*, 72: such "signs" of a return to life could be "quelque mouvement convulsif, un écoulement de salive, un changement de couleur. . . ." cf. André Vauchez, *La sainteté en occident*, 553 and notes.

121. Pierrette Paravy, "Angoisse collective et miracles au seuil de la mort: résurrections et baptêmes d'enfants mort-nés en Dauphiné au XVe siècle," *La Mort au Moyen Age*, (Strasbourg, 1977), 87-102 at 89.

122. *Becket*, vol. 1, 231-2, a case involving a three-year-old boy who "died" but who then seemed to move. Some of the bystanders conjectured that this was a sign of divine mercy, others, that it was movement due to entrapped gases.

123. *Diocesis Exoniensis Registrum Edmundi Lacy, pars secunda*, ed. G. R. Dunstan, Canterbury & York Society vol. 132 (1966), 217.

124. A good summary of the history of "limbo" in Didier Lett, *Faire le deuil d'un enfant mort sans baptême au moyen âge: La naissance du limbe pour enfants aux xiie-xiiie siècles, Devenir 7*, no. 1 (1995), 101-12.

125. Silvano Cavazza, "Double Death: Resurrection and Baptism in a Seventeenth-Century Rite," trans. Mary M. Gallucci, in Edward Muir and Guido Ruggiero, eds., *History from Crime: Selections from Quaderni Storici* (Baltimore, 1994), 1-31, with useful bibliography; and Judith Devlin, *The Superstitious Mind* (New Haven, CT, 1987), 64.

126. Cavazza, "Double Death," 26.

127. *Louis*, 128-9: *ad modum pueri mortui*.

128. Linehan, "Pedro de Albalat," 17: *si mortuus fuerit corpus non tradatur ecclesiastice sepulture*.

129. *Nicholas*, 128, 237, 245.

130. Mark Golden, discussing burials within the homes of classical Athens, suggests that this practice may not signify rejection of a more elaborate funeral, but rather the wish to have the child near, perhaps even for purposes of sympathetic magic. *Children and Childhood in Classical Athens* (Baltimore, MD, 1990), 85.

131. *Urban*, 440-1: *paraverunt cepelire extra cimiterium, eo quod baptisatus non esset*.

132. *Louis*, 134-6, and *Nicholas*, 551-8.

133. A. Bernard, *La Sépulture en droit canonique* (Paris, 1933), 117 n. 3, 134-5. This is the context of a statement in one of Boccaccio's tales (day ten, story four) about a pregnant woman who had apparently died: since "she had not been pregnant sufficiently long for the unborn creature to be perfectly formed, they

troubled themselves no further on that score; and . . . they buried her, just as she was, in a tomb in the local church." Boccaccio, *Decameron*, trans. G. H. McWilliam (New York, 1972), 750. Stable-burial may be merely practical in some circumstances, but one cannot ignore the manifest element of degradation that it entails—when in 1403 the nobleman Carlo di Luigi di Messer Roberto Adimari of Florence attacked a woman named Lucia Ducci at her home, he took her outside, "cut off her head and threw her body—and also her head—into a stable where the animals lay." *The Society of Renaissance Florence: A Documentary Study*, ed. Gene Brucker (New York, 1971), 101-2. Interestingly, Monica Green (personal comm.) suggests that "dead" infants might have been placed on dung heaps in the hope that the regenerative qualities of the dung would revive them.

134. On embryotomy and baptism see Laurent, *Naître au Moyen Age*, 221-2.

135. *quia per frusta et partes exiverat.*

136. *Louis*, 134-6: *in stabulo, in fimo vel palea*; the witnesses described the infant as lying in the stable for "a league," that is, the length of time it usually took to walk one league; leagues varied in length from region to region in medieval Europe.

137. Lett refers to the medieval development of special cemeteries for infants next to (consecrated) cemeteries: *Faire le deuil*, 106.

138. Y.-B. Brissaud, "L'infanticide a la fin du moyen âge, ses motivations psychologiques et sa répression," *Revue historique de droit français et etranges* no. 50 (1962), 240-2.

139. As, for instance, in an article by Ludo Milis, "Children and Youth, the Medieval Viewpoint," *Paedagogica historica* 29 (1993), 15-32.

140. J. Kroll and Bernard Bachrach, "Child Psychiatry Perspective: Child Care and Child Abuse in Early Medieval Europe," *Journal of the American Academy of Child Psychiatry* 25 (1986), 562-8, at 568.

141. Barbara Hanawalt, *The Ties that Bound: Peasant Families in Medieval England* (New York, 1986), 101, citing an article from the mid-1970s. As Eleanora Gordon suggests in "Accidents among Medieval Children" *Medieval History* 35 (1991), 154, it may not be so surprising that Hanawalt finds few infanticide cases in coroners' records and other legal sources, if as Gordon believes "in practice it was a crime left to the church to punish." As early as the late sixth to the late seventh centuries, Visigothic church councils urged joint action between bishops and secular judges in infanticide cases: D. King, *Law & Society in the Visigothic Kingdom* (Cambridge, 1972), 157, n. 6. For an example of a dispute between an ecclesiastical court and secular officers in the accidental deaths of three young boys (by drowning) see J. B. Sheppard, ed., *Literae Cantuarienses* Vol. 3 (London [Rolls Series], 1889), 288-91.

142. Brissaud, "L'infanticide," 232, 250.

143. Laurent, *Naître au moyen âge*, 164: "il n'est pas douteux que les infanticides étaient courants . . . "

144. Richard C. Trexler, "Infanticide in Florence: New Sources and First Results," in *The Children of Renaissance Florence* vol. 1 (New York, 1993), 51-2, from an

article originally published in 1973. Foundling homes were established in late-medieval Europe as alternatives to infanticide and abandonment, although high infant mortality within their walls was a perhaps unintended result, as John Boswell suggested.

145. In her *Growing Up in Medieval London* (New York, 1993), 44, Barbara Hanawalt continues to emphasize the fact that record sources do not indicate English children "being abandoned in great numbers" nor do they show "a widespread slaughter of innocents."

146. MS *Vat. Lat. 4015*, fol. 124ᵛ, fol. 127ʳ⁻ᵛ, fol. 132ʳ. They assumed that the woman had thrown her daughter into the water *ratione pauperitatis et miserie*. See Appendix.

147. *Becket*, vol. 2, 227-8: *in via projecit*.

148. *Dorotheas*, 229.

149. Susan C. M. Scrimshaw, "Infanticide in Human Populations: Societal and individual concerns" in Glenn Hausfater and Sarah Hrdy, eds., *Infanticide: Comparative and Evolutionary Perspectives* (New York, 1984), 439-62, at 443.

150. Philip Gavitt, "Infant Death in Late Medieval Florence: The Smothering Hypothesis Reconsidered," in McIntyre, ed., *Medieval Family Roles*, 137-53; Gavitt also raises questions about orphanages and infant death rates.

151. See Klapisch-Zuber, *Women, Family, and Ritual*, 104, n. 19; for the *Oculus Sacerdotis*, Pantin, *The English Church*, 199.

152. McLaughlin, "Survivors and Surrogates," 120-2.

153. "Childhood in Medieval Europe," in Joseph M. Hawes and N. Ray Hiner (eds.), *Children in Historical and Comparative Perspective* (New York, 1991), 38.

154. Arnold, *Kind und Gesellschaft*, 49-51, and McLaughlin, "Survivors and Surrogates," 157, n. 102.

155. Cantilupe, *AASS* 644-5, 666; MS *Exeter Coll. 158*, fol. 9ʳ; MS *Vat. Lat. 4015*, fol. 245ᵛ.

156. See David Ransel's comments in "Child Abandonment in European History: A Symposium," *Journal of Family History* 17, no. 1 (1992), 1-23, at 19-20.

157. *Becket*, vol. 1, 213-14, vol. 2, 245: *infans abjectus*.

158. Bodleian MS *Fell 2*, fols. 27ᵛ ff.

159. Fildes, *Wet Nursing*, 47-8. Klapisch-Zuber, "Blood Parents and Milk Parents" in *Women, Family, and Ritual*, 149, refers to cradles "equipped with a frame of arched ribs to prevent the covers from stifling the baby" in Florentine records; she then asks, "Were these frames also supposed to protect the child from being smothered?" by a wet nurse with whom the infant was sleeping. See Gavitt, "Infant Death," 145-6, for further comments on this cradle design and wet nurses as scapegoats.

160. *Nicholas*, 243-4.

161. *Urban*, 170-2: *ignorans penitus si ipsa esset in cause mortis filie sue . . . licet distaret satis longe ab ipsa in eodem lecto.*

162. *mater multo magis clamabat et dicebat.*

163. Sigal, "La Grossesse," 34.

NOTES TO CHAPTER 3

1. David Mechanic, *Medical Sociology*, 2d ed. (New York, 1978), 264.

2. Keith Manchester, "The Palaeopathology of Urban Infections," in *Death in Towns: Urban Responses to the Dying and the Dead, 100-1600*, ed. Steven Bassett (London, 1992), 8-14 at 8.

3. Eleanora C. Gordon, M.D., "Arthrogryposis Multiplex Congenita, A.D. 1156," *Developmental Medicine and Child Neurology* 38 (1996), 74-83, based on an English miracle in A. Jessopp and M. R. James, eds., *The Life and Miracles of St. William of Norwich by Thomas of Monmouth* (Cambridge, 1896), 273-4.My thanks to Dr. Gordon for sending a copy of this article.

4. *Louis*, 162-5.

5. Cecilia stated that she lived in *Santa Cruce, Regensis* diocese. If this is Ste-Croix-de-Verdon, just southeast of the old episcopal site of Riez, her trip would have had to cover at least sixty miles of far from level ground.

6. On occasion, pilgrims were "cured" en route to a shrine at the moment when the goal—the church or its spire—came into view. These vantage points became well known as a cult developed, as in Becket's case.

7. The mother's ability to recall specific dates (uncharacteristic of such reports) was probably due to these events having recently occurred: Louis's canonization process officially opened on February 29, 1308. For another example of specific dating in this process, see 145-6. For the dates of the hearing, see Margaret R. Toynbee, *S. Louis of Toulouse and the Process of Canonisation in the Fourteenth Century* (Manchester, 1929), 164. St. Michael's Plain is now engulfed by Marseilles suburbs.

8. *Urban*, 172-3.

9. Cantilupe, *AASS* 678; MS *Exeter Coll. 158*, fol. 21ʳ.

10. *Becket*, vol. 2, 125-6.

11. *Nicholas*, 185-6.

12. H. F. Delaborde, ed., "Fragments de l'enquête faite a Saint-Denis en 1282 en vue de la canonisation de Saint Louis," *Mémoires de la Société de Paris et de l'Ile-de-France* 23 (1896), 1-71 at 39-54.

13. *Plus quam millies tempore*, 40.

14. *Chiara*, 308-9, 427-8, 455-6, 503-4. Several witnesses mentioned this case at different points in the investigation, which suggests that it may have been more than usually "renowned" at the time.

15. Bodleian MS *Fell 2*, fol. 9.

16. *Nicholas*, 293-7: *digitum grossum*. Similarly, an English boy suffering a fistula in his right foot managed to support himself by balancing "with his right big toe grazing the ground," but usually he got about by crawling. *Becket*, vol. 1, 168.

17. *Urban*, 301-2: *Petrus Folqualquerii ac alii medici, tam physici quam etiam cirugici . . .* (in the 1370s).

18. *Nicholas*, 236-7.

19. St. Blaise continues to be evoked by modern Catholics seeking relief from throat problems.

20. *remanebit ita cicatrix ita quod erit vituperata.*
21. *AASS* I March (Antwerp 1668, repr. 1966), 683, #96: *maritare non posset.*
22. *Chiara*, 431: *Nos sumus victuperati de ista filia nostra . . . et potius vellem quod mortua esset quam viva.*
23. *Nicholas*, 586-7.
24. *Nicholas*, 515-6.
25. *Hippocratic Writings*, ed. G. E. R. Lloyd, trans. J. Chadwick et al. (Harmondsworth, 1986), 215; Roger K. French, "Scrofula (Scrophula)," in *The Cambridge World History of Human Disease*, ed. Kenneth F. Kiple (Cambridge, 1993), 998-1000, hereafter *CWHHD*.
26. *AASS* VIII October (1853 ed.), Mir. of Frideswide, 575: *Quae contactu regiae manus curari dicuntur.*
27. *Henry*, 122-3. The curative power of touch was also attributed to French kings.
28. *Dauphine*, 89, 310-1, 464-5, 467-8. On the same evening a scrofulous woman tried a similar approach, bursting into the queue and displacing a noble lady while ignoring the indignant shouts of the lady's squires. She too was cured by touching her neck to the noble feet, running home joyfully to give her parents the good news. Next year she was dead of the plague. *Dauphine*, 78-9.
29. *Louis*, 195-6: *ad eundum et ad laborandum.*
30. *Henry*, 120-2: *magna enim erat eorum vis amoris in filiam.* The commentator uses the term *iuvencula* in this case, possibly carrying the implication that she was what moderns might call a "poor kid" rather than a "child" plain and simple.
31. *Chiara*, 458-9.
32. *Chiara*, 351-3.
33. *Louis*, 184-6.
34. *Major copia medicorum.*
35. At the end of the four months, *de novo, . . . fecit sibi fieri unum beuragium, per quod credebat aliquod remedium provenire.*
36. Nancy G. Siraisi, *Medieval & Early Renaissance Medicine* (Chicago, 1990), 119, 146, and notes.
37. Joseph Shatzmiller, "Doctors' Fees and Their Medical Responsibility," in *Sources of Social History: Private Acts of the Late Middle Ages*, eds. P. Brezzi and E. Lee (Toronto, 1984), 201-8, at 206-7, contains accusations against certain doctors in Marseilles (1261) and Manosque (1298), for instance.
38. Bagellardus in John Ruhräh, ed., trans., *Pediatrics of the Past* (New York, 1925), 62-3, Metlinger at 92. As usual, many medieval medical opinions derived from classical exemplars.
39. *Becket*, vol. 1, .228-30, vol. 2, 255-7. And see the case of a month-old Italian child who screamed so strenuously and constantly, turning himself black, that the doctors feared he would be ruptured, *Chiara*, 379, 382-3.
40. *Laurent archevêque de Dublin*, ed. Plummer, 174.
41. *omnibus diebus vite sue custodire.*
42. *ego do tibi puerum meum . . . nisi mortuum vel sanatum.*

43. The scrotal hernia of a southern French child was supported by a truss until he was cured at age five. *Urban,* 196-7.

44. *Chiara,* 367-8, 371-3, 451-2.

45. On the other hand, in an example from the collection of Nicholas's wonders, a doctor refused to carry out surgery on an old man because he thought the patient would be in danger—given his age: *immo propter antiquitatem predictam medicus nolebat tangere ipsum ferro propter periculum persone.* Another witness refers to the danger (*periculum*) of surgery in the same case, *propter senectutem dicti avi . . . Nicholas,* 611, 613.

46. Siraisi, *Medieval & Early Renaissance Medicine,* 141, and Luke Demaitre, "The Idea of Childhood and Child Care in Medical Writings of the Middle Ages," *Journal of Psychohistory* 4 (1977), 461-90, at 476.

47. *Chiara,* 306-7.

48. *Nicholas,* 142-4.

49. *Becket,* vol. 2, 197-8: *mulieres . . . peritae;* for a little girl suffering the same type of rupture, see *Dorothea,* 378-9.

50. *AASS* VIII October (1853 ed.), Mir. of Frideswide, 588-9, corrected against Oxford Bodleian MS *Digby 177,* fol. 28[v.]

51. *commota nimirum erant super filio suo omnia viscera sua.*

52. She asked him where he had been and what he had seen; a most beautiful and elegant lady, he replied, who blessed his surgical wound and all the rest of him from his forehead to his feet; then she disappeared. The postcure vision and question-and-response constituted a hagiographical topos.

53. Siraisi, *Medieval & Early Renaissance Medicine,* 157-8, citing V. L. Kennedy's article on Robert Courson.

54. *Urban,* 252-3: *habita licentia a curia . . . si moreretur non esset in culpa.*

55. Shatzmiller, "Doctors' Fees and Their Medical Responsibility," 203-4, 207-8.

56. *Hippocratic Writings,* 215, 269. Of course, adults *do* suffer from stone, but of a different kind, usually associated with formation in the kidney rather than the bladder; the stones themselves tend to have a chemical composition different from children's.

57. Aldobrandinus in Klaus Arnold, *Kind und Gesellschaft in Mittelalter und Renaissance* (Paderborn, 1980), 118; Metlinger in Ruhräh, *Pediatrics of the Past,* 92.

58. Bagellardus in Rührah, *Pediatrics of the Past,* 59.

59. *Dorothea,* 465.

60. *Dorothea,* 343-4.

61. Edwin L. Prien, Sr., "The Riddle of Urinary Stone Disease," *Journal of the American Medical Association* 216, no. 3 (April 19, 1971), 503-7, at 504.

62. Mirko D. Grmek, *Diseases in the Ancient Greek World,* trans. M. Muellner and L. Muellner (Baltimore, 1989; first pub. as *Les Maladies à l'aube de la civilisation occidentale* (1983), 112. This work is an invaluable accompaniment to the study of diseases in history, whatever the period.

63. Prien, "Urinary Stone Disease," 504.

64. *Chiara*, 498-500; *Becket* vol. 1, 503-4.

65. *Nicholas*, 228-31, 247-9: *nescio quid faciam.*

66. *Urban*, 129-30, 216, 297-8, 470-1: *valde famesco* was a typical remark of recovering child victims of fever.

67. Occasionally the word "ague" is used for fevers in general as well as for malaria.

68. *Dauphine*, 392, 425-9, 435-6. In *Nicholas*, 668-9, there is a useful glossary of expressions under *febris* for types of fever encountered in central Italy; similar expressions are employed in southern French collections of cures.

69. Cambell, *Dauphine*, 504, working in that case with another *medicus*, Master Barberius, whom the editor identified as Guillelmus Barberius, surgeon of bishop Elzearius of Apt.

70. An indication of social distances — the lady claimed to know her servant only as "Huga."

71. *Louis*, 130-2, 284; about A.D. 1301.

72. *Sicut illi de quo sperabatur quod statim debebat expirare*, 284. For the custom, see E. Friestedt, "Altchristliche Totengedächtnistage und ihre Beziehung zur Jenseitsglauben und Totenkultus der Antike," *Liturgiegeschichtliche Quellen und Forschungen* 24 (1928), 40.

73. At the time this occurred, the father was about fifty-three. Peter, born when Poncius was around forty-eight, may have been especially dear to Poncius as, perhaps, the youngest of his male offspring.

74. *nutriebatur et iacebat in domo avi sui . . . in domo patris sui communis.*

75. *intraverunt lectum et dormierunt usque mane.* For the sharing of beds and other medieval customs involving sleep, see Maria Elisabeth Wittmer-Butsch, *Zur Bedeutung von Schlaf und Traum im Mittelalter* (Krems, 1990), esp. chap. 2, "Der Schlaf als Alltagserfahrung."

76. *Chiara*, 397-400. Cinctia was using a diminutive of the common name Lippus. Nicknames and affectionate forms of children's names, frequent in the southern European miracle reports, seem to be less common in the northern reports.

77. If Cinctia were as poor as she claimed, the doctor may have donated his expertise as an act of charity, which might explain his apparently dismissive attitude when the case seemed hopeless.

78. R. C. Finucane, "Pilgrimage in Daily Life," *Wallfahrt und Alltag in Mittelalter und früher Neuzeit*, Österreichische Akademie der Wissenschaften, philosophisch-historische Klasse, Sitzungsberichte, 592 (Wien, 1992), 165-217, at 204-5; Ronald C. Finucane, *Miracles and Pilgrims: Popular Beliefs in Medieval England* (London, 1977, repr. New York, 1995), 187.

79. *Urban*, 474-5: *infantes . . . et juvenes.*

80. *Urban*, 143-4.

81. For instance, in *Urban*, 183-4 and 189-90. Women who made a profession of healing by using elaborate "signing" techniques, however, might find themselves in trouble with the inquisition, as did a famous Venetian healer of the

sixteenth century, Elena Crusichi; Guido Ruggiero, *Binding Passions* (New York, 1993), chap. 4, "The Women Priests of Latisana."

82. Lundén, *Sankt Nikolaus*, 356.

83. *Urban*, 290-1.

84. *Urban*, 264-5: the father was *flens et lacrimens.*

85. *Urban*, 302.

86. *Ad parietem.* Turning to the wall in contempt or disappointment was a typical motif in deathbed descriptions; cf. the folklore surrounding the deaths of Henry II of England or Lorenzo the Magnificent, for instance. This gesture is briefly noted by Michel Vovelle in "The Relevance and Ambiguity of Literary Evidence," in *Ideologies and Mentalities*, trans. E. O'Flaherty (first published in Paris in 1982; Chicago, 1990), 30. Vovelle sees it as symbolic of a "bad death."

87. *Henry*, 103-6. Theologians might agree that spirits of the dead could by divine dispensation return to admonish the living; they might agree that hellish demons could possess the body; but they would probably not agree that spirits of ordinary Christian dead, such as those encountered in a London cemetery (which like a church was consecrated, i.e, hallowed ground), could possess anyone. The medieval public thought otherwise, however. On the other hand, it is not entirely clear exactly where Agnes was when attacked by invisible forces.

88. A demented Hereford woman who screamed horribly and seemed quite mad was beaten until the blood flowed, *usque ad sanguinis effusionem*, MS *Vat. Lat. 4015*, fol. 106ᵛ.

89. As reported, for example, in a London *Sunday Times* of September 18, 1994 (other examples are easily obtained) concerning a family—parents, grandmother, uncle, and cousins—who beat an infant to death in a Calabrian village: as the father put it, "his baby's death was unintentional but inevitable because the demon had had to be driven out." The chief exorcist in this case was the baby's uncle.

90. *Louis*, 214-6: Guillelmina *facta fuit amens seu demoniata . . .* and uttered *aliena verba et turpia et inhonesta.*

91. *cum quodam grosso baculo verberabat eam causa correctionis, et filia non senciebat, sicut dixit*, 215.

92. William's words were rendered by the notaries *rabiata sive furiosa*, and his remark concerning her behavior suiting her age, as *secundum etatem suam.*

93. *Louis*, 216-8.

94. Jesus had freed Mary of Magdala of "seven demons," Luke 8:2.

95. Augustus Jessopp and Montague Rhodes James, eds. and trans., *Thomas of Monmouth's The Life and Miracles of St. William of Norwich* (Cambridge, 1896), 203-4; cf. Finucane, *Miracles and Pilgrims*, 107-9.

96. Quoted in the old standard by T. K. Oesterreich, *Possession Demoniacal and Other Among Primitive Races, in Antiquity, the Middle Ages, and Modern Times*, trans. D. Ibberson (London, 1930), 8.

97. *Osmund*, 42-4.
98. Finucane, "Pilgrimage in Daily Life," 166-9.
99. *Becket*, vol. 2, 102-3.
100. *Becket*, vol. 1, 380-1.
101. *verebatur eum excommunicare*. This was possibly a reference to chapters twenty-three to twenty-five of the *Rule* of St. Benedict, directing that delinquent monks were to be excluded temporarily from the common life of the monastery.
102. Bagellardus in Rührah, *Pediatrics of the Past*, 37, 39; see also Metlinger in Rührah, 87.
103. *Hippocratic Writings*, 243.
104. *Chiara*, 310-1, 369-71: *erat stupor videre eam.*
105. *Nicholas*, 385-7.
106. Among the miracles of Coleta (d. 1447) in *AASS* I Mar. (Antwerp 1668, repr. 1966), 585, no. 241.
107. For further comment on this topic see Andre Sigal, *L'homme et le miracle dans la France médiévale* (Paris, 1985), 299-308 and Finucane, *Miracles and Pilgrims*, chap. 8.
108. *Nicholas*, 164-5, 383-4; see 668 for *exbruncii*; Mallus was also known as Nallus.
109. *Nicholas*, 598-600.
110. *Chiara*, 307-8.
111. *tunc vidit quod dictus puer habebat oculos suos ambos extra locum eorum debitum et pendebant cum nervis suis . . . usque ad extremum nasi sui.*
112. *Nicholas*, 109-11, 275-7, 433-4.
113. *in domo ipsius testis seu dicti eius viri.*
114. *statim et immediate oculi dicti Zucti . . . crepaverunt et pendebant per maxillas*, Nicholas, 276.
115. Reginald R. Darlington, ed., *The Vita Wulfstani of William of Malmesbury . . . and the Miracles*, Royal Historical Society, Camden Third Series, vol. 40 (London, 1928), 140.
116. *Urban*, 178-9: *claudens . . . oculum bonum.*
117. Cantilupe, MS *Vat. Lat. 4015*, fols. 186ʳ-209ᵛ, with an insertion of another miracle report (concerning Roger of Conway).
118. *pro receptione melioris lingue.*
119. In Ludlow one witness, who knew John from before his cure, watched—to her amazement, one assumes—as he touched his chin with the tip of his tongue.
120. See, e.g., Michel Mollat, *The Poor in the Middle Ages*, trans. A. Goldhammer (New Haven, CT, 1986, orig. published in French in 1978), especially Part 3 and 4.
121. *Dorotheas*, 451.
122. *Louis*, 244-6, 325. William called the excrescence *lippia* or *lepra.*
123. On the other hand, a different etiology is suggested in a six-month-old English infant who was said to have been stricken with the same ailment but cured in half a day following prayer to Henry VI. *Henry*, 114-5.

124. *Louis*, 173-6: *in membro suo naturali anteriori*. Dr. Eleanora Gordon notes that gangrenous ergotism (as opposed to the convulsive variety) always involved the extremities, never the genitalia (personal comm. of July 27, 1996); see also Ann G. Carmichael, "St. Anthony's Fire," in *CWHHD*, 989-90.

125. Though, it is true, medieval hospices and hospitals would appear to modern eyes anything but "secular." For the importance of worship among the inmates, see for example Nicholas Orme and Margaret Webster, *The English Hospital 1070-1570* (New Haven, CT, 1995), chap. 3. The girl was taken *domo sancti Anthonii*.

126. Her testimony is not easy to follow at this point: she says that *caro coxarum ex utraque parte coniunxit se* but a line later she talks of *crurium seu coxarum*, a difficult situation to visualize, as reported; the general sense, however, is clear enough.

127. *nec est apta ad viri consorcium*.

128. *Nicholas*, 618, *et aliis pluribus mulieribus de dicta contrata*.

129. *Urban*, 219, *mulieres multe*.

130. Jenny Swanson, "Childhood and Childrearing in *ad status* Sermons by Later Thirteenth-century Friars," *Journal of Medieval History* 16 (1990), 309-31 at 322.

131. *Becket*, vol. 1, 190-3, vol. 2, 234-7.

132. *Ut et mater ejus mortem optaret*.

133. Some in the household thought that her spirit might have been drawn out of her body and taken on a journey just as in the case of a local woman, Agnes, who recently had been cast into ecstasy and led about by St. Catherine to see the punishments and rewards of the dead, returning to her body five days later. Thinking that this might be a similar situation, everyone waited for Cecilia's spirit to return to her body, ending her trance-like condition. But it did not occur.

134. See, for instance, Geoffrey Rowell, *The Liturgy of Christian Burial* (London, 1977), 64-5.

135. *Henry*, 263-4.

136. *Becket*, vol. 1, 292-3. Monks would have been quite familiar with the appearance of venous blood, given their regular *minutio*, or monthly phlebotomy, which was thought to have prophylactic benefits.

137. *ut lepra videretur . . . elephantiae contagio*.

138. *Dauphine*, 65-7, 350-1. The name of this infirmity comes from the scriptural passage in John 20:17, Jesus's injunction to Mary Magdalen during their garden encounter immediately after the resurrection, not to touch him.

139. *Nicholas*, 559-60.

140. *Chiara*, 420-1, 422-3.

141. *Eo quod aliquantulum debilis erat*.

142. *Multis dominabus* — the title "domina" did not necessarily indicate noble rank in urban Italy.

143. *Henry*, 211-2, *Urban*, 292-3.

144. *Urban*, 471-2.
145. *Henry*, 284-6. The record states that he had *eadem contagiosa peste*, referring to the previous ailment, called (283) *peste pustularum*, a *plaga porriginosa . . . contagiosa valde et pestifera . . . ut leprosos . . . iam factus fuerat onerosus ut vix tolerari potuerit*, 285.
146. *Puerulus ante satis formosus*.
147. *[E]quitando, non equo ligneo (non baculo scilicet quo solent infantuli in suis lusibus uti)*. For this common medieval toy, see Löhmer, 159-64; Arnold, *Kind und Gesellschaft*, 70. Play and children's rituals are discussed by Nicholas Orme in "The Culture of Children in Medieval England," *Past and Present* 148 (Aug. 1995), 48-88. Such baubles, along with "gilded drums, and a thousand different kinds of toys" were condemned by the Dominican friar, Dominici: Ross, "Middle-Class Child," *History of Childhood*, 204.
148. *Urban*, 161; *picota vel vayrola*.
149. However, Ynez Violé O'Neill claims that this affliction is "now widely accepted" as influenza: "Diseases of the Middle Ages," *CWHHD*, 275.
150. *Henry*, 265-7; *sudore illo pestifero, quo circa hec tempora plurimi perierunt. The girl ad iam puberes annos pervenerat*.
151. The women who assisted were called *mulierculis* and *muliercule*; they were probably, like Anna, Belfeld's servants. In several of the reports investigated by papal examiners in Urban V's canonization process, victims were said to have been "nearly sewn into their shrouds" before signs of life reappeared; this had apparently become a late-medieval hagiographical topos.
152. *Urban*, 460-1.
153. *Becket*, vol. 1, 160-2, vol. 2, 229-33.
154. *promittens offerendum martyri puerum in medio Quadragesimae, Becket*, vol. 2, 230.
155. This remark by the twelfth-century monk anticipates a statement made next century by Bartholomew the Englishman, *viz.*, that a son is "loved most of all by his father when he bears a close resemblance to him"; from *De Proprietatibus rerum*, ed. and trans. Goodich, "Bartholomaeus Anglicus," 82.
156. *Becket*, vol. 1, 228-30, vol. 2, 255-7.
157. Goodich, "Bartholomaeus," 79; the Canterbury monk wrote *nescit quippe puer aliquis celare secretum*.
158. *infantem reperit a thalamo in aulam exteriorem elatum, extensum in area . . . , Becket*, vol. 2, 256. *Thalamus* in classical Latin is a woman's room or marriage bed.
159. Heinrich Fichtenau, *Living in the Tenth Century: Mentalities and Social Orders*, trans. Patrick Geary (Chicago, 1991, German ed. of 1984), 43. Of Queen Mathilda, Fichtenau reports, it was said that she never laughed or mourned "beyond measure," 139.
160. *Nicholas*, 150-1, 223-5, 286-9.
161. As Manfred put it, they prayed for the child's revival, *ne reciperent istam confusionem . . . quia verecundabantur multum quia dicta puella erat mortua in villa* [i.e., the village], *propter consuetudinem que est Tholentini quod mortui extra terram non reportantur intus sed sepeliuntur extra portam, et ipse et uxor eius . . . erant nobiles*

de terra, Nicholas, 224. However, this "custom" may have pertained only to very young children, as in this case; it would hardly be operable for Tolentino nobles who had died, for example, in battle with another city-state or while on business trips abroad.

162. See, for example, Valerie Fildes, *Wet Nursing: A History from Antiquity to the Present* (New York, 1988), esp. chaps. 2-5, and Christiane Klapisch-Zuber, "Blood Parents and Milk Parents," in *Women, Family, and Ritual in Renaissance Italy* (Chicago, 1985), 132-64.

163. *Dauphine,* 83-4, 353-7; *distincte et vulgarizato ac lingua materna explanato in romancio.*

164. *quamdiu ipse puer vitam duceret in humanis.*

165. "Während der Begriff *mortuus* bzw. *omnino mortuus* nur selten näher ausgeführt wird, finden sich bei *quasi mortuus* einige Erläuterungen. . . . Ein Fast-Toter konnte seine Glieder meist nicht bewegen, war stumm oder wies fast keinen Lebenshauch mehr auf." Christian Krötzl, *Evidentissima signa mortis. Zu Tod und Todesfeststellung in mittelalterlichen Mirakelberichten,* in *Symbole des Alltags, Alltag der Symbole: Festschrift für Harry Kühnel zum 65. Geburtstag,* eds. Gertrud Blaschitz et al. (Graz, 1992), 765-75, at 767-8.

166. *Dorotheas,* 28-9, 74-5, 129.

167. *Soranus' Gynecology,* 103-4.

168. Certain medieval medical writers, such as the Italian Paul Bagellardus, a contemporary of Metlinger, would have said that the "coolness" of the infant caused its vomit to be "green or livid." Paulus Bagellardus, *Libellus de egritudinibus infantium,* in Ruhräh, *Pediatrics of the Past,* 49.

169. *Dauphine,* 82-3, 143-5.

170. *Becket,* vol. 2, 258.

171. *Henry,* 60-1, 216-8, *e civitate famosissimos quosque medicorum; doctissimi quidem ac nominatissimi viri;* the archbishop was John Morton, in office from 1486 to 1500.

172. *Venenoso quodam spiritus maligni contactu languescere, Henry,* 217.

173. Golinelli's comment is apposite: "Naturalmente non si vuole con questo dare un carattere statistico 'reale' alle cifre, ma considerarle ragionevolmente indicative del prevalere e dell'effettiva presenza in un determinato ambiente storico di talune infermità piuttosto che di altre." He is speaking of Siral's work in particular, but also of such mathematical analyses generally. Paolo Golinelli, *Città e culto dei santi nel medioevo Italiano* (Bologna, 1991), 162.

174. Jürgen Jansen, *Medizinische Kasuistik in den Miracula Sancte Elyzabet: Medizinhistorische Analyse und Übersetzung der Wunderprotokolle am Grab der Elisabeth von Thüringen* (Frankfurt am Main, 1985), 30. In this interesting work, Jansen provides a German translation of each of the 130 miracles of the cult, along with secondary references to the illnesses, etc., as well as analyses of the material.

175. J. Kroll and Bernard Bachrach, "Child Psychiatry Perspective: Child Care and Child Abuse in Early Medieval Europe," *Journal of the American Academy of Child Psychiatry* 25 (1986), 562-8, at 565.

176. Arnold, *Kind und Gesellschaft*, 35-6.
177. Paternal involvement is examined by Didier Lett in "Des 'nouveaux pères' au moyen âge? Les fonctions paternelles dans les *Miracles de Saint Louis*," in *Conformité et Déviances au Moyen Âge*, Actes de deuxième colloque international de Montpellier, Université Paul-Valéry (25-27 nov. 1993), *Les Cahiers du C.R.I.S.M.A.* no. 2 (1995), 223-234. My thanks to M. Lett for this article.
178. Philippe de Beaumanoir, *Coutumes de Beauvaisis*, trans. F. R. Akehurst (Philadelphia, PA, 1992), 53, no. 126. Beaumanoir is noting valid reasons for a man's nonappearance in court: although allowed in case of his infant's natural death, "he can take a legal adjournment *even more properly*" in the case of accidental death, "for his distress excuses him." Emphasis added. This passage is noted by Didier Lett in his Thèse de doctorat d'Histoire, l'Ecole des Hautes Etudes, December, 1995, "Enfances, Eglise et Familles dans l'Occident Chrétien" (mid-twelfth to early fourteenth centuries), 210. I am grateful to M. Lett for permission to examine sections of his thesis.

NOTES TO CHAPTER 4

1. Frederick Rivara, "Epidemiology of Childhood Injuries," *American Journal of the Diseases of Children* 136 (May, 1982), 399-405; Sven Ove Samuelsen et al., "Temporal and Regional Trends in Fatal Childhood Injuries in Norway," *Scandinavian Journal of Social Medicine* 21, no 1 (1993), passim.
2. Barbara A. Hanawalt, *The Ties that Bound: Peasant Families in Medieval England*, (New York, 1986), 23-4.
3. Grenville Astill, "Rural Settlement: The Toft and the Croft" in G. Astill and A. Grant, eds., *The Countryside of Medieval England* (Oxford, 1988), 51-3, 60. Astill also calls attention (58) to the use of the house site for infant burials, both within and outside of buildings. For discussion and bibliography on early medieval Italian settlements, see Richard Hodges, "Rewriting the Rural History of Early Medieval Italy: Twenty-five Years of Medieval Archaeology Reviewed," *Rural History* 1 (1990), 17-36.
4. Adults, of course, were also at risk in using these structures. When Raynalda, eighteen, was descending the external steps leading from her father's house in Marseilles with her eighteen-month-old daughter in her arms, her dress snagged. As she bent down to try to free it, she lost her balance and she and the infant tumbled all the way down, "falling in a heap at the base of the steps." *Louis*, 239-41.
5. *Dorotheas*, 124, 334, 396-7.
6. *Becket*, vol. 1, 526.
7. *Nicholas*, 585-6.
8. *Chiara*, 379-80, 382.
9. Anne R. DeWindt and Edwin B. DeWindt, eds., *Royal Justice and the Medieval English Countryside: The Huntingdonshire Eyre of 1286, the Ramsey Abbey Banlieu Court of 1287, and the Assizes of 1287-88* (Toronto, 1981), 305, 399, 481; Martin Weinbaum, ed., *The London Eyre of 1276* (London Record Society, 1976), 27-8.

10. *London Eyre*, 19-20; Henry Summerson, ed., *Crown Pleas of the Devon Eyre of 1238* (Devon & Cornwall Record Society, n.s. 28, 1985), 60.

11. *Devon Eyre*, 97.

12. Michael Goodich, *Violence and Miracle in the Fourteenth Century* (Chicago, 1995), chap. 5, "Children as Victims," deals with accidentally drowned children; cf. esp. 93-7.

13. Hanawalt, *Ties that Bound*, 41.

14. *Henry*, 293-4.

15. Ellen Badone, *The Appointed Hour: Death, Worldview, and Social Change in Brittany* (Berkeley, 1989), 10.

16. Cantilupe, MS *Vat Lat 4015*, fols. 51ᵛ-54ᵛ.

17. The mother's weeping: *amare lacrimentem*. After the papal notary wrote the English exclamations "Alas, alas" he provided, for the benefit of his clerical readers, the Latin equivalent, *"Heu, heu."*

18. *adeo grossa et prope partum.*

19. It is described as a *vas* placed to receive water *fluentem ex stillicidio*.

20. Described as an interval equal to the time it would take for someone to walk from the door of the house to the entrance of the Franciscans' church, 120 paces away.

21. *effudit comprimendo mamillam suam lac.*

22. MS *Vat. Lat. 4015*, fols. 146ᵛ-157ᵛ, the events probably occurring on September 19, 1305.

23. It is not clear whether Alice and Hugh were on the same, or opposite, sides of the stream at this point. When Alice testified she said nothing about this warning.

24. The expression used of this area of the yard was *intra clausurum sive ovile*.

25. The same assumption that arose when some clothing was seen in the fishpond at Wisteston, below.

26. Thomas's father, William of Donington, was the brother of little William's mother, Alice. Thomas's grandfather was also named William.

27. *frigidum sicut lapis.*

28. Another witness was more specific: When the bystanders thought the boy had died, Agnes the servant of William of Donington, Sibilla wife of Robert Gunibald, and Matilda wife of Philip of Donington wanted to bind and join the child's hands and feet, according to the custom of the region, and hold a nightlong vigil for him before preparing him for burial. MS *Vat. Lat. 4015*, fol. 152ʳ.

29. He rode *cum equo festino gressu*.

30. *dolorem ferre nequiens.*

31. In this accident/miracle report, twelve witnesses were examined by the papal commissioners in 1307. Of these, six men claimed that they held their lands of the Mortimers, a family of the Welsh border region whose power had been growing through the thirteenth century. From their castle at Wigmore (three miles from Donington as the crow flies) the Mortimers in 1307 were repre-

sented by Lady Margaret, wife of Edmund Mortimer (d. 1304) and mother of Roger Mortimer (1287-1330), who became infamous in English history as the lover of Queen Isabella and the agent behind the murder of King Edward II. Five of the six witnesses claimed to hold their lands of Lady Margaret, one stated that he was a subject of Lord Roger de Mortimer. Radnor was one of the Mortimer holdings.

32. There is something puzzling about this sequence of events. Alice had already gone to Lord William's place when her son "drowned"; later, her husband saw his child apparently dead, then he too went to Lord William's, before his son's "revival." On his arrival, would he not have told Alice about their son? Yet she claimed that she learned of the accident *and the revival* of the boy that evening, so presumably this was her first knowledge of the event. Would John have kept the accident from his wife in order not to disturb her — or Lord William's dinner guests?

33. *torvo visu . . . furiosus.*

34. MS *Vat. Lat. 4015*, fol. 149ʳ. An early-fourteenth-century example of offering someone "a toast," a term coming from the practice of flavoring drinks with spiced toast.

35. MS *Vat. Lat 4015*, fols. 140ʳ-146ʳ.

36. The route of a Roman road runs through the present-day hamlet of Little Marcle, although there is a deserted medieval village site in the fields half a mile or so from the modern one. Given the descriptions contained in this report, "Little Marcle" of 1304/7 probably coincided with the modern site.

37. John was lucky; many children who played too near the water were less fortunate, as numerous coroners' records show. In 1265, for instance, ten-year-old Henry, while amusing himself in his father's yard, fell into a ditch of water. His father tried to save him, but "he did not succeed in doing this . . ." Charles Gross (ed.), *Select Cases from the Coroners' Rolls A.D. 1265-1413*, Selden Soc. vol. 9 (London, 1896), l.

38. The average withers height of modern cattle is about four and one-half feet; in the fourteenth to seventeenth centuries, it was roughly four feet, and about three feet eight inches in the tenth through thirteenth centuries. Sándor Bökönyi, "The Development of Stockbreeding and Herding in Medieval Europe," chap. 3 of *Agriculture in the Middle Ages*, ed. Del Sweeney (Philadelphia, 1995), 41-61 at 42-3. Even with admittedly shorter cattle in the tenth century, Heinrich Fichtenau tends to overstate livestock dwarfism in *Living in the Tenth Century: Mentalities and Social Orders*, trans. Patrick J. Geary (Chicago, 1991), 336.

39. See Joyce E. Salisbury's book *The Beast Within: Animals in the Middle Ages* (New York, 1994), for an introduction to this topic.

40. *Henry*, 178-81.

41. *tum strepitu . . . tum ululatu.*

42. *Becket*, vol. 1, 293. As William fitz Stephen wrote of twelfth-century London, "In winter on almost every feast-day before dinner either foaming boars, . . .

or stout bulls with butting horns, or huge bears do battle with the hounds let loose upon them." Trans. in *English Historical Documents*, vol. 2, eds. D. C. Douglas and G. W. Greenaway, 2d ed. (Oxford, 1981), 1029.

43. *London Eyre*, 14.

44. *Urban*, 455-6.

45. *et erat tota nigra in corpore velut corbo*, 455.

46. *Henry*, 275-6, The boy is described as *tum corporis exigui tum etatis imbecilli-tate. . . .* [yet] *vitrico tanquam patri obtemperans*.

47. These records contain other examples of kind, loving stepmothers and fathers.

48. *Urban*, 347-8; see E. J. W. Barker's comment in *Prehistoric Textiles* (Princeton, 1991), 69: "This habit of spinning while walking, or riding a donkey, seems to be fairly old in the north Mediterranean." The girl's accident occurred in southern France. For a discussion of children working in a more structured, urban environment, see Hanawalt, *Growing Up in Medieval London*, esp. chaps. 8 and 9.

49. MS *Vat. Lat. 4015*, fols. 157^v-165^r.

50. Ronald C. Finucane, "Pilgrimage in Daily Life. Aspects of Medieval Communication . . . [in] Herefordshire Villages." In *Wallfahrt und Alltag in mittelalter und früher Neuzeit* (International Round Table, Krems, Austria), (Wien, 1992), 165-217.

51. *ludere cum coetaneis suis . . . juvenili levitate.*

52. John notes that his son had been dressed *ut pauper*, i.e., in plain linen cloth (fol. 159^r).

53. MS *Vat. Lat. 4015*, fol. 159r, *commotis visceribus*.

54. *monstratus et exhibitus.*

55. *Becket*, vol. 1, 505.

56. *Dorotheas*, 366-7.

57. *Devon Eyre*, 30.

58. *Dorotheas*, 248-9; *exterritus timens puerum submersum.*

59. *Henry*, 17-9. This suggests, therefore, that Richard usually (*more solito*) took his grandson with him to the mill.

60. *Becket*, vol. 1, 202-3.

61. *Henry*, 21-3: *Namque ut proprium quodam modo infancium est quicquid manu arripuerint ad os protinus absque titulo discrectionis porrigere. . . .*

62. *Henry*, 141-3.

63. *Henry*, 193-6.

64. Bodleian MS *Fell 2*, fol. 33 (Edmund of Pontigny).

65. *Henry*, 93-4.

66. A loose translation of the narrator's theatrical-rhetorical version of her anguish, "Wretched me!" —*Ei heu me miseram*, etc.

67. Hanawalt, *Ties that Bound*, 176; and see 181: the "planting and harvest seasons were the most dangerous because parents were busy away from home."

68. Quoted by Luke Demaitre in his valuable article, "The Idea of Childhood and Child Care in Medical Writings of the Middle Ages," *Journal of Psychohistory*

4 (1977), 466; and in Shulamith Shahar, *Childhood in the Middle Ages* (London, 1990), 26.

69. *Becket*, vol. 1, 200-2, vol. 2, 238-9; see also Bodleian MS *Fell 2*, fols. 29-30, *Becket* vol. 2, 226-7; *Henry*, 207-8.

70. *Henry*, 62-3, 101-3, 209-11.

71. A. R. Malden, ed., *The Canonization of St. Osmund*, Wiltshire Record Society, vol. 2 (1901), 64-7, *iuvenes ipsius villate*.

72. *Osmund*, 65. Such attempts to escape the consequences of inflicting even accidental death would not have been unusual; contemporary English law included provisions for asylum.

73. In an earlier English example of the dangers associated with playing medieval quoits, the nine-year-old son of a priest struck in the head with a stone (exposing the brain's membranes) recovered after the wound was bound with linen. *Becket*, vol. 1, 341-2.

74. *Henry*, 37-8.

75. *Henry*, 237-9.

76. *Sicque ludus ille terminatur in luctu . . . plausus in planctum transit*, a play on words of which this miracle-collector was fond. See in the previous chapter, for instance, the phrases *in luctus gaudia vertit, in planctum plausus, in lacrimosa iocos, Henry*, 260-3, at 260.

77. *Dorotheas*, 249: [*I*]*n domo, in qua layci habebant convivium suum, sicut consuevit fieri apud eos in istis festivitatibus.*

78. MS *Vat. Lat. 4015*, fols. 123ʳ-140ʳ. For Cantilupe's cult, see Ronald C. Finucane, "Cantilupe as Thaumaturge: Pilgrims and Their 'Miracles'" in *St. Thomas Cantilupe: Essays in his Honour*, ed. M. Jancey (Hereford, 1982), 137-44, and Ronald C. Finucane, *Miracles and Pilgrims: Popular Beliefs in Medieval England* (London, 1977; repr. New York, 1995), 173-88.

79. Wisteston House, a building incorporating fifteenth-century work, was demolished within the last twenty years or so by the owner, who refused (in the late 1980s) to allow inspection of the site of nearby Wisteston Chapel, razed early in the present century. My thanks to Mr. and Mrs. Pye of Brick House Farm, Marden, for permission to examine their land for indications of the large fishpond in which little Joanna was said to have drowned. Medieval fishponds can still be identified in and around many English villages; cf. Trevor Rowley, *Villages in the Landscape* (Guernsey, 1987), 191-2.

80. In another source, Oxford *Exeter Coll. MS 158*, fol. 7ᵛ, the date for this event is noted as xjjjj.Kl.Maii in the second year of the miracles (which began in the first week of April 1287). The date of the accident, herefore, is likely to have been April 18, a Sunday, followed by St. George's day, on April 23d.

81. Joan and Joanna: it was common for children to be given a godparent's name.

82. John was *in dicto ludo pueriliter agens*, according to Joanna; but then, he was only four. He had died before the papal inquiry of 1307 took place.

83. They were *stupefacti et perteriti* at their discovery, as one of them testified.

84. *Quod non expediebat quod alii existentes in corea viderent hoc*, fol. 132ʳ.
85. What seems at first sight to be callous behavior was, apparently, often done in medieval England in order to escape fines levied on individuals or villages at the shire or county court: R. F. Hunnisett, *The Medieval Coroner* (Cambridge, 1961), 12. Most of the information in the following section is based on Hunnisett's book.
86. England was not unique in promulgating such laws: in 1366, after a girl fell into the water at a mill near Le Mans while washing clothes, "the locals feared moving the body without license from the secular authorities," but they did so anyway; Goodich, *Violence and Miracle*, 98.
87. *verba puerilia.*
88. Ralph's tale: *narrabat quedam verba solacii.* . . .
89. According to Adam, the image was hung up in 1288; his testimony indicates that in 1307—nineteen years later—it had already disintegrated. But medieval wax votives have survived intact after several hundred years, as shown by a discovery in Exeter cathedral during the present century; see U. Radford, "The Wax Images found in Exeter Cathedral," *Antiquaries Journal* 29 (1949), 164-8. For comments on the use of ex-votos as a means of documenting religious mentalities, see Michel Vovelle, *Ideologies and Mentalities*, trans. E. O'Flaherty (Chicago, 1990), 43-5, 93-5.
90. MS *Vat. Lat. 4015*, canonization of Thomas Cantilupe fols. 64ʳ-71ᵛ. Also found, in a fragmented state, in *AASS*, 696-704.
91. Dom Jacques Dubois and Jean-Loup Lemaitre, *Sources & Méthodes de l'Hagiographie Médiévale* (Paris,1993), 331-6.
92. Alternatively, he may have heard about the Hereford miracles years earlier but chose, for whatever reasons, not to appeal to Cantilupe until 1303.
93. The notaries helpfully define this object as "a little cart with one wheel which her father pushed in front of him with his hands" (*parvum currum unius rote quem pater ante se manibus pellebat*).
94. A pyx was a container that usually enclosed the eucharist or relics; here it held a liquid, somewhat like the ampules which contained water from the shrine of another Thomas, the murdered Archbishop Becket.
95. Medieval references to white or dazzling objects usually signified sinlessness, i.e., unspotted or unstained—"immaculate"—while black was often correlated with sin and Satan; junior devils were sometimes described as black men, "Ethiopians." Although the medieval liturgy employed specific colors for particular holy days, these color schemes were not the same everywhere, and there were several variant systems of color symbolism among the laity.
96. *Dorotheas*, 446.
97. Christian Krötzl, "Parent-Child Relations in medieval Scandinavia According to Scandinavian Miracle Collections," *Scandinavian Journal of History* vol. 14 (1989), 35.
98. *Dorotheas*, 395-6.
99. The whole sentence was, *Ecce! Ipsi venientes de conviviis iterum neglexerunt puerum!*
100. Cantilupe, MS *Vat. Lat. 4015*, fols. 165ᵛ-169ᵛ.

101. Hanawalt notes, in *Ties that Bound*, 176, that "It was common in many peasant societies for the parents to take swaddled children to the fields with them when they worked, where they were put in trees or laid on the ground. Although," she continues, "no coroners' inquests mention this practice . . ." it is clearly indicated in this miracle.

102. The animals and plow could be taken as deodand, as explained in the case of Joanna at Wisteston/Marden.

103. Amid an expanding universe of articles, reports, dissertations, and books on psychological, anthropological, medical, and sociological approaches to cross-cultural categorizations of human behavior as normal or deviant, an ancient but enjoyable, jargon-free classic is *Six Cultures: Studies of Child Rearing*, ed., Beatrice B. Whiting (New York, 1963).

104. *Dictionary of National Biography* and notices in Michael Prestwich, *Edward I* (London, 1988) passim.

105. Cantilupe, MS *Vat. Lat. 4015* fols. 188ʳ-203ᵛ, summarized in *Exeter Coll. MS 158* fol. 38ᵛ-39ʳ.

106. *in ictu oculi.*

107. The house was *non distante a castro nisi per iactum lapidis*, fol. 189ʳ.

108. *sicut ligantur infantes*, fol. 200ʳ, suggesting tying rather than, or in addition to, swaddling.

109. *Fuit capta ligata et retenta a vicinis ne exiret domum*, MS *Vat. Lat. 4015*, f. 202ᵛ.

110. MS *Vat. Lat. 4015* fols. 189ᵛ-190ʳ.

111. *erat frigidus ut lapis membra rigida ut lingnum* [for *lignum*] *aridum*, fol. 193ʳ.

112. *Cum dictus Willelmus scriptor apposuisset pennam ad pargamenum ut inciperet scribere inquisitionam* [sic] *de dicta morte*, MS *Vat. Lat. 4015* fol. 195ʳ.

113. Perhaps the coroners, preferring to avoid a "death" in the royal castle ditch, with the possibility of attributing at least some of the fault to royal agents, were only too happy to rid themselves of the inert form when minimal signs of life appeared.

114. Translators were appointed to attend such hearings to facilitate the proceedings, especially useful in the Cantilupe inquiry since the Herefordshire people, the papal commissioners were given to understand, had their own peculiar ways of saying things. Though linguistic localism was common in medieval Europe and England, in the Hereford region the proximity of Welsh-speakers may have made the situation even more complex (and see indications of language recognition, if not bilingualism, in the case of the Welsh mute, discussed in chapter 3).

115. Thus, about A.D. 1300.

116. John Havering was appointed Justice for Wales in April, 1300, Hugh Leominster was named Chamberlain for north Wales by Edward I in 1295, in which office he served until 1302, when replaced by Thomas Asthall. T. F. Tout, *Chapters in the Administrative History of Mediaeval England* vol. 6 (New York, 1933/67), 59, 61.

117. This is the first mention of "swellings"; after such a fall, bumps and scrapes on Roger's body would have been normal. In concluding their work on this case,

the papal inquisitors recalled the father, Gervase, who told them that he and Dionysia led a life no better than others, and that they had gone on pilgrimage to Hereford (some ninety-three leagues away) prior to Roger's birth, two or three times after that, and again after the miraculous revival of their son.

118. *Henry,* 156-9: *et quidem, fateor, negligenter satis*; the infant's being helpless: *imbecillitatem infantuli.* Given the infant's age, although at first sight it might seem that the commentator is deliberately overstating his helplessness—at least as far as his being able to walk is concerned—it is worth recalling that, for modern infants, the observed age range for ability to walk three steps alone is between nine and seventeen months.

119. *Urban,* 160-1.

120. Joseph F. Kelly, in a review of Chélini's *L'aube du moyen âge: Naissance de la chrétienté occidentale,* in *Speculum* 68 no. 4 (October, 1993), 1080.

121. Cantilupe, MS *Exeter Coll. 158,* fol. 28ᵛ: *Et ipsum fere per duos dies custodiebant ibidem si forte aliquod vite signum appareret in ipso.*

122. Robert G. Bolte et al., "The Use of Extracorporeal Rewarming in a Child Submerged for 66 Minutes," *Journal of the American Medical Association* (hereafter *JAMA*) 260 no. 3 (July 15, 1988), 377-9; "As far as we know, this is the longest time ever reported," 377.

123. J. Avery and R. Jackson, *Children and Their Accidents* (London, 1993), 95; see also J. A. Kram and K. W. Kizer, "Submersion Injury," *Emergency Medical Clinics of North America* 2, no. 3 (August 1984), 545-52, and J. H. Pearn et al., "Sequential Intellectual Recovery after Near-drowning," *Medical Journal of Australia* 1, no. 10 (May 19, 1979), 463-4.

124. A. E. Dick and D. Potgieter, "Secondary Drowning in the Cape Peninsula," *South African Medical Journal* 66, no. 22 (November 20, 1982), 803-6; J. H. Pearn, "Secondary Drowning in Children," *British Medical Journal* 281 (October 25, 1980), 1103-5. A fifteen-month-old boy fell into a pond one Tuesday morning, was pronounced dead at 4:45 that afternoon after resuscitation attempts had failed, "returned to life" about 5:15, but died next afternoon. *Sacramento* [CA] *Bee,* March 16, 1995.

125. James P. Orlowski, "Drowning, Near-Drowning, and Ice-Water Drowning" in *JAMA* 260 (1988), 391.

126. *Osmund,* 42-4; Krötzl, "Parent-Child Relations," 32, and see Reginald R. Darlington, ed., *The Vita Wulfstani of William of Malmesbury . . . and the Miracles,* Royal Historical Society, Camden Third Series, vol. 40 (London, 1928), 161, where a boy pulled from the water was taken home, *per pedes suspenso* and then put *ad ignem.*

127. *Laurent,* 170-1, *Becket,* vol. 1, 200-2, vol. 2, 238-9.

128. Orlowski, "Drowning," *JAMA,* 390.

129. *Nicholas,* 168-9.

130. *Nicholas,* 585-6.

131. *Chiara,* 509-10.

132. *Becket,* vol. 1, 505.

133. For a brief overview of alternatives, see Shahar, *Childhood in the Middle Ages*, 131-4.

134. As examples, cf. MS *Vat. Lat. 4015*, fol. 131ʳ, 133ᵛ, *Dorotheas*, 47.

135. MS *Vat. Lat. 4015*, fol. 66ᵛ.

136. MS *Vat. Lat. 4015*, fol. 201ᵛ.

137. *Nicholas*, 332, *et credebatur personas, que sciunt reactare ossa.*

138. Yves Bizet, *Les Guerisseurs, Les Rebouteux* (Sully-sur-Loire, 1992), passim, and Judith Devlin, *The Superstitious Mind* (New Haven, CT, 1987), 43-4.

139. *Henry*, 200-3. She was playing *more infancium lustrabat* but as a result of the accident, ended up *in modem fere placente planum.*

140. Gordon, "Accidents Among Medieval Children," 145-63, at 160.

141. *Louis*, 145-9: *faciunt coreas et vadunt cantando per terras et parant domus suas . . . de pannis, viz., chalonibus et aliis pannis melioribus quos habent.*

142. *corizando, cantando et saltando et tubis precedentibus.*

143. *Hey, Bernarde, et quid habetis vos? Intretis domum meam et quiescatis.*

144. His response was *Domina, dimittatis me ire*; as indicated, in Italy the title "*domina*" did not necessarily imply an elevated social position.

145. Oxford, Bodleian MS *Fell 2*, fols. 37-8.

146. *Becket*, vol. 1, 366; the Canterbury recorder also tells us, rhetorically, that the mother castigated herself since she "did not delegate anyone to protect errant childhood" (*vagabundae pueritiae*).

147. *Numquam aliquam bonam diem haberet, Dorotheas*, 176-7. In the south of France, when Moneta's eight-month-old son seemed to have died while she was out washing his wrappings, she was tempted to kill herself, fearing that her husband would blame her for their son's death: *Urban*, 478-9. The miracle-compiler attributed her thoughts of suicide, as such writers often did, to the devil.

148. MS *Vat. Lat. 4015*, fols. 123ᵛ, 129ʳ.

149. MS *Vat. Lat. 4015*, fol. 126ʳ⁻ᵛ.

150. MS *Vat. Lat. 4015*, fols. 123ᵛ, 126ʳ, 140ʳ: *virgo Sancti Thome.*

151. MS *Vat. Lat. 4105*, fol. 123ᵛ, *noluit accipere virum.*

152. On the other hand, the mother took the trouble to describe how the Hereford saint had benefited her son John, who was seeking to become a priest; the father Adam said nothing about this; MS *Vat. Lat. 4015*, fol. 129ʳ.

153. See appendix for this part of the process. The cardinals' deliberations can be read in Oxford, *Exeter College MS 158*, fols. 48v-52r and in Vauchez, *La sainteté en occident*, 633-47, a transcription of BN *MS. Lat. 5373A*, fols. 66r-69v.

154. Patrick Daly, "The Process of Canonization in the Thirteenth and Early Fourteenth Centuries," in *St. Thomas Cantilupe, Bishop of Hereford: Essays in his Honour*, ed. Meryl Jancey (Hereford, 1982), 125-35, at 135, for the papal ceremony of canonization itself. For the papal bull see, e.g., W. Capes, *Charters and Records of Hereford Cathedral* (Hereford, 1908), 192; liturgy in W. H. Frere and L. E. G. Brown, eds., *The Hereford Breviary (1505)*, Henry Bradshaw Society, vol. 40 (1911), and an earlier version in a fifteenth-century English

choir breviary, Bodleian *MS Laud misc. 299*, f. 467v: The full introduction was *Quedam namque puella etatis annorum quinque que tempore longo in quodam profundo staugno*[sic] *steterat mortua et submersa* . . . For additional information on Thomas's commemorations, see Philip Barrett, "A Saint in the Calendar: The effect of the canonization of St. Thomas Cantilupe on the liturgy" in Jancey, 153-7; another drowned and revived child was celebrated musically in a fifteenth-century motet: Brian Trowell and Andrew Wathey, "John Benet's 'Lux Fulget ex Anglia—O Pater Pietatis—Salve Thoma'" in Jancey, 159-80. The child was the son of Walter de Grafton of Oxfordshire, drowned in a water butt in 1289, MS *Exeter College 158*, fol. 11v.

155. *et litteris ac moribus informandum.*

156. *Per nos vel per vos provisum fuerit de ecclesiastico beneficio conpetenti, Registrum Radulphi Baldock* . . . [et al., London 1304-38], ed. R. C. Fowler, Canterbury and York Society, vol. 7 (London, 1911), 148.

157. *"Laurent archevêque,"* 171. *Hoc autem memoriale ab eventu fonti remansit, ut adhuc a tota vicinia dicatur: Hic est fons ubi Ernulphus submersus fuit.*

158. Miracles of St. Gertrude in *AASS* II Mar. (Antwerp 1668, reprinted 1968), 600.That Mary was living with the Beguines when her accident occurred, and her pilgrimage to Rome, suggest that she was predisposed to a religious life from an early age.

159. *Osmund,* 60-2.

160. *de huiusmodi infortunis multum condolentes . . . flexis ad terram genibus clamaverunt et oraverunt.*

161. *quomodo ipsa mortua fuit.* The scribes provided her with such expressions as *bene novit et recordatur . . . , postea bene scivit et sensiit . . . se esse vite restitutam . . .* (62).

162. Orlowski, "Drowning," 390, and see Avery and Jackson, who suggest that about 6 percent of near-drowning survivors were "left with a *severe* neurological handicap" (94-5, emphasis added), with presumably a larger percentage suffering moderate handicaps. Other medical research on neurological damage and concomitant linguistic debilitation in, e.g., K. Reilly et al., "Linguistic status subsequent to childhood immersion injury," *Medical Journal of Australia* 145, no. 5 (March 7, 1988), 225-8; F. D. Allman et al., "Outcome Following Cardiopulmonary Resuscitation in Severe Pediatric Near-drowning," *American Journal of Diseases of Children* 140, no. 6 (June, 1986), 571-5; R. S. Young et al., "Neurological Outcome in Cold Water Drowning," *JAMA* 244, no. 11 (September 12, 1980), 1233-5. My thanks to Jerome L. Kroll, M.D., for several of these citations concerning post-resuscitation debilities.

163. MS *Vat. Lat. 4015*, fols. 157ᵛ, 158ᵛ: *aliqualiter languidus.*

164. André Vauchez, *La sainteté en occident aux derniers siècles du moyen âge* (Rome, 1981), 514-8, discusses cases of stigmata during the fourteenth and fifteenth centuries, apparently by then more common among women, even though the medieval tradition was initiated in the thirteenth century by St. Francis.

165. *Dorotheas*, 396-7; 75-6, 289, 468-9; *Chiara*, 501-2.

166. Eleanora C. Gordon, "Accidents Among Medieval Children as Seen from the Miracles of Six English Saints and Martyrs," *Medical History* 35 (1991), 145-63 at 149; Gordon includes adolescents in her sample.

167. Barbara A. Hanawalt, *Crime and Conflict in English Communities, 1300-1348* (Cambridge, MA, 1979), 156.

168. Hanawalt, *Ties that Bound*, 180.

169. For example, the 1985 figures for deaths of children in home accidents in the United Kingdom was 66 percent boys, 34 percent girls, Avery and Jackson, *Children and Their Accidents*, 49. Canada for 1983: 64 percent boys, L. MacWilliam et al., "Fatal Accidental Childhood Injuries in Canada," *Canadian Journal of Public Health*, 78 (March/April 1987), 132. In 1985-86, analyses carried out in the state of Washington: in the age range zero to four, 61 percent were boys: Frederick Rivara et al., "Population-Based Study of Unintentional Injury Incidence and Impact during Childhood," *American Journal of Public Health* 79, no. 8 (August 1989), 992. In France from 1981-82, a study of a health authority near Paris indicated accidental injuries of 63 percent boys, 37 percent girls: A. Tursz, "Collection of Data on Accidents in Childhood: Problems of Method," chap. 3 of M. Manciaux and C. J. Romer, eds., *Accidents in Childhood and Adolescence: The Role of Research* (Geneva, 1991), 48.Based on 2,772 children's injuries reported in a 1988 national survey, "Boys had a significantly higher risk of injury than did girls": P. C. Scheidt et al., "The Epidemiology of Nonfatal Injuries among US Children and Young," *American Journal of Public Health* 85, no. 7 (July 1995), 932-8, at 934-6.

170. Avery and Jackson, *Children and Accidents*, 5.

171. MacWilliam et al., "Fatal Accidental Childhood Injuries in Canada," 134. See also Rivara, "Epidemiology of Childhood Injuries," 404: "The sex difference in injury rates has been often commented on but little explored. Why do boys have a higher injury rate than girls?"

172. Hanawalt, *Ties that Bound*, 182.

173. Gordon, "Accidents among Medieval Children," 149.

174. Avery and Jackson, *Children and Accidents*, 44.

175. A. R. Taket et al., "Mortality and Morbidity: The Available Data and their Limitations" in M. Manciaux and Romer, eds., *Accidents in Childhood*, 21-2. In another study of accidental mortality among children in the United States in 1975, it was found that 71 percent of the 4,446 victims between birth and nine years of age were under five. Leon S. Robertson, "Present Status of Knowledge in Childhood Injury Prevention" in *Preventing Childhood Injuries* (Ross Laboratories, n.p., 1988), 2.

176. Orlowski, "Drowning, Near-Drowning," 390.

177. M. A. Nichter and B. Everett, "Profiles of Drowning Victims in a Coastal Community," *Journal of the Florida Medical Association* 76 (1989), 253-6; H. Marcusson and W. Oehmisch, "Accident Mortality in Childhood in Selected Countries of Different Continents, 1950-1971," World Health Statistics Report (1977) 62.

178. In Gordon's study, the figure was about 56 percent, "Accidents among Medieval Children," 151. As noted earlier, according to modern studies, the primary causes of children's accidental mortality, excluding traffic-related incidents, are drownings (in which boys clearly outnumber girls) and burns. Avery and Jackson, *Children and Accidents*, 8, 48; MacWilliam et al., "Fatal Accidental Injuries in Canada," 133; Anna E. Waller et al., "Childhood Injury Deaths: National Analysis and Geographic Variations," *American Journal of Public Health* 79 no. 3 (March 1989), 310. Research published in 1994 indicated that of 20,402 children below age ten in the United States who drowned in the period from 1971 to 1988, 71 percent were boys, 29 percent girls. Ruth A. Brenner et al., "Divergent Trends in Childhood Drowning Rates, 1971 Through 1988," *JAMA* 271, no. 20 (May 25, 1994), 1606-8.

179. Arnold, *Kind und Gesellschaft*, 50-1, 120, and see Hanawalt, *Crime and Conflict*, 155.

180. A. M. Kemp et al., "Accidents and Child Abuse in Bathtub Submersions," *Archives of Diseases of Children* 70 (May, 1994), 435-8, a study based on forty-four cases in the United Kingdom in 1988 and 1989. J. M. Lavelle et al., "Ten-year Review of Pediatric Bathtub Near-drownings: Evaluation for Child-Abuse and Neglect," *Annals of Emergency Medicine* 25, no. 3 (March, 1995), 344-8, a study of twenty-one children in the period 1982-1992.

181. Patrick W. O'Carroll et al., "Drowning Mortality in Los Angeles County, 1976-1984," *JAMA* 260, no. 3 (July 15, 1988), 383.

182. Bartholomaeus Metlinger, *Ein Regiment der jungen Kinder*, in John Ruhräh, ed., trans., *Pediatrics of the Past* (New York, 1925), 77.

183. *Chiara*, 351-3. *dicitur puer omni sero balneabatur, ut moris est in patria pueros parvulos balneare . . .* The boy was about two months old.

184. *Dorotheas*, 229; *tinam seu vas balniandi pueros.*

185. Avery and Jackson, *Children and Accidents*, 94.

186. *Becket*, vol. 2, 227-8.

187. Hanawalt, *Ties that Bound*, 177-8.

188. Didier Lett, "Enfances, Eglise et Familles dans l'occident Chrètien entre le milieu de XIIe siècle et le début du XIVe siècle: Perceptions, pratiques et rôles narratifs," Thèse de doctorat d'Histoire, l'Ecole des Hautes Etudes en Sciences Sociales (Paris, 1995), 207-8, 264-6. I am grateful to M. Lett for sending me sections of his dissertation and allowing me to cite relevant passages, and also for sending me proofs of his article, "Les lieux périlleux de l'enfance d'après quelques récits de miracles des XIIe-XIIIe siècles," which is to appear in the no. 32 (Spring 1997) issue of *Médiévales*.

189. Avery and Jackson, *Children and their Accidents*, 44, 48-9, Rivara, "Epidemiology," 404, L. MacWilliam et al., "Fatal Accidental Childhood Injuries," 133-4; Waller et al., "Childhood Injury Deaths," 311; Rivara et al., "Population-Based Study," 993; Taket et al., "Mortality and morbidity," 21.

190. Barbara Hanawalt's coroners' records suggest this too: in about two-thirds of her cases, children's bodies were found by people who were not family members. Hanawalt, *Ties that Bound*, 184.

191. Krötzl, "Parent-Child Relations in medieval Scandinavia," 36.

192. *Becket*, vol. 2, 227-8.

193. Oxford, Bodleian MS *Fell 2*, fol. 34: *in clamores magnos feminarum more prorupit.*

194. *Nicholas*, 169: *occurrerunt ad predicta.*

195. *Dorotheas*, 78-9.

196. For loose smocks see, e.g., *Dorotheas*, 248-9 and *Henry*, 207-8.

NOTES TO CHAPTER 5

1. Barbara A. Hanawalt, *The Ties that Bound: Peasant Families in Medieval England* (New York, 1986), 184.

2. Composers of miracle collections no doubt emphasized parental grief for rhetorical effect, but in sworn depositions at canonization inquisitions, it is the parents and neighbors themselves who speak — though, it is true, in the Latin of the notaries.

3. Cicero to Titius in *Cicero: The Letters to his Friends (Epistulae ad Familiares,* V.xvi), trans. W. Williams, vol. 1 (Cambridge, MA [Loeb Classical Library], 1958), 395; and see 269, 273, 275-7, arguments repeated by the renaissance friends of Jacopo Marcello. Plutarch: "In Consolation to his Wife," *Plutarch: Essays* R. Waterfield, trans. (New York, 1992), 366, 365, 368-72.

4. Peter Brown, *The Body and Society: Men, Women and Sexual Renunciation in Early Christianity* (New York, 1988), 11.

5. Quoted by Margaret Alexiou in *The Ritual Lament in Greek Tradition* (Cambridge, 1974), 28.

6. Doris Desclais Berkvam, *Enfance et maternité dans la littérature française des XIIe et XIIIe siècles* (Paris, 1981), 123.

7. *Becket*, vols. 1, 228-30; 2, 255-7.

8. In Milton McC. Gatch, *Preaching and Theology in Anglo-Saxon England: Aelfric and Wulfstan* (Toronto, 1977), 97, 134, 234.

9. *The Coutumes de Beauvaisis of Philippe de Beaumanoir,* trans. F. Akehurst (Philadelphia, 1992), 711.

10. *Henry*, 286-8: *ululatusque et voces planctuose undique resonabant.*

11. *Dorotheas*, 366.

12. *Laurent*, 172.

13. MS *Vat. Lat. 4015*, fol. 143^r.

14. MS *Vat. Lat. 4015*, fol. 142^r; *Laurent*, 171.

15. MS *Vat. Lat. 4015*, fol. 202^r.

16. *collapsi fuissent ad terram quasi exanimes.* MS *Vat. Lat 4015*, fol. 159^r. In late twelfth-century England, a wall fell on a child asleep in its embossed wooden cradle. After calling on Becket for assistance, the mother collapsed and fainted. Two men coming upon the scene roused her with cold water, "as is the custom." *Becket*, vol. 1, 206-7, and vol. 2, 252-3.

17. *Dorotheas*, 75-7, 289, 392, 468-9; *Chiara*, 262-4: *percuteret capud ad murum.*

18. Margaret L. King, *The Death of the Child Valerio Marcello* (Chicago, 1994), 149. King cites a 1972 study of bereavement in modern adult life, and Antonia

Fraser's *The Weaker Vessel* (1984), on seventeenth-century English women. Though King points out the extent to which many of the Ariès ideas have been superseded, some of his concepts reappear in her theoretical treatment of premodern childhood.

19. MS *Vat. Lat. 4015*, fol. 152^r: *mulieres lacrimantibus*.

20. Bodley MS *Fell 2*, fols. 37-8: *more materno*.

21. *Vita Wulfstani*, 178-9: *de astantibus mulieruli contristanti*.

22. *Becket*, vol. 2, 94: *plorat uterque parens*.

23. Bodleian MS *Fell 2*, fol. 31: *eduxerunt matrem nimium se affligentem ne videret finem filii sui*.

24. *Vita Wulfstani*, 146.

25. Bodleian MS *Fell 2*, fols. 37-8.

26. Bodleian MS *Fell 2*, fols. 35-6: *more femineo*.

27. *Nicholas*, 133-4, 161-3, 261-4, 292-5.

28. For brother-sister relationships reflected in medieval miracles, see Didier Lett, "La sorella maggiore: 'madre sostituta' nei 'miracoli di San Luigi,'" *Quaderni storici* n. s. 83 (Aug. 1993), 341-53.

29. King, *The Death of the Child Valerio Marcello*, 153, 155. "Few children are mourned in written words by medieval authors, but by the time of the Renaissance, fathers express their grief." (193) This is true only if one is referring to authors of "literary" works. For Luther and Erasmus, see also Klaus Arnold, *Kind und Gesellschaft in Mittelalter und Renaissance* (Paderborn, 1980), 85.

30. *Becket*, vol. 1, 345-6.

31. Berkvam, *Enfance et maternité*, 136: the woman's lament, cast in these terms, had become, in the literature of the High Middle Ages, "*un modèle bien établi*." Berkvam finds that courtly love was the (literary) model for narrating motherly love, 141 ff.

32. *Becket*, vol. 2, 196.

33. *dolorem in mente quod nullum gaudium vel laetitiam potuit habere; vidit nimiam anxietatem et dolorem*, J. O. Halliwell, ed., *The Chronicle of William de Rishanger; The Miracles of Simon de Montfort*, Camden Society, vol. 15 (London, 1840), 82-83.

34. *Becket*, vol. 1, 231-2.

35. King, *Death of the Child Valerio*, 1 and 21.

36. *Dorotheas*, 340-1.

37. *Dorotheas*, 29, 289, 363-4. The dean of the church at Marienwerder told the papal commission that he had seen an account of this miracle written in the documents of the notary John Ulman, who had been commissioned by Bishop John and the cathedral chapter to record such events. The papal report contains this record, under date of September 30, 1395 (Dorothy had died on June 25, 1395.) The notary's record narrated how a certain little child, five months old, son of Gerke Gropeling and his wife, Donice, had been put into his cradle quite well but was found "dead" about midnight. Two well-known matrons, Tibde and Alheyt Lobdisch of the same village, also thought him dead.

38. *Urban,* 216-7.

39. Perhaps his reluctance to display his grief publicly was linked to the man's status; he was designated *dominus,* lord, of Belmont. *Urban,* 471-2.

40. *Becket,* vol. 2, 188: *pater secretius ploraturus in horto.*

41. *Becket,* vol. 2, 257-8: *non videbo morientem puerum.*

42. *Becket,* vol. 1, 190-3; vol. 2, 234-7.

43. Caroline Walker Bynum, *Jesus as Mother: Studies in the Spirituality of the High Middle Ages* (Berkeley, 1982, essay 4; see also for increasing tenderness toward medieval children from the twelfth century, Mary Martin McLaughlin, "Survivors and Surrogates: Children and Parents from the Ninth to the Thirteenth Centuries," in *The History of Childhood,* ed. Lloyd de Mause (London, 1976), 132-5.

44. *videns filium suum jam mori propinquum, amplectans eum cum brachiis, multum dolebat et anxiabatur pre nimio dolore, Urban,* 297-8.

45. Arnold, *Kind und Gesellschaft,* 37.

46. *Vita Wulfstani,* 163-7, occurring around 1220-21.

47. Several examples emphasize the deeper anxiety and grief reported of parents whose only child became ill or injured, e.g., *Louis,* 244-6, 320, 325; Dorotheas, 451.

48. *Nec hoc sicut virum deceret maturo gressu; set prepete cursu,* 164.

49. The editor notes that at this point the ms. reading is uncertain: *Quo vir inquit iure exute properas?* (164)

50. *et non minus crudeliter quam inhumane tractatur.*

51. Such examples of violent grief, attesting to the strength of parental love for their children, only highlight the despair that must have motivated one mother in a Pomeranian case. As Margaret held her son in her arms, warming him at the fire, a neighbor came in and asked why she was crying. Margaret, after explaining that her son had suffered severe pain from a kidney infection for a month, said "I would rather see the boy dead, than feed him and look at him, infected like this" (*Potius vellem videre puerum istum mortuum quam videre et nutrire eum sic infectuosum*). *Dorotheas,* 377-8.

52. David Nicholas, "Childhood in Medieval Europe" in *Children in Historical and Comparative Perspective,* Joseph M. Hawes and N. Ray Hiner, eds. (New York, 1991), 43; McLaughlin, "Survivors and Surrogates," 138-9.

53. Avery and Jackson, *Children and Their Accidents,* 1; Leon S. Robertson, "Present Status of Knowledge in Childhood Injury Prevention," *Preventing Childhood Injuries* (Ross Laboratories, 1988), 1-2; Amir Shanon et al., "Nonfatal childhood injuries: a survey at the Children's Hospital of Eastern Ontario," *Canadian Medical Association Journal* 146 (1992) 362. T. Gärling, in *Children Within Environments: Toward a Psychology of Accident Prevention,* T. Gärling and J. Valsiner, eds., (New York, 1985), 3: "Today the most frequent harm to children [in developed countries] is accidental injuries. About fifty years ago, diseases ranked clearly higher than accidents as a cause of death to children . . ." See also H. Marcusson and W. Oehmisch, "Accident

Mortality in Childhood in Selected Countries of Different Continents, 1950-1971," *World Health Statistics Report* 30 (1977), 65.

54. Barbara Schuh, *"Jenseitigkeit in diesseitigen Formen": social-und mentalitätsgeschichtliche Aspekte, spätmittelalterlicher Mirakelberichte* (Graz, 1989), 54-5; this figure excludes twenty-three children who were counted in another category.

55. For the claim that there were proportionally more females among late-medieval saints than during earlier centuries, see, e.g., Jacques Dalarun, "The Clerical Gaze," trans. A. Goldhammer, in Christiane Klapisch-Zuber (ed.), *A History of Women in the West*, vol. 2, *Silences of the Middle Ages* (Cambridge, MA, 1992), 41. For contraindications of women's improved status, see André Vauchez, *La sainteté en occident aux derniers siècles du moyen âge* (Rome, 1981), 317-8, 428-9,448; Judith M. Bennett, *Women in the Medieval English Countryside: Gender and Household in Brigstock Before the Plague* (New York, 1987), 197.

56. Vauchez, *La sainteté*, 550.

57. David Herlihy and Christiane Klapisch-Zuber, *Tuscans and Their Families: A Study of the Florentine Catasto of 1427* (New Haven, CT, 1985), 256.

58. Philip Gavitt, "Infant death in late medieval Florence: The smothering hypothesis reconsidered" in *Medieval Family Roles* Cathy Itnyre, ed., (New York, 1996), 148-9.

59. Schuh, *spätmittelalterlicher Mirakelberichte*, 54 n. 198: girls were "deutlich in den Hintergrund." Schuh does not indicate the distribution for gender, i.e., how many girls received cures of illness versus accidents, how many boys, etc., but 63 percent of all the miracles were cures of illnesses.

60. Pierre-André Sigal, *L'homme et le miracle dans la France médiévale* (Paris, 1985), 254: "[L]e pourcentage féminin est toujours plus faible parmi les miraculés jeunes que parmi les adultes." Commenting on a table concerning the cures of "les jeunes," Sigal notes "Une étude sur les enfants seuls n'est possible que pour la population masculine . . ." 261, n. 108, a conclusion with which I would not agree.

61. Bernard Cousin, "Deux cents miracles en Provence sous Louis XIV," *Revue d'histoire de la spiritualité* 52 (1976), 225-44, at 227: "[E]lle est plus nette envers celle des fils qu'envers celle des filles."

62. Eleanora C. Gordon, "Child Health in the Middle Ages as Seen in the Miracles of Five English Saints, A.D. 1150-1220," *Bulletin of the History of Medicine* 60 (1986), 506-7. Gordon's tabulation suggests that, of all the miracles she noted, about 87 percent involved cures of illness.

63. Susan C. M. Scrimshaw, "Infanticide in Human Populations: Societal and Individual Concerns," in *Infanticide: Comparative and Evolutionary Perspectives*, Glenn Hausfater and Sarah Hrdy, eds. (New York, 1984), 444; in the same collection of essays, see also S. Johansson, "Deferred Infanticide: Excess Female Mortality during Childhood," 463-85.

64. Assuming that medieval and modern trends are similar in this regard. For recent figures, see *Monthly Vital Statistics Report*, U. S. Dept. of Health and

Human Services (Centers for Disease Control and Prevention—National Center for Health Statistics), 43, no. 5, *Supplement* (October 25, 1994), 8 and 45, referring to final natality statistics for 1992. Interestingly, the sex ratio seems to vary with ethnic group.

65. Pierre-André Sigal, "La grossesse, l'accouchement et l'attitude envers l'enfant mort-né à la fin du moyen âge d'après les récits de miracles," in *Santé, médecine et assistance au Moyen-âge: 110e Congrès national des Sociétés savantes, Montpellier, 1985* (Paris, 1987), 32: "le voeu concerne davantage les garçons que les filles . . . ."

66. Cousin, "Deux cents miracles," 235, where Cousin also discusses his reasons for finding "une famille étroite, parentale, avec la nuance d'une sollicitude plutôt féminine . . ." around the sick child.

67. Since the whole of the sample of 490 children involved in accidents and illnesses shows a gender imbalance of more boys (67.5 percent) than girls (32.5 percent), these parental biases or preferences are already built in. The difference (relative to boys or girls) is a matter of further distinction within the overall male bias. For discussion based on a small sample of Louis's miracles, see Didier Lett, "Des 'nouveaux pères' au moyen âge? Les fonctions paternelles dans les *Miracles de Saint Louis*," in *Conformité et Déviances au Moyen Âge*; colloque . . . Montpellier, November 1993 (Montpellier, 1995), 223-34. M. Lett finds that in a few cases paternal concern for daughters was just as, or even more, evident than for sons.

68. David Nicholas writes, with admirable restraint, "There is some evidence, although it is by no means conclusive, that sons were preferred over daughters," in "Childhood in Medieval Europe," 37. Klapisch-Zuber notes that "The catasto [of 1427] reflects this tendency to discriminate between the sexes to the degree that certain individuals described their children by listing boys first although they were younger than the girls, while the inverse never occurred." Christiane Klapisch-Zuber, *Women, Family and Ritual in Renaissance Italy* (Chicago, 1985), 55; for disappointment at the birth of girls, see 101. In her study of fifteenth-century Lombard children in orphanages, Albini concluded that, in general, more girls were abandoned than boys. Giuliana Albini, "I bambini nella società Lombarda del quattrocento: Una realtà ignorata or protetta?" in *Nuova rivista storica* 68 (1984), 611-38, at 628-9, text and table, as well as note 90: "In generale le femmine abbondonate erano più numerose dei maschi." These are random samples from a very broad literature which seems to emphasize the preference for male over female children in medieval Europe. Preference for boys, of course, does not necessitate female infanticide.

69. *The Chronicle of Salimbene de Adam*, ed., tr. Joseph L. Baird et al. (New York, 1986), 9; emphasis added.

70. Herlihy and Klapisch-Zuber, *Tuscans and their Families*, 276-9.

71. Another factor that may have emphasized these regional differences is the expectation that certain types of cure could be obtained at particular shrines.

72. Bennett, *Women in Medieval English Countryside*, 59-62. Hanawalt, *Ties that Bound*, 11, 276.

73. C. Klapisch-Zuber, "Demographic Decline and Household Structures" and "'A uno pane e uno vino': The Rural Tuscan Family at the Beginning of the Fifteenth Century" in *Women, Family*, 32-5, 40, 58; David Herlihy, *Medieval Households*, 135, 137, 155. Klapisch-Zuber writes that (in rural Tuscany) the "total percentage of extended families is markedly higher than the usual rates for Western Europe in the early modern period [1427]," 40. But in rural Tuscany, the extended family was common; not so much within Florence itself, 58. Variant household types could also co-exist in the same region, e.g. in Tuscany's *contado* vs. Florence, and in the same region or city between rich (more children) and poor (fewer children). However, Herlihy also writes that in the 1430s the average size of Florentine families was 3.8, and in Tuscany in general 4.4: the large extended family was "seldom" a reality, 135. On 137, however, he refers to the Italian stem-family of three generations, distinguished from English conditions.

74. In her review article, Tamara Hareven, "The History of the Family and the Complexity of Social Change," *American Historical Review* 96 (February 1991), 95-124. In Fichtenau's words, "The question of nuclear versus extended family households has been a principal cause of division among medievalists," Heinrich Fichtenau, *Living in the Tenth Century*, trans. Patrick J. Geary (Chicago, 1991), 82.

75. E. M. Forster, *Where Angels Fear to Tread* (New York, 1975), 97.

76. Hanawalt, *Ties that Bound*, 89, 261.

77. Herlihy and Klapisch-Zuber, *Tuscans and Their Families*, 337, 352.

78. Avery and Jackson, *Children and Their Accidents*, 16.

79. Such as in MacWilliam et al., "Fatal Accidental Childhood Injuries," *Canadian Journal of Public Health* 78 (March/April, 1987), 133-4, discussing contrasting accident rates for children in rural and urban Canada.

80. Waller et al., "Childhood Injury Deaths," *American Journal of Public Health* 79 no. 3 (March 1989), 314.

81. For instance, see Bodleian MS *Fell 2*, fol. 31ᵛ; *Becket*, vol. 1.171-3; vol. 1.258-9 = 2, 263-6; vol. 2,153-5, and 167-8; *Vita Wulfstani*, 175-6; *Louis*, 169-71; and there has been much written about the ritual murder accusation (in which Christian children were imagined to have been murdered by Jews) by, e.g., Gavin Langmuir. In addition, child abuse is abundantly illustrated in coroners' records and trial transcripts, as well as hagiographical records.

82. For Muslim childhood in the Middle Ages, see, for example, Avner Gil'adi, *Children of Islam: Concepts of Childhood in Medieval Muslim Society* (London, 1992); the 1214 treatise is discussed by A.-M. Eddé in "Un traité sur les enfants d'un auteur arabe du XIIIe siècle," *Culture et civilisations médiévales, VII: Les Ages de la Vie au Moyen Age*: Colloque—Provins, March 16-17, 1990 (Paris, 1992); S. Kottek, "Childhood in Medieval Jewry as Depicted in Sefer Hasidim (12-13th Century): Medical, Psychological and Educational Aspects," *Koroth*, 8 (1984), 377*-395*.

83. Schuh, *spätmittelalterlicher Mirakelberichte*, 105: "Besonders interessante Informationen bieten Mirakelbücher über die Stellung des Kindes innerhalb der Familie, die der These einiger Historiker von der fehlenden emotionalen Bindung zwischen Eltern und Kindern widersprechen."

NOTES TO APPENDIX

1. Composed of William de Testa, collector of papal taxes in England, Ralph Baldock, bishop of London and—between April 21 and August 2, 1307— chancellor of the realm, and William Durand the younger, bishop of the French see of Mende

2. fol. 3v-4r.

3. fols. 29v and 128v. On fol. 73v, it is noted that on August 12, at the petition of the Hereford proctor, the proceedings were adjourned to Hereford. The commissioners duly traveled to Hereford, where they reconvened on Monday, August 28,1307. Fol. 123r of the ms., dated September 15, 1307, is titled "Second Part" of the process, "On the Proof of Miracles." Actually, the commissioners had been collecting miracle-evidence since the start of the process; this point in the ms. marked the start of their intensive examination of local witnesses to Thomas's wonder-working powers.

4. Margaret R. Toynbee, *S. Louis of Toulouse and the Process of Canonisation in the Fourteenth Century* (Manchester, 1929); similarly in other canonical inquests.

5. The other witnesses do not describe themselves as Mortimer's subjects, however.

6 *interfectum*—killed, not merely dead, *mortuus*.

7. For further discussion of the role of subjects and coroners in such cases, see Joanna's resuscitation, chapter 4.

8. *commotis vi[s]ceribus paternis.*

9. By the end of the sixteenth century, the manor of Marden (Broxash hundred) was believed to consist of six components—Sutton Freene, Verne, and Marden, Wistaston, Fromanton, and Valde—the latter four being referred to in 1307. John Duncumb, *History and Antiquities of the County of Hereford*, vol. 2 (1812), 127.

10. *ne perderent solacium suum*; or lose their "recreation."

11. *Cecilia filia tua Johanna iamdiu fuit* [*est* superscript] *submersa in piscaria.*

12. *Respondit quod eidem et filie sue visum fuit extunc frequenter in sompnis quod visitabant tumulum dicti domini Thome, et quod ibi orarent et reverterentur.*

13. For the need for assured means of subsistence before medieval a bishop would ordain, see e.g., J. R. H. Moorman, *Church Life in England in the Thirteenth Century* (Cambridge, 1945), 56; a pertinent canon (*Liber Decretalium Gregorii IX*, I.14.xiii) is cited by Peter Heath in *The English Parish Clergy on the Eve of the Reformation* (London, 1969), 17.

14. There are smudged lines in the ms. here, whose meaning is less than certain: *nisi fratres pr[a]emissa protestatione* [or, as Professor Susan Ridyard suggests, possibly *pro testatione*] *alias facta in isto processus a fratribus eiusdem ordinis* . . .

15. *matrina sive mater spiritualiter dicte Joanne.*
16. *Johannam ancillam Sancti Thome.*
17. *aqua supportante vestes suas quas elevavit super aqua et ipsa natante.*
18. *iacens stans vel natans.*
19. *in dicta piscaria erat aliquid submersum.*
20. *quod parvulus vel parvula erat submersus vel submersa in dicta piscaria.*
21. Hereford Cathedral Archives, *Marden Manor Court rolls* #R1112 (April-September, 1308), R1096, R1097, R1098, R1099. These rolls also mention others involved in the accident, such as Stephen and John de Pirebrok.
22. *ne ex tali clamore inciderent in tantum scandalum.*
23. *adeo pulchra et colorata. . . . ita pulchram nec ita bene coloratam.*
24. "For a female child two women and a man acted as godparents, and for males, two men and a woman." Hanawalt, *Ties that Bound*, 247.
25. *credidit tunc et adhuc credit quod dicta puella tunc haberet vitam in ea.*
26. *miliaria*, lit. thousand paces. Hereford is five and one-sixth (modern) miles from Wisteston as the crow flies. The English mile, prior to Elizabeth's reign, was reckoned to be about 1500 paces. R. E. Zupko, *A Dictionary of Weights and Measures for the British Isles* (New York, 1985), 248-51. As usual, there was much local variation.
27. The account of Joanna's resuscitation and other miracles was sent—along with a full report of Thomas Cantilupe's life—to the papal curia for further examination prior to canonization. Between August 14, 1318, and March 1320, the cardinals closely investigated twenty-four miracles; cf. Patrick Daly, "The Process of Canonization in the Thirteenth and Early Fourteenth Centuries," Meryl S. Jancey, ed., *St. Thomas Cantilupe: Essays in his Honour* (Hereford, 1982), 135. Joanna's was the first to be examined and the most extensively debated; report in Oxford, *Exeter College MS 158*, ff. 48ᵛ-52ʳ). In April 1320 Cantilupe was officially canonized, and among the miracles mentioned in the bull of canonization (W. Capes, *Charters and Records of Hereford Cathedral* (Hereford, 1908), 192), Joanna's is the first to be listed, as it is in Cantilupe's liturgy in a fifteenth-century English choir breviary (Oxford, Bodleian *MS Laud Misc. 299*, f. 467ᵛ).

SELECTED BIBLIOGRAPHY

Albanès, J.-H., ed. *Actes Anciens et Documents concernant le Bienheureux Urbain V Pape.* Paris: 1897.

Albé, Edmond. *Les miracles de Notre-Dame de Roc-Amadour au XIIe siècle.* Paris: 1907.

Albini, Giuliana. "I bambini nella società Lombarda del quattrocento: Una realtà ignorata or protetta?" *Nuova rivista storica* 68 (1984), 611-38.

Andrieux, Louis. "La Viatique et l'Extrême-Onction des enfants," II, "L'Extrême-Onction." *Revue Pratique D'Apologétique* 14, no. 158 (15 Avril 1912), 81-100.

Arnold, Klaus. *Kind und Gesellschaft in Mittelalter und Renaissance.* Paderborn: 1980.

Astill, Grenville. "Rural Settlement: The Toft and the Croft." In *The Countryside of Medieval England,* ed. G. Astill and A. Grant. Oxford: 1988.

Atkinson, Clarissa W. *The Oldest Vocation: Christian Motherhood in the Middle Ages.* Ithaca, N.Y.: 1991.

Attreed, Lorraine C. "From *Pearl* maiden to Tower princes: Towards a New History of Medieval Childhood." *Journal of Medieval History* 9 (1983): 43-58.

Avery, J. G., and R. Jackson. *Children and Their Accidents.* London: 1993.

Bennett, Judith M. *Women in the Medieval English Countryside: Gender and Household in Brigstock Before the Plague.* New York: 1987.

Berkvam, Doris Desclais. *Enfance et maternité dans la littérature française des XIIe et XIIIe siècles.* Paris: 1981.

Bernard, A. *La Sépulture en droit canonique.* Paris: 1933.

Blumenfeld-Kosinski, Renate. *Not of Woman Born: Representations of Caesarian Birth in Medieval and Renaissance Culture.* Ithaca, N.Y.: 1990.

Boswell, John. *The Kindness of Strangers: The Abandonment of Children in Western Europe from Late Antiquity to the Renaissance.* New York: 1988.

Bozóky, Edina. "Mythic Mediation in Healing Incantations." In *Health, Disease and Healing in Medieval Culture,* ed. Sheila Campbell et al. New York: 1992.

Brissaud, Y.-B. "L'infanticide à la fin du moyen âge, ses motivations psychologiques et sa répression." *Revue historique de droit français et etranges* 50 (1962), 229-56.

Buckley, Thomas, and Alma Gottlieb, eds. *Blood Magic: The Anthropology of Menstruation.* Berkeley: 1988.

Bynum, Caroline Walker. *Jesus as Mother: Studies in the Spirituality of the High Middle Ages.* Berkeley: 1982.

Cambell, Jacques, OFM, ed. *Enquête pour le procès de canonisation de dauphine de Puimichel contesse d'Ariano.* Torino: 1978.

Capes, W., ed. *Charters and Records of Hereford Cathedral.* Hereford: 1908.

Cavazza, Silvano. "Double Death: Resurrection and Baptism in a Seventeenth-Century Rite." Trans. Mary M. Gallucci. In *History from Crime: Selections from Quaderni Storici,* eds. Edward Muir and Guido Ruggiero, 1-31. Baltimore: 1994.

Cousin, Bernard. "Deux cents miracles en Provence sous Louis XIV." *Revue d'histoire de la spiritualité* 52 (1976), 225-44.

Daly, Patrick. "The Process of Canonization in the Thirteenth and Early Fourteenth Centuries." In *St. Thomas Cantilupe, Bishop of Hereford: Essays in His Honour,* ed. Meryl Jancey, 125-35. Hereford: 1982.

Darlington, Reginald R., ed. *The Vita Wulfstani of William of Malmesbury . . . and the Miracles,* RHS Camden Third Series, Vol. 40. London: 1928.

De Jong, Mayke. *In Samuel's Image: Child Oblation in the Early Medieval West.* New York: 1996.

Delaborde, H. F., ed. "Fragments de l'enquête faite a Saint-Denis en 1282 en vue de la canonisation de Saint Louis." *Mémoires de la Société de Paris et de l'Ile-de-France* 23, 1-71. Paris: 1896.

Demaitre, Luke. "The Idea of Childhood and Child Care in Medical Writings of the Middle Ages." *Journal of Psychohistory* 4 (1977), 461-90.

Devlin, Judith. *The Superstitious Mind.* New Haven, CT: 1987.

Dubois, Dom Jacques and Jean-Loup Lemaitre. *Sources & Méthodes de l'Hagiographie Médiévale.* Paris: 1993.

Fildes, Valerie. *Wet Nursing: A History from Antiquity to the Present.* New York: 1988.

Finucane, Ronald C. *Miracles and Pilgrims: Popular Beliefs in Medieval England.* London: 1977, repr. New York: 1995.

————. "Cantilupe as Thaumaturge: Pilgrims and Their 'Miracles.'" In *St. Thomas Cantilupe: Essays in His Honour,* ed. Meryl Jancey, 137-44. Hereford: 1982.

————. "Pilgrimage in Daily Life. Aspects of Medieval Communication . . . [in] Herefordshire Villages." In *Wallfahrt und Alltag in mittelalter und früher Neuzeit* (International Round Table, Krems, Austria), 165-217. Wien: 1992.

Gärling, T., and J. Valsiner, eds. *Children within Environments: Toward a Psychology of Accident Prevention.* New York: 1985.

Gavitt, Philip. "Infant Death in Late Medieval Florence: The Smothering Hypothesis Reconsidered." In *Medieval Family Roles,* ed. Cathy Itnyre, 137-53. New York: 1996.

Gélis, Jacques. *History of Childbirth: Fertility, Pregnancy and Birth in Early Modern Europe,* trans. R. Morris. Boston: 1991. First published as *L'arbre et le fruit,* 1984.

Golinelli, Paolo. *Città e culto dei santi nel medioevo Italiano.* Bologna: 1991.

Goodich, Michael E. "Bartholomaeus Anglicus on Child-Rearing." *History of Childhood Quarterly* 3 (1975), 75-84.

————. *From Birth to Old Age.* New York: 1989.

————. *Violence and Miracle in the Fourteenth Century: Private Grief and Public Salvation.* Chicago: 1995.

Gordon, Eleanora C. "Child Health in the Middle Ages as Seen in the Miracles of Five English Saints, A.D. 1150-1220." *Bulletin of the History of Medicine* 60 (1986), 502-22.

————. "Measurement for a Votive Candle: A Rite of Healing." *Storia e Medicina Popolare* 7, no. 3 (Rome, September-December 1989), 3-16.

————. "Accidents among Medieval Children as Seen from the Miracles of Six English Saints and Martyrs." *Medieval History* 35 (1991), 145-63.

————. "Arthrogryposis Multiplex Congenita, A.D. 1156." *Developmental Medicine and Child Neurology* 38 (1996), 74-83.

Green, Monica. "Women's Medical Practice and Health Care in Medieval Europe." *Signs: Journal of Women in Culture and Society* 14, no. 2 (1989), 434-73.

————. "Obstetrical and Gynecological Texts in Middle English." *Studies in the Age of Chaucer* 14 (1992), 53-88.

————. "Recent Work on Women's Medicine in Medieval Europe." *Society for Ancient Medicine* Review no. 21 (December 1993), 132-41.

————. "Documenting medieval women's medical practice." In *Practical Medicine from Salerno to the Black Death*, ed. Luis García-Ballester et al., 322-52. Cambridge: 1994.

Greilsammer, Myriam. "The Midwife, the Priest and the Physician: The Subjugation of Midwives in the Low Countries at the End of the Middle Ages." *Journal of Medieval and Renaissance Studies* 21, no. 2 (Fall 1991), 285-329.

Grmek, Mirko D. *Diseases in the Ancient Greek World.* Trans. M. Muellner and L. Muellner. Baltimore: 1989. First pub. as *Les Maladies à l'aube de la civilisation occidentale*, 1983.

Grosjean, Paul, ed. *Henrici VI Angliae Regis Miracula Postuma.* [Bollandists] *Subsidia Hagiographica* 22. Bruxelles: 1935.

Haas, Louis. "Women and Childbearing in Medieval Florence." In *Medieval Family Roles*, ed. Cathy Itnyre, 87-99. New York: 1996.

Halliwell, J. O., ed. *The Chronicle of William de Rishanger; The Miracles of Simon de Montfort.* Camden Society, Vol. 15. London: 1840.

Hanawalt, Barbara A. *Crime and Conflict in English Communities, 1300-1348.* Cambridge [MA]: 1979.

————. *Growing up in Medieval London.* New York: 1993.

————. *The Ties that Bound: Peasant Families in Medieval England.* New York: 1986.

Hareven, Tamara. "The History of the Family and the Complexity of Social Change." *American Historical Review* 96 (February 1991), 95-124.

Harley, David. "Historians as Demonologists: The Myth of the Midwife-witch." *Social History of Medicine* 3, no. 1 (Apr. 1990), 1-26.

Hausfater, Glenn, and Sarah Hrdy, eds. *Infanticide: Comparative and Evolutionary Perspectives.* New York: 1984.

Hawes, Joseph M., and N. Ray Hiner, eds. *Children in Historical and Comparative Perspective.* New York: 1991.

Herlihy, David. "Medieval Children." In *Essays on Medieval Civilization,* eds. B. Lackner and K. Phelp. Arlington [TX]: 1978. Reprinted in S. Ozment and F. Turner, eds., *The Many Sides of History,* Vol. 1, 155-73. New York: 1987.
———. *Medieval Households.* Cambridge, MA: 1985.
Herlihy, David, and Christiane Klapisch-Zuber. *Tuscans and their Families: A Study of the Florentine Catasto of 1427.* New Haven, CT: 1985.
Hunnisett, R. F. *The Medieval Coroner.* Cambridge: 1961.
Jancey, Meryl, ed. *St. Thomas Cantilupe: Essays in His Honour.* Hereford: 1982.
Jansen, Jürgen. *Medizinische Kasuistik in den "Miracula Sancte Elyzabet": Medizinhistorische Analyse und Übersetzung der Wunderprotokolle am Grab der Elisabeth von Thüringen.* Frankfurt am Main: 1985.
Jessopp, Augustus, and Montague Rhodes James, eds., trans. Thomas of Monmouth's *The Life and Miracles of St. William of Norwich.* Cambridge: 1896.
King, Margaret L. *The Death of the Child Valerio Marcello.* Chicago: 1994.
Kiple, Kenneth F., ed. *The Cambridge World History of Human Disease.* Cambridge: 1993.
Klapisch-Zuber, Christiane. *Women, Family and Ritual in Renaissance Italy.* Chicago: 1985.
Kleinberg, Aviad M. *Prophets in Their Own Country: Living Saints and the Making of Sainthood in the Later Middle Ages.* Chicago: 1992.
Kroll, J., and Bernard Bachrach. "Child Psychiatry Perspective: Child Care and Child Abuse in Early Medieval Europe." *Journal of the American Academy of Child Psychiatry* 25 (1986), 562-8.
Krötzl, Christian. "Evidentissima signa mortis. Zu Tod und Todesfeststellung in mittelalterlichen Mirakelberichten." In *Symbole des Alltags, Alltag der Symbole: Festschrift für Harry Kühnel zum 65. Geburtstag,* ed. Gertrud Blaschitz et al., 765-75. Graz: 1992.
———. "Parent-Child Relations in Medieval Scandinavia According to Scandinavian Miracle Collections." *Scandinavian Journal of History* 14 (1989), 21-37.
———. *Pilger, Mirakel und Alltag: Formen des Verhaltens im skandinavischen Mittelalter.* Helsinki: 1994.
Laurent, Sylvie. *Naître au Moyen Age: De la conception à la naissance, la grossesse et l'accouchement (XIIe-XVe siècle).* Paris: 1989.
Lemay, Helen Rodnite, ed., trans. *Women's Secrets: A Translation of Pseudo-Albertus Magnus's De Secretis Mulierum with Commentaries.* New York: 1992.
Lett, Didier. "Enfances, Eglise et Familles dans l'Occident Chrétien" [mid-12th to early 14th centuries]. Thèse de doctorat d'Histoire, l'Ecole des Hautes Etudes, Paris, 1995.
———. "Faire le deuil d' un enfant mort sans baptême au moyen âge: La naissance du limbe pour enfants aux xiie-xiiie siècles," *Devenir 7,* no. 1 (1995), 101-12.
———. "Des 'nouveaux pères' au moyen âge? Les fonctions paternelles dans les *Miracles de Saint Louis.*" In *Conformité et Déviances au Moyen Âge:* Actes de

deuxième colloque international de Montpellier, Université Paul-Valéry (25-27 novembre 1993). *Les Cahiers du C.R.I.S.M.A.*, no. 2 (1995), 223-234.

———. "La sorella maggiore: 'madre sostituta' nei 'miracoli di San Luigi." *Quaderni storici*, n.s. 83 (August 1993), 341-53.

Lloyd, G. E. R., J. Chadwick, et al., eds., trans. *Hippocratic Writings*. Harmondsworth: 1986.

Löhmer, Cornelia. *Die Welt der Kinder im fünfzehnten Jahrhundert*. Weinheim: 1989.

[Louis] *Processus Canonizationis et Legendae Variae Sancti Ludovici O.F.M., Episcopi Tolosani, Analecta Franciscana*, vol. 7. Quaracchi/Florence: 1951.

Lundén, Tryggve, ed. *Sankt Nikolaus av Linköping kanonisationsprocess*. Stockholm: 1963.

Malden, A. R., ed. *The Canonization of St. Osmund*. Wilts. Record Society, vol. 2. 1901.

Manciaux, M., and C. J. Romer, eds. *Accidents in Childhood and Adolescence: The Role of Research*. Geneva: 1991.

McLaughlin, Mary Martin. "Survivors and Surrogates: Children and Parents from the Ninth to the Thirteenth Centuries." In *The History of Childhood*, ed. Lloyd de Mause. London: 1976.

Menestò, Enrico, ed. *Il processo di canonizzazione di Chiara da Montefalco*. Firenze/Perugia: 1984.

Metz, René. "L'Enfant dans le Droit Canonique medieval: orientations de recherche" [1976]. In *La femme et l'enfant dans le droit canonique médiéval*, Variorum Reprints, I:9-96. London: 1985.

Milis, Ludo. "Children and Youth, the Medieval Viewpoint." *Paedagogica historica* 29 (1993): 15-32.

Morel, Marie-France. "Reflections on Some Recent French Literature on the History of Childhood." *Continuity and Change* 4:2 (1989), 323-37.

Nicholas, David. "Childhood in Medieval Europe." In *Children in Historical and Comparative Perspective*, ed. Joseph M. Hawes and N. Ray Hiner, 31-52. New York: 1991.

Niestroj, Brigitte. "Some Recent German Literature on Socialization and Childhood in Past Times." *Continuity and Change* 4:2 (1989), 339-57.

Occhioni, Nicola O.S.A., ed. *Il Processo per la Canonizzazione di S. Nicola da Tolentino*. Roma: 1984.

Opitz, Claudia. "Life in the Late Middle Ages," trans. Deborah Lucas Schneider. In *A History of Women in the West*, ed. George Duby and Michelle Perrot. Vol. 2: *Silences of the Middle Ages*, ed. Christiane Klapisch-Zuber, 267-317. Cambridge [MA]: 1992.

Orme, Nicholas. "Children and the Church in Medieval England." *Journal of Ecclesiastical History* 45, no. 4 (October 1994), 563-87.

———. "The Culture of Children in Medieval England." *Past and Present* 148 (August 1995), 48-88.

Paravy, Pierrette. "Angoisse collective et miracles au seuil de la mort: résurrections et baptêmes d'enfants mort-nés en Dauphiné au XVᵉ siècle." *La Mort au Moyen Age* [Colloque], 87-102. Strasbourg: 1977.

Platelle, Henri. "L'enfant et la vie familiale au moyen âge." *Melanges de science religieuse* 39, no. 2 (June 1982), 67-85.

Plummer, Charles, ed. *Vie et Miracles de S. Laurent archevêque de Dublin. Analecta Bollandiana* 33 (1914), 121-86.

Ransel, David. "Comments [in] Child Abandonment in European History: A Symposium." *Journal of Family History* 17, no. 1 (1992), 1-12.

Rivara, Frederick P. "Epidemiology of Childhood Injuries." *American Journal of the Diseases of Children* 136 (May 1982), 399-405.

Robertson, James Craigie, ed. *Materials for the History of Thomas Becket, Archbishop of Canterbury, Canonized by Pope Alexander III, A.D. 1173.* Vols. 1-6, Vol. 7 by Robertson and J. Brigstocke Sheppard, 7 vols. [Rolls Series]. London: 1875-85.

Ross, James Bruce. "The Middle-Class Child in Urban Italy, Fourteenth to Early Sixteenth Century." In *The History of Childhood*, ed. Lloyd de Mause. London: 1976.

Rowland, Beryl, ed., trans. *Medieval Woman's Guide to Health.* Kent, OH.: 1981.

Rublack, Ulinka. "Pregnancy, Childbirth and the Female Body in Early Modern Germany." *Past and Present* 150 (February 1996), 84-110.

Ruhräh, John, ed., trans. *Pediatrics of the Past.* New York: 1925.

Schuh, Barbara. *"Jenseitigkeit in diesseitigen Formen": social-und mentalitätsgeschichtliche Aspekte, spätmittelalterlicher Mirakelberichte.* Graz: 1989.

———. "'Wiltu gesund werden, so pring ain waxen pildt in mein capellen . . . Votivgaben in Mirakelberichten." *Symbole des Alltags; Alltag der Symbole: Festschrift für Harry Kühnel zum 65. Geburtstag,* ed. Gertrud Blaschitz et al., 747-64. Graz: 1992.

Schultz, James A. "Medieval Adolescence: The Claims of History and the Silence of German Narrative." *Speculum* 66 (1991), 519-539.

Scrimshaw, Susan C. M. "Infanticide in Human Populations: Societal and Individual Concerns." In *Infanticide: Comparative and Evolutionary Perspectives,* ed. Glenn Hausfater and Sarah Hrdy. New York: 1984.

Shahar, Shulamith. *Childhood in the Middle Ages.* London: 1990.

Shatzmiller, Joseph. "Doctors' Fees and their Medical Responsibility." In *Sources of Social History: Private Acts of the Late Middle Ages,* ed. P. Brezzi and E. Lee, 201-8. Toronto: 1984.

Sigal, Pierre-André. "La grossesse, l'accouchement et l'attitude envers l'enfant mort-né à la fin du moyen âge d'après les récits de miracles." In *Santé, médecine et assistance au Moyen-âge: 110e Congrès national des Sociétés savantes, Montpellier, 1985,* 23-41. Paris: 1987.

———. *L'homme et le miracle dans la France médiévale.* Paris: 1985.

———. "Le vocabulaire de l'enfance et de l'adolescence dans les recueils de miracles latins des XIe et XIIe siècles." *L'Enfant au Moyen-Age, Senefiance* 9 (1980) [Aix-en-Provence], 143-60.

Siraisi, Nancy G. *Medieval & Early Renaissance Medicine.* Chicago: 1990.

Stachnik, Richard et al., eds. *Die Akten des Kanonisationsprozesses Dorotheas von Montau von 1394 bis 1521.* Köln: 1978.

Stoertz, Fiona. "Suffering and Survival in Medieval English Childbirth." In *Medieval Family Roles*, ed. Cathy Itnyre, 101-20. New York: 1996.

Swanson, Jenny. "Childhood and Childrearing in *ad status* Sermons by Later Thirteenth-century Friars." *Journal of Medieval History* 16 (1990), 309-31.

Temkin, Owsei, ed. *Soranus' Gynecology*. Baltimore: 1956.

Thomasset, Claude. "The Nature of Woman." In *A History of Women in the West*, ed. George Duby and Michelle Perrot. Vol. 2: *Silences of the Middle Ages*, ed. Christiane Klapisch-Zuber, 43-69. Cambridge [MA]: 1992.

Toynbee, Margaret R. *S. Louis of Toulouse and the Process of Canonisation in the Fourteenth Century*. Manchester: 1929.

U.S. Department of Health and Human Services, Centers for Disease Control and Prevention — National Center for Health Statistics. *Monthly Vital Statistics Report*, 43, no. 5, Supplement of October 25, 1994.

Vauchez, André. *La sainteté en occident aux derniers siècles du moyen âge*. Rome: 1981.

Vecchio, Silvana. "The Good Wife," trans. Clarissa Botsford. *A History of Women in the West*, ed. George Duby and Michelle Perrot. Vol. 2: *Silences of the Middle Ages*, ed. Christiane Klapisch-Zuber, 105-35. Cambridge [MA]: 1992.

Vovelle, Michel. "The Relevance and Ambiguity of Literary Evidence." In *Ideologies and Mentalities*, trans. E. O'Flaherty. Chicago: 1990.

Waller, Anna E., et al. "Childhood Injury Deaths: National Analysis and Geographic Variations." *American Journal of Public Health* 79, no. 3 (March 1989), 310-15.

INDEX

AFT922